Tragedy in Crimson

TRAGEDY

in

CRIMSON

How the Dalai Lama Conquered the World but Lost the Battle with China

TIM JOHNSON

NATION
BOOKS
New York

Published by Nation Books,
A Member of the Perseus Books Group
116 East 16th Street, 8th Floor
New York, NY 10003

Nation Books is a co-publishing venture of the Nation Institute and the
Perseus Books Group.

Books published by Nation Books are available at special discounts for bulk purchases in
the United States by corporations, institutions, and other organizations. For more information, please contact the Special Markets Department at the Perseus Books Group,
2300 Chestnut Street, Suite 200, Philadelphia, PA 19103, or call (800) 255-1514,
or e-mail special.markets@perseusbooks.com.

The excerpt on page 192 from *Wolf Totem* by Jiang Rong, translated by Howard
Goldblatt, copyright © 2008 by Penguin Group (USA) Inc. Used by permission of
The Penguin Press, a division of Penguin Group (USA) Inc. The letter on page 249 from
Judge William P. Clark to Representative Sam Blakeslee is reprinted by permission.

Designed by Jeff Williams

Library of Congress Cataloging-in-Publication Data
Johnson, Tim, 1957–
    Tragedy in crimson : how the Dalai Lama conquered the world but lost the battle with
China / Tim Johnson.
        p. cm.
    Includes bibliographical references and index.
    ISBN 978-1-56858-601-4 (alk. paper)
    1. Tibet (China)—Relations—China. 2. China—Relations—China—Tibet.
3. Bstan-'dzin-rgya-mtsho, Dalai Lama XIV, 1935–   4. Bstan-'dzin-rgya-mtsho, Dalai
Lama XIV, 1935—Political and social views. 5. Bstan-'dzin-rgya-mtsho, Dalai Lama XIV,
1935—Travel—United States. 6. Johnson, Tim, 1957—Travel—China—Tibet. 7. Tibet
(China)—Description and travel. 8. Tibet (China)—Social life and customs. 9. Tibet
(China)—Politics and government—1951–10. China—Politics and government—1949-I.
Title.

DS786.J63 2011
294.3'923092—dc22

E-book ISBN 978-1-56858-649-6
                                                                    2010037497

10 9 8 7 6 5 4 3 2

For my wife, Tanya, and my mother, Jean

Contents

THE TIBETAN AUTONOMOUS REGION AND GREATER TIBET WITHIN CHINA

KAZAKHSTAN

Lake
Balkhash

MO

KYRGYSTAN

XINJIANG UIGHUR
AUTONOMOUS REGION

Ertis

PAKISTAN

Taklamakan Desert

GANSU

QINGHAI

TIBET
AUTONOMOUS
REGION

GREATER
TIBET

DHARAMSALA

Himalaya Range

Maquan

Yangtze

Mekong

LHASA

NEW DELHI

NEPAL

River Ganges

KATMANDU

SHIGATSE

Cho Oyu

BHUTAN

INDIA

Mount
Everest

Brahmaputra R.

BANGLADESH

Irrawaddy R.

YUNN

N

0   400 mi

0   400 km

MYANMAR

Bay of Bengal

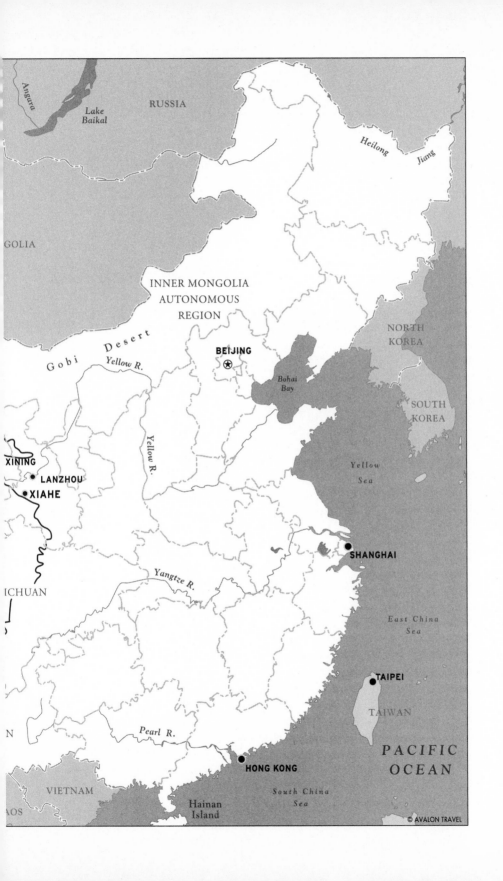

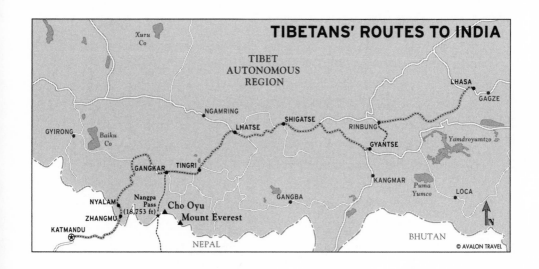

Introduction

THE BASIS FOR THIS BOOK IS SIX YEARS OF LIVING IN CHINA AND writing about the epochal changes that transformed the lives of hundreds of millions of people. When I first arrived in Beijing in 2003, the working environment for foreign journalists was not easy. The Ministry of Foreign Affairs required us to inform our minders every time we planned to take a trip out of the capital. Regulations also stated that we needed official approval for every single interview we conducted, including people on the street. In reality, most of us flouted the rules. We had to: We couldn't do our jobs waiting endlessly for approval and then travel with local Foreign Office minders constantly by our side. When we got caught outside of Beijing, local security officials would often demand that we write a *ziwo piping*—a self-criticism—acknowledging that we broke the regulations.

The atmosphere changed in early 2008. As part of its obligations to the international community for hosting the Summer Olympic Games, China relaxed the rules for foreign journalists. We no longer had to inform the ministry of trips or obtain permission for interviews, as long as the interviewees were amenable to taking questions. To its credit, China has maintained the more open environment after the Games. But some restrictions are still in effect. Tibet is off limits to journalists unless they obtain a permit, akin to a visa, which is rarely available. Indeed, Tibet is one of several topics that remain virtually radioactive for the ruling party. In journalistic shorthand, those topics are the three Ts and one F—meaning Taiwan, Tibet, and the Tiananmen Square pro-democracy movement crushed by Chinese troops in June 1989; the F refers to the Falun Gong meditation sect that rapidly expanded in China in the late 1990s before it was harshly suppressed and declared an "evil cult."

In 2007, a professor at the Hong Kong University of Science and Technology set off an academic brouhaha with an article in the respected *Far Eastern Economic Review*. Carsten A. Holz suggested that Western scholars held an often unacknowledged interest in not provoking China. First, those whose mother tongue is not Mandarin spend years mastering the language, an investment they don't want to go down the drain. Then when it comes to field research, scholars usually must cooperate with academics in China to collect data. Since China's research institutions and universities answer to the party, "surveys are conducted in a manner that is acceptable to the party, and their content is limited to politically acceptable questions," he wrote.[1] Others rely on prized key connections within the party or at major institutions to do research, constraining their actions. Not all China researchers feel pressure equally, Holz wrote, noting that political scientists and economists might feel it the most.

The article raised a ruckus among China scholars, some of whom protested Holz's charges. It was a prickly issue. No Western scholar would want to admit to tailoring research to maintain crucial access in China. And in fact, some bold enquiry on sensitive topics does exist. But I found the matter had substance—not only for academics but also for business executives willing to bend core principles of their companies in order to enter the huge China market, and even for some journalists who have made reporting from China their long-term career calling. An experienced China hand who suddenly finds himself or herself on China's "black list," unable to get a visa to attend conferences or confronting cancellation of residency, may face a major career setback. While the number of such cases may be small, perhaps a dozen or two dozen people, they have a large impact, causing many others to hesitate to conduct sensitive research in China or speak out about events there.

I've personally experienced the kind of pressure China can bring to bear. One day in November 2008, I received an email that gave me a jolt. The bureau chief in Washington for the media company that employs me, McClatchy Newspapers, wrote that Chinese diplomats in San Francisco were asking to see the chief executive officer to talk about my news coverage of China. The email arrived while I was traveling in Dharamsala, India, reporting on Tibetan issues. I wrote back that I had no idea what might be troubling China's Foreign Ministry. But my mind raced. It was hard to concentrate over the next few days. I knew that this level of interest in my work would certainly cause editors to exhibit extra care. It might even affect my own actions, perhaps subconsciously.

A month or so later, I was in Washington and asked the bureau chief what became of the meeting with the Chinese diplomats and the CEO. "They wanted to know about your book on Tibet," he said. I nearly fell on the floor, both in relief and in shock. How would the Chinese diplomats even know that I was writing a book, not to mention its subject? The answer was obvious. I hadn't had contact with Foreign Ministry officials for over a year. So the only way they could know of my plans to write a book (which I had shared with very few people) was if someone in China's state security apparatus had been monitoring my email and listening to my phone calls. This alone wasn't a surprise. Like all diplomats and foreign correspondents based in China, one presumes that state security agents monitor microphones installed in apartments, offices, and cars. China is increasingly free, especially for those Chinese or foreigners who have no interest in politics. But for anyone else deemed a threat or touching on sensitive topics, the state has a thousand eyes and a thousand ears. They had been listening to and watching me. They wanted me to know it, so they sent a shot across the bow of my employer. I found it chilling.

But what happened to me is amplified for Tibetans. This book unfolds over the course of a long journey, in reality a series of journeys over several years. It reveals the Tibetan experience through many perspectives, among them those of the nomad, the monk, the angry young exile, and the unique story of a young Tibetan woman with ties to the highest level of the ruling party. With each chapter, the chasm between Tibetan and majority Han Chinese comes into sharper relief. Behind largely fictitious verbiage pledging "autonomy," and while promising "leapfrog development," Beijing emasculates Tibetans. It has opened the floodgates to domestic migrants who weaken the Tibetans' grasp of their identity and culture. In my research for this book, I traveled to the frigid reaches of the high Himalayas, across

Nepal and India, and with the Fourteenth Dalai Lama on a lengthy speaking tour in the United States. The reader will observe how China has used its growing might to thwart Tibetans at nearly every turn, at home and abroad, in the digital realm and in the lawmaking halls of foreign capitals from Canberra to Washington.

If the writing contains a sense of urgency, it is because the endgame for Tibet has begun. The Dalai Lama is advancing in years, and the atheists of the ruling party claim the right to approve his eventual successor. As they have done with lesser lamas, they will ensure that his reincarnation is pliant to their interests. This is devastating to Tibetans. The renown of the Fourteenth Dalai Lama has elevated the Tibetan issue to all corners of the globe, and when his candle dies out, hopelessness may well set in. This story is not just about the fate of some six million Tibetans. It is about how the authoritarian party at the helm of a rising China treats those it perceives as a threat to its monopoly grip on power, especially when they wield alluring ideas about self-governance, human dignity, and religious freedom. In response, China uses bullying and heavy repression, and in the global arena it coerces its trading partners to accept its view of history. This doesn't only affect Tibetans. As China grows stronger in the future, it may affect every one of us.

My stint in China came to an end, and I have now been reposted to another part of the world. Perhaps that allows me some additional candor in describing my experience. I still have family history in China, though. My grandparents spent nearly the same length of time in China that I did, only eight decades earlier. My two daughters consider Beijing home. We lived there longer than anywhere else during their childhood. The younger girl attended a well-known Chinese elementary school, Fangcaodi (Fragrant Grass), for five years, and her spoken Mandarin could be mistaken for one of the native students. Yell out her Chinese name, Jiang Feifei, when she is on a playground or in a crowded area, and her head whips around. That is how closely she is connected to her Chinese identity.

While I am free to express my views candidly, many of those with whom I spoke cannot. I interviewed dozens of Tibetans over the course of more than two years. Only a few of them appear in these pages, and in some cases I have needed to change their names for their own safety, in which case I use a single Tibetan name. I have used real full names for all Tibetans quoted in chapters set outside of China. But even abroad, some Tibetans were reluctant to speak. One night at a dinner in the Boston area not long ago, a well-educated Tibetan whom I had met on a previous trip and who had agreed to collaborate with me on her family history suddenly broke down in sobs and begged me not to write about her, fearing the repercussions for family members still in China. This book is written in the hope that people like her may one day live without such fear.

TIM JOHNSON
Mexico City

chapter one

The Big Gamble

History? That's up to historians, up to legal experts. Let them say.
It doesn't matter. Past is past. What's important is future.

—*The Fourteenth Dalai Lama, Tokyo press conference,*
November 3, 2008

THE DAY OF MY INTERVIEW WITH THE DALAI LAMA, I AWOKE
excited and nervous. I had asked him questions in crowded press conferences and seen him speak more than a dozen times in theaters, hotel ballrooms, conference halls, and even an American football
stadium. But I had never had the chance to ask questions while having
his undivided attention. I had observed enough to know that he was
engaging and jovial yet eager to cut to the heart of a matter. I also had
heard that he could bring an interview to an end if he felt his inter-
viewer was asking ill-informed questions. Some fears lurked in the
back of my mind: If he were truly an enlightened being, the emanation
of the Buddha of Compassion, could he read my mind? Would I feel
exposed and vulnerable?

I staggered sleepily over to the window of my guesthouse in
Dharamsala, the Indian hill station, and peered down at the mon-
soon-season storm clouds already gathered over the Kangra Valley
below. The deep-throated sound of monks chanting their early morning prayers drifted up from the Tsuglagkhang Temple complex, which
sits on a saddle leading to the forested knoll where the Dalai Lama has
his office and residence.

I trundled down to the Coffee Talk Cafe on Temple Road and ordered a cappuccino and waffles with honey and jam. Itinerant Tibetan vendors were busy pushing their carts into place along the other side of the road to sell turquoise and coral jewelry and other wares to the Indian tourists flocking up from the broiling heat of the Punjab, the adjacent province in India's north, abutting Pakistan, known for its punishing extremes of temperature. The street scene was endlessly fascinating. Tibetan monks walked by, some noisily in groups, others in bowed-head solitude. Tibetan women in brightly colored striped aprons chattered loudly as they strolled by the backpackers and travelers arriving from all over the globe. When I turned around, the towering Dhauladhar Mountains provided a majestic backdrop. Not far behind them lay the border with China and Tibet.

Close to the appointment time, I walked down the hill through the temple grounds and out into a large courtyard. Further on was the yellow compound of the Dalai Lama, in front of which stood well-armed Indian security guards. The Indian government provides the same level of security to the Dalai Lama that it gives to cabinet secretaries and senior members of its own government. Off to one side is an entry hall, where both Tibetan and Indian security agents question visitors. A couple of days earlier, I had arrived for a meeting with the Dalai Lama's personal assistant and had forgotten my passport. They let me through only after questioning me at length, examining various press cards, and calling the assistant himself. Even though they recognized me this time, they flipped through every page of my passport and asked me further questions. After I removed keys and coins and other items from my pockets, a guard frisked me with a thoroughness I had only experienced at Israel's Ben-Gurion Airport. He patted around each leg and then felt my buttocks, groin, chest, and back. Satisfied with my harmlessness, they allowed me to gather my tape recorder and digital camera from the tray that had emerged from an X-ray machine, and signaled for me to walk to a yellow waiting hall.

I took a seat in an octagonal-shaped room, one of several waiting halls. A slight breeze came in through the open windows. Around me, a handful of women spoke in Chinese. Many of them clutched plastic bags of items like notebooks and incense. Soon, at least a dozen other people filled the cushioned benches against the walls of the small room. I wondered if all were going to see the Dalai Lama and if my meeting would be shorter than the planned forty-five minutes. I reviewed my questions and waited about twenty minutes before one of the Dalai Lama's polished young aides, Tenzin Taklha, appeared at the door and motioned for me to follow him. Tenzin spoke to me in American-accented English acquired during his childhood in New Jersey. His father was the Dalai Lama's elder brother, so today his boss is not only the most renowned Tibetan lama, or Buddhist teacher, on the face of the Earth but also his uncle.

Obtaining a meeting with the Dalai Lama—a pre-eminent religious figure who has risen to become a global icon of humanistic values— was not as difficult as it might seem. Eight months earlier, I had sent a letter to the Dalai Lama's office in India identifying myself as a journalist based in Beijing. I would soon be concluding a six-year stint as bureau chief in China for the third-largest chain of dailies in the United States, McClatchy Newspapers. I explained that I wanted to end my Beijing assignment with a book about the Tibet issue, written from the perspective of a journalist who had traveled to nearly every corner of China and was well aware that any book about the future of Tibet would also be about China's more muscular role in the world. A few weeks later, I turned up in India for a news event and made my pitch in person. I was in no hurry for the interview because I had much reporting still to do. A little more than six months later, I was beginning the book in earnest and sent an email to one of the Dalai Lama's top aides. Almost immediately, I received a response from Tenzin Taklha saying that an interview was scheduled for a date six weeks off. He suggested that I limit my questions and give him a heads-up about the topics. "Let me warn you that His Holiness tends to give lengthy answers to questions. This may result in you not being able to ask all your intended questions within the allotted interview time."[1]

I did as I was asked and prepared questions on Tibet's restive social situation and on the growing apprehension among Tibetans over the eventual death of the Fourteenth Dalai Lama, a septuagenarian who has entered his twilight years. Tibetans revere and venerate the Dalai Lama as a god-king, viewing him as a physical and spiritual manifestation of an aspect of the Buddha himself. I'd seen them break into tears or fall on the ground in prostration on seeing him. They believe that as a reincarnation of thirteen previous Dalai Lamas, he embodies the vast wisdom and insight of all of his predecessors.

Since Buddhism's appearance in Tibet around the seventh century, its followers have uniquely come to believe that a few hundred senior lamas, or *tulkus*, have mastered the death and rebirth process, choosing the manner of their rebirth and returning continuously to help humanity achieve enlightenment. Over the centuries, Tibetan Buddhism branched into four major schools, and the most revered in the largest Gelugpa tradition are the Dalai Lama and the Panchen Lama. By the seventeenth century, the Dalai Lama was established as the predominant political and spiritual power in central Tibet. In recent times, nearly all followers of Tibetan Buddhism, regardless of tradition, have come to venerate him as a savior being, and his prominence has grown far beyond the arc of the Himalayas.[2] In the world at large, although not in China, the Dalai Lama is an admired moral figure who espouses nonviolence and encourages humanity to cultivate loving kindness. He circles the globe several times a year meeting world leaders, elevating awareness about China's chokehold on Tibet, and speaking on pressing universal concerns such as global warming and nuclear proliferation. He's impishly good-humored and a media darling, winning headlines and television airtime wherever he goes.

But for all of the Dalai Lama's global fame, Tibetans are no closer to winning greater freedom under China. And China energetically vilifies him, calling him a diabolical mastermind who seeks to sever Tibet from the bosom of the motherland. In recent times, China has used its growing economic clout to threaten any nation that receives the Dalai Lama, warning of economic consequences. Even model democratic leaders of countries like South Africa and Costa Rica have heeded the warnings, urging him not to come or canceling his visa. The Fourteenth Dalai Lama's eventual death will mark a watershed, ridding China's ruling party of a prominent global critic beloved in many parts of the world, but also potentially radicalizing Tibetans despairing over their lack of a freer homeland.

Tenzin Taklha walked me to a spacious waiting room adjacent to the Dalai Lama's reception hall, up a hillock. Around the knoll were dramatic views of the valley dropping sharply below and the seventeen-thousand-foot peaks behind. Crows cawed from the wooded thickets around the complex, and hawks soared in the sky overhead, gliding on summer thermals. Tall, thin evergreens, known as deodars, cloaked the hill. I saw no monkeys as we walked, but I knew they were not far away. Buddhist chanting could be heard from the temple down the hill. The chanting was peaceful and resonant, reassuring in its baritone fullness. I was led into an empty room with many divans and coffee tables, and windows on all sides. Several people stopped by to assure me the interview would commence shortly. I looked out the windows to see a group of visitors lined up, ready to receive a brief blessing. Before I had time to think much about it, I saw the Dalai Lama amble up a driveway toward the line. He was grinning slightly, pressing his palms together in front of his chest in greeting. The visitors bowed slightly and expectantly, some wiping away tears. He walked slowly up the line, exchanging a few words with each one, clasping their hands between his, touching the packages of items that they had brought for him to bless. Before the Dalai Lama reached the end of the line, an aide signaled for me to enter his special reception room and wait for him there.

The room was simple and comfortable. A green Tibetan carpet covered much of the floor, and eleven *thangkas*, large embroidered religious scroll paintings depicting images of Buddha or other deities, hung from the walls. Two couches and four easy chairs in beige upholstery filled the room. A few other simple chairs were set against a wall. Fresh yellow flowers in modest vases graced several windowsills. An aide signaled for me to sit on the couch, indicating that the Dalai Lama would occupy a chair next to one end. I stood to await him. Three of the Dalai Lama's top aides entered first, including two personal secretaries and a Mandarin-speaking expert on Tibetan affairs. Then he entered smiling, squeezed my outstretched hands briefly, and sat. He wore his trademark crimson robe, with a mustard-colored tunic showing at the shoulder. Even his socks were crimson, and on his feet were lace-up brown leather shoes, which he did not remove. His left wrist bore a loose-fitting watch with a metal band. He wore the watch so that the dial rested on the part of the inner wrist where nurses often check one's pulse. Although he had been briefed already, I explained that I was an American journalist finishing a lengthy tour in China and writing a book on Tibet.

"I hope you're not brainwashed!" he blurted out, laughing heartily and clapping his hands together.[3]

The Dalai Lama spoke in conversational English, occasionally omitting a needed verb or mangling syntax and switching into Tibetan, looking to an aide for a colloquial translation. He turned attentive, asking when the book would be published and suggesting that a Chinese version would be useful. "The Chinese people have the common sense. So if they've got true information, then they will use common sense. But some of their leaders, hard-liners, one part of the brain where common sense develops is missing." Again, he laughed with gusto.

I told him of the travels I had undertaken in Tibetan areas, and we entered a discussion about the dramatic civil unrest that erupted across much of the Tibetan Plateau in March 2008. The unrest was intense and widespread, marking the greatest challenge by Tibetans to Chinese rule since the Dalai Lama had fled into exile nearly a half century earlier. The protests began peacefully, but in Lhasa, the Tibetan capital, rock-throwing mobs upended and torched cars, set bonfires, and left city streets in smoldering rubble, shocking many Chinese with the intensity of their anger. Following the Lhasa rioting, largely peaceful demonstrations broke out in more than a hundred other locations over subsequent weeks. Beijing immediately barred foreigners from entering Tibet, and tens of thousands of security forces poured onto the Plateau.

Curiously, a majority of the protests occurred a great distance from Lhasa, at the far reaches of the Tibetan Plateau, outside of what Beijing calls the Tibet Autonomous Region, unfolding in ethnic Tibetan areas of Sichuan, Gansu, and Qinghai provinces. I asked the Dalai Lama why those areas had shown such restiveness. He whispered something in Tibetan to one of the three aides in the room, and a map was quickly brought to a table. He then offered several explanations. Regional Communist Party officials in central Tibet exert "very, very tight control," he said. He paraphrased the Han Chinese party boss who was in charge of the Tibet Autonomous Region at the time, Zhang Qingli, who reportedly said after the Lhasa riot that those Tibetans who needed to be executed would be executed, a pledge carried out over the next year or so.

The Dalai Lama pointed to the outlying areas of the Tibetan Plateau. "These are the real border areas with China for last seven hundred years. These people are toughened. Before 1950, this area was controlled neither by Tibetan government nor by Chinese government. Warlords [controlled it]," he said. "They were something like semi-independent." Living in chaotic border areas for centuries has made Tibetans there rugged and even belligerent. "In these areas," he said, pointing to a Tibetan area of modern southeastern Qinghai province, "there's a saying that if the men of the household don't go out and rob and steal, then they aren't real men." He chuckled. Party officials in outlying areas, he added, have a history of more lenient control, and Tibetans can communicate with each other about their grievances in less fear. So after the initial spasm of violence in Lhasa, word spread more quickly in outlying areas, and they rose up peacefully.

I asked him about who would lead the struggle to protect Tibet culture and Buddhism once he passes from the scene. The Dalai Lama quickly began citing a number of young lamas. At the top of his list was the Karmapa, the twenty-something leader of one of four main streams or lineages of Tibetan Buddhism, the Karma Kagyu school. Handsome and charismatic, the Karmapa fled to India in late 1999 and has become very popular among Tibetan exiles. The Dalai Lama named others. "Many of these lamas have great potential," he said. Some remain working quietly in Tibet, fluent in Chinese and Tibetan, familiar with social conditions on the Plateau, and waiting for the right moment to seek exile or disposed to remain under watchful party eyes. He didn't immediately touch on a central question—his own reincarnation—a matter that deeply unsettles Tibetans these days and could have ramifications for the future of China.

The Dalai Lama was born in mid-1935, and the day when he may slip off to what Tibetans call the "heavenly fields" may not be so far off. Tibetans universally hope that religious tradition will follow its course and senior lamas using omens, oracles, and other hints will identify a young lad as his reincarnation, eventually installing him as the Fifteenth Dalai Lama. Many Buddhists believe that sentient beings endlessly cycle to new births. Tibetan Buddhists uniquely believe that a *tulku*, or reincarnation of a great Buddhist master, can channel his

mind stream (similar to spirit) to a new life, a young boy who will
share his enlightenment. Generally, an aged Dalai Lama leaves some
sign or hint, perhaps contained in a poem, about where to hunt for his
reincarnation. The Fourteenth Dalai Lama has said it is up to Tibetans
themselves if they think the institution of the Dalai Lama should continue. The reincarnation would come outside of China, where freedom is greater, he has said, and could even occur in a mystical process
known as *madey tulku*, in which his successor is reborn while he is
still alive, giving himself an opportunity to train the boy.

Gently, I asked the Dalai Lama when he might define the course of
his reincarnation. He demurred. Could he wait a decade? "I have to
ask my doctor," he said, chuckling. Then his eyes brightened with
higher than normal wattage. A brash prediction tumbled out, one I'd
never heard him make before. "I have no sort of assurance," he began,
"but I feel the Fourteenth Dalai Lama's life span may be a little longer
than the Chinese Communist Party's life span. I think this totalitarian
system, five years, ten years, I don't think its present ruthless sort of
policy will continue." At first, I wasn't sure if I heard correctly. So he
foresaw only a few more years for the Chinese Communist Party in its
present form? He nodded. It seemed like a rash prediction, even im-
petuous, signaling that the party architects of China's monumental
growth had their days numbered. He was personalizing the battle
with the Communist Party, just as its leaders had personalized the
battle over Tibet with him. Chinese leaders make it known that they
are awaiting the Dalai Lama's death, believing that it will sweep away a
major irritant.

A few moments later, the Dalai Lama again brought up how "this
narrow-minded way" of blaming him for the restlessness of Tibetans
had ensnared China's leaders. "They see one target—the source of
Tibet's problems," he said, indicating himself. "For the last twenty years,
they state occasionally [that] 'in order to kill a snake, you must crush the
head,' [or] 'in order to get rid of the flies, you have to remove the dead
meat.'" In fact, he said, Tibetans so closely identify with him that if
China wanted to crush resistance in Tibet, they'd have a bloody task on
their hands. "Ninety percent of Tibetans they'd have to kill," he said.

In essence, the Dalai Lama was throwing down the gauntlet. It was
a wager not just about life spans but about the weakness or strength of

an authoritarian social and political system. For decades now, he has skirmished with China over control of his homeland, demanding that Beijing offer greater freedom of religion and autonomy to Tibet even as China retains sovereignty. It is a topsy-turvy funhouse battle of weak and strong contestants, where the weak sometimes seems strong and vice versa. From most angles, the Dalai Lama is weak. His Tibetan followers revere him, but he is a god-king with no terrestrial realm. Chinese troops occupy his native land, which he fled in 1959 on the heels of a failed uprising. He presides over a government-in-exile in a small Himalayan town in northern India, where bands of monkeys clamber over buildings. Not a single country recognizes his government. He doesn't even own a passport. When he travels, he uses a yellow refugee document. In many ways, he is utterly power-less, just "a simple monk," as he likes to call himself. He even quips that he is homeless.

Yet the Dalai Lama has become one of the most recognizable lead-ers in the world, rising to the level of a universal moral figure along-side Nelson Mandela of South Africa, Martin Luther King Jr., and Mahatma Gandhi. The Dalai Lama can count among his friends and acquaintances current and former leaders of scores of countries. He can fill stadiums with his talks, and Hollywood celebrities jockey for photos by his side. He won the Nobel Peace Prize in 1989, adding mo-mentum to his secular calls for greater religious tolerance, compas-sion in human affairs, and better treatment of the environment. The Dalai Lama is powerless in a formal sense, but he wields significant soft power. In a world buffeted by economic uncertainty, nuclear peril, and environmental degradation, his urgent appeals for simpler, more humane approaches to global problems have broad appeal, and people listen to him.

For all his apparent weakness, the Dalai Lama makes China's leaders tremble in anger. They have few greater enemies. The Dalai Lama stands for much of what they detest—or fear. He espouses broad reli-gious freedom and has put in place a functioning democracy among Tibetans living in exile. His ideas resonate in both the East and the West. His followers adore him with a passion that the grim-faced engi-neers of the Politburo's Standing Committee can only dream about. It's hard not to think back to another era and recall a previous religious figure, Pope John Paul II, who helped bring an end to communism in his native Poland, and eventually all of Central and Eastern Europe. The Polish pontiff went down as one of the most acclaimed figures of the twentieth century. Now, as the twenty-first century gets underway, the Dalai Lama arguably has taken over the mantle as the universal moral voice and implacable critic of authoritarian rule. Like the Polish pope, the Dalai Lama has become a recognized figure around the globe, jousting at the familiar target of aging Communist leaders and their repression of ordinary people.

On the mainland, his denigration is constant. State television news-casters refer to him pejoratively simply as "Dalai," demeaning his posi-tion. Even as they heap vitriol on him, China bans his photograph, a first step at making him vanish. When he does pass away, Tibetans will be deprived of an irreplaceable figure around which to rally, and the world could well lose interest in the Tibetan struggle as just an-other case of a distinct ethnic group under the domination of a much greater power. In that sense, it is a life-and-death struggle—one that hinges on the life of Tenzin Gyatso, the puckish Tibetan monk who describes himself as a middling Dalai Lama. "This Fourteenth Dalai Lama not bad Dalai Lama but not a disgrace," he said once at a news conference, breaking into raucous laughter.[4]

For all his criticism of contemporary China, the Dalai Lama is quick to hail what the nation has achieved in the past six decades. During his first years in power, Mao Zedong showed he was "a true great leader." More recent years have brought a radical transformation of China's economy, and a dramatic repositioning of the nation in the globe. China has the high population, the military power, and the eco-nomic strength needed to claim superpower status, he said, but it doesn't have the moral authority to do so because of its repressive policies. He praised President Hu Jintao for setting the goal of build-ing a "harmonious society" in China but warned that "a harmonious society must build on basis of trust, not by gun, not through fear." As respect for religious and other freedoms increases, China will gain moral authority, he said. "If people from China become really very re-spectable superpower, then we Tibetans feel more proud to remain part of that."

TO UNDERSTAND THE TIBET ISSUE, it is fundamental to ponder what the Dalai Lama is pitted against in contemporary China, a behemoth of 1.3 billion people (equal to a fifth of humanity) and an increasingly powerful and prosperous force. During six years in China, I saw radical, mind-boggling changes to its cities. It was like watching one of those speeded-up films of alpine meadow flowers suddenly coming into bloom. Skyscrapers popped up before my office windows. Malls, highways, subway lines, and airports all materialized at breakneck speed. The Middle Kingdom was a teenager giddy with a growth spurt. During my time, it leapfrogged Britain to become the world's fourth-largest economy, then Germany to become third-largest, then grew on a par with Japan to vie for the number 2 spot. Few experts doubted that China one day would overtake the United States to become the world's biggest economy—the question was when. Some economists saw it happening well before the middle of the century.

In the late 1970s, the Communist Party veered from doctrinaire state planning and initiated "reform and opening up" economic policies, leading to uneven but dramatic growth. Never before in modern times have so many lives changed so quickly as in China. The World Bank calculated that China's economic miracle had pulled 400 million of its citizens out of poverty. Measuring on a variety of scales—from per capita meat consumption to the average floor space per inhabitant in urban areas—Chinese saw their lives improve. And along with the comforts came pride in growing national strength demonstrated by a succession of achievements. In 2003, China became a space-faring nation, later setting its sights on putting a man on the moon. In a global debut of its rising stature, China's capital hosted the most successful Summer Olympic Games in history in 2008, and its athletes captured far more gold medals than any other nation. A couple of years later, Shanghai hosted the 2010 World Expo, signaling its arrival as one of the world's most modern cities.

Like most foreigners in Beijing, I watched this transformation spellbound. The enormous material strides of China were at my doorstep. When I arrived in 2003, the majority of taxis cruising Beijing streets were rickety red Xiali sedans whose backseats crushed my knees. Even in winter, one would have to open the window to avoid

the exhaust fumes filling the interior. By 2006, all the Xialis were retired, and the city filled with bright new Hyundai and Volkswagen
taxis. They competed on the elevated ring roads of the capital with
luxury black Audis, the preferred car of the managers of state-owned
factories, and even with the occasional Lamborghini or Porsche. Near
the end of the decade, when a Chinese-American entrepreneur who
had made it big in restaurants took me for a ride in his $200,000 red
Ferrari Modena 360 sports car, we hardly drew any stares.

Beijing and Shanghai look like other major world cities these days,
stylish and modern. Gone are the residents wearing look-alike Mao-
style padded blue clothing and cloth-soled shoes. When we first got to
Beijing, commuters on the two subway lines would look drab and
even regimented. Within a year or two, many young people wore
sweat suits and sports clothing with conspicuous brand names like
Adidas and Nike. More recently, consumers in Beijing grew more
prosperous and sophisticated, dressing in upper mass-market casual
wear. Only migrants from second- and third-tier cities seemed to
dress in sports clothing.[5]

The astonishing speed of change left even longtime China experts
and scholars puzzling over the big picture. Much of China remains
opaque, but the trickle of information that once emerged—coming
from state-run media—is now a gusher. Tens of millions of Chinese-
language websites now populate the internet. News kiosks bulge with
magazines and newspapers. Newsletters are legion in many languages.
State-run China Central Television hosts channels in Mandarin, English, Spanish, French, Arabic, and Russian. After a visit to Beijing by
President Barack Obama in November 2009, U.S. Ambassador Jon
Huntsman Jr. voiced exasperation at the commentary from experts
opining on the results of the summit. "If you were here 10 years ago
and you're coming back for the first time, you don't know China. If you
were here two years ago and back again, you still don't know China. It
is changing so quickly and it is so dynamic that you've got to stay connected constantly to get a sense of what this means in terms of the future of China." Huntsman, who is fluent in Mandarin, said he doubted
that many people truly are experts on China. "I've come to the conclusion that 'China expert' is kind of an oxymoron. And those who consider themselves to be China experts are kind of morons."[6]

The extraordinary and steady growth of China's economy over the past three decades left many of its citizens optimistic even as others became restive over growing inequality and corruption. For three straight decades, living standards improved steadily. Some 560 million Chinese are under age thirty, and they have never known a year when conditions did not improve from the previous year. This boom-boom atmosphere created both extraordinary expectations and big illusions. One day, my office assistant returned from lunch with her friend, a researcher for Britain's *Guardian* newspaper, which has a bureau on a lower floor of the same building. She announced casually that the two of them were convinced that they would both one day become rich. I asked her what she meant. Did she mean that she'd own a nice apartment, perhaps a late-model car? No, she said, she meant rich, far wealthier than just middle-class. Perhaps her dreams were unreal, but she was not alone in her optimism. A Pew Global Attitudes Survey in the run-up to the 2008 Beijing Olympic Games found a whopping 86 percent of Chinese satisfied with the country's direction, far higher than any other nation on Earth.[7]

China's astonishing physical transformation coincided with a huge boost in pride—and a corresponding sensitivity to any slight by the outside world. The nation's rulers routinely jangle the nerve of historical resentment, saying that China's opponents sought to hinder its rise. School textbooks drill into students the details of China's "Century of Humiliation" prior to Mao Zedong's triumph with the 1949 Revolution. When tensions rose with Japan a few years ago, China quickly invoked the rape of Nanjing in 1937–1938, when invading Japanese troops killed a quarter of a million Chinese. With regularity, the state media summon up the memory of China's defeat in the Opium Wars in the mid-nineteenth century or the ransacking of the imperial summer palace in Beijing by British and French troops in 1860. When the United States is the target, memories are stirred of the U.S. bombing of the Chinese embassy in Belgrade in 1999. These resentments are against foreigners, rarely against Chinese, and never against party leaders. Most Chinese know little of the estimated thirty or so million who died of famine or weakness during Mao's disastrous Great Leap Forward at the end of the 1950s, or the two million who may have perished during the decade-long Cultural Revolution that began in 1966. Instead, any criticism is brushed aside by invoking the judgment attributed to former paramount leader Deng Xiaoping that Mao was "70 percent good and 30 percent bad."

Besides, Mao seems like a relic today, his portrait gracing the entrance to the Forbidden City with an enigmatic smile, his embalmed body resting a few hundred yards away in a huge granite mausoleum. Shifting from socialist ideology, the party today rests its legitimacy on sustained economic growth and broader opportunities. So far, it has succeeded. The gleaming big cities of Beijing, Shanghai, Guangzhou, and Shenzhen, where rising salaries have kept people largely content, provide ample demonstration. An implicit contract with the citizenry appears to be at work: As long as you don't challenge the Communist Party's monopoly on power, you can avoid trouble. In turn, the party will ensure steady growth of the economy and some increase in social mobility. For many people, that agreement works. They can manage the road bumps on the way to the "well-off society" that the party promises. Opportunities have expanded, like the prized chance to go to university. In the decade leading to 2008, university enrollments increased more than sixfold, to 21.5 million students. Fortunes seem within the grasp of any ambitious entrepreneur, partly because the rules of the game are malleable. Corruption and inequality are unavoidable side effects.

I went one day to see an economist from the China University of Political Science and Law, Yang Fan, to find that he'd moved from a dingy apartment block to a gleaming art deco–style complex near the Western Hills. I congratulated him on his move. I asked him about the many vacant apartments in the newly built complex. He said matter-of-factly that they'd all been sold, and the owners were absent. I asked to whom they'd been sold. "They are all owners of coal mines in Shanxi province," he said. I was astonished. The coal industry is notoriously dangerous in China, leaving 3,215 miners dead in one recent year.[8] By spending little on safety, mine owners were making huge profits. "They are really rich," Yang said.

As a journalist, I have talked to enough people to see the underbelly of China. The nation's economic juggernaut is leaving some people behind, among them the rural poor and some ethnic minorities. The

Communist social safety net—or "iron rice bowl" system—has largely vanished. China has moved from communism to a form of savage authoritarian capitalism. Health care, once almost free and universal, has slid out of reach under a brutal "pay or die" system. Millions of families struggle mightily when catastrophic illness hits. Education costs also eat a chunk of family budgets. Moreover, families of those who complain about the government face constant worry. Messing with party officials gets one labeled a "troublemaker," and so-called troublemakers fill China's prisons and a thousand or so "reform-through-labor" camps, compelled to toil for alleged crimes like "subverting state power" or "revealing state secrets."[9] Thousands also languish in "black jails"—the hidden penal system whose existence Beijing denied for years. There are plenty of issues to make one's blood boil, like the lack of property rights, environmental devastation, and abuses of power by local officials.

Occasionally disgruntled citizens would stop by my office, hoping to get my attention for articles, the only outlet they could find for their frustration. I knew the eyes of the state followed such people closely. One day, an organizer from heavily populated Sichuan province in the far southwest stopped in. Stocky and affable, Liu Zhengyou spoke with the thick burr characteristic of his native province. He was in Beijing to petition the government on behalf of apartment dwellers who he believed were not getting fair compensation for buildings being razed. I liked Liu and decided a few years later to visit him in his home city of Zigong while working on another story. Liu was effusive in his greeting and invited me into his modest home. His phone rang. It was an official from the Public Security Bureau. After speaking for a few moments in rapid-fire Mandarin, Liu hung up and said the official called "to invite me to have a cup of tea this afternoon."[10] It was the security bureau's way of telling Liu to watch his step because they knew he was talking to a foreign journalist. In case the point wasn't clear, as soon as Liu and I walked outside, a black Audi sedan with four men inside inched along behind us, trailing us through the city.

The threat of social unrest is the bane of the party. Officials fear little more than a sudden disturbance, fretting over the Mao dictum that "a single spark can start a prairie fire." On trips to outlying regions where minority populations are high, I saw that China's grasp on unity remains fragile. Secessionist-minded minority groups occupy huge chunks of its southwestern and western regions. Elsewhere, even amid runaway development, there are constant reports of trouble. More than half the population still lives in villages, and local party officials sometimes are abusive and corrupt. The state is already spending huge sums on security, fearful that enemies of the party could exploit its weak flanks.

Like other foreign reporters, I rushed around the country to look into why unrest had broken out. The causes were myriad and usually local. The eruption of anger would fizzle as fast as it began. But technology was changing the contours of unrest. Aggrieved people could use text messaging, tweets, and social networks like the Chinese QQ system to organize. Anyone angry over a perceived abuse could use a mobile phone to take photos or video and pass the images around on the internet. The state fought back with sophisticated censorship— the Great Firewall—and mobilized huge numbers of people to monitor signs of digital discontent. They molded public opinion on popular chat rooms, forums, and other internet venues. Wags soon gave the "guides" a nickname—the "Fifty Cent Party"—for the one-half yuan each would reportedly earn for every positive statement about government policy he or she posted on the internet. In a speech in mid-2008, President Hu Jintao hailed the work of those who were "setting a new pattern of public-opinion guidance."

Use of a word like *guidance* instead of *propaganda* or *censorship* is typical of the topsy-turvy world of contemporary China, where word choices are as likely to confuse as clarify. Beijing's "blue sky days" are a good example. In the years before the Beijing Summer Olympics, leaders fretted that the capital's severe air pollution would spoil the Games. They took increasingly dramatic steps to diminish pollution, closing factories around Beijing and in neighboring provinces, halting construction projects, and forcing private cars off the road one day per week. Eager to mark their progress, they used the yardstick of "blue sky days." In 1998, Beijing recorded only 100 "blue sky days." Every year, city officials would set a higher target for the number of "blue sky days" and beat it. The year before the Olympics, the city set a goal of 245 clear days and surpassed it by 1. Problem was, officials had altered standards and seemed to manipulate the data. Skies were clearing notably, but on many "blue sky days" one could barely see the sun through the smog. A "blue sky day," at least among some of us cynical foreign journalists, became a euphemism for any Alice-in-Wonderland claim contrary to apparent fact.

We could joke about it and send reports free of direct interference, but Chinese social critics posting their thoughts on the internet had to be circumspect and indulge in subversive creativity. In 2007, some Chinese bloggers began putting images of river crabs on their sites. It was actually nuanced social commentary on President Hu's slogan of "constructing a harmonious society" and a response to censorship. At first, when censors deleted blog posts, a daily occurrence in China, bloggers began to write that they'd been "harmonized." Chinese censors didn't like that cynical phrasing so they routinely deleted "harmonized" as well. Bloggers fought back. Since the Chinese word for "harmonize" in Mandarin sounds nearly the same as "river crab"—only using different characters—bloggers adopted the phrase "river crab" to mean "harmonized." Images of river crabs proliferated. A few years later, another strange critter appeared on the internet, the "grass-mud horse." No such beast exists. But the phrase sounds almost like a command to commit a most vile act against your mother. Soon, companies were making plush toys of "grass-mud horses," and Chinese would speak commonly of the beasts, all the while poking fun, making sly criticisms, and shielding themselves from sounding vulgar. Such wordplay gave many Chinese internet users a sense of a much more free information environment than their parents experienced. The majority of young Chinese savored these freedoms, accepting a world in which political activity is constrained.

Chinese can lend itself to direct expression. My apartment lease was a concise page and a half of type. But the party has also mastered ambiguous language. Vague and draconian catchall laws allow police to lock away anyone harming "the security, honor and interests of the motherland" or releasing never-defined "state secrets." On sensitive matters, words can mask underlying contradictions. Furiously capitalist, China's constitution still proclaims the rule of a "dictatorship of the proletariat" that "will follow the socialist road." In debates over Tibet, I noticed the lexicon of emotionally fraught words by all sides.

The Dalai Lama does not hesitate to call the Chinese system "totalitarian," which might apply more accurately to neighboring North Korea than to China. For its part, Beijing culls words to shape its portrayal of Tibetan history, a key battlefield, and brands the Dalai Lama as a "separatist" and a "splittist." By casting him as hell-bent on seeking independence for Tibet, the state appeals to the patriotism of the citizenry and averts discussion of real grievances harbored by Tibetans. No matter how many times he says he only seeks greater autonomy, China calls him a liar.

I have searched for an appropriate historical parallel for the situation of Tibetans. Some Chinese analysts have pointed out the hypocrisy of U.S. criticism of China's treatment of Tibetans when barely a century and a half ago its own Westward expansion left a trail of death for Native Americans. After hearing more Tibetans describe their grievances to me, I tended to look toward the U.S. civil rights movement as a historical mirror. Like blacks in the South, Tibetans say they simply want the protections of guaranteed freedoms enshrined in China's constitution and other laws. Just as I was delving into history books, Chinese Foreign Ministry officials began doing the same—only in reverse! They evoked the race of President Barack Obama to explain their Tibet policy. In November 2009, as Obama was about to make his first trip to China, Foreign Ministry spokesman Qin Gang suggested that Obama study U.S. Civil War history:

> I remember President Obama saying in a speech after taking office that he felt "a special gratitude" to President Lincoln because without Lincoln, he would not be able to become the first black president of America. He also said that President Lincoln played a unique role in upholding the country's national unity and territorial integrity. Dalai was head of the feudal serfdom of Tibet and he is now engaged in activities aimed at splitting the motherland and sabotaging its territorial integrity. . . . President Obama, as a black president, certainly knows well the great significance of the U.S. abolition movement initiated by President Lincoln. The old Tibet in the reign of Dalai enforced dark serfdom and he was head of Tibetan serfdom. In 1959, China completely abolished serfdom, which was a great step forward in the hu-

man rights cause. Such a move is of the same nature as the abolition of slavery by President Lincoln in the U.S.[11]

Lecturing President Obama on race and challenging him to reread U.S. history were signs of China's rising confidence, even chutzpah. One scholar at Tufts University in Boston wrote that it was a "cheap parlor trick" resulting from China's erroneous interpretation of Lincoln's opposition to slavery and the politics leading to the Civil War.[12] Unlike the American South, which voluntarily became part of the United States, Tibet was never asked in a formal way if it sought to come under Chinese dominion. Instead, Chinese troops invaded in 1950, and Tibetan envoys under duress acceded to a seventeen-point agreement recognizing Chinese dominion, a move that the Dalai Lama later rejected.

• • •

IN 2007 I GOT WIND IN BEIJING that a few diehard Tibetan Communists had grown sour on a government policy toward their homeland, which seeks to win over Tibetans by priming the pump of the regional economy while waiting for the Dalai Lama's death. To gather more information, I paid regular visits over a period of six months to a Tibetan academic in his early seventies with a remarkable personal history. The man, Jampal Gyatso, was a scholar associated with the Chinese Academy of Social Sciences, one of the nation's premier research institutions. Gyatso has a humble background but looks rather stately. A shock of white hair tops his head, and bushy white eyebrows peak over his rimless glasses. He is quick to smile, and his white teeth complement his ivory crown. Despite his years, Gyatso continues to keep an office at the academy, although I always saw him at his apartment in far northern Beijing, beyond the fifth of the concentric ring roads that encircle the city.

To get there, I took one of the new subway lines that proliferated in the period around the Beijing Olympic Games. The subway system now carries about five million passengers a day, and for a flat fare of just under thirty U.S. cents one can ride as far as one likes. At the station for Line 5, glass panels separate the platform from the tracks, and the approaching rail cars are fairly quiet compared to the noisy older subway systems in the United States. Inside each car, flat-screen monitors keep passengers occupied with bursts of advertising. A digital readout above the doors displays approaching stations. I got off at the elevated Lishuqiao South station and walked the half mile or so to Gyatso's second-floor apartment, where he greeted me with a cup of hot milk tea once I took my shoes off and put on slippers, as is customary in many homes in China.

This particular occasion was the fourth time I had dropped in on Gyatso. On earlier visits, I had pumped him for details about his upbringing in Batang in a verdant valley on the eastern edge of the Tibetan Plateau, where his family was so poor that one older sister was consigned to an orphanage. Prior to the Communist triumph in 1949, the area was a battleground between Maoist guerrillas, Nationalist soldiers, warlords, and bandits. Still etched in his mind was the day he stumbled onto a killing field outside of town littered with severed heads and mutilated bodies. At age eleven, following in the footsteps of an older brother, Gyatso joined a People's Liberation Army (PLA) song-and-dance troupe, getting a front-row seat for the Chinese military's efforts in the early 1950s to control and stabilize the Roof of the World. A couple of years later, barely a teenager, Gyatso found himself with the extraordinary honor of serving as the emcee and translator at the 1952 New Year's celebration in Lhasa for the Dalai Lama offered by the top regional PLA officers. "I was not allowed to approach him," he recalled. The god-king was a youth at the time, only four years older than Gyatso. "When the Dalai Lama saw me, he smiled at me and made a little motion with his hand."

During our earlier visits, I found Gyatso guarded against any criticism of China's policy toward Tibet. His family's poverty prevented him from developing much Tibetan national consciousness as a youth, and the Communist alternative seemed more enticing. Gyatso was finally admitted into the Communist Party in 1980, and his career soared as he supported its policies. He was also particularly close to the portly monk who was the number 2 in the Tibetan Buddhist hierarchy, the Panchen Lama. Many Tibetans describe the Dalai and Panchen lamas as the sun and moon in the religious firmament. For years, Gyatso had served as one of the personal translators of the Tenth Panchen Lama, and he grew to love and revere him.

The Panchen Lama had a tragic history. Initially a supporter of the ruling party's reforms in Tibet, he was eventually thrown in jail from 1968 until 1977, much of it in solitary confinement, for criticizing how those reforms were implemented. He was rehabilitated in the 1980s, by which time he had cast aside his monk's robes, married the granddaughter of a Han Chinese general, and fathered a child. In 1989 he died suddenly in Tibet under unusual circumstances, just a few months before party leaders would send tanks into Beijing streets to crush the Tiananmen pro-democracy movement, a move that would haunt the party for decades. Before his friend's death, Gyatso was authorized to write a biography of the Panchen Lama, but once published it was pulled off the shelves by the censors, who apparently couldn't stomach its repetition of the Panchen Lama's criticism of party failures in Tibet. On one of my visits, Gyatso offered me a photocopied English translation of the biography and allowed me to read it. No English publisher would touch the book either, partly because of what the translator described as its "Marxist passion" and its adulatory tone toward its subject.

On this particular day, perhaps because a level of trust had built between us, Gyatso opened up somewhat about his frustrations with China's policy toward Tibet. Beijing's leaders have pumped billions of dollars into projects in Tibet and yet have failed to raise standards of living rapidly. "The rest of China has developed much faster than Tibet. In 1980, income per capita in Tibet was 400 yuan a year (about $261), while the farmers around the Beijing area were earning just 100 yuan a year. But now farmers in the countryside earn 20,000 to 30,000 yuan a year while in Tibet it's only 4,000 yuan per year," Gyatso said, speaking in fluent Chinese rather than his native Tibetan. "Yes, the income of Tibetans is ten times greater than before, but people in coastal areas have seen their income grow a hundred or two hundred times." He said Tibetans hold real grievances over development policies, but incompetent party cadres on the Plateau cover up the dissatisfaction. "In ordinary times, they tell the central government that things are going well, that Tibetans support the central government very much. They cover up the problems and conflicts. When problems happen, they blame the 'Dalai Lama clique,'" he said, using the preferred party term for what it asserts is an exile cabal stirring up secessionist trouble.

Gyatso made clear that he didn't have much use for such explanations. In adulthood, he had the chance to encounter the Dalai Lama again, in Frankfurt in 1988, when he became the first Tibetan Communist Party member to see him in those years. "The Dalai Lama didn't recognize me. But he knew a little about me. He said, 'You were very young then but you are a research scholar now!' . . . It was the first time in thirty-three years that I had seen him." Following instructions from the United Front Work Department, which oversaw relations with ethnic minorities, Gyatso did not kneel before the Dalai Lama. "I just shook hands and gave him a *khata*," he said, referring to the white silk ceremonial scarf symbolizing purity and goodwill often exchanged at such meetings.

Gyatso has kept his disagreements with policy largely to himself—unlike the most widely known ethnic Tibetan in the Communist Party. That man, who like Gyatso is from the same town of Batang, is Phuntsok Wangyal, a feisty octogenarian known by one and all as Phunwang, a contraction of his name. Phunwang lives in Beijing, receiving few visitors and staying largely out of the spotlight. He is Tibet's earliest Communist, founding the regional Communist Party in the 1940s to fight against Tibet's feudal structures. He eventually fused his party with the Chinese Communist Party, abandoning a goal of independence for Tibet when it became clear that the Chinese party had reversed its policy of allowing minority territories to seek independence. He helped lead People's Liberation Army troops into Tibet in 1950, and for the next decade he collaborated with the Chinese administration, serving as the highest-ranking Tibetan in the party. In 1954–1955, when the Dalai Lama traveled to Beijing to meet Mao, Phunwang went as his translator. But like many key early advisers to Mao, Phunwang was cast off and ordered to prison in 1960, where he remained in solitary confinement for eighteen years. By the time of his release, Mao had died, and Phunwang eventually was rehabilitated, returning to his position as the leading Tibetan within the party.

As the new century broke, Phunwang's dismay grew. He observed the ongoing blockade against the Dalai Lama's return from exile and the stalemate in formal talks over the Tibet issue. He decided to take action, firing off lengthy personal letters to President Hu. In his first letter in October 2004, Phunwang told Hu that the ruling party was mistaken in believing that the Dalai Lama's eventual passing would resolve its problems. "Any notion of delaying the problem until after the 14th Dalai Lama dies a natural death is not only naïve, it is also unwise and especially tactically wrong," he wrote in a private letter that circulated later. If headway were not made on the Tibet issue, which was giving China a black eye internationally, he wrote, the death of the Dalai Lama could spark violence among radicalized young Tibetans. Phunwang said he saw "absolutely no contradiction" between the autonomy sought by the Dalai Lama and the goals of the party in Tibet. He urged Hu to accept the Dalai Lama's promise that he would not interfere in politics upon his return and would concern himself only with religious matters. "If the Dalai Lama whose fame and influence have become renowned in the four corners of the world were to return, it would reassure Tibetans who have long looked to the outside and those who have traveled into exile to be with him . . . as well as removing the need for thousands who annually make the journey to meet him in exile in spite of the danger."

MY TIME WAS RUNNING OUT with the Dalai Lama. More than an hour had already passed, yet I decided to ask him about the two elderly Tibetan Communists. Their names triggered immediate recognition. When I told the Dalai Lama that I believed Jampal Gyatso was torn between his belief in the Communist Party and his loyalty to his ethnicity, he shot back an immediate question: "How long have you [had] acquaintance with him?" I explained that it had been a half year. "Can you say that within that period, you have developed full trust?" I said I wasn't sure, but probably not. "No Tibetan who has common sense, I think, no one trusts the Chinese Communist Party."

The Dalai Lama certainly doesn't, and I was briefly puzzled at another point when I asked him if he'd ever seriously considered going to China during the past few decades. He noted that in 1983 he publicly expressed interest in visiting China and Tibet but that it led to nothing. When the Panchen Lama died in 1989, there was talk anew of his taking part in a nonpolitical visit for the funeral in China, but

between his own hesitancy about the false hope such a visit might en-
gender among Tibetans for his definitive return and Chinese indeci-
siveness, no visit occurred. "Recently, I received some sort of
indication they might allow me to go on some sort of pilgrimage in
Chinese lands," he said, explaining that it would be to Wutai Mountain, one of the four sacred Buddhist mountains in China, but China
would not allow a visit into Tibet during such a trip. Again, the Dalai
Lama weighed the political impact and decided it would go against
"my moral principle."

Without any prompting from me, the conversation drifted into a detailed discussion about the 1989 death of the Panchen Lama. The portly
lama died suddenly one evening while visiting Tashilhunpo Monastery
in Shigatse, the traditional seat of his power in the second most important city in Tibet. He was fifty years old and somewhat obese, and he
had just arrived at the high-altitude monastery from the lowlands of
Beijing. The official version is that he suffered a heart attack.

"There are quite strong rumors of his being poisoned," the Dalai
Lama said.

I had heard those reports, but it wasn't until the Dalai Lama entered a long explanation of the inconsistencies between the Chinese
government version of the death and the version of Tibetans at the
scene that I realized that these concerns would play into any decision
of his own ever to travel to China. He saw a possible unsolved murder
conspiracy in the Panchen Lama's death, one that would have vast
repercussions, including for how his own reincarnation might be selected. Before the Panchen Lama's early 1989 trip to his home
monastery, he had quarreled with then–paramount leader Deng
Xiaoping, arguing on behalf of Tibetans for greater freedoms in their
homeland, which was at the time under martial law, the Dalai Lama
said. Shortly before the trip, the Chinese government changed the
Panchen Lama's private physician and his bodyguard. On the day before his death, the Panchen Lama ate noodles in the evening, then felt
ill later on. His physician gave him an injection, but whether he died
right away or the next morning is unclear.

A year or two later, hopes soared that a definitive answer might
emerge about the Panchen Lama's death. A Tibetan lama was traveling from Tibet to the home of the Dalai Lama in India and bringing

with him a sample of the deceased Panchen Lama's hair. Such samples are routinely saved as religious relics. The hair sample would be submitted to rigorous scientific analysis to determine whether the Panchen Lama had been poisoned or not. But an extraordinary mishap occurred.

"When he reached Dharamsala, he didn't find it. He lost it," the Dalai Lama said, breaking into peals of laughter at the memory. "It was quite important!—this matter—but it was just carelessness that that happened." By now the Dalai Lama was shaking from laughter so hard he could barely get the words out. The treasured hair sample, possibly holding the secret to whether the Panchen Lama had been poisoned, and by extension whether the Communist Party might have had a black hand in reshaping the highest levels of Tibetan Buddhism, had simply vanished. Poof!

The interview slid to a close—nearly an hour and a half had passed. I walked out of the complex mulling the Dalai Lama's optimistic outlook on radical change in China. It was impossible to know if he would be right. Certainly few people had predicted the sudden fall of the Berlin Wall and the Soviet Empire in 1989. In hindsight, the signs of Soviet decay seemed clearer. But China is not like the Soviet Union. It has tallied one success after another. Man for man, the ministers and other high officials of the party seemed the equals of any in the Western world, if not in some cases more savvy. Moreover, abrupt political change in China might favor no one. It could lead to progressive strengthening of the security forces as they crush domestic chaos, moving even further from any democratic reform. As much as China's future interested me, I had already decided to travel extensively on the Tibetan Plateau, cross the Himalayas to Nepal, return to India, and visit the United States to assay what is at stake in Tibet. I wanted to know what conditions were like at the Top of the World and what made so many Tibetans flee as refugees over the Himalayas. I also wanted to peer into the inner workings of the exile movement and get a sense of how much China tried to stymie the Dalai Lama overseas. All this would lie in the days ahead.

For now, Tibet, its religion, and its god-king all seemed impossibly exotic, like an endangered orchid deep in the jungle. Perhaps it was a species on the brink of extinction. I didn't have a clue whether it could be saved. What I did sense, though, was that there might be something even more important than the endgame for Tibet. Perhaps more crucial would be to observe how a rising China behaves toward those it feels are weaker and in its way.

Today, it is the Tibetans. Tomorrow, those harmonizing about the glorious blue skies of China could be you and me.

chapter two

On Tibet's Periphery

It would take days to explain to you how tough our lives are
here. . . . We're under the gun. We Tibetans are on the lowest rung
among minorities. There is no freedom here.

    —*Tibetan monk at the Kumbum Monastery, Qinghai Province*

I TRAVELED TO TONGREN TO GAUGE THE FEELINGS OF TIBETANS IN
2009, a year after the massive series of protests around the Plateau.
Also known as Rebkong in Tibetan, Tongren is a large town with four
Buddhist monasteries, three of them set on outlying hills or in poplar-
filled valleys. It is in Qinghai province, to the north and northeast of the
Tibet Autonomous Region, which is a Chinese-created political entity
that comprises about half of the geographic territory where ethnic
Tibetans live. The town might seem removed from the heart of Tibet.
After all, it is closer to Mongolia than it is to the distant Tibetan capital
of Lhasa. One must cross seven hundred miles of often-desolate
mountain passes, permafrost-covered plateau, and high grasslands to
reach Lhasa from here. Indeed, Tongren is at the edge of the traditional ethnic Tibet region, and just a little to the northeast Hui Muslims and majority ethnic Han Chinese predominate. Yet despite its
location on the fringe of the Plateau, the surrounding region holds
outsized importance for the Tibetan issue, partly because of the intensity with which regional Tibetans regard their ethnic and religious
identity. The current Dalai Lama was born in a village no more an
hour's drive away. And I was discovering that it was in far-flung areas

of the Tibetan region where the itch for greater freedom seemed to manifest most openly.

I wandered into the vast Rongwu monastery and made my way through its labyrinthine pathways, looking for Tibetans to ask about the mood in the region. I found a shopkeeper who was circumambulating a temple with other pilgrims, and he grew animated at my questions. But like many Tibetans, he spoke Mandarin poorly, and I could barely make out what he said. He insisted that China's restrictions on the religious practices of Tibetan Buddhists amounted to ethnic repression. The more he spoke, the more rankled he became—and the less I understood. He mixed Tibetan words with heavily accented Mandarin, which was our only common language, and I got lost in the flow of speech. I was discovering that many Tibetans could not speak Mandarin with any fluency, only Tibetan. The two languages, while in the same broad language group, are not mutually intelligible. Tibetans can even have difficulty understanding each other because of dialectical differences between the far ends of the Plateau.

As I struggled to conduct interviews, a young Tibetan approached and addressed me in English. He gave me his Tibetan name, but the name I will give him to avoid causing him trouble is Robin. Barely eighteen years old, Robin was finishing up at a local high school, where he studied under volunteer foreign English teachers, the latest one a retired South African. He was of stocky build and modest height, and kept his longish jet-black hair swept straight back, accentuating his broad forehead. Like many Tibetans, the features of his face were full and soft, with a broad nose, a low eyebrow ridge, and a rounded jaw line. He had a wisp of a moustache and a small mole on his upper lip. His eyelids had only a slight epicanthic fold, less notable than Asians from farther to the East. He wore jeans and generic Chinese sneakers, and he moved with the grace of someone accustomed to life as a Tibetan nomad—his family heritage—and with confidence in his physical capabilities. Initially, I was leery of Robin, thinking it would be careless to talk to him for very long. As an experienced journalist in China, I found it worked better to grab snatches of interviews with a number of people in order to gather material quickly before police or local officials might intercept me. But Robin's good nature and easy smile, which showed off his bone-white teeth, won me over.

Besides, like a little mascot, he wouldn't go away. Eager to practice his English, he strolled by my side through the monastery, discussing the mood of local Tibetans.

High red and ochre walls towered above us to the left and right, broken by an occasional wooden gate leading into a temple courtyard or a monastic study center. Near the massive front entrance, we came across a long passageway filled with scores of wooden prayer wheels, essentially cylinders that spin on an axis, each about three feet high and painted in bright red, orange, yellow, and green. Tibetans of all ages walking by would instinctively reach out and turn the wheels, which are inscribed with holy mantras. Buddhists believe each clockwise spin of a wheel sends a prayer into the universe. At the gate of the monastery, a woman did prostrations—first kneeling, then extending her arms over her head, and dropping to the ground. A cloud of dust literally enveloped her head. In Tibetan Buddhism, the prostrations show veneration toward Buddha, purify the practitioner, and accumulate merit for future lives.

Robin described the region as a cauldron of tension. Tibetans still were infuriated by numerous arrests in the wake of the 2008 protests. But local Tibetans had not organized themselves. "They are very angry at the Chinese government and the Chinese people," Robin said. "But they have no idea what to do. There is no leader. When a leader appears and somebody helps out, they will all join." I pressed Robin to help translate for me as I searched out more Tibetans, and we set off for an area outside of the monastery. We found several nomads and heard tale after tale of civil disobedience in outlying hamlets. In one village, Tibetans burned their Chinese flags and hoisted the banned Tibetan Snow Lion flag instead. Authorities arrived there and detained nine villagers. One nomad, dressed in the traditional *chuba*, a long sheepskin coat, said anger among Tibetans at the Chinese government had been building and would not melt with time. "After I die," the fifty-three-year-old herder said, "my sons and grandsons will remember. They will hate the government."

We spoke in an open plaza outside the monastery's main gate. Around the perimeter were tall posts with mounted closed-circuit cameras offering unseen officials twenty-four-hour video of what was occurring. Such surveillance cameras are a constant feature in China's

trouble-prone areas. I had been to the large Kumbum Monastery, a
historic ancient Buddhist center two hours' drive from Tongren, and
monks there told me cameras kept an eye on the entire facility, including prayer halls. Wary of catching the attention of security officials, I suggested to Robin that we rendezvous at a quiet side entrance
to the monastery. After a quarter of an hour, I encountered Robin and
the herder again at a small courtyard, and as an obvious foreigner I
found myself still drawing curious stares. We moved into a stairwell to
remain out of sight, half whispering.

As we talked further, Robin revealed that his elder brother was
among the thousands of Tibetans detained in the wake of the rioting
the previous year. He was an accidental prisoner. The brother, a nomad, had taken a new girlfriend on a love trek to Lhasa, and they were
staying at a guesthouse in the center of the city when Lhasa erupted in
protest. He hid, but police came to inspect the guesthouse. The police
paid little attention to his girlfriend, who managed to slip away, but
they accused him of being a troublemaker because he'd come from
outside the autonomous region. They tossed him in a truck and piled
so many other detainees on top of him that he almost lost consciousness. Police held him for forty-eight days, keeping a hood over his
head for much of the time. Authorities transferred him several times
during his detention, and when he was finally freed, it was in
Lanzhou, the capital of Gansu province, outside the Tibetan region.
Police kept his shoes, sending him out the door barefoot. Robin told
the story in a matter-of-fact tone. I asked him if his brother was bitter
over the experience, and he said yes but there was little one could do.
The sun was setting, and as I took my leave, Robin said we should see
one another the next day. I agreed.

I ate dinner and postponed checking into a hotel until late evening.
It was a security precaution. At hotels throughout China, reception-
ists make photocopies of visitors' passports, and if they spot one with
the J-1 visa of a foreign correspondent, then they are required to notify security officials. In some areas of China, this is not a concern.
Along the booming eastern seaboard of the country, the presence of
foreign journalists generally does not trouble local authorities. But in
less prosperous areas, where rural discontent can be high, or in areas

of ethnic unrest, the presence of a foreigner can be a red flag for the local public security bureau.

I had learned from experience that rural police could hinder the work of foreign journalists, hauling us to stations for questioning, offering cups of tea while thumbing through our passports, always with a smile and assertions that it is for our own safety. With endless philosophical questions about differences between China and the West, such sessions could last half a day, and afterward police might insist that a bureaucrat from the local Foreign Affairs office accompany us to "facilitate" our interviews. In fact, the presence of such a government minder would put a chill on most interviews, shackling our ability to report freely. Technically, I was not in violation of any rule with my presence in Tongren as far as I knew. Yet I was wary because my visit came in late winter, both a festive and a tense time among Tibetans. They celebrate their New Year around then, but they also mark the anniversary of the March 10, 1959, failed uprising that prompted the Dalai Lama to flee to exile in India. Unrest routinely takes place on or near the anniversary, most notably in violent uprisings in 1989 and 2008. At the time of my visit to Tongren, the anniversary was approaching, and security forces were jittery.

I was also concerned about the safety of people I might interview. Journalists might face some inconvenience but would always go freely back to homes in the big cities. Those we'd interview remained behind—vulnerable. Annual surveys by the Foreign Correspondents Club of China showed numerous cases of ordinary citizens suffering harassment at the hands of police after speaking with foreign reporters. One horrible case stuck in my mind. It involved Fu Xiancai, a citizen who dared speak out against the forced relocations of hundreds of thousands of people caused by the construction of the huge Three Gorges Dam straddling the Yangtze River. Police repeatedly warned Fu to stop speaking with foreign reporters. One day in 2006, after Fu had spoken with a German television crew, thugs set upon him, breaking his neck. The government later said Fu had slipped on a path, hurting himself in a fall. A year later, a farmer in Heilongjiang province in northeastern China was sentenced to two years of reeducation through labor for speaking to foreign journalists about his campaign to recover and privatize farmland seized by the government.[1]

Morning arrived with a crisp chill. I walked along Tongren's main street, which was lined with two-story buildings, with little Tibetan influence to break the drab Communist architecture. Block after block, at street level it was a succession of shops. Many still had their facades covered with corrugated metal doors that slid down to protect them at night, making it look like an endless line of one-car garages. As I walked, I sniffed incense burning on small outdoor stands, giving off the aromatic air of burning juniper, a traditional Tibetan offering. A few Tibetans sat astride motorcycles, chatting in the street. The motorcycles were pulled in half circles, and carried a distinctive Tibetan fashion sense. Young Tibetan men throw a folded blanket or place a small woolen carpet over the seats of their motorcycles, and drape saddlebags behind them, giving the motorbikes a resemblance to the horses that once were the main mode of transportation in the region. On the street, young men pulled their cycles close together, almost as if they were atop horses gathered at a watering hole.

I found Robin waiting for me in a doorway near the monastery. He asked if I'd like to see his living quarters and have tea. We ducked through a gate and across a courtyard to a little apartment. The door opened, and I saw a young Tibetan woman, still in her late teens. Robin introduced her as a fellow student; she barely opened her mouth, stricken with shyness. In the center of the two-room apartment was a stove fed by kindling. The stovepipe exited through the roof. A bed extended across a slab of bricks. In typical Chinese fashion, one can place coals underneath to warm it.

Robin invited me to sit down and served me butter tea, which tasted salty. He offered me *tsampa*, which I'd never eaten. It is a staple in the diet of Tibetans everywhere. Often it is made with just roasted barley ground into flour and mixed with butter tea. Tibetans roll the wet doughy *tsampa* into balls and eat it. Sometimes the roasted barley is mixed with other ingredients, such as yak cheese, sugar, and salt, for a more substantial meal. Since the barley is roasted, it is easily digested and gives a quick energy boost. In many areas of Tibet, *tsampa* is eaten at all meals. Much can differentiate Tibetans from one another, including dialect, the school of Buddhism followed, and other regional variations, but sociologists note that all Tibetans are *tsampa* eaters. Chinese generally consider the barley meal primitive and backward, prompting Tibetans to cling even more tightly to *tsampa* as a symbol of their identity. Barley flour serves other purposes as well. Tibetans throw pinches of it in the air during marriage and birthday celebrations and at funerals. It is believed that *tsampa* throwing actually predates Buddhist beliefs, used as an offering to animistic gods. I took the small bowl that Robin offered me and gently made a ball with my fingers, poking a little in my mouth. He looked at me expectantly. I chewed and found it rather tasteless.

Robin played with his mobile phone. Its ring tone was set to a song supporting Tibet independence, and on it he kept a music video of the long-haired male singer Amchok Gompo, now in exile in Canada. He brightened up as he played the music video in the safety of the apartment. I watched with interest. Robin said he knew it would be risky if authorities caught him with the video on his phone. The song and video are prohibited, likely violations of state security laws barring any ethnic challenge to national unity. I peppered him with questions about his village, and Robin said I should come back at the end of the school term to accompany him home to the high grasslands. I voiced a strong interest. I had explained to him that I was writing a book about Tibet, and I said I would like to see how his family lived on the grasslands. As I walked out the door, he insisted that I should return. Within weeks, I began receiving text messages on my mobile phone. Some were simple—"How are you? Where are you now?"—while others would keep me posted on when his school term would end— "I will finish studying after 20 days." Eager to see his home, I waited until I was sure his school term had finished and contacted him. I received back an abrupt and surprising message: "Sorry, I'm afraid I can't. Because lots of reasons. I promise I will tell you later clearly (include reason), OK?" I waited further for the right moment to travel, delving instead into life in Beijing.

Months passed before I finally received a text message from Robin. It suggested I come to his village the following weekend. On a map, his home on the grasslands is not far from Tongren, but logistically it was easiest for me to approach from another direction. From Beijing I took a two-hour flight to Lanzhou, the capital of Gansu province, and then planned to hop buses several times to reach Xiahe, a major Tibetan town near Robin's home village. After landing in Lanzhou, I took a taxi to the bus station and inquired about the next departure for where I was headed. "You are not permitted to buy such a ticket," the stern looking woman behind the ticket window told me without looking up. Confounded by the answer, I figured she might have misunderstood. I repeated the question. "Not permitted," she barked, turning her back on me. I wondered if it was government policy to bar foreigners from reaching Xiahe, site of a huge monastery where restive monks had frequently protested. I decided to walk to a spot where taxis were taking loads of passengers to an intermediate point, Linxia, about two hours away. I climbed aboard. Fellow passengers said they also didn't know why a foreigner would be denied a bus ticket. At Linxia, the taxi driver stopped at the local bus station and whispered to a bus driver, who promptly signaled me to board. He charged me about three times the normal fare but allowed me to ride to Xiahe.

The trip took another two hours on winding roads that climbed up mountain valleys, many with dramatic views. It was early summer, and the yellow blooms of rapeseed, an oil-producing crop, exploded in color on terraced hillsides. We finally pulled into Xiahe, a bustling town about 9,500 feet in elevation, and it seemed I had passed out of Han-dominant China to a Silk Road entrepot with a mix of cultures and religions. Crimson-robed monks and nomads dressed in sheepskin strolled the streets, a sign that the town was largely Tibetan. So, too, did ethnic Hui Muslims wearing white skullcaps and often with wispy beards.

A Tibetan waitress with two long ponytails greeted me at a second-floor diner. She was friendly and inquisitive, displaying curiosity toward a Western customer. I told her I was a journalist, and she took that as an invitation to sit down across from me in the booth. We were alone in the diner except for another employee, who swabbed the grimy floor with a mop. We were interrupted by loud military-like chanting outside, and she led me to a back window. On a huge asphalted school playground across a small river, scores of olive-clad militia members were doing choreographed ninja-like drills. Each held a four-foot pole. Many had their shirts off in the heat. The security officers swung and thrust their poles in kung fu moves, chanting boisterously. The waitress said the troops were stationed at the school. They practiced twice a day in noisy drills that local Tibetans believed were designed to intimidate them. The troops were from the People's Armed Police, a paramilitary force responsible for border security and guarding against riot, terrorist attack, and other civil emergencies. Our attention turned from the drill, and I told her I'd like to speak with monks at the local Labrang monastery, one of the largest in China. She dialed her mobile phone, saying her brother was a monk and would be there in a few moments.

Minutes later, I was seated across from a thirty-nine-year-old Tibetan in crimson robes with intense dark eyes. His Mandarin was rudimentary, but we managed to converse. I asked about the mood in the town, and he said it was tense. Tibetans faced discrimination. "If you look at government offices, there are hardly any Tibetans. Tibetans go to university and study hard, and they can't get a job. This is my sister," he said, indicating the waitress. "She finished high school, and she can't find a job." He told me how, during protests a year earlier, police raided the monastery, took fingerprints of all the monks, made them sign papers in Chinese characters that many didn't understand, and ripped up all the photographs they could find of the Dalai Lama, whose image is banned across China.

His sister asked me a question I had difficulty answering honestly, not wanting to ruin their illusions: "Do you think there is any hope that His Holiness the Dalai Lama will come to Tibet in the future?" I hesitated, pondering how to respond. "We always pray for the Dalai Lama to come back to Tibet," she said, trying to stir me to speak. I said that many in the ruling party were waiting for the Dalai Lama to die, believing that his disappearance would resolve the problem. The monk blurted out: "This is impossible! Their thinking is wrong!" He and his sister competed to speak. "We really, really hate Chinese people," the sister said. I asked whether she used "we" to refer to all Tibetans including monks, who are supposed to have compassion for all sentient beings. "It isn't the monks. It's us young people." The monk began to recount the way the police manhandled people at the Labrang Monastery a year earlier. "They used their gun butts on our bodies and our heads." After a few more minutes, he dismissed himself to return to the monastery. I followed him out the door to look for a hotel.

I arose the next day marveling at the deep-blue mountain skies, with none of the smog that normally covers the cities of eastern China. Robin had arranged for a taxi driver to take me up the winding road onto the high rolling grasslands, where the Tibetan nomads set up tents in the warm summer months to be near their flocks of sheep and yaks. As we approached a large plain beside one village, I saw periodic piles of burning juniper branches along the road and a growing number of Tibetan horsemen dressed in ceremonial *chubas* with colorful sashes. As we drove on, the road was lined with Tibetans astride either motorcycles or horses, looking like they were waiting for someone. I saw hundreds of women and children standing in a field, many with brilliant crimson sashes around their *chubas*. Many of the children wore royal blue brocade jackets. The taxi driver explained that the senior *rinpoche*, or reincarnated lama, from the Labrang monastery was making his annual visit to the area, marking a major holiday. We got out to look more closely at the festivities, and I absorbed the stunning setting.

The grasslands extended for miles in each direction, without a tree in sight, rising into hills that disappeared into low-lying, leaden clouds. The yellow rapeseed patches, scattered among barley and wheat fields, added pastel colors to the wide-open panorama. I could barely make out clusters of colorful nomad tents and herds of grazing sheep on the distant hills. Suddenly the ground began to tremble slightly, then more strongly. I looked over to see horsemen galloping across the plain, their steeds bearing ceremonial saddle blankets. The tails of the horses were carefully braided. When the *rinpoche*'s convoy arrived, three police cruisers served as escorts as well as a number of other cars carrying Communist Party cadres. The driver suggested that we head on to Robin's village, and we rolled on across the grasslands, pulling up into a settlement of brick and mud houses set below a small monastery on a bluff. Robin, who had been calling the mobile phone of the taxi driver periodically to ensure our arrival, pulled up on a motorbike, grinning widely. He escorted me into a muddy courtyard and explained that his family had wanted to postpone my visit until the festival, which was a good pretext for a foreigner to visit and would clear any possible suspicion from falling on the family.

We settled down in his family's three-room, drafty home. I was both exhilarated by the extraordinary beauty of the surroundings and discomforted by the poverty of the village. A dung-fired stove sat in the middle of the largest room, which served as sitting and dining room as well as a bedroom in the evenings. Soon there were cups of butter tea all around. A big pile of bread and noodle soup appeared. As soon as I took a sip of tea, Robin's mother refilled the glass. The China I had grown comfortable in felt distant. Those around the table, except for Robin, spoke only the most rudimentary Mandarin. Striking up a conversation was not possible. Even so, the family switched on the television, rigged to a simple satellite system, and the Henan province TV channel blared out in Mandarin.

I asked Robin how many villagers could understand Mandarin. "They can speak a little Chinese, just so-so. When they need to use it, they use it. But they don't like to study it. Few Tibetans know Chinese well. If a Chinese truck comes here to buy something, they'll use it." What he described was a willful choice not to speak the main language of the nation, and I found the same situation again on other trips to Tibetan areas. Enthusiasm to learn English was great but to learn Chinese far less so.

Robin soon showed me his small room, lit with a bare hanging light bulb. Next to his cot were two metal lockers. He opened them and began pulling out volume after volume of English textbooks and notebooks full of handwriting, evidence of the many years he had labored to learn English. After a little more conversation, I realized how limited Robin's experience had been. He had never traveled to the Gansu capital of Lanzhou, nor had he been to Xining, capital of neighboring Qinghai province and only a two-hour drive from his high school. I asked him about what he studied in secondary school. "We studied Chinese history, Chinese politics, Chinese geography, world history, and world geography." And if you could choose what to study, what would it be? I asked. "I would study Tibetan history, Tibetan politics, Tibetan culture and customs, and English." And any Chinese subjects? "No."

Through the open door, I saw his mother puttering around in the courtyard. Earlier, she had worked with other villagers to pound out matted shorn yak wool into a flat felt rug. Now she was washing clothes. Robin saw my attention focused on his mother and talked about the hard labor that comprised much of the waking hours of his parents. "Every day, she cuts the forage for it to dry. She needs to go to the fields to weed them. She grows wheat. She goes from morning to night, very hard in season. In winter, she goes to the grasslands to herd the yaks with her sister. She also has to collect yak dung. Their lives are very hard. So we need to study hard. They are very old. My father is fifty-three. My mother is forty-eight."

Robin grabbed a basketball and suggested that we go out to the village court. I was surprised such a thing existed in the village. We headed down a dirt path, past huge piles of dung in conical structures that would serve as fuel for stoves, across a stream, and over to a packed earthen court in the middle of a field with two rudimentary goalposts at each end. Vast grasslands stretched away in three directions. He grabbed the ball and started to dribble. "I like Iverson," he said, referring to shooting star Allen Iverson. He reeled off the names of several other NBA stars—Dwyane Wade, Lebron James, and Kobe Bryant—only he used the Mandarin pronunciation, and it took me a minute to realize "Ke-bi" was Kobe and "Jie-mu-si" was James. NBA stars all have alternative Chinese names because fans in China can't pronounce their Western names. We played a game of Horse, in which we took turns taking shots from anywhere on the court.[2] Suddenly, I felt out of breath.

We were more than ten thousand feet up in the high grasslands. Little wonder I gasped. The sun's high-altitude rays bore down, and I sat on grass at courtside, shading myself. Robin kept shooting, and within half an hour at least ten other teenagers had congregated, some on horseback, a few on motorcycles. They spotted from afar that a game was in the offing, and one promptly started up. Trying to dribble the ball on the dirt court was a challenge, given that ruts in the packed dirt would make the ball take odd bounces.

At a break, I suddenly realized that the thin young man next to Robin was his elder brother, the one who was arrested in Lhasa during the 2008 protests. We sat down, and Robin translated as the brother recounted his treatment at the hands of the police following his arrest. The brother said he'd made the journey to Lhasa on a lark with a girlfriend. He'd never been before, and nearly everyone he knew ached to see the city. Robin interjected that all Tibetans long to visit the city. "Every villager hopes to go to Lhasa because there are so many famous Buddhist statues there. It's the Tibetan capital." Traveling is not easy, though, because police want to know the business of travelers, and they stop those seen as potential agitators. "Lhasa is a Tibetan place, but Tibetans can't go there," the brother said. "The Potala is our palace, but it is overrun with Chinese."

I spent part of the afternoon resting and reading in the cool shade while Robin returned to play more basketball. When I saw him again, he was excited. "While you were reading, I got a call from Southwest University for Nationalities. They said, 'You can come.'" This was particularly good news. The university is in Chengdu, a metropolis that is the gateway to Tibet from Sichuan province. It is also among the best of the universities scattered about China created specifically for the 108 million or so people who belong to the fifty-five ethnic minority groups apart from the majority Han Chinese. Tibetans are the most widely known of the minorities, but they are far from the largest group. The ethnic Zhuang, Manchu, Hui, Miao, Uighur, Tujia, Yi, and Mongolians all have greater populations than the 6.2 million Tibetans. The central government set up twelve universities that mostly enroll minority students, providing them with chances at largely segregated higher education. Robin had won a slot at Northwest University for Nationalities in the provincial capital of Lanzhou, but the Chengdu university was more prestigious. I asked if he ever considered attending a regular university alongside Han Chinese. He shrugged and said it was impossible. "There are so many universities in China, but they only take Chinese. I mean real Chinese, not *xiaozu minzu*," he said, using the Mandarin term for ethnic minorities.

In the course of several days, Robin and I discussed many aspects of the Tibetan dilemma, and I told him that his village was one of the "purest" Tibetan experiences I had had in multiple trips to the Plateau. Han Chinese were absent. None lived here. The Tibetan nomads and villagers seemed to dwell in a world of their own cultural identity, except for watching Mandarin-language television shows. If the Han majority was believed to be choking off the Tibetan minority, it was not readily apparent here. Robin listened patiently and suggested I'd get a fuller picture by talking to more people. I awaited his guidance and reflected back on encounters I had had in Dharamsala with people who said the struggle for Tibet had moved from Lhasa, where repression was fiercest, to outlying areas, like this northeast corner of Greater Tibet, where history had produced great Dalai and Panchen lamas, intellectual traditions ran deep, and local Tibetans were toughened by conflict.

Tibetans traditionally divide their homeland into three areas. To the east is Kham, a region of warriors. The vast central area around Lhasa is the holy seat of power and is known by Tibetans as U-Tsang. Amdo to the north and northeast is renowned for thinkers and intellectuals. The Amdo region is home to historic Kumbum and Labrang monasteries, two of the "big six" major centers of scholarship for the Yellow Hat, or Gelugpa, sect of Tibetan Buddhism, which is the largest of four schools and the one from which the Dalai Lama always emerges. Amdo also has a vibrant tradition of writing that goes on to this day in Tibetan-language blogs and essays.

A day later, Robin took me up a hill near the monastery and introduced me to a thirty-three-year-old monk. The monk was from the village but had spent six years in Lhasa at the famous Drepung Monastery, historically the largest of all in Tibet, housing as many as ten thousand monks nearly a century ago. Drepung is known for its high standards of learning, and the monk's bright eyes and alert manner indicated his cleverness. He told me that he was virtually a prisoner in the village. He was among scores of monks arrested at Drepung in Lhasa during unrest in 2008 and held for six months at detention facilities around Tibet and Qinghai. During his imprisonment, he saw the ways authorities coerced jailed monks to turn on each other. "Sometimes they say, 'We'll only let you out of jail if you turn into an informant,'" he said, drawing his crimson robe more tightly around him against a blustery gust. Jailed monks with relatives working as teachers or in government jobs faced particular pressure. "They say, 'We will take his job away.'" Still others are told they must hang photos of Mao Zedong in the shrine rooms in their family homes or face large fines.

When the monk told police he wasn't stirring up his brethren at Drepung, they caught him in a lie. They trotted out a video from the monastery's closed-circuit system in which he is clearly seen standing up with other monks urging rebellion. That made him a marked man. Other monks in jail told him they, too, were shown video of their own actions. When the monk was finally released, they told him he would not be allowed to return to Lhasa, only to his home village. "Of course, I want to go back. If there were an opportunity, I'd go now. But I'm not free. If I go somewhere, one or two people will follow me secretly." Then he would be forcefully brought back. I ask him whether the village might not be a better place than Lhasa—with its intense repression—to practice Buddhism. He demurred sharply, saying Tibetan consciousness is higher in Lhasa even with the repression, and activists insist that Tibetans cling fiercely to traditions. "There's no person in this village who tells people, 'You must protect customs.' So some people mix up Mandarin and Tibetan words," he says. The erosion is slow but steady, he said.

Robin and I headed back to his home. He remained excited about his imminent entry to university, though he didn't know whether he'd be able to afford the better one in Chengdu. He talked eagerly of his chance to study Tibetan language and culture as well as more advanced English. He felt pulled in several directions. On the one hand, he wanted to expand his knowledge of his ethnic roots and culture. He wanted to travel to Lhasa. On the other hand, he felt drawn away from Tibet. "I want to go abroad," he says. "I like English." Knowing the likely outcome of both choices, I felt a pang of sadness. After university, Tibetan graduates could strive for low-paying jobs as schoolteachers. A few might get government posts—if they had good connections. Other than that, options were few. Prospects for Tibetan entrepreneurs or professionals, like lawyers and accountants, were not good. And if Robin traveled and stayed abroad, the experience might be enriching but would inexorably begin to leach the "Tibetanness" out of him.

My visit to the grasslands came to an end, and I headed back to Beijing, where visions of Tibet exist in a parallel universe: The Dalai Lama is evil, and many Chinese feel the outside world misunderstands their policies toward Tibet, perhaps with malicious intent. Beijing felt like an echo chamber where the party line had been amplified to a feverish decibel. Newspapers and television newscasts uniformly slammed the Dalai Lama as an irredeemable separatist, using emotion-laden terms to deride Tibetans' quest for greater autonomy as a foreign-born plot to resurrect backward social systems. In the privacy of my own thoughts, I pondered possible ways to negotiate a deal with the Tibetans. Why not a "one country, two systems" arrangement like the one that brought Hong Kong back to China in 1997 from under British rule? Then I came to my senses. The Communist Party would cede no ground. A public with a growing sense of patriotic nationalism would see any concession as a sign of weakness, anathema to party leaders. Moreover, Tibet's resources and territory were too vital to China's interests. Tibet is rich in minerals and vital water. Himalayan glaciers provide the headwaters for seven of the mightiest rivers in Asia, including the Yangtze and Yellow rivers. China is believed to maintain four or five nuclear missile bases in Tibet.[3] Any ceding of ground to Tibetans would set a precedent, spurring other restive minorities to demand equal treatment. It would be a Pandora's box. Most Han Chinese I knew wanted to pull Tibet more tightly into Beijing's embrace rather than let up on a bear hug many Tibetans saw as suffocating.

Even our close Chinese friends, educated in foreign universities, would avoid discussion of Tibet, rolling their eyes at the futility of debate with what they saw as dogmatic foreigners starry-eyed over Shangri-La. One of them was a senior editor at one of China's biggest internet portals. She would grow testy when the subject arose. China has a legitimate claim over Tibet, she said, but the Western media ignored it and portrayed the Dalai Lama as morally superior. He's really just an astute political monk, she added, and the Western world plays into his hands. She went on to tell how one of her close Chinese friends living in London engaged in minor acts of defiance on the Tibet issue. Every time she entered a bookstore and saw books about the Dalai Lama, she said, the friend would pick them up from the section where they were displayed, whether "Religion" or "Self-Improvement" or "Current Events," and carefully relocate them to "Fiction." She hadn't been caught, and the act of disobedience seemed to do wonders for her own disposition.

The story resonated with me for days. I hadn't expected the editor to have such a visceral reaction to Tibet. But the fact is that in urban

China it is hard to find Han Chinese not nettled by what they see as misguided Western perceptions of Tibet. More than 400 million Chinese now regularly use the internet, and a good many see Chinese news reports and commentaries about erroneous foreign press reports. One frequent culprit is a wire service photograph of policemen beating Tibetan protesters, which has been mislabeled as occurring in China when it actually occurred in Katmandu, Nepal. Explanations from abroad that this might be the result of copyeditor carelessness have convinced few Chinese. Many believe in more nefarious causes.

For foreign journalists, there are few opportunities to raise questions with China's top leaders who are far removed from the press and public. Premier Wen Jiabao would hold one news conference a year at the Great Hall of the People, a huge meeting hall on Tiananmen Square, the massive plaza at the heart of Beijing. The first year, I dutifully held up my hand at the news conference, hoping to be called on out of the several hundred Chinese and foreign journalists present. It didn't take long to learn that operatives at the Ministry of Foreign Affairs had already selected a handful of journalists and told them to submit their questions. Most complied and stuck to their prevetted questions. That way, the premier, knowing an Indian journalist would be selected for a question, could quote from the Upanishads or the poetry of Rabindranath Tagore by memory, wowing the live televised audience with his erudition. The annual affair was a prearranged set piece. For his part, President Hu Jintao, the ruling party general secretary, never accepted interviews and rarely met the press, except on trips abroad where he might accept a single question or two.

On sensitive matters, such as Tibet, newspaper and television coverage would generally stick to a series of themes. The themes on Tibet were that the remote Land of Snows has been a part of China for at least seven centuries, that prior to the arrival of Chinese troops in the 1950s Tibet was hell on Earth, and lastly that China has administered Tibet in a benevolent manner, paying for vast development while allowing Tibetans to guide their own affairs.[4] News reports dutifully recounted the billion-dollar programs for bridge- and road-building programs, renovations of monasteries, hydroelectric plants, and other projects. Displays on the wonders of Chinese management of Tibet regularly filled the television airwaves and the exhibition halls in the capital.

On hearing of a new Tibet exhibit, I wandered down to the Minorities Cultural Palace, a large hall west of Tiananmen Square, where I saw a line of retirees snake along a sidewalk. Overhead, a large banner proclaimed, "Fifty Years of Democratic Reforms in Tibet." Many of the retirees were former workers at state-owned enterprises and had been given free tickets to enter the exhibition. The mood in line was upbeat, and many were enjoying the chance for an outing in pleasant weather. Because of the millions of young people still entering the workforce every year, retirement comes early for urban dwellers in China, with many women retiring at age fifty and men at age fifty-five. All those whom I could see were ethnic Han, who predominate in Beijing and in all of China, comprising 92 percent of the country's 1.3 billion people. Greeting visitors at the vast entry hall was a huge introductory placard, surrounded by bright red poinsettias, noting that barely half a century ago Tibet "was still a feudal serfdom under the despotic theocratic rule of officials, lamas, and nobles." The exhibition, the tablet noted, would outline the "remarkable achievements" Tibet has made under Communist rule. The entry hall led to three chambers, each with a different theme. One described the preliberation society in Tibet, in which tyrannical monks and lords ruled. Another championed the Chinese troops who "liberated" Tibet in the 1950s, and a third described the "happiness" of Tibetans despite "efforts by foreign countries and the Dalai Lama clique" to restore the old feudal system to the Tibetan Plateau.

Like many Chinese exhibits, the displays were long on statistics, such as the numbers of monks that once relied on compulsory, unpaid labor of peasants for their well-being. Next to one photo of a wretched looking Tibetan peasant, a placard said: "There were 2,676 monasteries in old Tibet whose 114,925 incumbents (12 percent of the Tibetan population) included 500 high-ranking monks and 4,000 with economic powers. None of these monks did manual labor because their living was supported by local farmers and herders." A display case housed heavy wooden stockades, wooden handcuffs, thumbscrews, foot fetters, and other instruments of torture. On central display was a wooden cage used to lock up prisoners. "Many monasteries housed criminal courts and prisons. They were therefore instrumental in the cruel punishment and execution of serfs," a placard explained. Outbreaks of disease, such as small pox, were rampant prior to the arrival of Chinese medical brigades, and peasants were routinely crippled by beatings that they received from their lords.

The exhibition portrayed the Dalai Lama and a handful of close aides as masterminds of ethnic unrest that surges periodically in Tibet. I watched as retirees shook their heads in disgust reading the damage toll from the 2008 riots in Lhasa, the Tibetan capital. Protesters set three hundred fires and destroyed 908 shops, as well as seven schools and 120 houses, displays said. Five hospitals were left in ruins, and eighty-four vehicles burned or smashed. And in the tragic human toll, eighteen innocent civilians were killed. Photos showed smoke billowing over Lhasa. No hint was offered of any grievances that might explain the violent opposition to China's administration of Tibet.

Only slight mention was made of the damage wreaked on Tibet's religious heritage during the Great Proletarian Cultural Revolution, the period of intense upheaval from 1966 until 1976, when Mao Zedong unleashed young radicals to smash the "four olds"—old customs, old culture, old habits, and old ideas. Red Guards across China went on a savage campaign to ransack museums, raze temples and shrines, and uproot vestiges of ancient heritage. Damage to Tibet may not have been worse than elsewhere in China but its Buddhist patrimony was ruinously devastated. Ethnic Han Red Guards as well as some Tibetan followers smashed and razed thousands of monasteries, stupas, and lamaseries. Priceless Buddhist relics, including handwritten sutras and other religious documents, were tossed in rivers or crushed in landfills. The Cultural Revolution's impact on Tibet was neatly brushed off in a small placard. "During the Cultural Revolution, Tibet, like other parts of China, suffered setbacks and losses. But the central government has done the best it could to offer assistance and guidance in the hope to reduce Tibet's losses to the minimum."

I approached several visitors to ask their opinion of the exhibition. Several foreign camera crews were doing the same thing. Perhaps because visitors had just passed a display of how the Western media slanted the news on Tibet to make China look bad, most were wary of being interviewed. "This exhibition is great!" an eighty-three-year-old

man who gave his surname as Wang said. Old Wang said he'd learned
a lot. "It's all so clear. It's obvious that in old Tibet, the serf owners and
the top lamas suppressed people cruelly." Another elderly man over-
rode the warnings of his wife to interject his opinion that the Dalai
Lama was misinformed about conditions in Tibet. "We see that his
thinking is not correct. The country gave him many opportunities,
but he didn't take them." The retiree said he was a former worker in
the state aviation archives, but his wife, muttering under her breath,
dragged him away before he could say more. In case anyone lacked
discerning powers over the exhibition, it offered a conclusion on a
placard:

> History makes fair judgments. During fifty years of
> development, Tibet has moved from darkness to light,
> dictatorship to democracy, and seclusion to opening up.

Beijing would like the world and its own citizens to conclude that
Tibet is open to anyone. But it is far from true. For all intents and purposes, Tibet is like a separate country with unique immigration rules.
As an accredited foreign journalist, I was barred unless invited to go.
Since an initial trip in 2007, I had submitted multiple letters and faxes
and made untold phone calls seeking permission to return to the Tibetan Autonomous Region, all to no avail. Foreign tourists, if they pay
hefty fees and do not have markings in their passport that indicate
they are journalists or diplomats, are generally permitted into Tibet.
But foreigners with specialized knowledge of the internal situation of
Tibet are generally barred, or allowed only brief visits, to prevent
credible reports about hardships there. Rather than moving from
"seclusion to opening up," China kept the curtain drawn on Tibet,
opening it only after much preparation and for brief periods. The few
foreign journalists who get in on government-sponsored trips find
minders at their side.

For the time being, I could only listen to what party cadres wanted
the public to know about Tibet in their once-a-year status report during the annual National People's Congress, the ceremonial legislature.
So I returned to the Great Hall of the People, the mammoth building
on Tiananmen Square, and ambled along the red carpets to an upper-

story salon with a Tibetan motif. On entering the room, one walks by a wooden divider that contains a huge painting of the Potala Palace and then sees elaborate and colorful murals. Three chandeliers illuminate the room. It is here that a Tibet informational meeting takes place on the sidelines of the National People's Congress each March. As I entered, I saw about two dozen officials behind microphones around tables set up in a U shape. Another equal number of their aides sat behind them. About half were dressed in elegant Tibetan attire, including some women in colorful headgear, interspersed with the political commissar of the People's Armed Police and other uniformed military officers. Leading the meeting was Jampa Phuntsok, a lanky Tibetan wearing a blue blazer, striped tie, and wire-rimmed glasses. By title, he was chair of the Tibet Autonomous Region government, but in actuality he took orders from the region's ethnic Han party secretary, who remains largely out of public view. At the time, Phuntsok was the most visible figure of government policy.

As a gaggle of journalists looked on from the back of the room, he and a series of other officials offered a bright assessment of how they have kept Tibet's economy growing vigorously, drawn foreign investment, protected the Plateau's fragile environment, and implemented programs for jobless Tibetan youth. At a final brief question-and-answer session, a scrum broke out for the microphone. One foreign journalist asked Phuntsok why authorities blocked foreign journalists from traveling to Tibet. Without a trace of mockery, he responded: "We very much welcome journalists from all over the world to Tibet to do interviews. We always say seeing is believing. . . . The 'problem' of not allowing foreign journalists to enter Tibet does not exist."

chapter three

Riding the Rails to Tibet

All nationalities in the People's Republic of China are equal. . . .
Discrimination against and oppression of any nationality is prohibited; any act which undermines the unity of the nationalities or
instigates division is prohibited.

    —The Constitution of the People's Republic of China,
    Article 4, Chapter 1

ON THE SKY TRAIN TO LHASA, A FEW THINGS ARE CERTAIN: THE
altitude will produce a stabbing headache, and yet through the discomfort the scenery unfolding outside the speeding train will be
among the most utterly strange and starkly beautiful on the planet. As
I boarded the train on my first trip, I dropped my ballpoint pens in a
plastic bag. I hoped it would contain the mess if the pens leaked from
the drop in air pressure as we chugged along the highest railway in the
world, keeping ink from spilling on my computer, small camera, and
clothes. This was no idle worry—it had happened to colleagues. Over
the next day and a half, the train would pull us ever higher onto the
Tibetan Plateau, finally crossing the Tanggula Pass, some 16,400 feet
in elevation, far higher than the highest peak in the continental
United States. At that altitude, sealed bags of snacks and chips puff up
like blowfish, ready to burst. People cradle their heads in pain, suffering high-altitude headaches, barely able to enjoy the majestic scenery
unfolding along the route. The air at such breath-taking elevations
contains only 60 percent of the oxygen that it does at sea level. We

would suffer the travails of high-altitude mountain climbing without ever strapping on crampons or clutching an ice axe.

Two colleagues who had joined me for the trip laughed and joked gregariously at lower altitudes, but as we climbed higher, the air thinned, and the conversation diminished. Soon we were short of breath despite the pressurized cabin. The conductor passed out air tubes that could be plugged into wall sockets for oxygen-rich air, and we took them as if we were a batch of wheezing emphysema patients. The train wended its way across vast expanses of Qinghai province into a largely treeless frigid plateau north of the Tibetan Autonomous Region, bound for the Roof of the World. In the dining car, the tables filled with a curious mix of government officials, a smattering of foreign tourists, and what appeared to be Han merchants and traders. We pulled out playing cards and whiled away the hours playing poker, allowing the cards to fall somewhat mindlessly in our oxygen-deprived state. After we tired of cards, we stayed glued to the windows, filming herds of yak amid patches of snow and keeping an eye out for Tibetan antelope. Under the clear blue skies, the occasional lakes in the distance would dissolve into mirages that blended with the horizon. At dark, as we lurched back to our compartment, I peered out the window. The moon had not yet risen, and all I could see was blackness and a few faint stars. No lights dotted the horizon. This is one of the few places in China where humanity has not pressed against me.

The comforting groan of the 3,800-horsepower engine in the custom-built locomotive disguised what an astounding engineering feat carried us onward. When the railway was inaugurated in mid-2006, China hailed it as on a par with construction of the huge Three Gorges Dam spanning the Yangtze River and with rocketing a Chinese astronaut into space a few years earlier. Like the other projects, the twenty-five-hundred-mile railway link from Beijing to Lhasa ran up a huge price tag—about $4.1 billion. It also was extraordinary in terms of technology, and China had reason to be bursting with pride.

Under my swaying railcar, the railway passed over frozen earth at extreme altitudes. Some six hundred miles of the rail line extends along permafrost more than thirteen thousand feet in elevation. I noticed that the train stayed mainly on bridges. To avoid melting the frozen earth, Chinese engineers devised their own technologies. In some areas of permafrost, a thin top layer of slush melts and refreezes daily with the rising and setting of the sun. Rather than build the railway on a causeway across the permafrost, which might allow heat from the trains to descend into the tundra and make it unstable, the engineers built hundreds of miles of bridges, often thrusting hollow concrete tubes deep into the ground, with coolants circulating to ensure that the permafrost remained frozen. Portions of the track are also passively cooled with ammonia-based heat exchangers. Sunshades protect sections of track. In more stable areas, huge stone slabs cover embankments. The trains themselves use cooling technology to prevent heat absorption by the tracks. Depending on one's outlook, one either feels snug or claustrophobic aboard the sealed train, unable to open a window but warmly protected from the freezing winds outside.

The rail line finalized a dream: Mao Zedong set out half a century ago to bind Tibet inexorably to China. Chinese historians maintained that Tibet had been an integral part of China since the thirteenth century, even though no written act or decree had surfaced to substantiate that claim, and history seemed far more ambiguous. But Mao knew that a rail line would be an inexorable cordon, and he sought to overcome the hurdle of construction. Getting armies of workers to toil so high up was not easy. At thirteen thousand feet, pulmonary and cerebral edemas can fell humans, swelling brain and lung tissue and causing a quick death. The only surefire treatment is going down to lower elevations. China asserts that none of the twenty thousand workers involved in the railway construction died from altitude sickness. Years earlier, I routinely traveled to high altitude in Peru and Bolivia, so I knew that I was prone to the nausea and severe headaches that such heights may provoke. It can be as bad as, or even worse than, a particularly nasty hangover. So I was taking a prescription medication commonly used by mountain climbers, Diamox, that causes one to breathe faster, metabolizing more oxygen and aiding in acclimatization. The drug also makes one's cheeks and fingers and toes tingle. I felt a prickly sensation in my fingers.

The railway is already altering Tibet. Once accessible only by air or by slow truck journeys along potholed roads lasting many weeks, Tibet is now open to any Chinese with the equivalent of $46 to pay for a one-way ticket on a hard seat (our soft sleeper berths cost $158) and a desire to head to the new frontier. The open door has many Tibetans worried that the railway is a wedge to allow Han Chinese to flood in and dilute their culture. "The railway link is a real danger," the Dalai Lama said. "Jobless people facing difficulty in Chinese mainland are coming to Lhasa." The railway line was engineered to keep the Tibetan permafrost stable, but its effect on the demographic stability of Tibetan society is another matter.

China's outlook on the railways has changed remarkably. At one time, trains evoked fear in China and symbolized foreign efforts to trample over a weakened, opium-addicted country ripe for exploitation. In anger, Chinese ripped up railroads. In 1877, on the inauguration of an unauthorized sixteen-kilometer railway built by British merchants from Shanghai to Wusong, the governor-general of Nanjing, Shen Baozhen, ordered it demolished.[1] A few decades later, foreign-built railways that upset the *fengshui* in the countryside partly led to the Boxer Rebellion at the turn of the twentieth century. An anti-Western sect known as the Righteous Harmonious Fists rose up and attacked churches, Christians, and foreign-built railways. In Shandong province, the Boxers destroyed two German-built rail lines seen as disrupting the harmony of the region, and mobs attacked the main rail link between Beijing and Tianjin. It wasn't until the 1949 Revolution that China began actively employing railroads as an imperial tool, useful for assimilating natives in outlying areas and thus stitching together China's mammoth human quilt. Despite much talk of ethnic harmony from China's leaders, the process was not smooth.

It never has been. For thousands of years, the Chinese considered their land to be the Middle Kingdom and those coming from outside to be "barbarians." Non-Chinese vassals paid tribute to the Chinese, who monopolized the sole right to rule "under heaven." Several times, foreigners breached the monopoly, most notably the Mongols and the Manchus, who founded the Yuan Dynasty (1271–1368 CE) and the Qing Dynasty (1644–1912 CE), respectively. But the ethnic Han, who come from China's central plains and are the most populous ethnic group in the world, successfully prevailed over outsiders, engendering an attitude of cultural superiority. After Mao Zedong brought China's Communists to power, he openly fretted in a 1953 essay about the tendency of "Han chauvinism." He said the problem occurred "to a serious degree and not just a matter of its vestiges. . . . Therefore, education must be assiduously carried out so that this problem can be solved step by step." The warning from Mao gained such currency that state fathers included the phrase "Han chauvinism" in the preamble to the 1982 constitution, pledging to safeguard minority rights. Today, ethnic minorities remain highly visible at national celebrations with their colorful costumes but deeply disadvantaged in day-to-day life, accounting for nearly 50 percent of the national poor.[2]

One needs only look at a map to see that the matter of ethnic unity is crucial for keeping China's territory intact. China officially calculates that it has fifty-five ethnic minorities, representing 8.4 percent of the country's 1.3 billion population. Some of those minorities have homelands on huge resource-blessed swaths of territory, and they face similar existential pressures from waves of Han migration. Looking at the situation of two other minority groups may portend what lies ahead for the Tibetans.

The first are the Uighurs, Central Asians who look Caucasian, speak a Turkic language, and generally are Sunni Muslims. The Uighur homeland is in the arid far northwest, an area that China designates as the Xinjiang Uighur Autonomous Region. The situation of a second group, the Mongols, descendants of Genghis Khan and the powerful Mongol Empire, which once stretched from Eastern Europe to the Korean Peninsula, may mirror what will happen if Han migration into Tibet continues at a steady torrent. Today, Mongols are a partitioned people, spread across three national boundaries. More than five million live in China, mostly in the Inner Mongolia Autonomous Region or in abutting Liaoning province in the northeast. Some three million live in the Republic of Mongolia, an independent landlocked country of steppes to the north, and another million live in Russia.

The Tibetans, the Uighurs, and the Mongols are not the largest ethnic minorities in China today. The Zhuang, Manchu, and Hui Muslims are more numerous. But the Tibetans and Uighurs have huge cultural, linguistic, and religious differences with the majority Han. Indeed, both groups say religion is core to their identity and feel deeply aggrieved over restrictions on its practice. Those two groups, along with the Mongols, are concentrated in vast border regions. If China were to face a significant secession drive from any of the three groups, it would face the prospect of a seriously dismembered territory. The Tibet and Inner Mongolia autonomous regions each comprise one-eighth of China's landmass. The Xinjiang Uighur Autonomous Region is one-sixth of China. Together, the three autonomous regions make up over 42 percent of the nation's territory. And that doesn't even take into consideration that ethnic Tibetans live in an area about twice the size of the Tibetan Autonomous Region. Take Greater Tibet into account, and what is at stake is half of the Chinese nation.

The experiences of the Uighurs and Mongols differ in some ways from that of the Tibetans, but there are also similarities, notably in the way China's leaders proclaim a hollow autonomy for each group, move large numbers of minorities who are obstructive, and jail or exile those who demand greater freedoms. To better understand the Uighur and Mongol experiences, I searched out two strikingly different women, similar mainly in their vocal support for their own ethnicity. China labels one of the women a "separatist monster" and a terrorist instigator, but her followers call her the "Mother of all Uighurs." She was sent into exile a few years ago and now works from an office nearly shouting distance from the White House. The other woman is a brainy former Marxist philosopher who runs a small gift shop of Mongolian handicrafts in the city of Hohhot, quietly promoting the Mongol cause and advocating for her husband, a long-serving political prisoner.

WHEN THE WORST RACE RIOTS in more than a decade in China erupted in the nation's far northwestern region in the summer of 2009, the ethnic group thrust into the news was largely unknown outside of Asia. Even the name of the group was hard to pronounce for newscasters, who needed tips like "WEE-ger." Unfortunately for the Uighurs, they did not have a spiritual or political figurehead akin to the Dalai Lama who could speak English and make news by rubbing shoulders with Western politicians and titans of industry. The closest the Uighurs have to a global spokesperson is an accidental leader, Rebiya Kadeer, a diminutive former businesswoman living in exile in the United States. On one of my trips to Xinjiang, I reached Kadeer from my cell phone. She was traveling in California. A translator was also on the line, and Kadeer spoke in her native Uighur language. My strongest recollection was that I had to hold the telephone away from my ear because she seemed so strident. But the more I learned about Kadeer and her extraordinary personal sacrifices, the more intent I became on meeting her. I finally got the chance during a visit in late 2008 to Washington, DC.

For our interview, I was summoned to a suite in a building on Pennsylvania Avenue favored by trade associations and lobby groups that want to be near the nexus of power. The building is diagonal to the Eisenhower Executive Office Building, a Washington landmark that houses some of the White House staff, including the National Security Council. While the address suggests clout, the offices of the Uyghur American Association are low-end. In fact, there are no fixed offices. The multiple tenants of the suite—which include the embassy of Palau, various lawyers, and the National Abstinence Education Association—use office space on an as-available basis. The day I came, Kadeer's right-hand man went looking among offices for an empty one we could occupy.

A few minutes later, Kadeer walked in. Her most distinguishing feature is the way she wears her hair—in two long, loosely braided pigtails that extend to her mid-back. She wore a deep vermillion wool jacket with light black trim atop an embroidered red blouse with a stand-up collar. On her head was a *doppa*, a small boxy velvet skullcap traditional among Uighurs. It sat on the back of her crown, showing her thick hair, which is liberally gray, and she wore the hat with one of its corners high. Her skin was a healthy olive color, accentuating her dark eyes and thick eyebrows. She smiled easily and projected a softer image than what I had imagined through the static-filled mobile phone interview from half a world away. Kadeer speaks rudimentary Chinese and even less English, though she had been in exile in the States for a number of years, so we spoke again through a Uighur translator, and her remarkable story poured out.

Born into poverty as the daughter of a gold miner in the Altai Mountains, Kadeer rose to become a successful merchant in Urumqi, the largest city in Xinjiang and a hub for commerce to Central Asia. She began trading in sheepskins, moving on to textiles and scrap iron. Amassing capital, she built a department store and then moved into real estate development and production of foodstuffs. By the early 1990s, her business acumen had made her the seventh richest person in China.[3] She built her fortune despite little formal education, never attending university, and while raising eleven children. As she grew more powerful, trading extensively with newly independent Central Asian nations, the party sought to bring her into its ranks, inviting her as a delegate to the National People's Congress, the ceremonial legislature in Beijing where she dined at banquets with mighty party leaders. All the while, she developed a sense that laws purportedly designed to provide equality to minorities, such as the Uighurs, were actually applied to weaken them and force their assimilation.

"I never thought of being a leader in my life. I thought someone would appear. At the end of the day, it turned out to be me," Kadeer said. Using her post, Kadeer began to speak out, asking why resources such as oil and cotton were being exploited in Xinjiang by the central government with no benefit to the ethnic Uighurs. "Under six decades of Chinese rule, Uighurs are just struggling for their daily survival." Kadeer talked of going to see Wang Lequan, the forceful longtime party boss in Xinjiang, and finding that like most Han Chinese he could not speak Uighur despite more than a decade in the region. Soon she realized that she was getting favored treatment. "The Chinese government allowed me and a few other Uighurs to get rich to show how great their policies are."[4]

As her husband, a scholar, raised questions in newspaper articles about the legitimacy of China's historical claim over Xinjiang, Kadeer said she grew weary of taking part in government entities like the National People's Congress, which she saw as "a complete waste of time."[5] So she spoke out about the influx of ethnic Han migrants pouring into Xinjiang, regulations banning Uighurs from discussing politics at weddings and funerals, and the lack of their presence in any positions of power. The migration issue made many Uighurs seethe. Since 1949, ethnic Han have grown from 6 percent to about 40 percent of the region's twenty-one million people, slightly trailing the 45 percent (a little more than nine million people) who are Uighur. Some Uighurs say the Han treat them like colonial masters, asking them to put on traditional costumes at a whim for their entertainment.

Kadeer bristled at superficial displays of ethnic harmony that are common at political events, where minorities are cast as exotica. "They make Uighurs dance on those occasions, and make us sing songs to show how happy we are."[6] By the time of a U.N.-sponsored conference on women in Beijing in 1995, Kadeer was allowed to participate, but only with three Chinese women at her side at all times translating for her. "My relationship with them reminded me more of one between a hostage and her kidnappers," she later wrote.[7] After denouncing bloody repression of a Uighur uprising in Gulja in early 1997, Kadeer was stripped of all her official posts. In 1999, authorities charged and convicted her of "leaking state secrets" after she tried to give newspaper clippings to a visiting U.S. congressional delegation. She spent nearly six years in prison. China released her on medical parole in 2005 on condition she go into exile to the United States, joining her husband, who had already fled. Security officials warned her not to speak out against China from abroad or her family members remaining in her homeland would pay the price.

That price was dear. One day in April 2006, her phone rang in a Virginia suburb of Washington. It was her daughter Rushangul calling on a mobile phone from Xinjiang, where several security agents were beating two of her sons, one of them severely. The agents instructed the daughter to tell her mother that she was to blame for what was happening. "She was screaming, jumping and telling her mother that police were beating Ablikim," said Alim Seytoff, a family friend who's the director of the Uyghur Human Rights Project.[8] Kadeer could barely recount the incident when I saw her, breaking into sobs on several occasions. That same year, a white van surged across a yellow line in Fairfax County, Virginia, and rammed the Hyundai carrying Kadeer. At least one press report said the van then backed up and rammed the Hyundai again.[9] Seytoff said the FBI later told Kadeer's office that the van had been rented by the Chinese embassy in Washington.

When overseas supporters nominated Kadeer for the Nobel Peace Prize in 2006, party leaders were incensed. Her activities "clearly show that she wants to destroy the peace and stability of Chinese society. Those actions do not conform to the requirements of the Nobel Peace Prize," said Xinjiang's governor, Nur Bekri, a fellow Uighur, who also

ridiculed Kadeer's qualifications to speak for the ethnic group. "To call
Rebiya the 'Mother of all Uighurs' is absolutely preposterous."[10] More
recently, Beijing has taken to calling her "an ironclad separatist collud-
ing with terrorists" who is "unceasingly fanning unrest within and
outside of China."[11]

China has tried to stick Kadeer with the "terrorist" label, laying a
series of small-scale bombings and a larger terror attack in the city of
Kashgar days before the 2008 Olympics at her feet. In fact, the armed
resistance has an older history that goes to the heart of China's claims
that Xinjiang has been an "inseparable part of the unitary multi-eth-
nic Chinese nation" since ancient times, roughly two thousand
years.[12] China's dominion in parts of Central Asia, pulled into its economic orbit from the Silk Road trading route, dates back much of that
time, but this dominion was often through local monarchs sub-
servient to Chinese dynasties rather than a military presence.[13] Twice
in the past century, as China languished from civil war and invasion
by Japan, Uighurs sought to establish independence under their preferred name for the region, East Turkestan. A Chinese warlord ended
the first republic, a year after it was established in 1933, with help
from the Soviet Union. A second republic set up in 1944 lasted for five
years until the People's Liberation Army marched in after the founding of modern China. Since the 1980s, separatists have carried out a
smattering of attacks, which Kadeer has decried.

But the September 11, 2001, Al Qaeda terror attacks in the United
States, and subsequent arrests of Uighurs in Afghanistan, gave China
ammunition to devise an effective two-pronged strategy to discredit
the Uighurs. Around the Muslim world, Beijing portrayed Kadeer's
flight into exile to Washington as a sign she was a lackey of the West,
hoping that would limit Muslim solidarity with—or worse, armed assistance for—disgruntled Uighurs. "They tell the Muslim world that we
are bad Muslims because we like the West," she said. But in European
and North American capitals, Chinese diplomats describe radical
Uighurs as Al Qaeda–linked terrorists, a charge not easily dismissed.
The U.S. military caught dozens of Uighurs in militant training camps
in Afghanistan in 2001 and placed them in the Guantanamo Bay holding camp in Cuba. Washington eventually shipped many of them to
Albania, Bermuda, and Palau to avoid returning them to China, where

they might be mistreated. China's strategy effectively left the Uighurs adrift, as both the West and Muslim nations remained largely indifferent to their plight. Like nations everywhere, Islamic countries do not want to offend China, the world's rising superpower. While Tibetans get plenty of good press, the Uighurs bemoan their fate. "There is little international sympathy for us," Kadeer said.

As our meeting wound down, Kadeer suggested that Beijing was putting a tighter squeeze on Uighurs in Xinjiang, hoping that they would respond violently, thereby justifying a harsher crackdown. I paid little heed to the remark. Like many frequent travelers to Xinjiang, I was enchanted by the history of the region but didn't suspect ethnic tensions might explode in a broad and violent fashion, exposing the fissures left by decades of repressive rule. After all, it was easy to become captivated by Xinjiang's past as home to the ancient Silk Road that brought heavily laden camel caravans from East and West. Its oasis cities still were redolent of Central Asia. Walking around old market areas, with Uighur artisans clanging on copper bowls and ewers, carving wood, and knotting carpets, hints of the ancient Silk Road come alive. Bakers along the dusty streets pull round flatbread flecked with green onion from deep tandoori ovens, chatting with each other while sipping on blood-red pomegranate juice. At street-side butcher stalls, skinned sheep hang upside down from meat hooks, drained of their blood. Further along, vendors wearing the traditional skullcaps sell mounds of grapes, apricots, wolfberries, apples, pears, and melons, alongside walnuts, raisins, and mounds of exotic spices.

Closer observation, though, reveals that ethnic Han and Uighur live side by side in uneasy proximity. Among the signs are the "time wars" that leave clocks and watches set to two distinct settings. By edict of the government in far-off Beijing, all of China observes the same time. So even though China is roughly the size of the continental United States, it has only one time zone, not four. In Urumqi, Xinjiang's capital, clocks at all schools, government offices, train stations, and airports are set to "Beijing time." But in reality, there is a two-hour difference in longitude between Urumqi and Beijing, so it can be dark out at 10 AM on a winter morning or still light at 11 PM on a summer evening. The Muslim Uighurs ignore "Beijing time." They set their watches to their own unofficial time, two hours earlier, matching the rhythms of the sun. They awake later and keep their businesses open later than the Han. The different pace of Han and Uighur lives is a metaphor for the abyss that exists between the two groups in Xinjiang.

A few months before race riots would leave nearly two hundred people dead on the streets of Urumqi, the large industrial capital of Xinjiang, I spent a few days in Khotan, a Uighur oasis on the southern edge of the Taklimakan Desert, the second largest wasteland of shifting sand dunes in the world, after the Sahara. The desert is so harsh that the locals call it "The Place of No Return." Occasional windstorms can kick up enough sand to block the sun for days on end, and on my visit a thick haze of suspended dust cloaked the city. One evening, I joined a fellow foreign journalist traveling through the city, and we headed to one of the few hotels that served beer. The doorman guided us to the bank of elevators and told us to go to the karaoke bar on an upper floor. Some young Han Chinese were also headed there, and in the span of the elevator ride we'd already exchanged jovial words and demonstrated mutual curiosity, deciding to continue the conversation over drinks. The music throbbed, and I struggled to follow the conversation. It turned out that several of the young men worked for the State Grid, the huge power transmission and distribution company. The fellow sitting next to me was in his mid-twenties, and I congratulated him on landing such a good job out of university. After further chitchat, he leaned over and asked me, "Are you scared?" I thought I misheard, so I asked him to repeat the question.

I'd already grown accustomed to an almost instinctive and unapologetic Han Chinese view of Uighurs as backward and even treacherous. One human rights monitor put it to me in an interview like this: "The general perception of Uighurs has shifted in China at large. Now mention 'Uighurs,' and it's, 'Oh, dangerous terrorists!'"[14] Moreover, Han living in Xinjiang could easily sense Uighur resentment over economic disparities between the two groups, which are wide. And they were spooked at how Uighurs were clinging more tightly to Islam, with women wearing head coverings and even partial burqas like those commonly worn in Afghanistan. So I knew what my drinking buddy was getting at when I asked him if he meant whether I was scared of the local Muslims. He nodded his head and pronounced by way of explanation: "They hate us."

Of course not all Uighurs see Han Chinese as unwanted occupiers. Some Uighurs have prospered under Chinese rule and aspire to achieve equality while riding the Han economic juggernaut, even at the cost of losing Uighur language and identity. It's hard to gauge how many they number. As in all of China, independent opinion surveys on sensitive political matters are not allowed. China's affirmative action policies include preferences for minorities on university admission and a partial exemption from "one-child" birth control policies. Beijing poured development money into Xinjiang, which now boasts twelve modern airports and thousands of miles of new highway and railway. Xinjiang prospers from oil, gas, and wind energy investments, booming construction, and agro-industry. Under a "Go West" development plan begun in 1999, Xinjiang's economic growth rates routinely top those of the nation as a whole. One of the conduits of investment began much earlier, under Mao, who sent about 175,000 people, mostly from the army, to form the Xinjiang Production Construction Corps, a unique entity that built farms, towns, and cities and took charge of much of the region's security. The Corps, known locally as the Bingtuan, actively recruited Han Chinese to settle the frontier, a campaign that many Uighurs viewed as a plan to swamp and weaken the Uighur population. Today, 88 percent of the Corps' 2.5 million employees are Han Chinese. Despite the dilution of the Uighur population, the surrounding area is still known as the Xinjiang Uighur Autonomous Region, even if the "autonomy" in the name is less than it appears. As in Tibet, the governor in the region is an ethnic minority, assisted by a Han deputy. The figure who calls the shots is the party secretary, and he has always been a Han male.

In Xinjiang, Uighur and Han worlds are often parallel, rarely overlapping. Uighurs seldom obtain jobs in the oil and gas industries, transport, manufacturing, communications, or construction.[15] Uighurs complain of job discrimination, leaving them largely confined to trade and business, and they lag far behind the Han in education, health, and employment. Their most serious grievances revolve around broad constraints on religious practice and around policies they say destroy their culture and way of life. Throughout Xinjiang, party cadres bar Muslim youth under eighteen years of age from entering mosques. Unlike other parts of the Muslim world, loudspeakers do not blare sermons outside mosques. Even the muezzin daily call to prayer is muted. Local imams are barred from providing social and educational services to the faithful, and thus their influence is limited.[16] On occasion, party leaders in some Xinjiang municipalities have banned fasting by government officials during Ramadan, the holiest month in the Muslim religious calendar. They've also ordered men to shave off their beards and women to remove their veils.[17] In some Xinjiang towns, police confiscated passports of Uighurs, ensuring that they did not attempt a pilgrimage to Mecca by themselves, as all physically able Muslims are expected to do at least once in their lifetimes. China seeks to closely control which Muslim citizens can go each year on government-sanctioned pilgrimages to Saudi Arabia. The widespread discontent has prompted some journalists to call Xinjiang "China's other Tibet."[18]

The most thoroughly Uighur city in Xinjiang today is Kashgar, which also happens to be the most westerly city in China, a short drive from the towering Pamir Mountains and near the border with Kyrgyzstan. A city with a history dating back two millennia, Kashgar is considered the cradle of Uighur culture and pride, and it is where complaints have grown loudest that Beijing is dismantling Uighur civilization under the guise of modernization. The old city, with its warren of dusty alleys, traditional markets, and mud-brick courtyard homes, has a timeless appeal that draws some 1.5 million tourists a year to see the physical embodiment of the rich history of the Uighurs. Kashgar flourished as a key stopover for caravan trade routes linking China with Central Asia and Europe. Marco Polo passed through the oasis in the 1270s. The resilient city bounced back after being sacked by Tamerlane and Genghis Khan, but Kashgar has now largely lost its battle to Chinese authorities, who say the old city is vulnerable to collapse from earthquakes and suffers from poor drainage. They have razed most of the architecturally unique city center, deeming traditional homes "old and dangerous buildings," and sent the residents to live in boxy, concrete apartment blocks on the city's outskirts.

By 2010, bulldozers had leveled much of the old market behind the towering Idh Kha Mosque, which dates to 1442, and were well on their way to a wholesale dismantling of eight square kilometers comprising the center of the city, replacing them with faux Islamic architecture buildings suitable for a heritage theme park and characterless glass-and-steel shopping centers filled with Han migrant storekeepers.[19] Some sixty-five thousand houses were being torn down. Plans are to wipe out and rebuild fully 85 percent of the city, affecting some 221,000 people.[20] Nearly every night on television, authorities publicized the relocation of inner-city dwellers to the rows of apartment blocks on Kashgar's outskirts. The programs show Uighurs gleefully dancing in front of their new residential towers and portray city fathers as sick with worry about the loss of life that a major earthquake might cause. Chinese leaders say they have consulted with residents about the urban demolition and renewal, and offered them a say in redevelopment.

Uighurs say they have simply been summoned to meetings and informed of compensation schemes and relocation timetables. Some families are giving up residences where relatives have lived for hundreds of years. Anger goes deeper than just compensation. Some Uighurs say authorities seek to get rid of mazelike alleyways that might breed terrorists. There is no doubt that for some Uighurs, the living conditions in the mid-rise apartment blocks lined up in neat rows on Kashgar's outskirts are an improvement. But underlying the relocations are broader issues of cultural preservation and lack of consultation about development. Han business owners appear poised to manage the downtown area, controlling markets and further marginalizing Uighurs, some of whom burn with rage.

On one trip when demolitions were just getting under way, I went to the outskirts of Kashgar and quickly drew a crowd of Uighur women shouting in anger over their relocation. One large woman with a head covering began to cry, holding her wrists together to signal being handcuffed. My Uighur translator said her relative had been detained and jailed for protesting the low compensation offered by the government and the tenfold increase in price earned by city officials when they released the land to developers. As she became more agitated, my translator froze up. When I pressed him, he would only say, "We are not alone," signaling with his eyes several Uighur men in jackets standing off to the side listening to the conversation. It was time to leave.

Traveling in Xinjiang, I grew accustomed to trying to spot the state security officials assigned to follow my moves. In Urumqi, I got so addled by the close tailing of my myriad taxis throughout a full day that when I spotted one of the security agents enter the lobby of my hotel to sit and wait for my next move, I approached him and said in Chinese, "Why don't you just leave me alone?" I explained that I had permission from the Foreign Ministry to be in Xinjiang. He smirked slightly and didn't say a word, getting out of his chair and walking out the lobby door, only to return a few minutes later.

The security presence in Xinjiang is extensive, but it wasn't finely tuned enough to halt a sudden venting of ethnic frustrations in the summer of 2009. The initial spark for the explosion, remarkably enough, occurred in a toy factory on the other side of China, about two thousand miles away in Guangdong province, factory zone to the world. The Hong Kong–owned Early Light (Xuri) Toy Factory in the city of Shaoguan employed eighteen thousand workers. Some of them were Uighur, transferred to factory jobs in the humid tropics of southeast China as part of a make-work plan that had already moved some two hundred thousand Xinjiang residents to coastal regions. Beijing said the transfer program, begun in early 2008, would help provide jobs to 1.5 million surplus workers in Xinjiang. Uighur advocates disputed that, saying the government had coerced Uighur households with threats of large fines to send their young adults, especially women under age twenty-five, as a way to assimilate them more easily. Many Uighurs could speak little Mandarin and did not mix with other migrants. In late June 2009, a rumor spread that several Uighur workers raped a Han woman who wandered into their factory dormitory. Enraged Han workers marched on the dormitory, and in the early morning hours of June 26 they wielded lengths of steel torn from cots, wooden staves, and paving stones to attack the Uighurs. By dawn, police tallied two dead Uighur men and 120 or so injured people, mostly Uighur. Internet censors immediately barred a short video of the riot, in which Han workers seemed to be the aggressors.[21]

State media offered scant information about the melee. Anxiety levels back in Xinjiang rose after text messages arrived from workers at the factory saying the bloodshed had been worse than state media suggested. Foreign media accounts also raised questions. The British newspaper the *Guardian* quoted a Han worker saying he personally helped kill seven or eight Uighurs. "We used iron bars to batter them to death and then dragged them out and put the bodies together," he told the paper.[22] Uighurs in Urumqi called for punishment of the perpetrators of the toy factory brawl. On the balmy evening of July 5, 2009, several hundred gathered at the city's People's Square to demand justice. More Uighurs arrived, and soon they were pushing over guardrails, smashing buses, and torching police cars. Rioters chased and tried to kill Han passers-by, and they set fire to hundreds of shops. By dawn, the streets were littered with glass shards, bloodstains, and overturned vehicles. Two days after the riot, as authorities still tallied the death toll, a Han backlash occurred. A crowd armed with clubs, lead pipes, axes, and meat cleavers gathered on the streets, intent on avenging the massacre. They stormed into Uighur neighborhoods, smashing windows of Muslim shops and upending cars. The official death toll from the initial rampage and the backlash riot stood at 197 people, with more than 1,700 injured. State media said two-thirds of the fatalities were Han.

Nerves remained raw all summer in Urumqi, and Han residents of the city, who comprise about 75 percent of its 2.3 million population, grew frustrated by lack of action to punish Uighurs and to ensure their own safety. Then police unwittingly made matters worse. On August 31, authorities sent a text message alert to Urumqi residents. "Recently, several residents were attacked by hypodermic syringes. . . . Please don't panic," the message said.[23] Some Uighurs were jabbing unsuspecting Han with needles in a vengeance tactic that generated more anxiety than any conventional weapon might have, leveraging tiny pricks into widespread fear. Every time Han Chinese felt a wince of pain, like a mosquito bite, they thought they had been jabbed. Within four days, more than five hundred residents had shown up at local hospitals, saying they'd been pricked on buses or in public areas. Rumors spread that Uighur attackers had needles infected with HIV or hepatitis. On September 3, angry Han Chinese crowded into

People's Square and shouted, *"Wang Lequan xia tai!"*—calling on the long-standing secretary general of the autonomous region to step down for not ensuring their safety. Han mobs beat any suspected Uighur needle-wielder, adding to the death toll.

Party Secretary Wang, the longtime strongman of Xinjiang, held onto his job, and the government demonstrated its strength. Twenty-six people were sentenced to death for the rioting, mostly Uighurs.[24] Worried that foreign agitators might be stirring up trouble, officials sent Xinjiang back to the digital Stone Age, pulling the plug on the internet. They blocked email, text messaging, and international phone calls. In a sense, the moves showed the party's true colors—that it was willing to take virtually any step necessary to ensure that minority unrest would not destabilize its grip on power. If it took dropping Xinjiang into a communication black hole, so be it. Ten months passed before Xinjiang's seven million internet users would have access again. By early 2010, Beijing had nearly doubled the security budget for Xinjiang, a sign that party cadres would be better prepared should Uighur unrest shake the region again.[25]

IN CONTRAST, BEIJING HOLDS UP the Inner Mongolia Autonomous Region as a model of ethnic harmony, but the reality is that ethnic Mongols have become weakened by state policies to the point that few oppose them. Harmony, then, is also acquiescence to the power of the state.

Rights activists recommended that I travel to Inner Mongolia to speak with one of the few Mongols publicly challenging this trend. Like some Mongols, she goes by a single name, Xinna, and I flew to Hohhot, the provincial capital of Inner Mongolia, to meet her. Like Rebiya Kadeer, the Uighur crusader, Xinna was an accidental activist. The 1995 arrest of her husband, a Mongol university professor, forced her to fight for the life of a man who is now one of China's longest-serving prisoners of conscience. In the process of publicizing her husband's plight worldwide, she also became an advocate for her ethnic Mongolian community and for greater freedom under China's one-party system.

Hohhot is a modern city with many ethnic Mongolian flourishes. Streets and store signs are in Mongolian script as well as Chinese, yurt-themed architecture graces the city, wolf and deer totems are everywhere, and some park benches have a Mongol saddle motif. The ethnic touches are only skin-deep. Hohhot these days is primarily a Han city. Fewer than 10 percent of the metropolitan region's 2.6 million inhabitants are Mongols. Indeed, only 17 percent of the Inner Mongolia Autonomous Region's residents are Mongol, and they are confined largely to nomadic settlements and ethnic oases in a larger sea of Han. It wasn't always this way. At the time of modern China's founding in 1949, the Mongols outnumbered Han Chinese in the region 5 to 1. By the most recent census in 2000, the proportion stood at 4.6 Han Chinese to every 1 Mongol. The population transfer has been steady over the decades, virtually engulfing the ethnic Mongolian population. A growing number of Mongols have adopted common three-syllable Chinese names and lost the ability to speak their own language, ceding steadily to a "harmonized" identity.

Xinna speaks Mandarin fluently but clings to her Mongol roots, listening to ethnic music and surrounding herself with crafts unique to her culture. She makes a living by selling Mongolian handicrafts. I found her shop in a district near the Inner Mongolia Normal University, off a nondescript alley. Her three-room store brimmed with handmade items, books in Mongolian, and other cultural artifacts. Tapestries of shaggy wild horses on the steppes and posters of Genghis Khan hung from the walls. Wooden carvings of wild two-humped Bactrian camels filled one shelf, alongside miniature leather saddles and other knickknacks. Near piles of CDs of Mongolian music sat a wooden two-stringed instrument, known as a *morin khuur*, its wooden neck in the form of a horse head and its strings made from dried deer sinew. Xinna lovingly picked up objects and explained their importance to Mongol culture. She spoke like a schoolteacher, her former profession.

Like the Kurds in the Near East, ethnic Mongolians are spread across multiple international boundaries. The greatest number live in China's Inner Mongolia Autonomous Region, but they have far less freedom to protect their culture than those to the north in Mongolia, an independent country that for much of the twentieth century was under the sway of the Soviet Union but is now a multiparty democracy. Xinna and I chatted about the cultural differences between

Mongolians on the two sides of the border. The differences are most notable in the arts, she said, walking over to the section of her store with music CDs. "There are more and more Mongolian songs and fewer and fewer songs from Inner Mongolia. It's because of ideology. These songs from Mongolia have lyrics that worship life and love. Inner Mongolian songs are much more ideological. You know that song, 'Armed to Protect Our Country'?" she asked me.[26] I was unfamiliar with it, but I got her point.

It was evening time, her store was closing, so we walked to an ethnic Mongolian restaurant, where Xinna ordered steaming dishes of roast lamb, butter soup, and tea with stir-fried millet. Platters of cheese arrived, and so did glasses of sour milk. Her mood turned serious as she talked of the discrimination that Mongols face in seeking jobs. A recent case particularly irked her. Not long before, a Chinese company posted a public job advertisement at the nearby campus of the Inner Mongolia Normal University, which has the highest percentage of Mongol students in the region. The ad stated that the company would only accept applicants who had been taught in Mandarin, not Mongolian. "When the students saw the poster, they were very angry," Xinna said. "If you are good in Mongolian but not so good in Mandarin, you are not needed. It's a reality."[27]

This was a common refrain from young ethnic Mongols educated in their own language. Some insisted on studying Mongolian culture and history at the university level even though it would hurt their job prospects. One graduate of the Mongolian Studies Department of the Normal University, a young woman named Nabuqi, ran a small kiosk selling dairy products; she had been unable to parlay her Mongolian language degree into a better job. "Even someone with a doctorate in this field finds it difficult to find a job. They can get a job only if they are good at another foreign language, like English or Japanese, or at doing special research," she said.[28]

I later called an exiled human rights activist, Enghebatu Togochog, of the Southern Mongolia Human Rights Information Center, which operates out of his New York City apartment. He said that laws protecting Mongol language and culture looked good on paper but are routinely ignored. "It is said that it is an official language. But in meetings, they don't use Mongolian," he said. "If you want to send a letter and you address it in Mongolian, they won't deliver it. It's really useless."[29]

Xinna had recently come back from a rare visit to her husband, who goes by the single name Hada. In the early 1990s, Hada, a former university professor, ran the Mongolian Studies Bookstore in Hohhot, where Mongol intellectuals gathered to discuss ways to preserve Mongol identity and culture. In 1992, Hada organized the Southern Mongolian Democratic Alliance to obtain greater autonomy for Mongols as guaranteed by China's constitution. As time passed, he grew more bold in his calls for greater freedoms, writing a book titled *The Way Out of Southern Mongolia*. In mid-December 1995, a dozen police raided the bookstore and arrested Hada. After a closed-door trial, he was convicted of "splitting the country" and "engaging in espionage" and given a fifteen-year sentence.

Instead of throwing Hada in a local prison, authorities sent him to a prison in Chifeng City, a thirteen-hour train ride from Hohhot, making trips there difficult for Xinna and their son, Uiles, who has written periodically about his visits with his father. Authorities always videotape and record his conversations with his father at Chifeng No. 4 prison, the son says. When they meet, the two are separated by a glass window and speak through a telephone. If they break into Mongolian, the telephone connection ends. They are only allowed to speak in Mandarin. Uiles said in 2009 that his father has been wearing the same worn and tattered sweater in prison for the past thirteen years. He and his mother have been denied the right to offer him clothes, medicines to treat recurring phlebitis in his leg, or books. "Newspapers we order for him were not properly delivered to him. Some of the newspapers were sporadically given to him, but the editions related to politics and world news were confiscated. He has never been allowed to read any books there," Uiles said.[30]

For all the harshness of Hada's imprisonment, he is lucky not to have received a death sentence, which are routine in China and have often been used against minority dissidents. The ethnic unrest in Lhasa in March 2008, and in Urumqi in July 2009, brought about more than three dozen death sentences. China executes more people than the rest of the world combined, human rights groups say, but it doesn't provide data on executions, saying such information is a state secret. In the year 2008, Amnesty International estimated that China executed 1,718 people. Under Chinese law, there are sixty-eight categories of crimes—including homicide and aggravated assault, but also including nonviolent crimes such as smuggling, tax evasion, and embezzlement—that can result in the death penalty. Foreign opponents of capital punishment say China uses it disproportionately against ethnic minorities, especially those convicted of leaking state secrets, violating security laws, or threatening national security. Draconian state security laws make almost any rumblings by ethnic minority activists punishable by long prison terms or capital punishment. It adds a level of fear to the expression of any grievances.

Older Mongolians are acutely aware of how fragile their culture is. They remember the decade-long Cultural Revolution, which began in 1966, and the tumultuous campaigns targeted at any sign of non-Han ethnicity. "When I left elementary school, nobody talked to me in Mongolian," Wang Heixiao, a former well-regarded ethnic Mongolian dancer who heads the Hohhot Bureau of Culture, told me over tea in his office. "You weren't allowed to talk in Mongolian. You weren't allowed to study in Mongolian. My school was shut down. I was sent to the countryside." Wang said he recovered an ability to speak Mongolian after the ideological tumult passed, but the language has become less relevant to his daily life. Like many Mongols, he married a Han woman and adopted a Han name. His son, in his mid-twenties, speaks only a little Mongolian. "The language environment here is Mandarin," he said.

The falloff in students opting to receive a Mongolian-language education has been dramatic, an indicator of the erosion of ethnic culture and the pull of Han culture. In 1986, some 380,000 students received a Mongolian-language education, but at the time of my visit state media reported that the number had fallen to 240,000 students. "Some parents think their children are better off if they go to school in Mandarin," said Dalai Duren, principal of the Xing An Road Ethnic Primary School. "If the students want to study outside of Inner Mongolia, the instruction is in Mandarin." The principal said he is worried. "If we lose our language, we will lose our culture."[31]

Other factors make ethnic unity nearly impossible. While Mongolians in China, Mongolia, and Russia all share a language, they don't share the same alphabet. As a result of imposition from the former Soviet Union, those in Mongolia spell with the left-to-right Cyrillic alphabet, while those in Inner Mongolia use a classical script that goes from top to bottom. The international border between Mongolia and the People's Republic of China is guarded closely, and ethnic Mongolian traders from the Chinese side say they are routinely given close scrutiny upon returning from the other side. "They check the cell phone and look for information. They check the camera. They kept me for half a day while they went through my things," Sengge Renqin, a trader from Inner Mongolia, told me over lunch one day. "The majority of Mongolian people feel upset about it, but they don't say it."[32]

Railways were crucial in allowing the torrent of Han Chinese to move into Inner Mongolia. In the 1990s, amid a global boom in demand for cashmere, tens of thousands of Han farmers flocked to Inner Mongolia to raise goats for their wool. The subsequent overgrazing led to the speeding up of desertification and the regularity of massive dust storms sweeping across northern China. To halt the damage, the central government began policies in the 1990s to force the relocation of some 650,000 nomads and herders from their ancestral pastures to urban areas. This "ecological migration" has turned Mongolian herders into environmental refugees, moved off their traditional pastureland. They are landless people in their own land. Using slogans such as "recovering grassland eco-system" and "combating desertification," officials have made grazing livestock on grasslands subject to harsh punishment and heavy fines.

That Inner Mongolia may represent a harbinger of what could occur in Tibet, in terms of not only demographic composition but also maintaining language and cultural identity, is of concern to the Dalai Lama. I heard him publicly fret about the status of ethnic Mongolians at a press conference in Tokyo, saying that unchecked migration of Han people had weakened Mongolian culture. He said that Tibetans and Uighurs were within their rights to resist such migration. "In the autonomous region of [Inner] Mongolia, Mongolians became a minority," he said. "That is our real anxiety. If in Tibet and in Xinjiang the local people become a minority, it's very difficult to preserve culture."[33]

Xinna understands that sentiment. She said she sees little hope of saving the Mongol way of life in China in the long term. "We used to be the hosts here," Xinna said. "Now we feel like guests in our own land."³⁴

BACK ON THE TRAIN to Lhasa, we wobbled back to the dining car shortly after daybreak, eager to take in the panoramic views of snow-capped peaks out of both sides of the speeding train. At one end of the car, a digital readout informed us of the train's speed, the altitude, and the outdoor temperature. The hostesses, dressed in lilac outfits and headscarves, brought us hot tea, porridge, pickled vegetables, and eggs. My appetite was low, and a slight headache throbbed, but the haze-free mountain air and the majestic landscapes that unfolded in a moving postcard outside kept us in a reverie. Sitting in cozy comfort while gazing on the chilly scene outdoors, I found it hard not to admire the railway. From the outside, the green-and-yellow eight-wagon train looked fairly normal. But even the railcars themselves are special, made with the know-how of Canada's Bombardier, a mass transit and aerospace giant. The double-paned windows did not open, preventing sudden decompression from changes in altitude and protecting against subzero temperatures outside. Coated windows shielded against ultraviolet radiation. From the special high-powered locomotive to the reinforced undercarriages of the wagons, built to withstand shards of windblown ice and blizzards, the train was exceptional. Water in the toilets was heated to prevent it from freezing, and all sewage and waste-collection systems were contained, to be emptied at special collection points rather than leaving waste along the tracks, as is the practice elsewhere in China.

The railway whooshed across thirty-three overpasses built to allow endangered antelope and other wildlife to pass through the line. Months before our trip, a scandal erupted over a faked photograph showing some twenty antelope roving peacefully under a railway bridge. The state television broadcaster named it one of the ten best news photos of the year, but some internet users voiced suspicions over how calmly the antelopes seemed to trot next to the roaring train. Experts say Tibetan antelopes are easily disturbed by even the slightest sound. The photo was later shown to be a montage, and the photographer confessed that he had combined two separate photos. "I have no reason to continue my sacred career as a newsman," he said in quitting his job. What the photographer, Liu Weiqing, didn't say was that state media had published his work extensively, raising no red flags in their eagerness to portray the Tibet railway as harmless to the environment. Whether the railway will harm the environment isn't yet clear. What has become clearer is that the railway was designed in part to ease the exploitation of mineral and energy resources in Tibet for China's voracious industrial appetite.

Before China began the railway project, it undertook a survey project lasting seven years and costing $44 million to determine if the Chinese name for Tibet—Xizang, or "western treasure house"— would live up to its billing. The survey showed that it did. Initial reports identified mineral beds estimated to contain thirty million to forty million tons of copper, forty million tons of lead and zinc, and billions of tons of iron ore. It was a eureka moment for China, the world's biggest consumer of both copper and iron ore, and signaled it might alleviate the nation's massive dependence on foreign minerals, which it needs to fuel steel plants, build cars, and make electronic products. Moreover, the high-grade iron ore and copper deposits found on the Tibetan Plateau offer better grade ore than those found elsewhere in the country.

In a Xinhua news article, a senior official in the China Geological Survey Bureau also said northern Tibet contains "large or super-large" deposits of gas and oil shale. "These deposits will fundamentally ease China's shortages of mineral resources," the official said, adding that new mineral discoveries on the Plateau potentially are worth $128 billion.[35] Early word of the mineral discoveries prompted a cry of concern from the Dalai Lama himself. "I appeal to all foreign mining companies and their shareholders thinking about working in Tibet to consider carefully about the ethical values when embarking on such a venture," he wrote in a 2003 open letter.[36] Years later, his office issued another statement saying the exile government is "deeply concerned that the increased mineral extraction activities would have large adverse social and environmental impacts on the Tibetan Plateau and further beyond."

The railway will make extraction of minerals far more feasible, and it has also slashed the cost of transporting goods into Tibet. Initial estimates are that the train is bringing three tons of freight on average for each of the 2.8 million people living in the Tibet Autonomous Region. Cargo transport costs have also dropped to a third of what they were before the train was built. Many Tibetans today are deeply ambivalent about the railway, seeing the need for development but seriously worried about the influx of migrants.

I reflected on the numerous letters and faxes I had sent to the Foreign Ministry seeking permission to visit mining camps and other sites in Tibet, all to no avail. On this trip, a German reporter friend, a Mexican photographer, and I were slipping into Tibet as tourists. We had tried and failed to get a government permit to enter as journalists. No foreign journalist can enter Tibet without such a permit, and they are hard to come by. But we'd found a travel agency in the provincial city of Lanzhou that was willing to issue us tourist permits, and we decided to try our luck. We were uncertain over what awaited us.

But for the moment, the spectacular vista out the windows enthralled us. We saw grazing herds of yaks, mirage-filled lakes, isolated Tibetan farmhouses with their distinctive four-corner turrets, and endless frozen tundra. Other passengers chatted endlessly or surfed the internet on their mobile phones, which always seemed to have a signal aboard the train, a sign of China's growing technological prowess. By late in the afternoon, the train pulled across the Lhasa River, and the holy city of Tibet's capital loomed into view.

chapter four

Holy City or Devil's Land

Tibet is totally controlled by the Chinese government. Under these circumstances, it's impossible for Tibetans to change the destiny of Tibet. Tibet can only change along with China.

—*Tsering Woeser, Tibetan writer, December 2009*

MOST FIRST-TIME TRAVELERS DISEMBARKING FROM THE TRAIN IN Lhasa feel awe at entering a city once so inaccessible. For centuries, the towering wall of the Himalayas to the south and the arduous journeys through inhospitable terrain in other directions kept foreigners at bay. Dozens of intrepid adventurers, eccentrics, teachers, and missionaries had tried to reach the capital. But the journey required months of preparation and caravans of pack animals. Moreover, Tibetans showed hostility to foreigners broaching the holy city. By the early twentieth century, the virtual blockade weakened. A smattering of Asian traders and diplomats took up residence, and a steady number of Europeans, North Americans, and fellow Asians found their way into the breathtaking sight of the Potala Palace, the enduring landmark of Tibet.

The Potala was the seat of one Dalai Lama reincarnation after another, and its size epitomized the power that the god-kings of Tibetan Buddhism held over the populace. The palace, finished in the mid-1600s, is a towering structure containing a thousand rooms and stretching a quarter mile from end to end, the world's largest such palace. For more than three centuries after it was finished, the Potala was considered the world's tallest occupied building. It is only thirteen stories tall, but from atop a hill its white, ochre, and yellow façade towers over the Lhasa plain. Its height symbolizes the divine realm looking over the mortal world. Inside, it contains no end of shrines, prayer rooms, monks' dormitories, and courtyards. Its inner sanctuaries house some ten thousand statues, countless *thangkas*, and relics of bygone lamas.

It was early evening, and we stumbled out of the train lugging our backpacks to find several people from a local travel agency waiting for us. They placed white silk *khatas* around our necks and took us to a local tourist hotel a bit removed from the center of the city. We were delighted to be in the city but exhausted from our journey, and a little put off by the insistence of the travel agency employees that we discuss our stay in Tibet that evening. We were a tad nervous because we knew that we were blatantly skirting China's rules that foreign journalists obtain special permits to enter Tibet. The travel agency in Lanzhou had issued us tourist permits after we told them we were vacationing journalists who wanted to visit the Mount Everest Base Camp near the border with Nepal. It was a ploy on my part in pursuit of a story. Little did I know at the time, it might forever block my return to Lhasa.

My purpose was, in fact, to go to Everest Base Camp in Tibet (there is a separate, more popular base camp on the Nepal side of the mountain). An editor had suggested the trip half a year earlier, and his inquiries about my preparations were insistent. The first message noted an article in an adventure magazine about the assortment of wild-eyed mountaineers and ill-prepared business tycoons flocking to the base camp to climb Everest, which straddles the border between Nepal and Tibet. Mountaineers can use either of two base camps on their Everest attempts, one on the Nepal side of the mountain or another on the Tibet side, which is cheaper but less popular. "Made me think there's a good story to be done next spring as the Everest climbing season approaches," he wrote. I noted the difficulty in getting permission from China to make the trip. Secretly, though, I was quite excited at the prospect. I did a little research and discovered that Everest had become a magnet for fame seekers. A year earlier, a Polish *Playboy* playmate had scaled the mountain, followed by a New Zealand double amputee using carbon-fiber prosthetics. He suffered new frostbite and required further amputation of his fingers and legs. But he'd parlayed the experience into a career as a motivational speaker.

When I told the editor I might not get permission to travel to Tibet for the Everest story, he didn't find that convincing. "Just tell them you want to climb Everest. They seem to not think anything of letting people with no remote qualifications go in to make the effort." Well, that strategy seemed to have some flaws. I wasn't going to strap on crampons and try to take my out-of-shape body up a 29,035-foot ice-covered mountain, but I clearly had to find a way to make this story happen. Two months later, another nudge arrived by email: "By the way, what's the Everest climbing schedule?"

I wrote to the Foreign Ministry in Beijing pleading my case, noting that my intention was to interview foreign climbers trying to scale the world's highest mountain. They suggested I should work through the Foreign Affairs Office in Lhasa, which oversees visits by foreigners, a bureaucratic leftover of a Marxist-Leninist system in which visits by foreigners must be accompanied. New faxes flew, and I pestered them to the point where they ordered my office not to call again but simply wait for an answer. Problem was, time was flying by. The two-month Everest climbing season was about to begin, and I felt uneasy, not wanting to wait a year. That's when my German colleague suggested that we go in on "vacation." I knew the plan was too clever by half, but he'd been to Tibet several times previously, and I saw no harm in trying.

That evening, we sat in the hotel lobby in Lhasa and explained to the travel agency employees that we wanted to charter a four-wheel-drive vehicle and take a trip to Everest Base Camp. After some whispering, they offered what we considered an absurd price. We felt they saw us as easy targets. Since we had not signed a contract, we felt no obligation. The meeting ended politely, but with unhappiness all around. We decided to acclimate for a few days in Lhasa, meet some people, and get a different estimate from other travel agencies. A day or two later, we came across an agency with a Tibetan owner. They offered us a more reasonable price. It seemed our problems were solved. But we still lurked carefully around Lhasa, worried that we might be stopped and expelled as unwelcome journalists.

Our anxious amblings about Lhasa were far from the first by nervous foreigners. In 1924, an indomitable fifty-five-year-old French woman undertook a journey by foot to Lhasa, determined to become the first Western woman to explore the city. Her fluency in Tibetan and the experience of previous trips to outlying Tibet gave Alexandra David-Neel some confidence. She disguised herself as a beggar pilgrim to allay mistrust. She and a young Tibetan lama, who would later become her adopted son, traveled on foot at night to avoid suspicious inquiries. No foreigners were permitted to penetrate so deeply into the country, making her trek an outlaw's journey. "I walked for forty-four days, crossed a dozen peaks with snow up to my knees, slept in icy caves like a prehistoric woman, without food, almost barefoot, the soles of my moccasins being worn out by the rocks in the road," she would later write. When they finally slipped into Lhasa, lost among swarms of pilgrims celebrating a religious festival, their faces were blackened by charcoal, and she wore yak-hair pigtails and a fur hat. "For two months I was to wander freely in the lamaist Rome, with none to suspect that, for the first time in history, a foreign woman was beholding the Forbidden City."[1] Eventually, she detected suspicion among Tibetans that forced her departure from Lhasa. She left for Sikkim and went on to Europe.

Much of Lhasa would be unrecognizable to David-Neel. Modern cars ply its paved streets instead of pack animals lumbering along muddy paths. Vegetables fill its markets, grown by migrant workers in greenhouses near Lhasa, alleviating the once-monotonous diet of barley and dried meat. Glass-enclosed coffee bars offer Wi-Fi with their lattes, and mountaineering shops hang out displays of Oakley sunglasses and high-end rucksacks. From far off, the city still looks majestic, spread under the Potala's shadow. But today it is clean and tidy, a far cry from its condition a century ago. Foreign travelers in times past were almost uniform in their disgust. "The city which appeared so stunning from a distance was in reality squalid and filthy beyond belief. The streets were filled with stagnant pools, and dogs scavenged among the rubbish; the buildings were dark and fetid; the people were sullen and ragged; the city was unpaved, unsewered and unlit, like a survivor from the Middle Ages."[2] Yet Lhasa has lost some of its soul, and as we walked along its streets, we realized that Tibetans were a minority. Han migrants drive nearly every taxi, and Han and ethnic Hui Muslims own most shops, a sign of the marginalization of Tibetans. One account says that of thirteen thousand shops and restaurants in Lhasa, barely three hundred are owned by ethnic Tibetans.[3] Signs are not just in Tibetan script but also Chinese characters of equal or larger size.

We walked to the large public square in front of the four-story Jokhang Temple, the most sacred and historic in Tibet, constructed nearly fourteen hundred years ago. It was there where signs of immortal Tibet flourished. We heard the "clack-clack" of pilgrims, mainly elderly women, prostrating themselves, using rawhide kneepads and wooden planks on their hands that hit the paving stones first as they fell to the ground. The scene transfixed us. Smoke poured out of four large incense burners in front of the temple, and we peered into a shrine where hundreds of yak butter candles cast a yellowish glow. We then walked the pilgrim circuit that goes around the temple and encompasses much of the Old City, circumambulating with devout Tibetans and sensing we were near the divine soul of Tibet.

Chinese historical narratives, disputed by Tibetans, say Tibet was incorporated into China in the thirteenth century under Kublai Khan, when the Mongol Empire dominated both countries and most of Asia. As conqueror, Kublai Khan was the founding emperor of the Yuan Dynasty, and under his rule the Mongol aristocracy converted to Buddhism and sought spiritual guidance and moral legitimacy from the Tibetan theocracy. Thus began what scholars call the "priest-patron" relationship in which the Yuan government pledged to protect Tibet against foreign invasion and received loyalty in return. The relationship was based on mutual respect and responsibility rather than notions of sovereignty. It wasn't until a later dynasty, the Qing, founded by Manchus from Manchuria in the seventeenth century, that the imperial court sought to rule Tibet, dispatching high commissioners and enacting laws that would facilitate governing Tibet for more than two centuries before the system collapsed with the end of imperial rule in 1912.

As we ambled around the city during the next day or two, visiting temples and taking photos, I reflected back on conversations I had

had with Tsering Woeser, a fiery young Tibetan writer and poet based in Beijing whom I had befriended. Woeser writes the most widely read blog on Tibetan issues in China, and her criticism of state policies has left her under constant surveillance. Woeser has a foot in several worlds. Her grandfather was an army officer under the Chinese Nationalists, and her father served in the People's Liberation Army. Ethnically, she is a quarter Han and three-quarters Tibetan. She was born in Lhasa and lived there for years as an adult but was forced in 2003 to move to Beijing, returning subsequently only for short visits.

I asked her about how Lhasa had changed in recent years, and she talked about the city's increasing Chinese patina: "I was born in 1966, during the Cultural Revolution. Let me tell you about Lhasa at that time. On the top of the Potala, there were five huge boards with five characters on them:

毛主席万岁

which means 'Long live Chairman Mao.' I think you can tell what Lhasa's condition was at that time." In more recent years, she said, Chinese city planners and migrants had renamed most streets and landmarks in Lhasa, giving places "names of interior cities like Jiangsu Road, Guangzhou Road, and Qushui County. Besides Lhasa city, there is a square called Taizhou Square. Taizhou is [President] Hu Jintao's hometown. So when you are there, you cannot have the feeling of being in Lhasa, because you walk on Jiangsu Road, visit Taizhou Square, and see Fujian Road and Guangzhou Road." She said she'd seen nomads arriving in Lhasa on pilgrimage only to find themselves lost in the city because they could not read Chinese signs and did not know the newly imposed Chinese names. "Restaurants and hotels all have Chinese names. These nomads were strangers in Lhasa, getting lost."

Beijing relaxed migration rules to Tibet in the mid-1990s, and a heavy flow of people since then has transformed the city's population and urban character. At the time of the 1949 Revolution, Lhasa's population was no more than 30,000 people. Since then, city boundaries have grown more than twentyfold, and the most recent population estimates say 257,400 people dwell in the capital. But that figure counts neither a sizable military presence nor a floating population of "temporary" miners, construction workers, traders, and other migrants.

Government officials dismiss reports that Lhasa has lost its Tibetan character, asserting that the population of the Chengguan district that includes Lhasa remains 63 percent ethnic Tibetan. I couldn't find anyone outside Chinese government circles who believed that figure. Foreign scholars say as many as two-thirds of Lhasa residents are non-Tibetan today.[4]

What is indisputable is Lhasa's new seamy underbelly, replete with karaoke bars, massage parlors, gambling dens, and whorehouses. A favored riverside picnic site of Lhasa residents, Gumolingka Island, has become a Chinese-style karaoke and shopping complex. The outskirts of the city offer new self-contained developments with all the red-light entertainment possibilities a migrant might want. "In cities like Beijing, brothels do not dare to do business in the open. But in Lhasa, they not only operate publicly, they are even open during the daytime," Woeser said. "The mobsters come from Sichuan province and the Northeast. There is one nightclub where the boss is an official from the Public Security Bureau. There are five hundred prostitutes every night in that nightclub."

A U.S. State Department human rights report on China cites estimates of ten thousand sex workers in Lhasa and Shigatse, the number 2 city in Tibet, and adds that "some of the prostitution occurred at sites owned by the CCP [Chinese Communist Party], the government, and the military."[5] Brothels in Lhasa number in the hundreds, it added. Widespread prostitution is one of the reasons Tibetans now painfully dub their once-holy capital "Devil's Land." Lhasa has become a kind of theme park for visiting Chinese, marketed even as a good place to hold a wedding ceremony. The completion of the railway to Lhasa speeded up the pace of change, as builders braced for the influx of tourists and the growing army of Han soldiers, bureaucrats, and shopkeepers arriving weekly to engrave China's seal indelibly on Tibet.

Such desecration of Lhasa is among the reasons why exiles clamor for Tibetans to be given greater autonomy over their own affairs. For long periods, Beijing ignored appeals from the Dalai Lama to hold talks over how Tibet is governed. Following meetings with the Dalai Lama's elder brother in mid-1992, officials from the ruling party severed all formal communication with the Dalai Lama's office in India for a decade, even briefly shutting down informal channels. But by the turn of the twenty-first century, China's international trajectory and foreign policy and trade goals required that it placate foreign critics on several touchy matters, including Tibet. China desperately sought entry into the World Trade Organization after fifteen years of marathon negotiations. It won the right in mid-2001 to host the 2008 Olympic Games, and it set as a priority the successful carrying off of the Games as a display of its national strength.

Amid those developments, the Dalai Lama's elder brother, Gyalo Thondup, who had lived for long periods in Hong Kong and spoke Mandarin, visited Beijing and renewed informal contacts. Years later, Gyalo Thondup would tell foreign journalists what he told the party cadres: "If you want Tibetans to be a part of China, you must treat them as equals. . . . The Chinese are treating the Tibetans like a conquered land and a conquered people."[6] Aware that the simple existence of talks with the Tibetan exiles would mollify some critics of China, the party acceded to formal negotiations, which began in September 2002 and stretched through multiple rounds into the beginning of the next decade. From China's perspective, the talks could buy time and drag on. Since the Tibetans agreed to keep details of the talks confidential, criticism was muted. Talks took place about once a year, and China offered no confidence-building gestures, saying that the existence of the talks was concession enough. "Our Chinese counterpart made very clear how gracious the Chinese government was to allow us to come to Beijing to talk," recalled Kelsang Gyaltsen, one of the two senior Tibetan negotiators.[7] Only once did China accede to a round of talks outside China, in 2005 in Switzerland. Otherwise the Dalai Lama's envoys are required to come to the mainland for the rounds. Often the Tibetan negotiators have been ushered on tours of remote areas of the mainland to see how other minority groups live.

On occasion, the negotiations seemed to enter into substantive terrain. By 2008, the Chinese negotiators asked the Tibetan exile side to present a paper explaining what the Dalai Lama meant by "greater autonomy" for Tibetans. The Tibetans later offered a ten-page explanation that said most of what they sought was compatible with China's constitution. It stated that Tibetan should be respected as "the main spoken and written language" throughout Tibetan regions and that schooling should be in Tibetan. The document said the state should not interfere in religious practices, such as the recognition of reincarnations, and allow monasteries to enroll any number of monks or nuns that they wish. It called for Tibetan leaders to have a say over exploitation of natural resources and be given the right to protect the environment. Public security should be put back in the hands of local Tibetan officials. On a sensitive issue, it called for Tibetans to have control over the flow of ethnic Han settlers into Tibet. "It is not our intention to expel the non-Tibetans who have permanently settled in Tibet and have lived there and grown up there for a considerable time," it said. "Our concern is the induced massive movement of primarily Han but also some other nationalities into many areas of Tibet, upsetting existing communities, marginalizing the Tibetan population there and threatening the fragile natural environment."[8] Lastly, tackling the issue of "Greater Tibet," the document insisted that all areas where Tibetans live should be combined under one administrative entity rather than divided into multiple entities, such as the Tibet Autonomous Region, and separate autonomous counties in the provinces of Qinghai, Gansu, Sichuan, and Yunnan.

Within days, a top party official lashed out at the document, saying it contained "obscure words" and revised interpretations of the constitution intended to give Tibetans "the rights of an independent state." The high degree of autonomy sought by the Tibetans is "exactly the same as 'semi-independence' and 'covert independence.'"[9] The paper appeared to go straight in the trash bin, and as China rode out a global recession and found less need to placate critics, its position hardened. The Chinese envoys dismissed their Tibetan counterparts as empowered only to talk about the conditions for the Dalai Lama's eventual return to China before his death, not the demands of a wider Tibetan community. "The so-called 'Tibet government-in-exile' is utterly illegal. It can neither represent Tibet nor the Tibetan people," a statement from the United Front Work Department, the party entity that handles ethnic matters, said following a ninth round of talks in early 2010. Du Qinglin, the United Front's chief negotiator, indicated to the Xinhua News Agency that the Dalai Lama was out of touch by making any demands of China. The Tibetan god-king should "respect history, conform with the times, clearly understand the reality, and cast aside illusions," Du said.[10]

ON THE MORNING OF OUR DEPARTURE for Everest, we packed our bags into the four-wheel-drive vehicle in high spirits. It seemed that we might get to the foot of the world's highest peak within two days, with the climbing season in full swing. The car made only one stop out of Lhasa, pulling over at a warehouse next to some fifty-five-gallon drums containing contraband fuel. As the driver filled the tank, we noted markings on the drums that indicated the fuel had been waylaid from the military. Topped up, we sped along the highway toward Shigatse, the first stop, about 220 miles to the west. The two-lane highway hugged the edge of a tributary, which further downstream joins with other rivers to become the mighty Brahmaputra, one of the grand arteries of Asia. As we climbed from Lhasa, the occasional stands of riverside poplar disappeared, and the landscape became both stark and majestic. I savored the blue sky and the occasional raptors floating on thermals overhead. Between the high ridges on either side of the road, we occasionally caught glimpses of massive, sunlit, snow-covered Himalayan peaks, which would quickly disappear as the highway wended on. The air grew chillier the higher we went and signs of settlement scant. At narrow bends, the river hundreds of feet below turned into a cascading torrent. After three hours, we pulled off at an overlook to stretch. We tossed stones to see who could send one across a scree slope to hit the river.

Suddenly, a black Buick sedan careened along the highway toward us. Its occupants spotted our off-road vehicle and lurched toward it. Two men in civilian clothes hopped out. One man barked in rapid-fire Mandarin that they were tourism police from Shigatse and ordered us to follow their vehicle to Lhasa. I felt butterflies in my stomach, anxious that my determined efforts to get to Everest had been stymied. There was little choice. As we piled back into the vehicle, the mood was glum. The driver said he was to drop us off at a Lhasa coffee shop, where we would be questioned. There, security agents took the driver into an adjacent building, while we entered the coffee shop. The turn of events grew even odder. The manager arrived from the larger travel agency that we had rejected. He demanded to see our documents and studied our journalist visas. Over the next hour or two, he lectured us about Chinese law, and peppered us with questions about why we had broken the regulations regarding obtaining permits to come to Tibet. His attitude was more akin to a security official than a service manager. My German friend excused himself to get something out of the vehicle. In the parking lot, he encountered the stricken Tibetan driver, who told him that the security agents who interrogated him provided a detailed log of our activities since our arrival in Lhasa. We had been monitored for many days. The log included each taxi trip we had taken, what we discussed with the driver, and where we had gone.

In the coffee shop, I felt as if I had passed through a looking glass. We found ourselves again discussing with the official why we hadn't used the services of his travel agency. I was flummoxed. We were ensnared in a bizarre trap in which state security and commercial interests intermingled. And now we were in a fix. But I detected that there was a way out if we gave him business. I told him that I still wanted to hire his company for a day-long trip to see a glacier near Lhasa and that I was determined to make it to Everest Base Camp and might be ready to pay his price for the trip. He appeared pleased, but he hedged on whether his company could take me, insinuating lingering problems, suggesting we meet again the following day. We returned to the Barkhor area for dinner, mulling what we had learned about the surveillance of our activities. We looked for closed-circuit cameras and spotted a few.

For different reasons, my two colleagues chose not to join me as I paid for the more expensive trip to Everest Base Camp and was given permission to go. After two long days of driving, we finally pulled into a camp near the Rongbuk Monastery at the foot of Mount Everest. Crude signs adorned a few of the fixed canvas tents at the site, announcing "Snow Land Guest House," "Hotel de California," and "Everest Teahouse." The tents were cozy from yak dung stoves inside, and smoke curled into the sky overhead. The guide, a Tibetan, found us tent lodging. I moved slowly, careful not to let altitude sickness get the better of me and impede a dawn departure for the final few miles to base camp, where climbing expeditions from all over the world awaited good weather to scale the mountain. I slept snugly, feeling a tingling sensation in my cheeks and fingers, one of the slight side effects of my high-altitude medication. All that disturbed the quiet was an occasional sound of rockslides crashing down the surrounding slopes.

To my amusement, I awoke to find the two travel agency employees looking wretched. Mountain sickness had brought them down, giving them the equivalent of severe hangovers. Neither would accompany me up to the higher base camp, and the Tibetan guide said he would deliver me and return right away to the lower camp. I'd be alone to do my work at last. I loaded my gear on the back of one of the horse-drawn carts that regularly ferry visitors up to the glacial plain of the base camp. The cold wind whipped along, biting through my clothing. Yet even with the discomfort, the sight of Everest towering ahead, with wind blowing plumes of snow off its flanks, was exhilarating beyond belief.

The base camp was divided into four areas atop a boulder- and rock-strewn glacial plain. One quadrant was for Chinese military climbers, and the other three were for foreign expeditions. My guide helped me put up my tent in the shadow of a latrine (one of only two permanent structures) in what appeared to be the area reserved for budget climbers and scruffier expeditions. He promised to be back in a day to check on me. Then he disappeared. My head pounded, and I was desperately short of breath, but I was pleased to be left to my own devices.

I lay down for a while in the tent, coping with the thin air at seventeen thousand feet, higher than I'd ever been in my life. Virtually no plant life exists at that altitude, and little stirred on the rock plain except for a few birds and a scattering of mountaineers puttering around camps. Occasionally, jangling bells from yak caravans laden with climbing equipment broke the quiet. The shaggy yaks can carry cargo as high as twenty-three thousand feet above sea level, and well-financed expeditions used them to carry loads up to an advanced base camp. Yaks have three times more red blood cells than ordinary cattle, are half the size, and have huge lungs, perfect adaptations for high altitude. Their heavy coats allow them to survive temperatures as low as 40 below zero (which is about the same in Fahrenheit and Celsius). My guide had kindly procured several yak-hair blankets, and I wrapped them around my sleeping bag and outer bivouac shell, ensuring against extreme cold. My food for the next few days consisted of sardines, crackers, granola bars, instant noodles, and dried fruit.

After a short rest, I went exploring. Across the way, I discovered the expedition tent of Wim Hof, an affable bearded Dutchman. Known as "the Iceman," Hof had a knack for surviving extreme cold. He'd already run a half-marathon barefoot and in shorts above the Arctic Circle, chalked up a Guinness World Record for swimming eighty meters under arctic ice, and survived submerged in a tub of ice for more than one hour. His latest scheme was to climb Everest in shorts. It was madness, and there he was, glad to be interviewed. In other tents were an assortment of adventurists, including an ultra-marathoner from California and a couple of exuberant Frenchmen who lacked both equipment and high-mountain experience. They would rely on the weather reports and fixed climbing lines of major climbing expeditions. And if they got in trouble in the "death zone," the area above 26,000 feet where frozen corpses of climbers litter the landscape, they would rely on the goodwill of fellow mountaineers for rescue. It struck me as foolhardy, and I only hoped they wouldn't end up like the Indian climber who froze to death in 1996 lying in a fetal position in a tiny cave at 27,890 feet. His frozen feet jut out on to the trail, and experienced mountaineers refer to him simply as "Green Boots." "It's one of the most horrible, humbling experiences I've ever had, walking over those dead bodies. A lot of times you have to step over their limbs," an American veteran guide on Everest, Daniel Mazur, told me.[11]

I carefully conserved energy at base camp—literally. Unlike climbers with the major expeditions, I was a bare-bones camper with no generator. I took photographs sparingly and turned on my computer only to download photos and video, afraid that my camera and computer would run out of juice. To my astonishment, my mobile phone worked. China's largest mobile operator set up a temporary trailer at another site, and climbers told me that they could get a signal high on the mountain.

By the second day, my body adjusted better to the altitude, and I ventured behind a ridge over to a separate camp, where the biggest expeditions have set up. One of them, Himalayan Expeditions, even had a large white double-insulated "Tiger Dome," where climbers warmed themselves near a wood stove, sipped cocktails, and gazed out through transparent panels at the glorious view of Everest. A New Zealand guide, Mark Woodward, let me peek inside. There were chairs and couches and a widescreen plasma television. "We watched *Crash* last night, and *The Good Shepherd* the other night," Woodward said.[12] By the third day at the base camp, I had finished my interviews and packed up and rendezvoused with my minders down the hill. To their relief, I said my trip was over and they could drop me off at the Lhasa airport, a long day's drive away. During the trip, the Tibetan guide spoke to me in English so the other two minders would not understand. He described how the public security bureau allowed him to work as a guide under the condition that he report each month on all his contacts with foreigners. He said the two travel agency employees were keeping an eye on him as well as on me.

Wherever I'd been, I'd seen crews with huge earthmoving machinery building roads, erecting bridges, and damming rivers. China is developing Tibet at great expense—and exploiting its key resources—in the certainty that raising living standards through economic development will win Tibetan hearts and minds. President Hu Jintao describes the policy as "going down the road of development with Chinese characteristics and Tibetan flavor." As it digs up valuable ore, the Chinese government is building modern highways, hydroelectric dams, and other huge infrastructure projects. Little input from local Tibetans is solicited for the development. Tibet is clearly also a strategic buffer for China on its flank with potential rival India and a geographically valuable site for part of its nuclear arsenal. The Tibetan exile government asserts that China maintains nuclear missile bases near Lhasa, Nagchu, and Nyangtri, abutting the border with India. I had witnessed the stresses on Tibetan society, including population social engineering in which hundreds of thousands of nomads are moved each year from their traditional pastoral grounds to special settlements. Add to that an influx of Chinese-speaking migrants and constant vilification of Tibetan monks, traditionally esteemed as the most learned strata of Tibetan society, and it's not hard to forecast that the palpable accumulated tension in a city like Lhasa would soon find a vent.

About six weeks after my return to Beijing from Lhasa, I got a polite telephone call summoning me to an urgent meeting at the Foreign Ministry, a strikingly modern building set along the Second Ring Road. I would be meeting with the head of the Information Department for North America, Europe, and Oceania, quite a senior official. A young diplomat from Shandong province, my usual point of contact, ushered me into a small meeting room off the lobby of the ministry. Bouquets of flowers graced the tables between large comfortable armchairs. Tea was brought in. I looked around, thinking that such rooms were the scenes of innumerable diplomatic demarches between Chinese and foreign diplomats. I knew I was about to get a dressing down. The senior official arrived and politely launched into an account of his own background. Then he looked down at his notepad.

He said I had recently been to Tibet, and he began to read excerpts from a recent article I had written. He noted that I did not have permission to travel to Tibet as a journalist and I did so against regulations. He said that I asserted in an article that foreign reporters are generally allowed in Tibet just once a year on tightly organized trips and that China's policy is repressive toward Tibetans. He summed up by saying that my writings were not true and were "unacceptable" to the Chinese government and that they could jeopardize not only the status of the newspaper company in China but also the good relations developing between the People's Republic of China and the United States. Such an assertion seemed preposterous to me, and our conversation grew a bit testy. But it became clear that the meeting only amounted to a quiet warning. We said our good-byes. Back in the office, I jotted a blog entry about my dressing down and quickly got the kind of nationalist response I had grown used to. "Western journalists have never been fair in their reporting," a Chinese reader posted in response. "They only want to bash China to make themselves look good."

The official scolding deepened my interest in Tibet. The diplomat's assertion that my reports were "not true" underscored the difficulty of arriving at any common understanding about Tibet among Han Chinese, Tibetans, and interested foreigners. Beijing and the Dalai Lama cannot agree even on the meaning of *Tibet*. To Beijing, it is the Tibetan

Autonomous Region, an area established by the ruling party in 1965 that makes up roughly half of ethnic Tibet. To the Dalai Lama, Tibet is the larger area where ethnic Tibetans live, including parts of four other provinces. Nor can the two sides agree on the meaning of *autonomy*. For the ruling party, autonomy in Tibet means that minorities have a say as long as they do so through the channels of a Leninist party that punishes any criticism of the party's actions. For Tibetans, genuine autonomy means they have the power to determine policies in education, culture, religion, social development, and demographic composition to foster and protect those Tibetans living on the Tibetan Plateau.

If defining such present-day terms is tough, analyzing Tibet's history is even more problematic. Both sides have sought to write history in their own favor, molding and presenting facts to their benefit. A crucial period in Tibet's history began a century ago, and it is essential to understanding Tibet's claim to a unique standing in the world. That was when the Qing Dynasty came thudding down in a heap, ending a succession of Chinese imperial dynasties that stretched over two thousand years.

From Beijing's perspective today, what followed from the Qing's collapse in 1912 was an aberration, a period when Tibet took advantage of China's temporary weakness caused by foreign powers feasting on the Middle Kingdom's edges. As warlords roamed China, the Thirteenth Dalai Lama, seeing advantage in the turmoil, expelled all Chinese officials and troops from Tibet and sent China's then-provisional president, Yuan Shikai, missives that were virtual declarations of independence. For the nearly four decades that ensued, Tibet was largely a de facto independent state, although independence was never recognized by China, nor was it formally acknowledged by any other power. The tide changed with the triumph of Mao Zedong's guerrilla army in 1949, and when Mao stood on the balcony of Tiananmen Gate outside the Forbidden City, Beijing immediately laid claim to Tibet. A year later, the People's Liberation Army launched a full-scale invasion, marching into eastern Tibet but stopping short of Lhasa. The world, distracted by war on the Korean peninsula, ignored Tibet's appeals.

Under duress, a disheartened Tibetan delegation in Beijing reluctantly signed a seventeen-point agreement that gave up claims of independence, acknowledging Chinese sovereignty over Tibet in exchange for recognition of the rights of Tibetans to regional autonomy and religious freedom. The Dalai Lama sent a congratulatory telegram to Mao but later disavowed the agreement when it became clear it did not cover all areas where ethnic Tibetans dwelled. For most of the 1950s, an uneasy coexistence unfolded, with Chinese troops enforcing land redistribution and social reforms in Kham and Amdo, the Tibetan areas outside the Dalai Lama's traditional reach. By late 1955, revolt broke out in Kham, and the Chinese responded with fierce bombardment of monasteries and towns. The clashes led Tibetans there, known as Khampas, to form an armed resistance movement. By 1958, the CIA made its first arms drop for a guerrilla campaign that never gained much momentum.

Refugees fleeing Kham for Lhasa brought jarring news of the vast social and political reforms imposed there by the Chinese. By early 1959, Lhasa boiled with tension. On March 10, 1959, thousands of residents swarmed the Dalai Lama's summer palace, the Norbulingka, amid rumors that the Chinese army had laid a trap for him, using the pretext of an invitation to a song-and-dance performance to snatch the god-king. The city, already teeming with pilgrims for a prayer festival, mobilized in protest. By March 17, the PLA shelled parts of the city, including the Norbulingka. That night the twenty-three-year-old Dalai Lama slipped out and began his journey to exile. Less than a week later, the Chinese army had taken control of the city and hoisted the Chinese flag over the Potala Palace.

With the Dalai Lama gone, party cadres moved to impose collective ownership of land on Tibet. Over much of the next decade, Mao's vision transformed Tibet along with the rest of China, only to be interrupted by a decade of calamity known as the Proletarian People's Cultural Revolution (1966–1976). During that period, Mao called on youth to attack all authority other than his own in a period of upheaval that rivaled Stalin's Great Terror in the Soviet Union. Gangs of Red Guards comprising both ethnic Han and Tibetan youth destroyed thousands of monasteries and hounded monks out of their robes. With Mao's death in 1976, Beijing's policies toward Tibet relaxed to the point that then-paramount leader Deng Xiaoping told the Dalai Lama's elder brother, Gyalo Thondup, that Beijing was willing to discuss any issue apart from Tibet's independence.[13] Beijing moved to revitalize Tibetan culture and language, and sought to improve economic conditions on the plateau. But even as an air of hope wafted through Lhasa, in a history that would repeat itself later, the relaxation led emboldened monks to the streets in protest—perhaps misreading the level of support for Tibet abroad. Four major riots erupted in Lhasa in October 1987, in March and December 1988, and again in March 1989. The two March protests coincided with the always-sensitive March anniversary of the Dalai Lama's flight to exile. The riots led to the imposition of martial law in Tibet.

In subsequent years, and propelled by astonishing sustained economic growth, China hurtled past one milestone after another. It launched a manned space mission in 2003 and headed for the hosting of the 2008 Olympic Summer Games, a source of huge national pride and a symbolic showcase of its reemergence as a world power. But some Tibetans had a different idea. Deeply frustrated by the Dalai Lama's continued exile, they saw the run-up to the Games as a chance to grab the spotlight for their own cause and embarrass China. A collision of interests brewed, coming to a head when monks at Lhasa's big three monasteries staged a series of protests. They had several festering grievances, among them anger over an increase in "patriotic education" classes imposed on them by the party. The classes had increased in frequency to punish monks for celebrating five months earlier when the U.S. Congressional Gold Medal was given to the Dalai Lama. On March 10, monks at Drepung Monastery—one of the big three Gelugpa monastic centers in Lhasa—hit the streets, leading to dozens of arrests. For the next three days, protests by monks at the Ganden and Sera monasteries also unfolded peacefully.

Then mayhem erupted. By nightfall on March 14, 2008, the city of Lhasa lay in smoldering calamity. According to government accounts, rioters set some three hundred fires, and heavily damaged or destroyed 908 shops, seven schools, and 120 houses. They ransacked or ruined five hospitals and ten banks. Protesters overturned or torched eighty-four vehicles. At a minimum, eighteen ethnic Han civilians, one police officer, and three Tibetan rioters lay dead, according to the Chinese government, although Tibetan exile groups said as many as two hundred people were killed during the rioting and its aftermath.

The spark for the day's melee was a confrontation in late morning between police and monks at the Ramoche Temple. As monks scuffled with security forces, Tibetan bystanders threw rocks at police. Fires broke out, and more Tibetans joined in. Videos played later on Chinese state television showed Tibetans pulling Chinese off motorbikes and bludgeoning them, shattering shop windows, and looting stores. "These lawless people launched assaults on the street-side shops, primary and middle schools, hospitals, banks, power and communication facilities and news agencies along the major streets in Lhasa, set vehicles on fire, chased and attacked passengers, and attacked department stores, telecommunication services outlets and government offices," Jampa Phuntsok, who was then the Tibetan chairman of the Tibetan Autonomous Region, said in Beijing.[14]

The detailed chronology of the rampage and subsequent police crackdown were never fully clarified, and censors went into panic mode. Only one foreign correspondent was in the city at the time, James Miles of the *Economist*, and he was confined largely to his hotel before being ordered back to Beijing. Authorities sent foreigners out of Tibet and imposed a lockdown that lasted for months. State television newscasts repeated video images of the rioting with lengthy tributes to innocent loss of life. Among the victims were five female clerks, age eighteen to twenty-four, burned to death at a clothing store when rioters set the store afire. One of the 382 people wounded in the rioting was a Han man whose left ear was sliced off by assailants. Rioters cut out "a piece of flesh as big as a fist" from the buttock of one wounded policeman.[15] In the days and weeks after the Lhasa riot, unrest spread across the entire Tibetan Plateau. It marked the biggest and most widespread ethnic upheaval to challenge the ruling party since it came to power, surpassed only by the Uighur riots more than a year later. Foreign monitors said 125 documented protest incidents occurred between mid-March and early June, a majority of them in ethnic Tibetan areas outside the Tibet Autonomous Region that China designates as Tibet proper.[16]

Responding to outrage among ordinary Chinese across the nation, the government pledged to mete out exemplary punishment for those responsible. Incensed Chinese authorities blamed the Dalai Lama and his followers overseas for instigating the riot, accusing them of using the pre-Olympic period as a platform to gain visibility. "The Dalai clique has cried out that the Olympic Games is the 'last chance for Tibetans.' They took great pains to organize, mastermind and fan the recent rioting in Lhasa and some other places," Ye Xiaowen, head of the State Administration of Religious Affairs, wrote.[17] In a memorable turn of phrase after the rioting, the Communist Party secretary of Tibet, Zhang Qingli, told the *Tibet Daily*, "The Dalai Lama is a wolf wrapped in robes, a monster with a human face and an animal's heart."

In the months after the protests, the refrain from the state media, party officials, and Foreign Ministry spokesmen was that the Dalai Lama and a criminal cabal around him had secretly planned and instigated the Lhasa riots, stirring up Tibetans despite the contentment of the majority. The spasm of violence left many Han Chinese puzzled and angry, asking in internet forums why Tibetans were so ungrateful for the $45 billion or so that Beijing had poured into Tibet since the beginning of the decade for development. Open racism poured out from both sides. The crackdown after the riots netted more than forty-four hundred arrests across Tibetan areas, responding to the government's desire to bring stability and crush any hope for a recurrence of trouble. By one account, eighty-four Tibetans were sentenced for crimes committed during the Lhasa riots within a year or so, and press reports citing foreign exile groups said at least six of them were given death sentences.

One late afternoon in Beijing, I went back to see Tsering Woeser, the prominent Tibetan poet and writer. She lives with her husband, Wang Lixiong, a Han Chinese intellectual, in a small high-rise apartment in Tongzhou on the far eastern outskirts of the capital. Tibetan paintings, scrolls, tapestries, and photographs covered the walls, and in one corner a string of multicolored Tibetan prayer flags hung over a photograph of the Dalai Lama. Woeser is a petite woman in her mid-forties, given to stylish scarves and large jewelry. On this day, she was wearing a yellow cotton sweater over a black leotard. Large silver earrings dangled from her ears, and a trace of pink lipstick brought out color in her face. We sat down on stools, and sipped some mugs of hot tea. A long period had passed since the Lhasa unrest, and I asked her how she felt about the future.

"I am pessimistic," she began. "Tibet is totally controlled by the Chinese government. Under these circumstances, it's impossible for Tibetans to change the destiny of Tibet. Tibet can only change along with China. However, the Chinese government is a rather despotic dictatorship, so the possibility of change in Tibet is quite low. . . . If it takes a long time for change to come, the future of Tibet will not be promising. That is because when you go to Tibet now, you discover that Tibetan traditions, culture, and the environment have been seriously damaged. The damage is accelerating. The marginalization of Tibetan people in their own homeland is racing along."[18]

The situation has a personal dimension for Woeser. Her father, a former army deputy commander in Lhasa, passed away in 1991, but her mother, sister, and brother still live in the Tibetan capital. She doesn't visit Lhasa much any more because of the close monitoring to which she is subject by the state security apparatus as a prominent Tibetan dissident. She doesn't want to bring her family trouble, so she only telephones them and keeps conversations short. Already, police have told her "that I will probably end up in prison if I don't keep my mouth shut."[19]

She considers herself a Tibetan exiled in Beijing and must maintain her Tibetan friends at arms length for fear of bringing the state security's focus on them. Mainly, she remains in her apartment, updating a blog on Tibetan matters and writing her poetry and essays, waiting for change to come. She is unable to leave China. In 2007, she applied for a passport so she could pick up a writing award in Norway, but the application was rejected. Her husband went in her place to receive the award. She filed a lawsuit seeking to overturn the denial. The case went nowhere. "They still refuse to give me the passport."[20]

Our conversation turned to the ongoing talks between Beijing and the Dalai Lama's envoys, and she said it was important to keep them going even without tangible results. "It's better to have some contact than no contact at all. From another angle, the dialogue can have some historical value. When we look back, we can see that Tibetans kept making continual efforts to change the situation." She said that Tibetans within China understand that the negotiations are likely to lead nowhere, but Tibetan exiles may have illusions. "I think they should understand that the dialogue will not achieve anything. I've found that they still have illusions about this dialogue, which is wrong because this is just a show. The Chinese government is playing it to the world."[21]

A few months earlier, an unusual dissonant chord had sounded amid the propaganda chorus on Tibet, and it heartened Woeser. It came from the Open Constitution Initiative, a small group of scholars, several of whom are graduates of the Beijing University law school, the most prestigious in the country. The scholars said they had conducted a month of field research in Tibetan areas and concluded that Tibetans were airing reasonable demands in their protests. The group's twenty-eight-page study noted an acute sense of alienation among young Tibetans arising from a lack of economic opportunity.[22] It cited deficiencies in schools, including woefully poor teaching of the Tibetan language. And it confirmed exile charges that ethnic Han and Hui migrants are given an edge in competing for jobs, while banks deny Tibetan business owners loans.

> Large numbers of Han and Hui have been drawn into small businesses, food services and tourism industries. The people drawing the greatest benefits from the thriving are the incomers, the non-Tibetans; and because Tibetans lack capital and skills, this is contributing to them becoming increasingly marginalized. In Lhasa, there are Sichuan restaurants everywhere, run by people from Sichuan. Taxi drivers are mainly non-Tibetan outsiders from Henan, Sichuan, Hunan and Shaanxi. Travel agencies are nearly all owned by outsiders, and the tourist souvenir and handicraft trade in the stores around the Barkhor are mostly owned by Hui from Gannan and Qinghai, and not Tibetans. Many items of Tibetan handicrafts come from Yunnan, they come from Zhejiang, and they come from Nepal.[23]

The report said the riots intensified the views among many Han Chinese that minority groups in the nation's west, including the Tibetans, are "remote and backward barbarians." It said the repeated and intense repetition of video images of the riots in Lhasa in the state media led some Chinese to "form feelings of racist sentiment toward the Tibetan masses as a result." For their part, Tibetans subject to targeted security measures around the time of the Olympic Games, including intrusive searches at airports, felt even more acutely their separateness from the majority Han. "I went to Beijing representing a certain company in Lhasa to participate in training by the Central Communist Youth League," one young woman told the group, "and because I was Tibetan not a single hotel let me stay. I got angry and argued, saying what they were doing was racist!"

The report said a new aristocracy had formed in Tibetan areas made up of local party cadres who build networks, siphon off aid for their personal benefit, and fail to address local problems. When social conflicts emerge, the local Tibetan party officials quickly blame the troubles on "foreign forces" rather than their own incompetence. The report cited diehard Tibetan Communist Baba Phuntsok Wangyal in dismissive remarks about the incompetence of local Tibetan party cadres, who blame separatist forces (known in Chinese lingo as "splittists") for all of Tibet's problems. "They take every opportunity to play the splittism card, and while on the face of it they shout about anti-splittism, in reality their personal interests are involved. They are unable to admit their mistakes and instead put all of their effort into shifting accountability onto 'hostile foreign forces.'"

The afternoon was growing late, and I peppered Woeser with a few more questions, asking her how Tibetans would react if the Dalai Lama died in exile, unable ever to return to his homeland. "Tibetans in China have not seen the Dalai Lama for the last fifty years," she began. "One of the biggest dreams for Tibetans is to meet the Dalai Lama during their lifetimes. The reason many Tibetans took part in the [March 2008] protests was to appeal to the Chinese government to allow the Dalai Lama to return to Tibet." But his return seems increasingly unlikely. How disconsolate Tibetans react once the Dalai Lama dies could prove to be a major test for China. "Their grief will be so great that they may carry out even bigger protests to express their loss. It could create a situation that the Chinese government would be at a loss to deal with." I told Woeser about the Dalai Lama's prediction that he would outlive Communist rule, and she shrugged it off, saying experts with whom she was in touch were divided. Some believe the ruling party is growing stronger, while others say corruption could bring it down in short order. "Some estimate the collapse could happen in ten years. Others say fifty years."[24]

I left Woeser's apartment wondering if I would ever see her again. Other dissidents I knew were already in jail, and the thin protection offered by her renown overseas would not shield her indefinitely. Ordinary Tibetans didn't have that protection, and some were fleeing China on an unimaginable cross-Himalayan journey to Nepal and India to lay eyes on His Holiness. I recalled the cold spring nights at Everest Base Camp and knew what I endured was a romp compared to the midwinter treks of Tibetans across glacier fields with nothing on their feet but tennis shoes.

chapter five

Over the Himalayas

They are shooting them like dogs!

—*Romanian mountaineer Sergiu Matei on seeing Chinese border guards opening fire at Tibetans crossing into Nepal*

SO MUCH ICE COVERED THE WINDOW OF THE GUESTHOUSE IN THE high Himalayas of Nepal that I could barely detect that it was snowing outside. The plastic cup of water I'd left by my bedside was partially frozen. I punched through the ice layer with my pen to get at the water and quench a raging thirst from the dry mountain air. My hosts were a Sherpa couple, devout Buddhists who regularly provided temporary shelter to groups of Tibetans making their way across the eighteen-thousand-foot mountain trails toward Katmandu, the Nepalese capital. The guesthouse was about a three-day hard hike from the mountain pass that divides Nepal and Tibet. I'd been here almost a week, waiting for a late-night knock that would signal the arrival of a group of Tibetans making their way along the underground railway.

The last my hosts had heard, the group had departed Lhasa. If everything were to go as planned, they would take buses or trucks to Tingri, a desolate village on a high plateau in southern Tibet just over thirty miles from the border with Nepal. Then they would begin a perilous journey on foot, walking only at night to avoid being spotted by Chinese border guards or nomads and farmers serving as informants. Chinese guards could catch and throw them in a remote jail—or shoot them. The Tibetans couldn't wear the thick clothes one needs at high altitudes. Such bulky clothes might draw attention from informants observing as they left Lhasa. So they had to survive the high Himalayas with inadequate protection from the frigid temperatures. Frostbite and snow blindness loomed as real threats.

Most Tibetan refugees cross in winter, the most inclement time. Curiously, it is safer. High up the Himalayan pass, wintry temperatures stabilize the ice and snow fields, making it easier to avert the deadly crevasses that yawn open, swallowing those who don't watch their footing. Also, the Chinese border guards don't patrol so often in the cold season, preferring to remain in their heated mountain huts. Once the Tibetans cross into Nepal, they face further dangers. Nepalese police and soldiers routinely shake down Tibetans for the little cash they have in their shoulder bags. So for the first few days, Tibetans sleep in the open, avoiding villages with police bases. All told, the journey from Tingri to the safety of a refugee center in Katmandu, the Nepalese capital, takes about two weeks.

The routes across the Himalayas are well trodden. For centuries, traders leading yak caravans have crisscrossed the mountains. Indeed, the Tibetans and Sherpas of Nepal speak a language with the same roots and can largely understand one another. In recent decades, yak caravans diminished, while human traffic over the mountains burgeoned. Anywhere from a few hundred to three thousand or four thousand Tibetans walk out of their homeland each year on the way to temporary or permanent exile. It is an erratic exodus, rising when tensions in Tibet ebb and falling when border security tightens. For most Tibetans, the walking journey is the only way out of their homeland. It is illegal for them to leave China without passports, yet obtaining a passport can be difficult for ordinary Tibetans. So they walk for days and nights across some of the most forbidding high-mountain terrain on Earth. The lucky ones come in small groups and pay modest amounts to guides. Others come equipped only with hearsay knowledge of the route. The exodus, not widely known in the West, belies China's claim that all is well in Tibet. The journey across the snow-laden and windswept Nangpa Pass, at 18,753 feet, is simply too arduous for anyone except those dead set on leaving China and escaping to South Asia.

Eager to learn more about the migration, I flew from Katmandu to Lukla, the drop off point in eastern Nepal for trekkers and those venturing into the high Himalayas. Lukla has what many consider one of the world's most dangerous airports—a two-thousand-foot inclined runway with a 12 percent grade. At the bottom end of the sloped runway is a fence, and after that a two-thousand-foot drop into a deep valley. Only twin-engine aircraft with overhead wings can land in Lukla easily. Our flight had already been postponed a day because of foggy weather. Luckily, decent weather arrived, and Himalayan crags surrounded us as we bucked to a stop and climbed out of the de Havilland aircraft. It was still early morning, and we began our nine-hour hike up to Namche Bazaar, a thriving village in a horseshoe-shaped mountain saddle that is on the main hiking route to reach the base camp for Mount Everest on the Nepal side of the world's highest mountain. Most trekkers and mountaineers stop in Namche, as everyone calls the place, to acclimate for a day or two to the high elevation. It is crowded with internet cafés and bakeries, the last settlement where one can get a frothy coffee and a pizza before heading into the forbidding and breath-sapping high Himalayas and a steady diet of rubbery freeze-dried food and granola bars.

When trekkers in the 1990s arrived in the village in greater numbers, the Sherpas running guesthouses began to replace their rustic wooden structures with sturdy stone lodges. Then came bakeries, pizzerias, and internet cafés with satellite hookups. Some café owners built outdoor terraces to let hikers take in the ever-changing alpine scenery, most spectacular when spring brings an explosion of rhododendron and magnolia blossoms. Word soon spread among backpackers that Namche offered a window into the culture of the Sherpas, hardy mountain people often used as porters and Himalayan guides. No roads climb to Namche; thus there are no vehicles, only cobblestone walkways. Nearly everything that keeps the village alive must come on the backs of porters or by a heavy-lift Russian-made Mi-17 helicopter that ferries timber, large appliances, and other heavy goods by charter. I'd seen porters with huge amounts of cargo. One scooted past me on a mountain trail despite a load that included five cases of beer, heavy bags of rice, noodles, and assorted other goods. They earn as little as $3.50 a day. "They are like little trucks. Some of them can carry 120 kilograms [264 pounds]," Pemba Gyaltsen Sherpa, manager of the well-established Khumbu Lodge, told me.

Unbeknownst to many of the foreign trekkers acclimating comfortably in the stone lodges, Namche is smack on the underground railway route for scared Tibetan refugees. At some lodges, the Tibetans sneak in late at night, rest a day or so without leaving their rooms to avoid being seen, and then leave before dawn. The exodus is an escape valve for Tibetans, with repercussions both inside and outside their homeland. Some Tibetans cross over the Himalayas to see the Dalai Lama and deepen their religious training. Others are teenagers sent by their parents to get a Tibetan-language and English-language education in India in schools run by the Tibetan government-in-exile. A few flee troubles at home. Others seek better economic opportunities abroad, displaced by Han migrants in Tibet's new economic hierarchy. Many of those who cross do not intend to stay abroad. Some want a better education and religious training but seek to return to Tibet years later—even if they must cross the Himalayan pass again. They often return impressed by the freedoms they've experienced in India and with new pride in their heritage instilled by the organized communities of exiles.

The underground railway keeps a degree of information flowing back and forth between Tibet and the diaspora. All newcomers are formally debriefed at refugee centers in Katmandu and Dharamsala, providing a wealth of information to the Tibetan government-in-exile about conditions in their home regions. As the days go on, I found the use of the term "underground railway" ever more apt in relation to the Tibetans. Just like the underground network of routes and safe houses operated by abolitionists that allowed thousands of black slaves to escape from the southern United States to free states in the north in the nineteenth century, the system for Tibetans is similar, run by fellow Buddhists sympathetic to their plight. The guesthouse where we stayed was like many that cater to Western trekkers. The proprietors used coded telephone messages to learn when new groups are likely to arrive. Travelers at the guesthouses were usually oblivious to the drama playing out in the basement or back rooms. If they spotted the escapees, they were likely to mistake them for local Sherpas, not Tibetans arriving from harrowing journeys.

As days went by, we hiked to higher valleys to ask trusted contacts if they'd heard word of the group of Tibetans. We arrived in the village of Kunde, a bleak, rocky hamlet at an elevation of 12,600 feet, and stopped at the hospital founded by Sir Edmund Hillary, the famous New Zealand conqueror of Mount Everest. The remote clinic has treated hundreds of Tibetan refugees over the years, and a health worker with decades of experience said the vagaries of high-mountain weather could bring calamity to underequipped refugees. "Some are unlucky," said the worker. "They get caught in a bad snowstorm." If they are really unfortunate, the refugees arrive at the hospital with severely frozen fingers and toes that must be removed. "The frostbite treatment is not to amputate right away. You wait for demarcation of dead tissue and live tissue. It can take up to a couple of months."[1]

The medic told me about a frostbitten young Tibetan staying at the small Tsamkhang Monastery above the hamlet. I met Pema Tsering, who slowly removed his right canvas tennis shoe and showed me his frostbitten toes, blackened as if by the plague. Tsering was eighteen years old, although his young face gave him the appearance of a teenager in middle school. Tsering didn't flee Tibet for the usual reasons—a desire for religious freedom or flight from political persecution. He said he left because his parents died and he didn't get along with an elder brother in his remote village in central Tibet. So he and a fifteen-year-old brother decided to flee. In preparation for fording streams on the high pass, they brought plastic bags to put over their feet, a common practice. Tsering was too tired to put on a plastic bag at one stream, and his right foot got soaked and froze. Like most refugees, they ate no hot food on the journey, consuming only some dried meat, dried fruits, and *tsampa*. They mixed the *tsampa* with water or snow to make a paste. During rest times, they crawled into empty plastic garbage bags to sleep.

When I asked Tsering whether he had any desire to travel to India to meet the Dalai Lama, he looked at me blankly. I asked again. "I've never heard of the Dalai Lama," he said sheepishly. A Tibetan nun looked on and shrugged. I had never met a Tibetan who didn't know about the Dalai Lama, and the Tibetans I talked to usually responded to his name with signs of deep reverence. Even amid the relative freedom of Nepal, Tsering was giving me a quick lesson on how Chinese-run schools in Tibet had made young Tibetans wary of confessing any awareness of a high lama regarded as a virtual traitor to the motherland.

Tibetan refugees crossing the Himalayas find that extreme weather isn't the only hazard. They also must contend with China's "border management" policy carried out by marksmen with high-powered rifles. The policy came to the fore in a dramatic incident on September 30, 2006, captured on video by a group of foreign mountaineers. Chinese guards hoisted their rifles and took aim at an unarmed group of Tibetans walking through a snowfield toward the Nangpa Pass. The incident unfolded in full view of some sixty mountaineers and porters at a base camp for Mount Cho Oyu, a peak near the pass. As shots rang out, a seventeen-year-old nun slumped to the snow, fatally wounded. Two other Tibetans also appear to have been hit but kept moving. One of the mountaineers later posted the video to mount-everest.net, a website devoted to Himalayan climbing. "They are shooting them like dogs!" Romanian mountaineer Sergiu Matei is heard saying on the videotape. In the chaos after the shootings, one of the Tibetan escapees made it to base camp and was found trembling in fear in an outhouse. Back at the guesthouse on the Nepalese side, the subject of the shooting came up one night, and our host had something to add. It turned out that the "very scared" Tibetan survivors of the Nangpa Pass shooting later arrived at the very guesthouse where I was staying. "The group leader had a bullet hole in his pants," our host said.

The group of Tibetans never turned up, waylaid for some unknown reason. It wasn't until much later that it became clear that a dramatic falloff had occurred in refugee crossings around the period of large-scale Tibetan unrest in China in early 2008. That year, only 627 Tibetans fled into Nepal, and just 691 did so in 2009. The dwindling numbers are the result of tighter border control and from growing Nepalese cooperation with China to establish a "Great Wall of Stability in Tibet" to check migrations of those wanting to see the Dalai Lama.[2]

I returned to Katmandu, one of the smaller hubs for the 145,000 or so Tibetans now living in exile. The vast majority (101,000) reside in India, and another 16,000 or so live in Nepal. The rest are scattered around the world. I found frustrations high among second-generation exiles born in Nepal and India with little or no possibility of obtaining citizenship and numerous restrictions on business and travel. Some have done well, getting university degrees and finding jobs with aid organizations, embassies, and travel agencies catering to trekkers, often rising higher than non-Tibetans in their towns and cities. Still, they feel rootless and angry over their stateless status, restlessly searching for a way to bring change to Tibet, a land that most of them have never known.

One night in Katmandu, a Tibetan acquaintance brought together a dozen of his friends to talk about their frustrations with the Dalai Lama's "Middle Way" approach to China, the policy pursued since the late 1980s to seek genuine autonomy for Tibet rather than full independence from China. The young exiles gathered around the restaurant table were mostly under age thirty and university-educated. They looked cool, even hip. Several wore fashionable down jackets with jaunty silk scarves, sunglasses tucked away in pockets. They could have been rugged adventurers posing in a Patagonia catalog. Some spoke vernacular English honed as tour guides or on trips to the West. The cosmopolitan streak came from having relatives living in exile in Britain, Switzerland, Canada, and the United States. Candles illuminated the restaurant because another blackout had hit Katmandu. Conversation was animated.

A young Tibetan herbal doctor, Tashi Dorje, turned to me and said exiles should pool their resources and obtain land for a new country. "We can buy an island," he said, warming to his theme. "We can have our own national TV, passports, so that we can enjoy the facilities of a citizenry, of a free nation." Others pounced on him, ridiculing his idea, asking why Tibetans should settle on land not historically theirs. Later, he turned to me and said quietly he would be ready to take up a gun for the Tibetan cause. "If you can blow up a railroad track, it means more than a protest."

Most of them had neither formal papers nor passports, toting only refugee identity cards. Their rights were sharply restricted. In Nepal, they did not even have the right to protest. They pined for a Tibet they knew only through the stories of their parents. Their longing seemed ethereal and wistful. Yet they bantered in Tibetan, wolfed down Tibetan food, and said all their friends were fellow exiles. They said they wanted a free and independent Tibet, not a region under China's thumb. All voiced hopes that a free Tibet wouldn't be just another Third World backwater, yet they couldn't articulate clearly how to build a country without China's potent backing. They revered the Dalai Lama but grew strongly animated in declaring that his diplomacy with China hadn't worked—and would never work. Independence, they reiterated, was the only path. And to get there, they said, required protests, demonstrations, and even stronger actions. The conversation turned to a widely known exile poet and activist, Tenzin Tsundue, whose radical tactics have won him both fame and stints in jail. "For many in the young generation, he is a very big inspiration," the eldest of the group, a thirty-three-year-old Tibetan exile radio journalist, said to me. "He has sacrificed his own personal livelihood and career."

A few months later, I traveled to India and had a chance to meet Tenzin Tsundue. I spotted him in a crowd, and it was easy to pick him out. Tsundue wears a broad red headband wherever he goes. He says it represents his pledge to work every day for the freedom of his homeland and that he will never take it off until Tibet is an independent country. "Only an independent Tibet can guarantee the survival of Tibet, nothing else," Tsundue said later as we ate Tibetan food at a hotel restaurant in Dharamsala, the Indian hill station that is the seat of the Tibetan government-in-exile.[3] Tsundue, sitting across from me, was fidgety and full of impatient energy. Large horn-rimmed glasses gave him a studious appearance, and his broad face featured a slight moustache and goatee.

Tsundue is known for what he himself calls "capers," flamboyant publicity stunts that embarrass China over the Tibet issue. He made a name for himself shortly after graduating from Loyola College in Madras, daring in 1997 to travel overland on foot to Tibet. "I was arrested by the Chinese authorities, beaten up, interrogated, starved and finally thrown out of Tibet after keeping me in their jails for three months in Lhasa and Ngari," he wrote to me in an email.[4] Tsundue's fearlessness at confronting Chinese authorities on their own turf— even at the cost of beatings and jail—brought him to the attention of other Tibetan exiles frustrated at the lack of progress in seeking greater freedom for Tibet. He carried the banner of restless youth unwilling to wait forever for China to loosen its grip on Tibet.

Young radicals like Tsundue are occasionally said to be anti–Dalai Lama, which they deny. They revere the Dalai Lama as a Buddha, and they adhere to principles of nonviolence. But Tsundue said their inter-pretation of nonviolence is more aggressive. "For us, non-violence is not a strategy. It's a principle of life. But our non-violence is not the Dalai Lama's non-violence, where it's all talk, talk, talk. The younger generation's non-violence is confrontational, aggressive non-violence. Where there is injustice, we go there and fight. We will receive the beatings. We will go to jail. We will fight court cases," he said.[5]

His big media pop came in January 2002, when he learned from newspapers that China's then premier, Zhu Rongji, was to visit Mum-bai and stay at the thirty-story Oberoi Towers, a five-star hotel on Nariman Point that overlooks the Arab Sea. Tsundue went nearly a week ahead of the visit to scope out the site, finding scaffolding on one exterior section. During the visit, Tsundue waited outside for Zhu to leave the hotel for a meeting at a museum, guessing correctly that security agents would relax with his departure. It was then that he snuck past guards and climbed the scaffolding. Workers, rather than security guards, were the first to spot him as he shinnied up the building. "When I climbed up to, like, five floors, they said, 'Why are you doing it? Come down! This is really scary!' . . . I just kept on climbing up," Tsundue related.[6] When he reached the tenth floor, workers were still shouting at him to come down. The activist kept climbing. By the time he had reached the nineteenth floor, masses of Indians had flooded the street to watch his stunt. He didn't know it at the time, but an Indian news channel was broadcasting live from the scene. People were gathered on the roofs of neighboring buildings to watch.

Tsundue then unfurled a large red banner with "Free Tibet" lettered on it. He draped a Tibet flag from the scaffolding and tossed leaflets to the crowds below. "I was there for quite some time, shouting slogans and throwing leaflets. . . . My throat dried up and I was tired."[7] Look-ing through the window into the building, he saw Chinese dignitaries glaring at him in shock and surprise. Since the hotel's windows were sealed, workers had to fetch screwdrivers to unscrew the window frame to allow security agents to get at Tsundue and pull him out of the limelight. The court case for the stunt dragged on for two years, and he said he had to appear before the judiciary some twenty times before receiving a simple and final legal reprimand.

But the media storm was an intoxicating display of power for Ti-betan activists used to powerlessness. In 2005, Tsundue read in the newspapers that another Chinese premier, Wen Jiabao, was to visit Bangalore, the high-tech hub that is considered the Silicon Valley of India. The Tibetan took the calculated risk that Wen, an engineer, would visit the city's Indian Institute of Science, the premiere scien-tific research center in the country. Wary of new stunts by Tibetans, authorities had cordoned off youth hostels where Tibetans often stay and banned Tibetans living locally from leaving their houses. Tsundue evaded the security by staying at an Indian hostel. He slipped onto the institute campus a day before Wen's arrival and climbed up a rain-water pipe to the roof of the majestic main building. He spent the night on the roof. Unbeknownst to him, the Chinese premier was to come to the very building he had scaled. Once Wen arrived and as he gave a speech on the ground floor, Tsundue scaled a tower on the building and appeared on a balcony, where he unrolled a banner, brandished a Tibetan flag, and let loose a flurry of printed flyers. "I gave a long speech in Hindi and in English. . . . It was a hugely dramatic protest," he said. The massive number of journalists there for the premier's speech focused on the Tibetan activist's latest exploit instead.

By the time President Hu Jintao visited India in 2006, authorities had wised up to Tsundue's knack for scaling buildings and disrupting such visits. They slapped an official detention order on him for four-teen days not to leave the hill station of Dharamsala. Wherever he went for that period, fifteen plainclothes officers in four cars and two motorcycles accompanied him. Some of the cops would even follow him into the toilet. As the date of Hu's visit drew near, the local super-intendent of police summoned Tsundue and pleaded with him to con-duct no protests. "And then he warned me, 'If you breach this detention notice, we will have to deport you.' I said, 'When I breach this notice in a few days, please do just that. I *want* to confront China face-to-face in my *own country*. Please deport me.'"[8] As it turned out, other Tibetan exile groups picked up the cause, mobilizing hundreds of Tibetans to travel from Dharamsala to New Delhi to protest in Tsundue's place. In exchange for a pledge from police to allow safe passage for the demonstrators to Delhi and a guarantee of protection once there, the Tibetan activist decided to stay put in Dharamsala.

I sat down with Tsundue while five hundred or so Tibetan exiles were congregated in Dharamsala for an open-ended weeklong discussion about the future of Tibet. Many had come from Europe, Canada, and the United States, and the mood was high-spirited. The diaspora's most important thinkers had arrived, and the door was open to all, including those who rejected the nonviolence espoused by the Dalai Lama. The exiles divided into subgroups with certain themes to discuss, such as whether to continue on the path of negotiation with China. The Dalai Lama receded from view for the week, not wanting to influence open discussion.

"There are many people who I've read about or whose emails I've read, but I've never met them before. When you do come together, you feel good. We are strong," Tsundue said.[9] But he admitted that getting Tibetans to voice their views without waiting for cues from the Dalai Lama was difficult. For decades, the Dalai Lama had voiced his hope that Tibetans could construct a democratic culture, voicing their opinions freely and shaking off habits of submission to the religious hierarchy. But such habits are ingrained. No matter how much the Dalai Lama tells Tibetans to speak their opinions and make up their own minds, many cannot help but offer total submission to the god-king. "The whole mind-set is so dependent and so awed by the presence of the Dalai Lama. It's not just leader-subject, or even Gandhi and the Indian people. It's much more than that. The people worship His Holiness as the Buddha. He's a Buddha in real life. People say, 'I will even die if you say. You make the decision, and I will follow,'" Tsundue said.[10]

Tsundue's flair for disrupting international diplomacy has inspired many young Tibetan exiles, but it is a broader organization of Tibetan youth that most infuriates China. Beijing despises the Tibetan Youth Congress, a nongovernmental organization that gives the greatest voice to the frustrations of exile youth. Widely known simply by its initials, the TYC claims to have thirty thousand members in the diaspora and is by far the largest independent exile organization. It was set up with the blessing of the Dalai Lama in 1970 to give voice to young people. Its early leaders are now among the grand old men of the Tibetan exile struggle, their radical years tempered with age. They include Lodi Gyari, the burly diplomat who operates from a brownstone in Washington, DC, as the Dalai Lama's chief negotiator with China and the senior diplomatic envoy to the world. The TYC increasingly charts a different path from the Dalai Lama, who for more than two decades has said he can accept Chinese sovereignty over Tibet as long as his homeland enjoys full autonomy. For its part, the TYC has stuck by its founding objective of independence for Tibet. A statement of the group's aims on its website calls on each member "to struggle for the total independence of Tibet even at the cost of one's life."[11]

China has singled out the TYC as a radical hotbed and even a terrorist organization. Following the month-long eruption of riots in ethnic Tibetan regions in early 2008, a commentary on *People's Daily Online*, which reflects party thinking, declared that the Tibetan Youth Congress "does not have much difference essentially with Al Qaeda and Chechen terrorists."[12] The commentary said TYC leaders helped organize a deadly rampage in Lhasa on March 14, 2008, and schemed to set up guerrilla squads. "They incited Tibetan youths to go in for underground activities, and spy on railways and water conservancy and power grid projects in Tibet and numerous barracks of the military area command," the commentary said, suggesting that the reconnaissance was for potential terrorist attacks. It added that the TYC had joined with four other exile groups to create the "Tibetan People's Uprising Movement" to destabilize Tibet and weaken China's control there.

At about the time the commentary was published, I was in my office in Beijing and telephoned the president of the Tibetan Youth Congress, Tsewang Rigzin, at its headquarters in Dharamsala, and asked him over the static-filled line if his group supported the use of violence in fighting Chinese control of Tibet. He sounded tentative. "I'm not sure," he said, pausing for a few seconds. "Our struggle has been nonviolent so far."[13]

Rigzin was in Dharamsala at the time of my later visit, and on meeting him I found him to fit the part of a banker more than a bomb thrower. Indeed, his idealism seemed steeped in the civic activism that sprouts in California coffee bars, not in the radical militancy of armed guerrilla actions. Rigzin was wearing a tan sport coat and an open-collar shirt. His hairline was receding, and he spoke the idiomatic English of a well-settled immigrant to the United States. He was in temporary residence in Dharamsala, having left his wife and children behind in Vancouver, Washington, to assume the presidency of the TYC for a three-year period. Rigzin was born in Sikkim in northeast India. His Tibetan parents, like many new exiles, worked with picks and shovels cutting mountain roads for the Indian Public Works Department and lived in roadside camps.

When Rigzin was four, the family moved to Karnataka in southern India, where he attended a school for exiles. With the help of an elder brother, who had joined the Indian army, Rigzin enrolled in Mysore University, where he studied English literature, political science, and sociology.[14] He never graduated. During his second year, his father urged him to put his name in the hat for a U.S. resettlement program. In the late 1980s, Congress had approved a plan to sponsor a thousand Tibetans to come to the States. Rigzin balked at his father's request. "I said, 'A thousand Tibetans out of all the Tibetans that we have, I don't stand a chance.' I said, 'It's not going to happen.'"[15]

It did happen, though, and at age twenty-two Rigzin found himself on a jetliner for Los Angeles, part of a group of Tibetans accepted into the program. Organizers settled him into an apartment in Santa Monica with three other Tibetans. Each one was given $50 a week. "It was a big change, a big shock. I'd never been abroad before. . . . When I first got there, I had mixed feelings about it. I said, 'Maybe this is not the right place for me,'" Rigzin recalled. Unemployment was high, and the only job he could find was making espressos at a mall, later moving to inventory control at a jewelry factory in Burbank. When the 1994 Northridge earthquake struck in the Los Angeles area, Rigzin feared that his job was no longer stable. So he moved to Minneapolis, which had a larger Tibetan community. He got a temporary job filing documents at a local bank, which later merged with Wells Fargo. After some intensive training, he got a full-time job handling corporate trusts and internet banking. Without a college degree, he found himself with a full-fledged career as a banker.

After a decade or so in Minneapolis, he moved with his wife and two children to Portland, Oregon, where he had relatives. While working at another banking job, he found his free time completely taken over by activism. "I was never satisfied with what I was doing for my country because I had to go to a job, I had to take care of my family. There were times when I was spending my whole annual vacation on activist stuff."[16]

Rigzin said he felt "this fire burning inside me" to do more for the homeland of his parents and fight "all the evil policies being implemented by China to wipe out the Tibetan nation and Tibetan people."[17] So with the backing of colleagues in the TYC, Rigzin ran for president and won. He scoffed at the charges made by China that his organization was actively training insurrectionists. I read to him one of the latest news reports in which Beijing said police had seized "a lot of offensive weaponry in some Tibetan Buddhist temples or lamaseries, as a clear proof to the violent nature of the TYC." The Xinhua News Agency cited a Ministry of Public Security spokesman saying authorities had recovered 178 guns or rifles, 13,013 rounds of ammunition, 359 knives or swords, 3,504 kilograms of dynamite, 19,360 detonators, and two hand grenades, all ready for use by Tibetan militants. "Their next plan is to organize suicide squads to launch violent attacks, according to our investigation," the spokesman said.[18]

Rigzin described the allegations as fanciful and untrue and pointed to a TYC statement that Tibetans had never been known to use such weaponry. "In its 39 years of existence, the TYC has not been involved in a single incidence of resorting to terrorism," the statement said, adding that "all TYC campaigns in the past have been peaceful."[19] There was much that Rigzin declined to discuss, such as whether the organization had collaborators inside Tibet and what role they might play. Like a practiced politician, he responded, "No comment." He insisted that Tibet should be independent. "China has been saying internationally that Tibetans are happy under China. But it's completely the opposite. It's been reflected in these uprisings. We cannot live under China. We can live with China as our neighbor but not under China."[20]

If Rigzin was less than candid about whether radicals among the Tibetan exiles might turn to a guerrilla campaign against China, one of his predecessors—a former head of TYC—laid out his own vision of how a violent campaign might unfold. I visited Lhasang Tsering at his modest Moonbeam Bookshop in Dharamsala. Tsering, a poet and writer, openly seethes at the concept of negotiating with China. "We've waited for thirty years for the Chinese government. Are we going to wait for three hundred years, or three thousand years, for the Chinese people to tell us, 'You are going to get nothing'?" Tsering asked with a sneer. "We are going to be wiped out in another thirty years. It is now or never, do or die." As another Tibetan looked on, shaking his head in vigorous agreement, Tsering said a new guerrilla campaign should begin against Chinese targets within Tibet. "Without going into tactical details, the one and only effective way to strike at the soft underbelly of China's increasingly market-oriented economy is to target their industries, their power supply, and communications inside China through acts of sabotage. While there'll be no intention to kill, we recognize there will be loss of life on both sides."

That a grassroots insurrectionary campaign could ever succeed against a far superior Chinese force seemed improbable to me. I had already seen the blanket security surveillance in Lhasa and knew that China considered social stability in Tibet to be a top priority. To be sure, the contemporary peace-loving image of Tibetans obscures a bare-knuckle history with episodes of notable belligerence. Before the 1949 Revolution, large monasteries commonly deployed squads of ruffians. Heinrich Harrer, the Austrian who lived in Lhasa for five years in the 1940s, wrote of the "monk thugs" guarding some monasteries. "The worst of them belong to the unauthorized but tolerated organization of the Dob-Dobs, or monkish soldiery. They wear a red armband and blacken their faces with soot," Harrer wrote. "In the war against the Chinese Communists they formed a battalion which gained a reputation for courage. In peacetime, too, they have opportunities for getting rid of their superfluous energy, as the Dob-Dobs of the different monasteries are always at war with one another."[21]

More recent history illustrates that failure is likely even when a foreign government backs Tibetan insurgents. In one of the little-known sideshows to the Cold War, the U.S. Central Intelligence Agency armed, financed, and helped train Tibetan guerrillas for more than a decade until it abandoned the fighters in 1969 in the interests of a broader U.S. agenda. None other than the Dalai Lama's two elder brothers, Gyalo Thondup and Thubten Jigme Norbu, coordinated U.S. assistance and training for the rebels. Even before the arrival of American aid, armed fighters in the Kham region had already formed hit-and-run armed militias calling themselves Four Rivers–Six Mountains, after the predominant geographical features of the Kham region.

In March 1957, prospective Tibetan insurgents had been flown to a secret U.S. military base in Saipan in the South Pacific for training in how to read maps and use light arms, as well as guerrilla warfare tactics and operating RS-1 hand-generated radio transmitters and receivers. A bit of English language training was thrown in, too. Soon, unmarked B-17 aircraft began dropping guerrillas, supplies, and light weaponry into Tibet, usually on moonlit nights.[22] The CIA trainers later hauled Tibetans to Camp Hale, situated between Aspen and Vail in the Rocky Mountains of Colorado, a place chosen for its similarity to the physical features of eastern Tibet. The camp trained more than 250 Tibetans through 1964.[23] The instructors, unable to master the Tibetan names of their charges, assigned them random American nicknames.[24] To boost the Tibetans' fighting spirit, American trainers showed them war movies like *Viva Zapata!*, *Roger's Rangers*, and *Merrill's Marauders*. For their air jumps, the Tibetans were taught to scream "Geronimo!" as they fell.[25]

By 1960, fewer than fifty insurgents had been dropped into Tibet, and only a third of them survived. The larger and better-equipped Chinese troops were giving the guerrilla forces a spanking. Tibetan fighters were long on bravery, opting to take on Chinese troops in frontal attacks, but short on tactical guerrilla strategy. So the CIA pulled the insurgents away from Chinese forces into relative safety in Mustang, a scrap of remote arid Nepal jutting into Tibet and bounded by the high Dhaulagiri and Annapurna peaks. The project, code-named ST Circus, was one of the CIA's longest-running covert operations against a foreign government. While U.S. assistance remained minimal, the Tibetans conveniently fit into Washington's plans to destabilize and overthrow communist regimes around the world.

The first winter in Mustang was bitter. Some Tibetans froze to death. Others ate their shoes to survive. More Tibetan volunteers flocked to Mustang, compounding food shortages. But the rebels began chalking up some successes, and further U.S. airdrops arrived. In October 1961, a hit-and-run mission by forty Tibetan horsemen against a Chinese jeep and truck traveling along the main road between Lhasa and Xinjiang proved an extraordinary success. After killing the Chinese soldiers, the rebels rescued from one of the vehicles a blue satchel containing 1,500 pages of bullet-riddled, blood-stained documents—a treasure trove of intelligence. Among the papers were two dozen issues of a classified People's Liberation Army journal, *Bulletin of Activities*, and other documents that provided deep insight into rumblings of discontent in the military, frank discussion about the discord between Beijing and Moscow, and admission of the failure of the Great Leap Forward, Mao's disastrous industrialization drive that left millions of Chinese dead from famine. A former CIA trainer of the Tibetans called it "one of the greatest intelligence hauls in the history of the agency."[26]

The rebels tallied a few more successes, including planting sensors that allowed Washington to detect nuclear tests at Lop Nor in the northwest Xinjiang region. But by the mid-1960s Beijing had moved abundant PLA forces into Tibet and constructed enough roadways to mobilize quickly. The last CIA airdrop to the rebels occurred in 1965. By 1969, President Richard Nixon's rapprochement with China signaled the death knell for the Tibetan rebels. The order came from CIA headquarters to shut down Operation ST Circus. The Tibetans were once again on their own.

Decades later, China is resurgent, and the Tibetan struggle is on a knife's edge. The Dalai Lama has put a brake on the radicals, wary that violence could harm global support for the Tibetan cause. Yet he also says he wants stronger political leaders to emerge in the diaspora. In his twilight years, the Dalai Lama hears the rumblings of discontent among frustrated young exiles but sticks to his stance on nonviolence. He voices exasperation and weariness when speaking about the Chinese leadership, but he does not display bitterness. Indeed, he suggests compassion for the ruling party leaders. Those who perpetrate injustice, he says, face long-term consequences of karma, which is to say they will suffer in a future life for any cruel actions in this lifetime. So they deserve forgiveness. Tibetans, meanwhile, must not harbor negative feelings toward the Han Chinese and must instead reach out to them.

Yet at times it seems that one can spot ambiguity in the Dalai Lama's position. He knew of CIA assistance to Tibetan fighters four

decades ago and never publicly expressed any hesitations about it. Indeed, John Kenneth Knaus, the CIA case officer who trained Tibetan
agents and later led the Tibet Task Force in the early 1960s, recounted
in his book how he and the Dalai Lama met twice, once in 1964 in a
meeting that was somewhat chilly and again thirty years later. "I
opened our conversation by recalling our earlier meeting and the
irony that I personally dislike firearms but was then supplying them to
his people," Knaus wrote. "This must have seemed to be the embodiment of the moral quandary he had faced then and that continues to
trouble him to this day."[27] Moreover, the Dalai Lama's charitable trust
fund accepted $180,000 in annual donations from the CIA, as well as
$75,000 a year to run Tibet Houses in New York and Geneva, for an
undetermined period.[28]

During a talk the Dalai Lama gave in Boston, I was startled when I
heard him talk about forgiveness and yet interrupted himself with the
following thought: "If you really want revenge, keep calm and think
deeply, what is the best way to hit back?"[29]

It is among the questions that reverberate around Dharamsala, the
quaint Indian town that is the nerve center of the Tibetan exile movement. There, a tiny government-in-exile tries to keep alive the hopes
and aspirations of people who feel their culture is being smothered by
China. Most Tibetans are steeped in Buddhism and believe in the im-
permanence of all things. Everything will change. Tibet will soon slide
evermore tightly into China's grasp, or it may take a surprising lurch
in a different direction. No one knows for sure. Even the famed
Nechung state oracle of Tibet has yet to offer a prediction.

chapter six

Dharamsala

We will have to remain in exile for a longer period than expected.
We will have to settle mentally as well as physically.

— *The Dalai Lama, speaking to exiles in northern India in 1959*

MONSOON RAINS HAD LASHED THE HIMALAYAN HILL STATION OF
Dharamsala before my arrival, and the downpours had made a mess
of the road to the higher mountain district where I was headed. Rains
had washed away some of the asphalt, leaving gaping potholes and
bare ruts. I boarded a tiny white Maruti Suzuki taxi, and it kicked its
way up toward a district some locals call "Little Lhasa." It didn't take
long to see that the hip settlement on a pine-covered spur of the
mountains lies solidly on the international travelers' circuit. Along the
roadside were coffee bars, restaurants offering Italian and Mexican
food, yoga studios, and bookstores. Western backpackers wandered
the streets, with orange shawls bearing the Hindu symbol for "Om." It
no longer felt quite like India, but neither did it seem like Tibet. Most
travelers had come to catch a glimpse of the most famous resident
here, the Dalai Lama, who lives and works on a wooded knoll with a
panoramic view of the Kangra Valley below. When he comes out, it is
usually in a convoy of vehicles protected by high-level Indian security.

The proper name for the district is McLeod Ganj, and the headquarters of the Tibetan government-in-exile is just a mile or so down the
road. The district is named for Sir Donald Friell McLeod, who was a
lieutenant governor of nearby Punjab during the British Raj. The British
established Dharamsala as a garrison town, placing a cantonment on

the ridge of a mountain with a commanding view. By the 1850s, the higher districts of McLeod Ganj and Forsyth Ganj sprang up, filled with cooks, cleaners, tailors, and merchants catering to the resident British army. An endearing neo-Gothic stone church, St. John in the Wilderness, still stands in a forest of Himalayan cedar trees between the two districts. Among the crumbling tombstones is a memorial to Lord Elgin, the British viceroy who so loved Dharamsala that he suggested before his death in 1863 that it be made the summer capital of India. That dream died with him. Dharamsala was already falling into decay in 1905, when a devastating earthquake killed 19,800 people. The church was one of the few buildings left standing.

Eventually some bungalows and villas were rebuilt in the cool forests around McLeod Ganj and Forsyth Ganj, perched 6,800 feet up in the Himalayas, but following the birth of independent India in 1947 and its bloody partition, Dharamsala fell back into drowsy obscurity. Owners of the villas fled back to Lahore and New Delhi, and a new hibernation began for a hill station that would soon become akin to a spiritual Las Vegas, drawing seekers from around the world.

Upon the Dalai Lama's exile from Tibet in 1959, the Indian government first directed him and his followers to Mussoorie, another hill station, only later providing sanctuary in and around Dharamsala's McLeod Ganj. Indian Prime Minister Jawaharlal Nehru, wary of disrupting his pro-China policy, wanted to keep the Dalai Lama away from the capital, where the Tibetan leader would have easy access to endless foreign dignitaries. But because of the religious affinity between Indians and Tibetans, and the sympathy that many Indians felt for the Tibetan refugees, India set aside agricultural land and settlement areas along the flanks of the Himalayas and in the south of India for the eighty thousand or so Tibetans who escaped their homeland in the year after the Dalai Lama's exile. The arrival of the Dalai Lama and his retinue in McLeod Ganj in 1960 stirred the district back to life. The young Dalai Lama occupied what was known as Swarg Ashram. In the first years, most Tibetans figured their exile was temporary. But after a decade, they began to rebuild the institutions they had left behind, erecting temples, monasteries, and schools.

When my taxi arrived in McLeod Ganj, I found half a dozen roads converging from odd angles onto the main square. Buses and jitneys loitered there, as did vendors, onlookers, and dogs. To one side, at the edge of a sharp mountain slope, was a dilapidated wooden-frame store set up by Parsee merchants back when Lord Elgin still came to the town to escape the heat of the northern Indian plains. It bore a sign reading, "Nowrojee & Son, Est'd 1860," the district's oldest shop. The sign also declared that the vendors were "Wine & General Merchants," only the "Wine &" had been clumsily painted over. On a windowsill, five soft drink bottles and two jars filled with candies were on display. Inside, the day's fresh Indian newspapers lay on a countertop. The store served as the town's sole news kiosk.

Past the newspaper display, rays of sunlight illuminated dust suspended in the still air of a much larger hall. It was once the main sales area but now served as an antiquated museum. Dusty candy jars lined shelves. Old-fashioned tin advertising signs from a bygone era were nailed to the walls. "Glaxo Biscuits," announced one. "State Express Cigarettes—the world's premier high-class cigarette," said another. A box proclaimed that it contained "Rangaroon teas from the peak of the Darjeeling tea district." The proprietor, a well-groomed man in his fifties, Parvez N. Nowrojee, said the district and his own family had interwoven histories. It was his great-great-grandfather who arrived from Karachi and set up the store to attend to the influx of British civil servants and soldiers arriving each hot season to the hill station. The store was the center of all activity during the colonial times, selling wine and petrol, ammunition to protect against feral beasts, and homemade aerated cream sodas and ginger ales, as well as handling auctions of property.

"When I grew up here, it was a sparsely populated town," Nowrojee recalled. "It's basically because of His Holiness that people came here." A constant trickle of Tibetan exiles arrived over the years, seeking to be near the Dalai Lama and to settle down. Even as locals profited from the influx of Tibetans, they felt a little swamped. About eight thousand Tibetans now live in McLeod Ganj. "Some time ago, they used to call this 'Little Lhasa' until we Indians got up and said, 'You'd better not do that because we don't want to become Lhasa only. This land belongs to us!'"[1] Nowrojee said the Tibetan government-in-exile sends many newer Tibetan arrivals to other Tibetan exile communities scattered around India.

For a decade or two after the Dalai Lama's arrival, the hill station remained sleepy. "It did not have much tourism because Kashmir was doing well." The peaceful Vale of Kashmir in northern India had attracted a variety of foreigners, most famously George Harrison of the Beatles, and travelers flocked there for the serenity of Srinagar's Dal Lake, where flower vendors with names like "Mr. Wonderful" paddled flower-laden *shikaras*. But the flow of travelers to Kashmir dried up in the early 1990s as separatist militants and Indian security forces battled, making the region unsafe. By then, the Dalai Lama's fame had soared, and travelers and Buddhist seekers turned Dharamsala into a hot destination. They came from all over: some to study Buddhism, others to do trekking in the mountains, still others to soak in the spiritual ambience of a community with a distinct Tibetan air. "The place is on the international map," Nowrojee said. At certain times of the year, one group predominates—young Israelis, most of them at the end of their mandatory military service and eager to blow off steam. "They don't learn Buddhism, but they just found the place a haven for themselves. In fact, there's a joke going around town that it's time they had a rabbi, there are so many of them."[2]

The Pema Thang Guesthouse, one of many that had multiplied around McLeod Ganj, was up a hill from the square, and I toted my bags to a second-floor room and walked out on a wooden balcony to take in the scenery. Tibetan prayer flags fluttered from many rooftops, some of which had Tibetan architectural flourishes. Back inside, I spied a note on the nightstand with a warning: "Doors and windows should be shut when leaving your room as monkeys may enter in your absence." I returned to the balcony to scan the branches for any rustling that might betray the smaller rhesus and larger gray langur monkeys. Downstairs, guesthouse manager Sonam Dorje chuckled when asked if monkeys really would enter the building. "Sure, they'll come in your room if you let them! They can turn everything upside down." From then on, I made sure to latch the screen door and windows. My first trip out was to stroll about, take in the international flavor of the town, and look for old-timers.

Wall posters advertised an endless series of debates on Tibet, film nights, drop-in yoga classes, massage and Reiki courses, meditation training, and other services for the traveler. "Ear & Body Piercing," said one. "Vedic Astrologer: Consult and Learn Indian Astrology," said another. A half-dozen roads make up the settlement, and many are filled with shops selling traditional Tibetan handicrafts, banners, and incense. Bookshops brim with rare and popular titles on Tibetan Buddhism, meditation, history, and culture. Fluttering above many buildings was the Snow Lion flag that Tibetans use as their national symbol, and Tibetan music wafted from numerous small restaurants. It didn't take long before I was in front of the restaurant Taste of India. Handwritten signs in the window touted the establishment in Korean, German, Chinese, Hebrew, Hindi, and English, a testament to the polyglot travelers in McLeod Ganj. The proprietress inside, Nisha Sarin, offered me cardamom tea. "The businesses like massage and yoga are just mushrooming. . . . There used to be only ten to fifteen restaurants, and now in all of McLeod Ganj there are at least a hundred fifty restaurants."[3]

In the early 1980s, only two buses a day brought tourists from New Delhi, she said. Now, up to eight buses arrive each day. Prosperous Indians from the Punjab, usually Sikh families, drive up to Dharamsala during the summer months to escape the heat of the plains and gawk at the international hodge-podge of McLeod Ganj, where it is common to see Westerners dressed as Tibetan monks and nuns. Dharamsala's airport was expanded a few years ago, and now accepts fifty-seat turboprops arriving from New Delhi each day, weather permitting.

As we sipped tea, Nisha Sarin pulled out a photo of a world map on which visitors to her cooking classes had stuck pushpins to identify their home countries. "I think I have covered more than two hundred countries now." My wife had taken a class from Ms. Sarin a few days earlier and was astonished to observe her speaking Hebrew. "I do speak some Hebrew," she told me, adding that it was necessary to explain spices to Israeli tourists.[4] I had already noticed other signs of Israeli influence on the town. At one shop selling papier-mâché handcrafts from Kashmir, among the articles on display was a mezuza, which is traditionally affixed to door frames in Jewish homes.

The guesthouse had a somewhat sporadic internet connection, making it necessary to visit one of the dozens of internet cafés in the village. As I searched my email, I couldn't help but hear a young foreign woman nearby using a headset and speaking to a friend through a free

internet service. Chatting in Spanish, she spoke animatedly with relatives in Guatemala. She explained that she had just come out of a ten-
day silent retreat at a local Buddhist center and hadn't uttered a word
to anyone during that period. The words tumbled out of her. When it
was clear that the conversation was dying down at the far end, she
asked her relative if there were anyone else at home in Guatemala with
whom she could speak. She hungered for conversation.

Filling the other chairs of the internet café was an eclectic mix—
tonsured monks, backpackers from Australia, hippie Europeans, Indian intellectuals, and (from a quick glance at the screen next to mine)
a handsome young Tibetan Lothario responding to a love email written to him by a smitten foreign woman. The internet connections
weren't the fastest in the world, but McLeod Ganj and the Tibetan exile community are deeply digitalized. Young exiles are constantly online sparring with unseen Chinese counterparts in the digital realm
over the situation of Tibet. I'd already seen exchanges on sites like
YouTube every time a pro-Tibet or pro-China video would go up.

A typical exchange occurred on a music video promoting Tibet independence.[5] An internet user, presumably Chinese, used the name
"HisPhoniness" and wrote the following post: "His Phoniness Daliar
Lama is a money hungry dollar chasing monk politician who has
ruled for 70 years over the indian tibetans with his autocratic theocratic nepotistic rule. Down with daliar lama and his elite wealthy
aristocratic family, then tibetans will have true freedom."

A quick response came from a Tibetan using the name Dorje168:

China is the World Leader in:
    1) Lying
    2) Torture
    3) Racism
    4) Brutality
    5) Executions
    6) Repression
    7) Slave Prisons
    8) Internet Censorship
    9) Human Rights Abuse
    10) Vulgar Lowlife Speech

"A lie repeated a hundred times becomes the truth."
—Chairman Mao

Such back-and-forth occurred in English, rather than Tibetan or Chinese, and probably didn't change anyone's mind, but it allowed the two sides to vent and engage in creative exchange.

I wandered out of the café and decided to drop in on Lobsang Wangyal, a handsome Tibetan in his thirties who sports a black pony-tail and an earring. Wangyal is a talented entertainment entrepreneur, photojournalist, artist, and operator of an internet site that aggregates news on Tibet. His garret office atop a building had panoramic views of the snow-capped Dhauladhar range. The office itself was painted orange and lilac, with bright curtains covering floor-to-ceiling windows. For the last few years, Wangyal had also produced an annual Miss Tibet pageant, which drew as many as five thousand people to a local arena. Posters of the pageant adorned the office walls. One had a likeness of a shapely young Tibetan and read, "Celebrating 50 Years of Tibet on the World Stage." When I asked him why he sponsored a beauty pageant, he smirked, "I like pretty girls." He was an unapologetic bon vivant. A blue brassiere hung from a peg on the wall. But rather than discuss the pageant, he was in a mood to talk about the erosion of Tibetan culture. "Every day, I'm getting more Hindi words and more English words in my Tibetan conversation," he said. His brother emigrated to Vermont, and his niece has become American-ized. "My niece is twelve years old. He speaks to her in Tibetan. She answers in English." Wangyal takes pride in the dignitaries that routinely make the journey to Dharamsala to consult with the Dalai Lama. "Fifteen years ago, who would have thought that Nancy Pelosi, the third most important politician in America, would come here?"[6]

But he was disturbed by the rootlessness of both the tourists passing through the exile town and the Tibetan youth seduced by the charms of the backpackers. Of the foreigners, he said, "All of them are seekers. I don't know what they are seeking. They are lost and confused. Since there are no shortcuts in Buddhism, I think they will grow more confused." Some of the younger Tibetans joined the moonlit raves and smoke *charis*, or hashish, with the visitors. "You see all these Tibetans hanging around waiting to be picked up by Western

women." Like many Tibetans, Wangyal was not economically self-suf-
ficient in his ventures of running pageants and sponsoring art shows.
His brother in Vermont sent him an occasional remittance of American dollars.

For younger Tibetans, the pull of the West is strong. Those Tibetans who emigrate to Europe, Canada, or the United States often
come back with tales of success. Coincidentally, while I was in
Dharamsala, I heard an update about a Tibetan journalist who had
helped me search for refugees in Nepal. A year had passed, and I
learned that he'd moved to New York City, temporarily leaving his
wife and daughter behind in Katmandu. Wherever we had gone in
Nepal, he used his video camera, preparing footage for a documen-
tary he hoped one day to produce. Profoundly patriotic, he longed to
do more for Tibet, even to the point that he said he'd be willing to pick
up a rifle to fight. I was surprised at the news of his move, so I wrote
him, and he quickly responded:

> It's exactly a year now that I am living in New York and working in
> New Jersey. I have been out of touch with media for so long, I really
> miss doing it. But life is now taking me a different alley that I don't
> know and am discovering slowly.
>
> My documentary really was one of the biggest blows. It is still in-
> complete. Sometimes, I didn't have equipment, sometimes I don't have
> resources and now I don't find enough time to complete it. But I will
> complete it whenever it is possible. If you plan to come to New York,
> just let me know and we could do some catching up.

The circle of foreign residents in McLeod Ganj is not large. A few
reside year-round, and others drop in each year to hear public teachings by the Dalai Lama. One of them was Phil Void, whose twinkly
eyes, sizable girth, bushy gray-flecked beard, and long ponytail make
him an instantly recognizable presence in town. More than three
decades ago, Void was studying for a doctorate in Sanskrit and Tibetan languages at Columbia University when he faced a dilemma: He
loved both rock 'n' roll and studying Buddhism, and he didn't know
what to pursue. So he consulted the resident sage of Dharamsala,
telling the Dalai Lama about the new rock anthem on Tibetan inde-

pendence that he'd composed and asking him for advice. "He looked at me with a funny smile and a look that bore right through me. His Holiness said, 'You have a special talent for these songs.'"[7]

That did it. Void had already ditched his birth name, Philip Hemley, taking the Buddhist-sounding name Phil Void instead. He then scrapped his academic ambitions, touring with fellow Buddhist musicians in a band they dubbed the Dharma Bums, after the Jack Kerouac novel. Void recounted this story over a beer at the bar of the Hotel Tibet. Near the bar was another of the erstwhile band members, Maura Moynihan, an activist, singer-songwriter, and daughter of the late Sen. Daniel Patrick Moynihan, who was U.S. ambassador to India under two administrations. Void recalled that when he first came to McLeod Ganj in 1975, a single tourist bungalow welcomed visitors. A decade later, progress still lagged. "There were no taxicabs. The road between the temple and the library was a goat path."

The natural beauty of the mountain setting is still largely undisturbed. Forests of chir pine, Himalayan oak, rhododendron, and deodar trees cover the mountainsides. Far below in the valley, patches of rice and wheat fields and tea plantations differ in their shades of green. Walking around McLeod Ganj, I was always aware of the Dhauladhar range that rises to the east, reaching heights of seventeen thousand feet or so. Some days, azure skies rose above the serrated peaks, while other days treacherous and unpredictable weather cloaked the mountaintops. McLeod Ganj pulsated with the sounds of Tibet.

One day at dawn, I heard the chanting of monks at the Tsuglakhang, the Dalai Lama's temple, on a ridge five minutes' walk from the guesthouse. At the temple's entrance, Buddhist faithful prostrated toward the throne, where only the Dalai Lama may sit. Some of the women held wooden clappers in their hands, falling on their knees and then sliding gracefully forward in a full prone position. Inside the temple were huge *thangkas*, depicting fierce deities or tranquil mandala images. Behind the temple were kitchens where monks prepare tea in huge cauldrons—up to six feet across—for the thousands of monks and nuns that routinely arrive for public teachings of the Dalai Lama.

Near the entrance was the Tibet Museum, which chronicled events of the 1950s. It made the case that Tibet enjoyed independence for the period between the fall of imperial China in 1912 and the arrival of Communist troops on the plateau in 1950. Mural-sized photos hung from the walls, and display cases held Tibetan bank notes, stamps, and passports. One case held the handmade folded paper that served as the passport of a onetime finance minister, Tsepon Shakabpa. The explanation on the display said, "It bears stamps of many countries, which granted visas and transit permits to Shakabpa. The passport bears visas from countries like India, United Kingdom, United States, Italy, Switzerland and France." China, of course, contends that the slip of handmade paper has no meaning.

Another case held postal stamps. Only later did I find the display less convincing than it first appeared. Lhasa issued stamps in 1912, 1914, 1933, and up into the 1950s. But the isolated kingdom never joined the international body recognizing the world's postal stamps, meaning the handful of foreigners mailing envelopes to the outside world from within Tibet had to use Tibetan stamps on an outer envelope. Once the envelope reached the border, it would be ripped open, and an inner envelope bearing stamps from India or Nepal recognized by the International Philatelic Union would be mailed onward. This awkward process symbolized Tibet's ambivalence about integrating with the larger outside world.

During the decades of self-governance, Tibet remained insular, and few Tibetans exhibited much desire to connect with the outside world. It wasn't until World War II that Tibet created a Bureau of Foreign Affairs, partly to deal with the American forces "flying the hump" from India over the Himalayas to air bases in southwestern China in the war effort against Japanese forces. Only when the war ended, and as Maoist troops gained strength, did Tibetans awake to the challenge. But efforts to rally support for their independence were met largely with indifference by newly independent India, Britain, Russia, and the United States.

The lack of timely steps to get international recognition for independence was only one of the many yin-yang riddles in the Tibet dilemma. On the one hand, the exiles appeared entirely impotent. Back in Lhasa, the Dalai Lama once ruled from the imposing Potala Palace, where he could sit on pillow-festooned thrones looking down on the humans tilling the barley fields below. Today, he works out of a one-story office and claims to have removed himself from the government-in-exile he set up, serving only as a senior adviser and not on day-to-day affairs.

Daily administration of Tibetan exile matters occurs down the hill at the compound of the Central Tibetan Administration, which is overseen by a rheumy-eyed lama who is the prime minister. The compound of yellow wooden buildings and brick chalets has the quaint air of other minuscule seats of government I had visited, like Belmopan, Belize, or in various Pacific and Caribbean isles. There are offices for seven ministries: Home, Education, Security, Finance, Health, Information and International Relations, and Religion and Culture. There's also a supreme justice commission, an auditors' office, a public service commission, and a building for the parliament-in-exile. It takes four minutes to walk from one end of the compound to the other. If one doesn't pay attention, one could miss the Finance Ministry or walk past the staircase that leads to the Education Ministry. The compound is so quiet that one day two lads used the dusty open parking space to play cricket, a game once foreign to Tibetans but now familiar to those who have attended Indian colleges and universities. The exile government's powers are limited. Its security force can make no arrests. Its tax office can forcibly collect no taxes. The department of international relations has no formal relations with any foreign government. When monsoon rains make the roads impassable here, the Tibetans are not empowered to fix them themselves. Mainly, the government looks after the social interests of the exiles and moves Tibetans gently from their theocratic past toward democratic rule.

Yet despite its weakness, Dharamsala wields a paradoxically outsized role on the world stage. A constant flow of foreign politicians, entertainment figures, prominent scientists, and religious leaders arrive for meetings with the Dalai Lama when he is in town, which is about half his time. Less than a week after my arrival in McLeod Ganj, the guesthouse proprietor informed me that I should find new lodging because a delegation of six Australian legislators was about to arrive and they had reserved my room in advance. Without the Dalai Lama, most of the foreign dignitaries would likely never come. But China's relentless demonizing of the exile government has imbued it with a certain importance as well. Beijing accuses the bureaucrats and lamas of Dharamsala of conspiring to stir up riots and pry the Tibetan Plateau from Beijing's grasp. For all the fire that the Chinese dragon breathes about conspiracies hatched in this Himalayan backwater, one might think the place would burn with a feverish desire for emancipation of a lost homeland. But the fever is notably low grade. Dharamsala has none of the revolutionary zeal of Ramallah in the West Bank, nor does it simmer with the anti-Castro–type conspiracies that roil the Miami of Cuban-Americans. Instead, it whirrs with quiet vibrations more in tune with spinning Buddhist prayer wheels.

No one was at the reception desk of the parliament-in-exile, and I paused to determine how to notify the Speaker that I had arrived for an appointment. Penpa Tsering, a husky former restaurateur in his mid-forties, finally emerged and brought me to his Speaker's office. He wore a short-sleeve cotton shirt, khaki pants, and Teva-style sandals. A blue blazer was slung over the back of his high-backed swivel office chair. The yellow sofa had a thick Tibetan rug thrown over the seat. His upright desk was slightly cluttered, and a big set of headphones with an attached microphone lay atop papers. Tsering had short-cropped hair and a broad face. I realized that I'd already seen him around McLeod Ganj astride his Royal Enfield Bullet, a motorcycle made by a former British weapons manufacturer that has since become an Indian company. Its onetime motto: "Made like a gun, goes like a bullet."

We made small talk for a few moments about the modesty of the government-in-exile before he suddenly stood. "Let's take a walk," he said amiably, ushering me out the door. He took me to a nearby room with more than a dozen black-and-white mounted photos, showing sessions of the parliament-in-exile after each election. The first parliament had thirteen members who were sworn in on September 2, 1960. Three parliamentarians were selected for each of the three traditional regions of Tibet—U-Tsang, Kham, and Amdo—and one representative was picked for each of the four major schools of Tibetan Buddhism. Over the years, the Dalai Lama pressed exiles to set up more exemplary forms of democratic government, and by 1991 the parliament had grown to forty-three seats with an established system of elections every five years. The Dalai Lama can appoint another three representatives, for a total of forty-six seats. A decade later, the exile government's prime minister was empowered to nominate his own ministers with minimal input from the Dalai Lama.

"This is our parliament hall," Penpa Tsering said as we strolled into a medium-sized room with an array of desks lined around the Speaker's dais. Behind it was an elevated seat. "This is the seat for His Holiness." The parliament meets twice a year, normally in March and September, for sessions that last about ten to fifteen days, "depending on the work load." With some pride in the evolution of the parliament, he added: "We consider Westminster as our grandfather, and Indian democracy as our father. We are the son."

It's a shoestring operation. Senior members of the exile government make about 15,000 Indian rupees a month, or about $300. They and their families get free schooling for their children as well as free health care and modest housing. But other benefits are minimal. "Even for me, the Speaker of the Parliament, we get 15 rupees—how much is that? 30 cents?—for lunch each day."

In most groups with all-powerful leaders, moves to democratize usually come from the grassroots. A peculiarity of the exile Tibetan movement is that the reverse is true: The push for democracy has come from the paramount leader, the Dalai Lama, and the grassroots has resisted. I asked the Speaker about this, and he responded: "We don't see the Dalai Lama as an ordinary person. We see him as an incarnation of the Lord of Compassion, Avalokiteshvara. Because of that, people don't want His Holiness's powers to be devolved. In our case, it's always been His Holiness who wanted more democracy, and the people who didn't necessarily want it." As the Dalai Lama has increased the pressure on Tibetans to take the reins of their destiny—and not look to him to make all substantive decisions—they have figuratively kicked and screamed, begging him to remain in absolute charge. In 2003, a committee set up to redraft the constitution to enshrine more democratic powers sent a petition to the Dalai Lama imploring him not to make them go ahead with the task. The petition said in part:

> Your Holiness is the eye and heart of the Tibetan people. Your Holiness is the soul of the Tibetan nation and its spiritual and temporal polity. The Tibetan people, both in and outside Tibet, look to your Holiness

with absolute reverence and hope. No leader of a democracy enjoys as much trust from people as Your Holiness does. From this perspective, the existing system does reflect genuine democracy. Therefore, we appeal to Your Holiness not to ask us to constitute the committee. Instead, kindly, continue to take responsibility as our leader.

In some ways, this goes to the nub of the Tibetan exile dilemma. The Dalai Lama is a megawatt global figure, elevating the Tibetan cause in arenas around the world, inspiring tens of millions of people. In his shadow, few Tibetan exiles have emerged as genuine political leaders, casting their own light. The few well-educated Tibetans stepping forward with political opinions often don't get much traction. After all, why let mere mortal Tibetans make decisions when a divine presence could do it? The Dalai Lama describes himself as a simple monk. Yet his followers see him as infallible. The religious aspect of their adoration cannot be stripped away, even when he commands them to take more responsibility for themselves.

When the Dalai Lama convened some five hundred or so leading Tibetan exiles from around the world to come to Dharamsala for a week in late 2008 to discuss the Tibetan plight, he literally holed up in his residence during the discussions to avoid sending cues about his viewpoints. Afterward, when participants largely endorsed his nonviolent approach of seeking autonomy for Tibet rather than returning to a demand for full independence, the Dalai Lama said he took no part in the discussions. "I had no direct involvement," he said.

Those most hesitant to express their views are ordinary laypeople, generally not the monks and nuns of the Buddhist clergy. At the time of my visit, nine of the forty-three legislators were monks and nuns, and Tsering said they often spoke up the most. But even senior lamas feel constrained. The prime minister, Samdhong Rinpoche, is said to have offered his resignation twice in disputes over whether to act independently of the Dalai Lama. The prime minister is one of the leading Tibetan scholars of Buddhism, and as a *rinpoche*, an honorific literally meaning "precious one" that is given to important reincarnations, he is treated with deference by all. But Samdhong Rinpoche said his job was to "anticipate the Dalai Lama's unstated thoughts and direct his efforts to their realization." Such a view underscored the weakness of exile democracy, and one critic of the exile government, the writer Jamyang Norbu, said it echoed more "the fawning of the grand eunuch in a decaying Oriental court than the free and candid expression of a democratically elected leader."[8]

So while awaiting cues from the Dalai Lama, parliamentarians pass laws regulating the functions of cabinet departments, how voluntary donations are tallied, and how the government operates. In actuality, the laws are akin to internal regulations of a self-governing entity that practices a measure of internal democracy. The total annual operating budget of the government-in-exile is $4 million. That amount covers the salaries of some six hundred fifty employees in Dharamsala, spread around the fifty-three Tibetan settlements in India, Nepal, and Bhutan and in eleven Offices of Tibet in New York, London, and other foreign capitals. The Speaker said the money comes from three sources. First are direct voluntary contributions from Tibetan exiles. Every Tibetan in India is asked to contribute the equivalent of $1 a year, while those living in the West give $48 annually. Public servants of the exile administration also kick back a portion of their modest incomes. The personal office of the Dalai Lama contributes roughly a third of the annual operating budget, donating money raised from royalties from the dozens of book titles sold around the world under the Dalai Lama's name. The final third comes from other contributions and a 4 percent tax for administrative costs put on social welfare grants earmarked for Tibetan exiles. While the total budget is modest, Tibetans seem to be doing better than their Indian hosts. As the Speaker escorted me back to his office, he brushed aside a poor Indian beggar with an infant in her arms who approached us with her palm out. She was a fixture at the compound. The exile government hires Indians, mainly women in saris, to do manual labor around the compound. Tibetan exiles won't work for such low wages.

Critics of the Dalai Lama and the exile movement sometimes suggest that foreign intelligence agencies, particularly the CIA, channel money to Dharamsala as a way to strengthen a group that is a key adversary to the ruling party in China.[9] A State Department document from the mid-1960s mentions that the CIA had been providing $15,000 a month to the Dalai Lama at the time, but no further documents indicated whether, and when, the payments were halted. The

Speaker said the CIA payments were stopped in 1968, when President Richard Nixon began making overtures to Mao Zedong over renewing U.S. diplomatic relations with Beijing. Washington still provides significant money to Tibetan exiles, but much of the money goes to support independent organizations, like the Tibetan Youth Congress, the Voice of Tibet radio station, and the Tibetan Centre for Human Rights and Democracy. At best, I could find no year in which such payments to these groups amounted to more than $1 million. Costlier are some $2 million in annual U.S. payments to support refugee reception centers in Katmandu, Nepal, and in New Delhi and Dharamsala. All Tibetan refugees crossing the Himalayas pass through the centers.

Lots of additional money flows to the Tibetan exiles for specific development projects in health, education, and welfare. I dropped into the office of the finance minister, Tsering Dhundup, a no-nonsense sort who did his university studies in Missoula, Montana, to get a better explanation of where the money comes from—and found again that the fund-raising prowess of the Dalai Lama was critical. "We always get a large sum of money from His Holiness's pocket. People offer a lot of money to His Holiness, and he in turn offers it to the Central Tibetan Administration." The minister said development projects came in at about $12.4 million for the most recent year, paying for renovation and construction of housing in settlements, ongoing health care, and other programs.

The miniscule nature of the government-in-exile begged the question: Do the exiles have the know-how to govern Tibet if for some sudden reason China ceded real autonomy? I asked the minister, and his answer wasn't entirely satisfactory. He noted that much of the billions of dollars in capital investment that China has poured into Tibet did not go for the benefit of Tibetans themselves. Rather, the investment was to facilitate resource exploitation, exercise political control, or serve other purposes. He said Tibetans with genuine autonomy would receive major help in development from outside the People's Republic of China. "If the PRC agrees to give genuine autonomy to Tibet, I don't think the multinational companies will run away from Tibet. On the contrary, I think they will rush in," he said. The minister brushed aside further queries about the capacity of Tibetans to self-govern on a large scale, reeling off three reasons to ease concern. "We have a leadership incomparable to other leaders in the world," he said curtly. "The commitment and devotion of the Tibetans is the second thing. And thirdly is our commitment to nonviolence. If Tibetans started acting like Palestinians, we would be nowhere."

Occasional news reports indicate that the coffers of the Dalai Lama are quite ample. Not only does he give a substantial portion of the royalties, donations, and bequests that he receives to the Central Tibetan Administration, he also offers his generosity to needy causes around the world. "Everything he gets, he gives away," said Tenzin Taklha, the Dalai Lama's nephew and aide. Some of those around the Tibetan leader even voice quiet vexation at what a soft touch he is at appeals for assistance. When trustees decided to shut down the department of religious studies at Florida International University in 2009, one of the professors there, Dr. Nathan Katz, asked the Dalai Lama, a personal friend, to send a letter in support of the program. The Dalai Lama went further. His assistant wrote a letter to FIU President Modesto A. Maidique saying that the Dalai Lama would put up $100,000 of his own funds to help save the department. "I fell off my chair," said Katz, who befriended the Dalai Lama while studying Tibetan language in the 1970s.[10]

When an earthquake devastated Haiti in early 2010, killing some two hundred thousand people and leaving another million homeless, nations scrambled to offer assistance. Half a world away, China dispatched a sixty-member search-and-rescue team, partly to search for some of its own trapped nationals, eight members of a UN police peacekeeping presence in Haiti. China and its domestic Red Cross offered a donation to Port-au-Prince of $5.4 million. For his part, the Dalai Lama gave 100,000 Swiss francs (about $93,200) for Haiti relief efforts. The relatively small size of Beijing's efforts drew comment. "In Latin America, many countries have noted that the Chinese response, while admirable, was more consistent with a small, activist country than with a rising global superpower. More Haitians may ultimately be pulled from the rubble by the various teams from Belgium, Iceland, Poland and Turkey than by the Chinese responders," one American commentator said.[11]

The tentative steps by Tibetan exiles, under tremendous prodding by the Dalai Lama, to take control of their own governmental affairs are commendable. But the exile government is as bureaucratic as any small administration. More impressive is another aspect of exile life— one of the great successes of the exile experience: the independent education and child care system set up by the Dalai Lama and operated for many years by his younger sister. In the sylvan hills above McLeod Ganj, the headquarters of the Tibetan Children's Villages oversees education for thousands of Tibetan children. Word of the schools has spread far and wide in Tibet, and a multitude of parents have sent their children on the perilous trip over the Himalayas to spend years under the tutelage of the schools.

The TCV, as the system is widely known, comprises eighteen schools and vocational centers across thousands of miles of India. It may be one of the most potent weapons in the exile arsenal. An extraordinary number of the students educated in the system eventually sneak back into China—with a firm grasp of freedom, a strong sense of Tibetan culture, and a command of English as well as Tibetan. China stifles the flow of information between Tibetans at home and in exile by filtering the internet, intercepting and monitoring telephone calls, and posting sharpshooters along the frontiers. But the human trickle over the mountains allows Tibetan communities on both sides to hear reliable firsthand testimonies.

The director of the TCV system, Tsewang Yeshi, acknowledges that graduates of the schools are given help to return to Tibet. "Despite the difficulties, obstacles, and extreme conditions back in Tibet, if there are individuals who want to go back because of family or homesickness, if they choose to go back, we have every reason to support them materially. If they return, it's a good thing. Otherwise, Tibet without Tibetans, it would be a losing battle." The headmaster said that over the past five decades, the system had enrolled about forty thousand youngsters and that sixteen thousand were currently students. About 65 percent of the students are relatively new arrivals who had come to India in the past seven or eight years, usually without their parents. I asked him how many students he believed had returned to China after receiving a TCV education. "I can easily tell you that three thousand students made it back."[12]

My mind raced back to one cold evening in a Tibetan ethnic region of Sichuan province. It was the spring of 2008, and scores of disturbances and protests had erupted across the Tibetan Plateau. After two days of traveling, I made it to Litang, a town at a nosebleed elevation of 13,100 feet with a monastery known for restive monks, and stumbled into a Tibetan-owned hostel. After I dropped my bags, I wandered into the hallway, where a young Tibetan woman said, "Hello. Where are you from?" Her accent in English sounded Indian, and I quickly asked, "Did you go to school at TCV?" She told me that she'd spent close to a decade in TCV schools but wanted to come home. We touched briefly on the lockdown of the town, but she pursed her lips, and I knew it was better to stay away from sensitive matters. It became clear later that there were thousands of young men and women like her across Tibet. Educated as youngsters by a Communist Party that claimed to have brought modernity to a feudal society and rid the region of its chief "slave owner," they later studied in schools where portraits of the Dalai Lama hung on each schoolroom wall.

At the Tibetan Children's Village schools, a majority of the children have no parents nearby, or even in India, so they live in housing clusters with foster parents, usually about thirty-five children to a couple. The schools are entirely reliant on charity but have raised abundant funds in places like Japan and Germany, partly due to the aggressive fund-raising role by the Dalai Lama's sister. Many of the children have individual sponsors. The children are taught in Tibetan during elementary school. English is the language of instruction in the higher grades. Opportunities for university study are not abundant for secondary school graduates, and only about 40 percent go on to higher education.

In asking about the prospects for the other students, I made a rather surprising discovery: Those who do not obtain sufficiently high marks on university entrance exams often go into the Indian army, where special units of Tibetan soldiers operate. The oldest is the Special Frontier Force, a mountain commando unit created after India's rout in the short but intense 1962 Sino-Indian border war. The Tibetan commando unit was conceived as a guerrilla force that could operate behind Chinese lines in the event of a new war. Rather than putting the Tibetans under army command, the unit was put under the Research and Analysis Wing, India's intelligence agency. Another paramilitary unit, the Indo-Tibetan Border Police Force, was also created at the same time, priding itself on its members' sense of adventure and daredevilry.

The TCV director said he believed about three thousand to four thousand Tibetan students had gone into one of the two units, and many were recruited at the gates of the TCV schools straight after graduation. He downplayed the military option for the students: "Many may have joined not out of patriotism but out of not getting other job opportunities." I voiced astonishment that thousands of young Tibetans had gotten modern military training, even as the Dalai Lama advocated for nonviolence and peaceful conflict resolution. He bristled slightly. "Our struggle is not military. It is not realistic. It's suicidal. It's a waste of human life."

Around the surrounding mountains, nearly every aspect of life is touched by the Dalai Lama's influence. The schools enjoy his grace and gather global donations as a result. Throngs of travelers come to get a glimpse of the god-king or to soak in his healthful aura, filling the guesthouses and patronizing the boutiques, bookshops, internet cafés, and snack bars. The karma has been good. But some merchants feel uneasy. They think Dharamsala's days of glory may come to an end with the Dalai Lama's passing. They fear the Himalayan hill station will sink back into obscurity.

But down the hill in the Kangra Valley, a tall, handsome, twenty-something Tibetan monk dwells atop a Buddhist monastery, meditating and offering teachings to his own followers. In his free time, he studies English, listens to hip-hop music on his iPod, and plays video games. The Dalai Lama treats him like a son, admiring the youth's own daring escape over the Himalayas from Tibet in late 1999. The young monk is the Karmapa, number 3 in the Tibetan religious hierarchy and the latest reincarnation of the most ancient lineage in Tibetan Buddhism. Some Tibetans see the Karmapa as the likely unifying leader in a post–Dalai Lama era. That they look to the Karmapa is a sign of their profound hopes—or illusions.

chapter seven

The Karmapa

They've already recognized me. They can't unsay what they've said.
—*The Seventeenth Karmapa, speaking of China's vetting of him*

ONLY A HALF HOUR'S DRIVE DOWN THE ROAD FROM THE DALAI
Lama's compound, on the large plain below Dharamsala, one comes
to Gyuto Tantric Monastery in the farming village of Sidhbari. On
the rooftop of the main temple hall is a set of rooms intended to ac-
commodate visiting lamas. An open-air walkway surrounds the
rooms, offering panoramic views. Emerald green rice paddies
stretch toward the foothills flanking the plain. Ever-present crows
caw in the distance. Within the monastic compound, the yellow-
and-white buildings offer their own vivid coloration. Bright Tibetan
banners flutter, and orange and crimson monks' robes hang to dry
on rooftop clotheslines. The garret rooms are the dwelling place of
the second most-venerated Tibetan Buddhist lama in exile today:
the Karmapa.

His given name is Ogyen Trinley Dorje. Still a young man, he is
handsome and strapping, built with the muscular frame of someone
who would be a formidable opponent on the sports field. He walks
with youthful grace and exudes a sense of vigor. He listens to hip-hop
and likes computers, X-Men comic books, and video games. He
sometimes wears his prayer beads wrapped loosely around his left
wrist, hanging over his gold wristwatch, a casual stylistic choice befit-
ting his generation. The Karmapa keeps his hair trimmed to a stubble

and wears rimless glasses. His face is round and well proportioned, and his eyes so neatly almond-shaped that they give him the look of countless bronze statues of the Buddha. Taken by his good looks, one swooning American fan introduced him during a tour in the United States as "His Hotness."[1]

Tibetan exiles view the charismatic young lama as a natural bridge in a post–Dalai Lama era, a unifying figure on whom they can place their trust. Quite uniquely, Beijing does not question his religious standing, nor does it heap the kind of vitriol on him that it reserves for the "Dalai clique," which it describes as a criminal cabal. Although the Dalai Lama shies from speaking of the Karmapa as his protégé, he has taken him closely under his protection. When foreign dignitaries come to see the Dalai Lama, he often suggests that they meet the young Karmapa as well. Many Tibetan exiles view the Karmapa as a key player, if not the crucial one, to guide them once the Dalai Lama passes on. Posters around Dharamsala proclaim him as "Tibet's Rising Sun."

In some ways, the Karmapa's personal history mirrors that of the Dalai Lama, although it occurred decades later. He, too, fled Tibet under duress from the Communist Party, crossing the Himalayas to India, where his international following has grown further. But his story also contains complexities and byzantine political intrigues that may foretell some of the difficulties that lie ahead for Tibetans—inside and outside the borders of China—after the passing of the Dalai Lama. India seems to view him with suspicion, for murky reasons, and he faces internecine challenges from two other monks who contend to be the rightful reincarnation. Legal moves prevent him from setting foot in Rumtek Monastery in Sikkim in northern India, which may be the repository of some of his sect's most valuable artifacts, including the mystical Black Crown, a holy symbol fundamental to one of the Karma Kagyu sect's core rites.

Tibetan Buddhism comprises four major schools, or sects, and the Dalai Lama's Gelugpa school is the largest. It is often called the "yellow hat" sect because of the distinctive headwear of senior monks in the order. The Karmapa heads the Karma Kagyu school, which was the most powerful sect until four centuries ago, when the Dalai Lama's order took dominance. Tibetan Buddhism also has the Nyingma and Sakya schools, each with its own transmission techniques, practice, and philosophy. Non-Tibetans sometimes refer to the three major non-Gelugpa sects as the "red hats" to distinguish them from the dominant "yellow hats." The Karmapa lineage is the longest unbroken line of reincarnate lamas in Tibetan Buddhism, dating back to the twelfth century. Successive Karmapas served as spiritual advisers to Mongolian khans and to Chinese emperors. From the beginning of the Karmapa lineage, more than two centuries would pass before the advent of the Dalai Lama line of reincarnations.

One could place the starting point for the modern history of the Karmapa lineage in the Oberoi Grand Hotel in Calcutta in early 1981. The previous reincarnation, the Sixteenth Karmapa, who had opted for exile decades earlier, some time before the Dalai Lama, temporarily occupied a large suite there. He was only a few months away from perishing from stomach cancer. One night, after taking a glass of orange juice, he turned to a trusted disciple named Tai Situ—one of his four "heart sons"—and handed him an amulet wrapped in yellow brocade of the kind Tibetans often wear around their necks. "This is a very important protection," the Sixteenth Karmapa told his disciple. "In the future, it will confer great benefit." He offered no further explanation. Nine months later, the Sixteenth Karmapa died in a hospital near Chicago.

Upon his death, Tai Situ and the other three heart sons gathered. All were senior reincarnate lamas, or *rinpoches*, of the Karma Kagyu sect. They formed a council of regents to oversee affairs of the order and to organize a search for the Karmapa's reincarnation. But the agreement fell apart three years later. By the end of the decade, followers were growing impatient for a reincarnation to be located. In the early 1990s, Tai Situ Rinpoche said he remembered the amulet that the Karmapa had given him, offering little explanation for why it took him more than a decade to check inside of it. He said he opened the amulet to find a simple prediction letter. The key verses of the letter read:

From here to the north [in] the east of [the Land of] Snow
Is a country where divine thunder spontaneously blazes.
[In] a beautiful nomad's place with the sign of a cow,
The method is Döndrub and the wisdom is Lolaga.

[Born in] the year of the one used for the earth
[With] the miraculous, far-reaching sound of the white one:
[This] is the one known as Karmapa.[2]

At a meeting of the four *rinpoches* in 1992, general agreement emerged about what the letter meant: The Karmapa was to be reborn in a specific valley in eastern Tibet. Although a search party had yet to leave, the letter predicts the names of both the current Karmapa's mother (Loga, a Tibetan diminutive of Lolaga) and father (Karma Döndrub) as well as the name of the settlement where the boy would be found, Lhathok, which means "divine thunder," a name given by the Sixteenth Karmapa. Another hint indicated that the boy would be born in the Tibetan year of the Wood Ox.

Later that spring, a search party of monks on horseback braved a blizzard near the nomadic settlement in eastern Tibet. They came across a couple of yak herders with their nine children, one of them a boy of seven who was fondly called Apo Gaga, or "happy, happy brother" in Tibetan. The nomads told the monks that when the boy was born, rainbows appeared in the sky and a vibrant sound similar to the blowing of a conch shell rang out for more than an hour—all key auguries in Tibetan Buddhism of a reincarnation. The boy's elder sister recalled the strange vibrating purr that accompanied the birth. "We heard what we thought was the sound of a thermos, which sometimes can vibrate and hum from the pressure inside. So we looked for it inside, but then the sound seemed to come from the outside, and when we looked outside, the sound seemed to come from inside. We could not find it. Then it seemed to come from near mother's bed, and we thought it was a bumblebee, but nothing was there. As time went by, the sound grew louder and louder, and the whole family heard it clearly."[3]

Once the baby had grown into a small boy, word arrived that a search party was nearby. The boy packed his clothes and loaded them onto his favorite goat, certain that he would accompany the roving monks to their monastery, which he described accurately in some detail in their presence even though he had never visited. The holy men determined that the boy was the reincarnation of the Karmapa and whisked him to the Tsurphu monastery, forty miles west of the Ti-betan capital, for enthronement and intensive religious training.

In a huge installation ceremony at the monastery in September 1992, as monks waded among throngs of pilgrims offering tea and saf-fron rice, Chinese authorities presented the young incarnation an offi-cial letter, encased in red brocade, proclaiming him a "Living Buddha," the Chinese term for a reincarnated lama. It marked the first time the Chinese Communist Party had ever recognized an incarnate lama, and behind the action was a shrewd political motive. Under decades of repressive Chinese rule, Tibet had grown short of "Living Buddhas." The Dalai Lama had fled into exile, taking thousands of monks with him, and the Panchen Lama had died a few years earlier. After the en-thronement, the moon-faced boy became far and away the highest lama remaining in Tibet, and China hoped to mold him into a patri-otic figure to help legitimize control over religious affairs in Tibet.

Like thousands of other monasteries, his home monastery had been devastated by radical Red Guards during the Cultural Revolution sev-eral decades earlier. Eager to uproot Tibetan Buddhism, the Guards destroyed hundreds, if not thousands, of monasteries and threw price-less Buddhist relics into rivers. They left Tsurphu monastery, which dates back an extraordinary eight centuries, completely uninhabitable. But slowly, the monastery was rising again. The previous Karmapa had sent funds from India to reconstruct the remote seat of his order, perched fourteen thousand feet high in the mountains. Luckily for the new Karmapa, bad roads isolated the monastery, and political com-missars and party cadres largely left it alone.

But as the 1990s unfolded, political pressure grew on the young lad. He was taken to Beijing on an official visit in 1994, and state media gave him intense coverage, quoting him as saying he supported the ruling party and its then paramount leader, Jiang Zemin. A year later, the party overruled the Dalai Lama and installed its own "soul boy" as the Eleventh Panchen Lama, and as time passed, it demanded that the Karmapa recognize the younger lad as legitimate and even prostrate be-fore him as a religious superior. Making matters worse, China denied entry to several of the Karmapa's key exiled religious teachers, namely, Tai Situ and Gyaltsab Rinpoche, and refused to let him travel to India to receive religious teachings from them. The relationship between teacher and pupil is crucial in Tibetan Buddhism, since teachings are often oral, and empowerment comes from one-on-one transmission of the dharma, the instruction of the sutras, and the recitation of mantras. Some two hundred Tibetan monasteries joined a petition to Beijing asking that the Karmapa be given access to his teachers, but Beijing ignored the appeal. And in a final aggravating circumstance, he and his advisers feared that they would be asked to denounce the Dalai Lama publicly, which none of them wanted to do.

The Karmapa, barely fourteen at the time, and key aides hatched an escape plan, developing secret codes to avoid raising suspicions over the tapped phone lines at the monastery. Even the Karmapa's parents were kept in the dark. In the waning days of 1999, the teenaged lama announced that he was beginning a twenty-one-day retreat in isolation. In preparation for the escape, an attendant used monastery funds to buy a jeep, ostensibly to oversee projects near the border with Nepal and to launch a search party for a *tulku* thought to be living high in the Himalayas. In fact, the lama was surveying mountain escape routes.

On the night of December 27, the young lama penned a letter in his room stating that he was leaving Tibet to have access to his teachers. He said he was turning against neither China nor its people, and he would one day return. A cook, who was in on the escape, put some kung fu videos on the downstairs television and prepared hot soup to lure guards in from the wintry night. Upstairs, as the Karmapa's tutor chanted devotions and rang bells to feign that the retreat was progressing normally, the high lama slipped off his crimson robes and put on a down jacket, blue jeans, a cap, and spectacles to alter his appearance. He dropped out of a window and stealthily crept along a roof to the waiting four-wheel-drive vehicle. He and several tutors and trusted aides began their eight-day flight from China.

Four decades after his predecessor relocated across the Himalayas to Sikkim with his top aides, foreseeing turmoil in Tibet, the Karmapa and his retinue followed in their footsteps. During days of driving, the boy monk would routinely get out of the jeep to walk around military checkpoints, catching up with his party on the other side. Chinese minders quickly discovered the escape and intensified inspections at border checkpoints. But the party found a crossing into windswept Mustang, a part of Nepal that juts into Tibet, where the escape vehicle bogged down in ice. The members continued on foot and horseback, climbing over snow-covered sixteen-thousand-foot mountain passes before reaching a small heliport, where they paid $1,000 for the one-hour flight to Pokhara, then traveled on to Katmandu and Dharamsala.

The Karmapa's arrival in exile electrified Tibetan Buddhists in Dharamsala and created headlines around the world. Chinese authorities downplayed the getaway, never mentioning his discontent at being separated from his teachers. China stated that the letter the Karmapa left behind explained that he had gone to India to pick up "musical instruments required to conduct Buddhist ceremonies."[4] It also said his aim was to retrieve the Black Crown, which had been carried by his predecessor to Rumtek Monastery in Sikkim. China made a savvy move with the allegation, invoking a potent religious tool of liberation that is core to Kagyu beliefs, and suggesting a plausible motive for the trip.

The Black Crown embodies what non-Buddhists might see, depending on their outlook, as a rather fantastical belief. Tibetan Buddhists of the Kagyu sect believe the crown has the power to open the subconscious of those who set eyes upon it. Mere sighting can bring enlightenment. The history of the crown dates back six centuries to the Ming Dynasty, when the Yongle Emperor realized that the black crown he saw hovering over the Fifth Karmapa's head was the "Vajra Crown," an aura of wisdom energy seen only by the enlightened. The emperor had a physical representation of the black crown made as a gift, studded with sapphires and a rare large ruby, wishing for all to see it and receive its power of enlightenment. Devotees believe the indestructible spiritual crown is woven from the hair of ten thousand female angels. During the rare Black Crown ceremony, the Karmapa enters a state of meditation to merge his mind with Chenrezig, the Buddha of Compassion and his boundless loving kindness. As resonant reed horns sound, he takes the eight-inch-tall Black Crown from a silk brocade cylindrical box and places it on his own head, steadying it with one hand. The Karmapa recites the mantra *Om Mani Padme Hum* (which means "the jewel is in the heart of the lotus") and exchanges his limitless awareness for the sufferings of those present, transmitting blessings to each witness to the degree that he or she is capable of receiving them.

The crown controversy followed the Karmapa to his new home. While exiles celebrated the Karmapa's arrival, India treated it with deep suspicion, hearing rumors he had been purposefully sent by China as a spy and questioning how he had escaped under the nose of heavy Chinese security. A security detail was assigned to him, and his movements were circumscribed. He wasn't even permitted to go down to the main temple of Gyuto Tantric Monastery from his rooftop living quarters for thirteen months. Eventually, he was allowed to meet the international media, and he heaped scorn on China's explanation of the letter describing the reasons for his flight over the Himalayas. "I said in the letter that I left because, although I had for a long time, persistently and repeatedly, requested permission to travel internationally, I had never received it and so I had to leave. I did not in the letter mention the Black Crown, the Black Hat. Why would I want to retrieve that from India and bring it back to China anyway? The only thing that would be served or accomplished by doing so would be to place that hat on Jiang Zemin's head."[5]

For most of his first decade in exile, India also barred the Karmapa from traveling overseas, worried about offending China and still not completely convinced that he wasn't a Trojan horse for Beijing. India finally relented, and the first time I went to see the Karmapa was shortly after his first overseas trip, which took him nearly three weeks in late spring 2008 to the New York City area, Seattle, California, and Boulder, Colorado. I was among a group of foreign journalists. Indian security agents required us to leave our cameras and tape recorders with them before climbing to the Karmapa's reception hall. He was asked whether he had enjoyed the trip. "It was wonderful! I found some freedom," he beamed, breaking into English from his normal Tibetan.[6]

In the States, the Karmapa made some headlines. He gave an interview to the PBS show *Religion & Ethics Newsweekly*, which noted that at one appearance in Seattle, he told followers that he liked to read X-Men comic books, but then attendants stopped giving them to him.[7] The Karmapa is also known to like listening to hip-hop music on his iPod and play games on a Sony PlayStation. Some of the back and forth with journalists was about his isolation in Gyuto Tantric Monastery. He was asked if he'd like to reach out more to Chinese followers, of which he has many. "If I get a chance, I want to do this. I'm not sure I'll get this chance. It's difficult, as you see, to connect with the outside world." It's difficult even for him to reach out to his parents, who were arrested in Tibet for a brief period after their son's flight to India and remain under close monitoring. The Karmapa only rarely speaks to them by telephone, sending messages mainly through a sister. Asked if he'd like to return to Tibet for a visit, he sounded rather wistful. "Of course, because I want to see my parents."[8]

During the brief meeting, the Karmapa seemed good-natured and self-assured but contemplative and little given to laughter. Above all, he seemed vigorous and energetic, traits that have helped him build an enthusiastic following. The attention on the Karmapa as a future pan-Tibetan leader has grown because of the Dalai Lama's advancing age. Tibetans pray for the Dalai Lama's long life but also fret about what looms ahead. Until recently, exiles considered it taboo to speak of the Dalai Lama's eventual passing. But his health has hit a few speed bumps, with two hospitalizations within the space of a few months, reminding Tibetans of their leader's mortality.

On one brief stay in a New Delhi hospital in October 2008, doctors removed the Dalai Lama's gallbladder in a three-hour operation. Recovery was speedy, and the Dalai Lama would later say that his physician described his body as that of a man in his sixties, not his seventies. Indeed, the Tibetan leader has no visible health woes. He walks with a relatively firm gait, exercises every day before dawn, and enjoys an unfailingly serene, positive outlook on life. A few coffee-colored splotches darken the skin of his upper arm, and he wears glasses, which he removes frequently to clean. He travels overseas on a dozen or more trips a year, some of them extended, and suffers little jet lag. I've seen him fall ill with a cold and recover within a day or two. As a result of the hospitalizations and concern about his advancing age, the Dalai Lama has responded to questions more frequently in public about what may occur with his eventual passing, melting some of the hesitance associated with the issue.

The Dalai Lama's advancing age has turned the spotlight on the Karmapa. But for all the hope that Tibetan exiles have put on him, the Karmapa cannot replace the Dalai Lama. He's already a *tulku*, or reincarnation in the lineage of another lama, and cannot be considered a reborn Dalai Lama as well. Moreover, dalai lamas emerge from the Gelugpa school of Tibetan Buddhism. For the Karmapa, the head of another school regarded in some quarters as a rival, to take on a leadership role that has until now been held by a senior Gelugpa lama would represent a significant shift in protocol and convention. On the other hand, such changes have already been characteristic of the present Dalai Lama's career in his efforts to promote the welfare of the Tibetan people and the preservation of Tibetan identity. Tibetan exiles increasingly say the young Karmapa could become a temporary unifying figure, perhaps even serving as a regent for the fifteen to twenty years it would take for a Dalai Lama reincarnation to be found and come of age. This thinking has become more than idle chatter among Tibetan exile leaders.

Many of them had gathered in Dharamsala in late 2008, convened urgently by the Dalai Lama to debate strategy toward China and the future of the Tibet movement. China seethed over massive protests in Tibet that had embarrassed the nation in the run-up to the Beijing Summer Olympic Games. Talks between the two sides had halted and appeared on the verge of complete breakdown. The Dalai Lama did not hide his disappointment. "My trust in the Chinese government [is] now thinner, thinner, thinner. . . . Things are not going well. I cannot pretend that something [is] okay. No, I have to accept failure."[9] His tone was matter-of-fact. He said that it was time for Tibetan exiles to pass judgment on the future of his Middle Way policy and the Tibetan movement, and that was why he had convened the historic forum of exiles. In reality, the six-day forum was also designed to chart the course for when the Dalai Lama passes from the scene. Given his huge global renown and headline-generating ability, many exiles fretted about that future day.

The debate took place behind closed doors, but participants spoke openly afterward. One of them was Tenzing Chonden, an electrical engineer living in Southern California who also served as a member of the Tibetan parliament in exile. A veteran Tibetan activist, he responded bluntly when I asked him what he feared about the Dalai

Lama's passing: "If the Dalai Lama is not there, that moral authority is not there to guide Tibetan people; then you can certainly predict that people will do desperate things." As the week wore on, it became apparent that all of the fifteen working groups were studying the issue of future leadership of the Tibet movement. The Seventeenth Karmapa's name was on the tongues of many participants. At least five working groups listed him as a suitable candidate, more than any other person.[10] Participants at the forum noticeably perked up when I asked them about the Karmapa. "He's young, he's charismatic, and he's smart. Among the younger generation, he is very, very popular," Lobsang Sangay, a Harvard Law School fellow, told me outside an auditorium as the forum drew to a close. Sangay said the normally turbulent period after the death of a Dalai Lama could be avoided by tapping the Karmapa early on as a temporary leader, or regent, seeking a pan-Tibetan figure above sectarian disputes. Moreover, the young lama retains strong links to Tibet, where his parents still live. "He has a unique background of being born and brought up in Tibet, endorsed by the Chinese government, and having a large following in Tibet. He is one of the very few lamas who have a direct connection with Tibetans inside Tibet. That makes him attractive."[11]

The Dalai Lama had declared the Karmapa to be a "very, very important" religious figure, and advised him closely. But he had also praised other prominent lamas, including the young reincarnation of his former teacher, Ling Rinpoche, and had not indicated in which direction he was leaning. In public discussions, the Dalai Lama encouraged Tibetans to think unconventionally about the succession issue and to embrace even radical change. He'd offered a number of scenarios, some of them with clear forethought of the political impact on China, others with a social dimension. He'd suggested that after his passing, a new senior religious leader could emerge through a democratic vote among lamas, not unlike the way the College of Cardinals meets after the death of a Roman Catholic pontiff to elect a new one. Or a leader might be picked strictly based on seniority. If Tibetans wanted to adhere to tradition, and still find the institution of the Dalai Lama relevant, he has said, then the reincarnation must be born in religious freedom, outside of Chinese control. "If my death comes when we are still in a refugee status, then logically my reincarnation will come outside Tibet," he said in Amritsar, India, in late 2007.[12]

But even then, senior lamas should not stick to ritual on the appropriate candidate. "Now time has come," he said in a news conference in Dharamsala in late 2008, "female[s] should take more active responsibility on world peace, on promotion of human compassion. Therefore, Dalai Lama's reincarnation could be one female reincarnation." Searching deeply into theological possibilities, he'd also suggested that Tibetans could use an esoteric practice called *madey tulku* in which he would pick his reincarnation while still alive. Such bifurcation of spirit, or mind stream, in the bodies of two different people does not trouble senior lamas. "It is quite common practice. Nowadays in Tibet, at least as far as I know, two persons before death chose their reincarnation," he said.[13] Following that practice would allow the Fourteenth Dalai Lama to play an assertive role in selecting and educating his replacement and would shorten the period until Tibetans have a new adult leader. It would also foil Beijing's efforts to hijack the finding of a successor.

China asserts it has veto power over all Tibetan Buddhist reincarnations, including the Dalai Lama. In mid-2007, the State Administration for Religious Affairs announced that it held the sole power to approve any reincarnation.[14] The government offered no religious reasoning for the decree, offering instead a nationalist argument that it was designed to ensure that "the selection process cannot be influenced by any group or individual from outside the country." The move, which marked the first time the party openly claimed such authority, was an opening salvo in the religious battle that will occur with the Dalai Lama's passing. As the Dalai Lama tries to keep his successor independent of Beijing's control, China will certainly dismiss that successor as illegitimate. It likely will coerce lamas in Tibet to support a candidate palatable to Beijing, orchestrating its own "reincarnation" and exercising strong control in his youth to ensure the lad would be raised as a loyal servant of the motherland. Thus there would be a scenario of dueling dalai lamas, one considered legitimate by Tibetan exiles and many, if not most, Tibetans on the Plateau and the other considered a faux. Having multiple pretenders to the throne has happened in the past, not only for dalai lamas but also for other reincarnations. Indeed, the widely recognized Seventeenth Karmapa faces challenges from two other men who claimed to be the rightful leader of the Karma Kagyu sect.

Whomever the mantle falls on to take a larger role following the Dalai Lama's death, the challenges awaiting him or her would be daunting. Adoration of the Dalai Lama and a practice of submission to his views have unified Tibetans behind his policy of nonviolent engagement with China, even though many (and possibly a majority) of Tibetans disagree with his stance to accept Chinese sovereignty over Tibet. That unity conceals the frustrations among Tibetans over the lack of results from the policy. Any leader less venerated than the Dalai Lama may struggle to keep Tibetans unified. Yet along with such challenges, other variables may be in play. The future of Tibet rests on many fulcrums, including whether China's social situation is kept stable and the shifting political landscape inside the ruling party, which will undergo a leadership change in 2012 or 2013. Moreover, it is common for China to reappraise a policy that has brought about international censure—such as vilifying the Dalai Lama—when something dramatic happens, such as his death. A reappraisal could bring sharp shifts in policy. A generational change might allow the Karmapa, if he is tapped, to succeed where the Dalai Lama has failed. Even an interim leader could usher in new possibilities on the Tibet issue.

Eager to gauge the outlook of the Karmapa on such issues, and to further take his measure, I sought another interview with him at Gyuto Tantric Monastery on a subsequent trip to India. I found the atmosphere a bit more relaxed. No Indian guards toted rifles at the entrance. But procedures remained onerous. To arrange a meeting, one must seek a letter of invitation from the Karmapa's office at the monastery to give to the Superintendent of Police in Dharamsala, a procedure stricter than to see the Dalai Lama and a remnant of Indian suspicion that lingers over the young lama. The day I sought the letter, guards at the temple were frisking all visitors thoroughly before entering an anteroom, which was filled with a gamut of pilgrims ranging from the deeply pious to the downright zany. Sitting on one bench was a quiet Japanese nun and a Greek tourist. A tall European with his hair in a ponytail sat impassively meditating on another bench. A Canadian woman to my side had spent five years at the yoga ashram of Ramana Maharshi, the now-deceased Hindu sage of south India, before switching to Tibetan Buddhism once she set eyes on the Karmapa. She spoke of her devotion to the young lama, and her zeal unnerved me. I let the conversation descend into a lull.

Nearby, a gregarious Sikh wearing a bright turquoise turban and matching dress shirt recited poetry to whoever would listen. He seized on my glance toward him and marched over to me. "I am H. S. Nirman, at your service," he said, presenting me with a business card. Nirman had already received a blessing from the Karmapa and was elated. Before I could pull back, he reached over and grabbed my hand and that of my wife, asking where she was from and exclaiming over what he considered her exotic appearance. On learning that she was Nicaraguan, he peppered her further and then pulled a pamphlet of poetry from his bag and began to declaim in a stentorian voice. Soon he was enthusing over what an extraordinary coincidence that we should meet there—behold the wonder!—offering us a free copy of his pamphlet of poetry and departing with all due huzzahs.

As he walked out the door, the tall European with hoop earrings and a goatee stirred to life. My wife and I whispered to each other our curiosity about him, so she piped up.

"We were wondering where you're from."

He gazed at us fixedly and responded: "What do you mean by that?"

"What country are you from?"

He looked at her as if it were a moronic question. "Where I was physically born or where I've come from in previous lives? Where I was born doesn't have much meaning."

Oh, we both said, looking at each other and rolling our eyes. A Tibetan attendant who was serving tea chuckled and interjected, "He's a monk. He won't give you an answer the first time. He'll try to teach you first." My wife pressed ahead, eliciting that he was Swiss-born of Belgian parents and that he'd spent nearly three decades floating in and around Tibet and the Himalayas. He'd taken on a Tibetan name, Lama Norbu Repa, and had been present when the Karmapa, then age seven,

was enthroned in Tibet in 1992. Afterward, he spent two years over-
seeing restoration of a twelfth-century dilapidated monastery in Tibet,
eventually returning to Europe to set up a dharma center in France.

Our companion veered the conversation in an unexpected direction
when we touched on the Karmapa's multilingual abilities (he was advancing in English and Korean and already speaks his native Tibetan
and fluent Mandarin). The fact that he is still a young man must help
in learning foreign languages, my wife suggested. Norbu Repa again
looked in disbelief and said, "If you say so." He paused. "He doesn't
seem young to me." He suggested that anyone with sufficient awareness could gaze into the Karmapa's eyes and see an ancient soul containing the wisdom of the ages. In fact, his followers say the Karmapa
uses one illuminated eye to gaze at the outside world and the other to
look inwardly to the infinite depths of his own consciousness.

I obtained approval for the interview, which was to be a few days
later. In the interim, I saw the Karmapa on his twenty-fourth birthday,
when some five hundred people gathered in the temple below the
Karmapa's living quarters. About half were lamas and nuns, some of
them from the West. He came in wearing a crimson and gold robe
and sat on an elevated seat before the multitude, sitting cross-legged
on the floor. Behind him was a higher throne, and on it was a card-
board cutout of the Dalai Lama in a semi-lotus position. A chorus of
monks chanted in a spectral aural display using sacred throat singing:
They hit one bass pitch and a second overtone at the same time. The
Karmapa did not address the followers, many of whom fanned themselves against the rising June heat. A couple of days later, I'd seen him
appear before school kids at the Tibetan Children's Village up the hill,
where he spoke in Tibetan for half an hour about the need for environmental protection. The Karmapa largely shuns politics but has
embraced environmentalism in his public presentations. "We are all
interdependent," he said, speaking in a low voice. "Every animal has a
role to play in the ecology by being a part of the food chain. If you remove one layer, the entire chain is affected. . . . By saving wildlife, you
are ultimately helping yourself."[15]

On the appointed Saturday morning, I arrived at the monastery
for an 11 AM audience to find a full waiting room. Many people appeared to be foreign followers, including visitors from Hong Kong

and Taiwan. The Indian security guards patted us down but allowed me to take in a digital recorder and my wife to tote a digital camera and serve as photographer. As we waited with the others, an aging Indian security officer with dyed jet-black hair approached me and said, "Can I have a copy of your good questions, sir?" I explained that I had emailed the questions ahead, and the monastery should have a copy. "He wants your questions to be nonpolitical," a Tibetan attendant whispered to me.

After a lengthy wait, we climbed the four flights of stairs to the Karmapa's rooftop aerie, removed our shoes, and took seats in plastic deck chairs arranged in the hallway. The faint sounds of monks chanting reached to where we were sitting. Attendants hustled in and out of the reception room, signaling various pilgrims to enter. A Taiwanese lady behind me broke into sobs repeatedly as she waited, overcome with emotion at her imminent face-to-face contact with the Karmapa. She and her companion carried large bags of items to be blessed. Her friend said the two had just arrived in India and were making an annual trip to have their spiritual batteries recharged. A commotion sounded in the stairwell, and a sizable Australian legislative delegation arrived. I had seen its members repeatedly around Dharamsala earlier in the week. Several of the legislators quizzed each other on protocol as they took off their shoes and put *khatas* around their necks. "Just say 'Holiness.' You don't need to say 'Your Holiness' because that's just for the Dalai Lama," I overheard one Australian say to another, mistakenly.

Another hour passed, and we were ushered into the sunlit reception room. Large Tibetan *thangkas* hung from the walls. A large blue and orange traditional Tibetan rug mostly covered the green, wall-to-wall outdoor carpet. The Karmapa was standing, and he walked slightly forward in greeting, clasping my hands, and studying me from behind his wire-rim glasses, appearing to remember me from a previous visit. A single aide sat on the floor off to the side to serve as a translator, only occasionally interjecting when the young lama's English failed him. We sat down, the Karmapa on a striped divan at the head of the room with his legs folded under him. A yellow folder lay before him, apparently notes from his previous meeting. A small bonsai tree graced one table to his left, and a table to his right held knickknacks, including a nautilus shell. He asked if we would be following the list of questions I had emailed, and when I noted there were some additional subjects, he shrugged and indicated it would be no problem.

I brought up that I had recently attended a large exhibition in Beijing in which the government celebrated the Dalai Lama's flight into exile half a century ago, saying it corresponded with the liberation of Tibet from serfdom. Was Tibet a feudal society prior to the arrival of Chinese troops in the 1950s? "Outwardly, Tibet might have been a very, very feudalistic country. But we have to ask two questions. You must look at the heart of Tibetans. Were they happy or not? That is one question. Another thing we have to ask is, is the modern development taking place in Tibet beneficial to Tibet or not?" He made a reference to the new railway leading to Tibet and questioned whether it harmed the environment. "Are we really bringing something good, playing with the Tibet environment today? These questions we have to ask ourselves, and search into our hearts." The Karmapa segued into the violent unrest that had shaken the Tibetan Plateau a year earlier, saying many Tibetans risked their lives to give voice to their discontent under current Chinese policies. "It is evident that they are not happy today."[16]

The Karmapa rocked back and forth ever so slightly in his seat. Occasionally, he rolled his eyes in a comical way. His answer made me think back to the interview with him months earlier. Then, he was critical of China's repression of Tibetans, saying it was at the root of unrest. "Because there are no human rights living under the Chinese, some of them stood up. That's the reason for the spring uprising," he said at the time. Like the Dalai Lama, the Karmapa emphasized that it was the state repression ordered by Chinese rulers, not ordinary Han Chinese themselves, who were responsible. "Since I am born as a Tibetan, I really care about Tibetan people and the Tibetan community. At the same time, I also love Chinese. I make no distinction between Chinese and Tibetans."[17] He quickly added, though, that China is far more powerful than Tibet and its leaders bear more responsibility for the well-being of people there.

I asked him why ordinary Chinese appeared to be growing more interested in religion, and the Karmapa responded that "maybe they need a spiritual path or spiritual practice for something like a happier life." China's extraordinary economic development, he added, has left some citizens with "some emptiness, some vacuum, something missing." Economic development alone is not enough to satisfy the human soul, he said, even if China is changing in monumental strides. "It's external progress and development. It's just like a fat pig, just growing and growing on the outside but not on the inside." A little surprised at his increasing confidence to criticize China, I asked if he ever worried that China would take away its recognition of him as a divine reincarnation, and he shot back: "They already recognized me. They can't unsay what they've said."[18]

The Karmapa, in my interview with him and those with other journalists, shunned speculation that he might play a political role in a post–Dalai Lama era. "There are a great many Tibetan people who are doing a wonderful job serving the vision of His Holiness and implementing his vision. I try to do my best, too, but in terms of future roles that I might assume, I'm already the Karmapa. That's my role and it's already one I feel quite weighed down by." He shied away from a question about what he would do if he were asked by popular appeal from Tibetans to assume the leadership of the Tibetan movement in the future. "It's really quite an involved issue. In order for anyone to assume the role of leader of the Tibetan people, it's important to have historical context or at least an examination of the historical context. For anywhere between 800 and 900 years, the Karmapa has been a very apolitical figure, a person who has concentrated solely on spiritual leadership, not involved in any way with governmental leadership. So I think it would be very difficult to change that historical pattern overnight and turn the role of the Karmapa into something more than strictly a spiritual teacher."[19]

We chatted about his personal life. He arises most mornings at about 5 AM for his morning Buddhist rituals and study of scriptures and texts. He receives guests later in the morning. He also receives tutoring in English almost daily and regular tutoring in Korean so he can communicate with his many followers in South Korea. The Karmapa said he likes classical music and the New Age Irish singer Enya. He doesn't watch much television but likes to surf the net. "I often look at the BBC website," he said, but he does not use email. His sister, Ngodrup Pelzom, lives in the compound, and it is through her that he stays in touch with other family members. A natural restless quality envelops him.

In other interviews, he has said that he sometimes turns to video games to blow off steam. "I view video games as something of an emotional therapy, a mundane level of emotional therapy for me. We all have emotions whether we're Buddhist practitioners or not . . . and we need to figure out a way to deal with them when they arise. So, for me sometimes it can be a relief, a kind of decompression to just play some video games. If I'm having some negative thoughts or negative feelings, video games are one way in which I can release that energy in the context of the illusion of the game. I feel better afterwards."[20]

The Karmapa does not tire of studying and wished he had more opportunity to do so rigorously. He told an Indian journalist that he wants to study psychology and science. "There has been no real opportunity to pursue serious study in these subjects. I want to study modern science in the near future and I hope to enroll in a university for formal education. Modern science and Buddhist philosophy are complementary and beneficial to each other."[21]

Echoing warnings by the Dalai Lama, the Karmapa has said Tibetans don't have time to waste in the battle to preserve their culture. He reacted vigorously to one journalist who suggested that Tibetan exiles were assimilating into their Indian hosts:

> I feel the situation of Tibet is dire and that people in the world need to pay more attention to it. The situation is not one where we can take our time and wait 10, 20, 30 years to see what happens, what conditions might change because the danger is so great that much of our culture could be lost and the chances of restoring our culture greatly diminished. So it's actually quite a hot potato that we have here. We have to do something quickly. In the language of your question, if we were to wait 50 years, we would be in danger of losing a great chunk of Tibetan culture that could not be recovered.[22]

I asked the Karmapa if he was free to leave the monastery when he wanted. He said he circumambulated the grounds but did not leave the compound frequently. More often, he just roamed the rooftop terrace of the temple. "You see the terrace," he signaled out the window. Asked if he felt caged by India's continuing security concerns, he said, "It's difficult to explain. It's better than Tibet."

I puzzled over why India felt it necessary so many years after his arrival to keep a leash on his activities. Again in the spring of 2010, the Indian government declined to grant permission to the Karmapa for a month-long European trip and a second trip to offer teachings in the United States.[23] The reasoning for such refusals was a bit murky. But key factors were the rivals within his own order and the ensuing legal and media battles. One of the rivals openly calls himself the Seventeenth Karmapa; travels around Europe, the United States, and East Asia to offer teachings to tens of thousands of followers; and controls the karmapa.com website. He's not quite a doppelganger because his physical appearance is quite different from that of the far more widely accepted Karmapa endorsed by the Dalai Lama. But he's got powerful patrons, including a popular Danish Buddhist ex-boxer with thousands of followers. A lesser challenger is from Sikkim and has told the media that all three men should be given tests of spiritual mastery. "I am ready to show my powers but all the claimants should also be there in the sacred room of Rumtek monastery," said the man, Dawa Sangpo Dorje.[24] The disputes echo the shadowy and age-old conflicts that have torn at Tibetan Buddhism over the centuries, some of them involving charges of poisoning and even murder.

One of the disputes emerged from frictions between the four "heart sons" of the Sixteenth Karmapa after his passing. The most senior among the four, Shamar Rinpoche, who is commonly called the Shamarpa, later accused another, Tai Situ, of making up the prediction letter out of whole cloth. He demanded that forensic experts examine the letter and determine if the Sixteenth Karmapa indeed wrote it in his own hand. Tai Situ flatly refused, saying handwriting analysis was not a traditional procedure in the recognition process. The Shamarpa suspected a plot was afoot. When a supportive *rinpoche* sent him word about a boy in Lhasa who claimed to be the reincarnate Karmapa, the Shamarpa sent a trusted lama to investigate. Upon his return, the Shamarpa grew convinced that he had found the true reincarnate, named Trinley Thaye Dorje. In 1994, the boy and his family escaped Tibet to New Delhi. There, the Shamarpa arranged for his enthronement as the Seventeenth Karmapa. Despite his claims, he has never gained the upper hand.

These events might seem to be minutiae of an internal conflict of concern only to members of one Tibetan Buddhist order. But significant assets—and the fate of the Black Crown itself—may lie in the balance. A lawsuit over the dispute ensnarls the Kagyu order's estimated $1.2 billion in assets, including its most important exile monastery, Rumtek, and the priceless boxes of spiritual treasures, relics, and texts stored there.[25] Some say the Black Crown lies in a Rumtek vault, although the Shamarpa is said to allege the crown is only a replica and that Tai Situ has stolen the real crown, a charge he denies.

It's all enough to make an outsider's head spin. Sifting for truth in the intrigue, I consulted one of the Karmapa's Western collaborators, who suggested taking a broad historical view in which such conflicts have been rife. In the past, he said, when disputes about recognition would arise, one of the candidates would sometimes die suddenly. In fact, history is replete with allegations of dalai and panchen lamas who consumed a poisoned meal or died mysteriously at a young age. In some cases, regents were suspected of hastening the earthly passage of their young charges, eager to hang on to the privilege of their own posts. Four dalai lamas in a row died prematurely from 1805 until 1874.[26] The Ninth Dalai Lama was a cherubic boy enthroned in 1810. The English explorer Thomas Manning, who arrived in Lhasa in 1812, met him when he was seven and was taken by him. "The lama's beautiful and interesting face engrossed all my attention," Manning later wrote. "He had the simple, unaffected manners of a well-educated princely child. His face was, I thought, poetically and affectingly beautiful." By 1815, the boy was killed by a cold that progressed to pneumonia, just two months past his ninth birthday.[27] The Tenth Dalai Lama was placed on the Golden Throne in 1822 but died when he was just twenty or twenty-one years old. His regent was suspected of slowly poisoning him.[28] The Eleventh Dalai Lama entered the "heavenly fields" in 1853 at the age of seventeen, and his successor died at age eighteen. During the reign of the four short-lived Dalai Lamas, various regents held great power, as did the Panchen Lama.

It will take skill for the shepherd's son who is the most recognized Karmapa to find his way past obstacles once the Dalai Lama is no longer there to guide him. Ordinary Tibetans may pray for him to take a political role, pushing him toward leadership, wanted or not. He may well find that crossing the high Himalayas to freedom was a minor feat compared to navigating the political gusts and crosswinds that toss about those seeking a resolution to the Tibet issue.

Far away, across the Loess Plateau of China, and down an alley in an area east of Beijing's Forbidden City, dwells a young Tibetan woman about the same age as the Karmapa. She, too, is a Buddhist, one with a singular birthright from her bloodline. Her father was a top Tibetan lama who was jailed for a decade by the ruling party. On regaining his freedom, the lama took off his robes, married, and had a daughter. History has forged a unique role for her, although her path has been circuitous. It involved schooling at a posh private academy in Southern California and weekends in the company of Hollywood actors. More recently, she's earned a PhD in Beijing, acceding to the direct suggestion of President Hu Jintao to attend his prestigious alma mater. It is yet to be seen if her inner loyalties are to her ethnic Tibetan brethren or to the ruling party that guided her education.

Whatever the case, if the Communist Party keeps its grip on China, the young woman may be summoned to help it bring stability to Tibet, playing a key role domestically. Just as the Karmapa's star is rising abroad, so too destiny may hold a special role for a woman known as the Princess of Tibet.

chapter eight

The Princess

Truth is timeless. It always remains the same. Undoubtedly, there were mistakes in my petition. But I have never been wrong in speaking up.

—The Tenth Panchen Lama, speaking to ruling party leaders in Tibet in 1987, two years before his death

AS THE TWO HIGHEST REINCARNATED PRIESTS IN THEIR GELUGPA Buddhist tradition, the Dalai and Panchen Lamas guide each other from lifetime to lifetime, continually returning in successive rebirths. In the past, when the system worked, tradition called for the wise elder to take the younger as a disciple, and when one would die, the other would play a pivotal role in identifying the reincarnation. The two lamas reigned in different regions, with the Dalai Lama ruling from the Potala Palace in Lhasa and the Panchen Lama presiding over a sprawling monastery in the city of Shigatse to the west, with its own ruling elite. Relations have sometimes soured between the two high lamas, especially over Lhasa's claims to governing rights over Shigatse, and the Chinese have attempted to use this rivalry to their advantage. One Panchen Lama (the Ninth) fled to Mongolia after a dispute with the Thirteenth Dalai Lama over taxes to finance a standing army. At other times, Panchen Lamas have sought closer relationships with Beijing.

When China strengthened its control over Tibet on the heels of invading troops in the 1950s, the two Tibetan religious leaders were both in their teenage years, the Panchen Lama three years younger than the Dalai Lama. As they matured, the two adopted different strategies. As the Dalai Lama veered toward conflict with the Communist Party, the Panchen Lama was popularly seen as "pro-Chinese." When the Dalai Lama fled to exile in 1959, the Panchen Lama remained behind, lauding the ruling party's ideals and viewing it as a lesser threat than the sometimes antagonistic religious order in Lhasa. The party quickly named him vice chair of the Chinese People's Congress, finding in him a useful puppet. But the Panchen Lama was to become a pebble in the shoe of Mao Zedong and a courageous but tragic hero to many of his fellow Tibetans. By 1962, when he was barely twenty-four years old, the Panchen Lama produced a lengthy critique of the party's troubled policies in Tibet that Mao would call "a poisoned arrow shot at the party."

The Panchen Lama's critique, couched in Marxist language acceptable to the party, was a call for change in policy toward Tibet. It lambasted the imprisonment of ten thousand Tibetans and blamed local party cadres for trying to eradicate Buddhism, reducing the number of monasteries in the Tibet Autonomous Region from twenty-five hundred in 1959 to about seventy within three years. The strangulation of Buddhism "is something which I and more than 90 percent of Tibetans cannot endure," he wrote. Starvation was on the rise, and the party had failed to improve conditions from Tibet's dark feudal past. Critics pounced on the Panchen Lama, and in 1964 they subjected him to fifty days of abuse and humiliation, declaring him an "enemy of the party, enemy of the people and an enemy of socialism." Four years later, he was dumped into prison for a decade. By the time of his release, he was nearly shattered. He took off his robes, abandoned the celibacy that is routine for most Tibetan monks, and married a Chinese woman, who gave birth to a daughter. It was the first time in more than six centuries that a Panchen Lama married a woman and fathered a child.

After living in Beijing for several years, I discovered that the Panchen Lama's daughter resided only five or six blocks away from our apartment, a bit to the east of the Forbidden City, just off of the principal artery, the Boulevard of Everlasting Peace. Her residence was behind the Chang An Grand Theater, an eight-hundred-seat venue that is a premier spot to see Peking Opera, situated along a typical alleyway, known as a *hutong*, lined with an assortment of modest shops and a public toilet. In the summertime, men would sit on the sidewalk playing Chinese checkers or mah-jongg. There were no special markings on the high gray walls, only a huge metal gate with a peephole for the guard to peer through at arriving visitors. Like many such courtyard dwellings, the outside walls revealed no hint of the property inside, which turned out to be an island of serenity despite its proximity to a ten-lane boulevard.

The Tenth Panchen Lama himself had resided in the historic compound, and now it belonged to his immediate family. The full name of his daughter is Yabshi Pan Rinzinwangmo, which means "wise holy woman," but nearly everyone calls her Renji. Curiously for China, where the revolution largely obliterated class differences, Renji also bears the honorific title "Princess of Tibet," with the state's blessings. When I first met her a few years ago, she was in her mid-twenties, living in Beijing after a decade of studies in the United States. She greeted me in English with a distinct California tinge. It didn't take long to see how she has a foot in three worlds—Tibet, China, and the West. She is half ethnic Tibetan and half Han; her mother was a Han medical student. Renji grew up in a household surrounded by Tibetan monks, and Tibetan remains her native language. Even though she has never received extensive religious training, many ordinary Tibetans revere her as an embodiment of her father, who died when she was barely five and a half years old.

The Han Chinese also embrace her. Renji's maternal great-grandfather was a former army general under the Kuomintang, or nationalists, who battled and eventually lost to the Communist revolutionaries. He moved over to the Red Army, and the family burnished its credentials under the Communists. Through a quirk of history, Renji's mother developed a direct relationship with Hu Jintao, the general secretary of the party, and the Chinese leader signaled that her daughter had a promising future in politics. Hu and other party leaders saw Renji as a potential bridge across the chasm that separates Beijing and Lhasa. Many Western diplomats and scholars have befriended Renji, respecting her Western education and understanding of Western values as well as the special role handed her as a potential unifying force on the difficult matter of Tibet.

It took me a handful of encounters with one of her aides to persuade her to see me. She was busy studying for a doctorate in finance and didn't want to be bothered with interviews. I finally gained an audience after pestering the aide with numerous emails and seeking him out repeatedly for meetings to present my case. On the appointed day, I made my way to her compound. When a guard let me in, I observed a large parking area, a small garden, and a three-story main house with some outbuildings. Attendants first ushered me to see a third-floor shrine to the deceased Tenth Panchen Lama, where candles burned under his large painted image. Multicolored cylindrical prayer flags hung from the ceiling, and photographs adorned the walls. After a few minutes, I was taken to a large sitting room with a massive painting of Mount Everest on a wall. The sitting room was quite formal, typical of Chinese meeting rooms, with large overstuffed chairs arranged around the walls and side tables to hold cups of tea. A bouquet of roses adorned a low table in front of the sofa at the head of the room. An attendant entered silently and offered me hot butter tea and a small plate of fruit and chocolates. She quietly reentered every quarter hour to refill my cup.

When Renji walked in the room, her attendants stood. She beamed and extended her hand. She had the healthy bronze skin tone of Tibetans. Her hazel hair was a little longer than shoulder length, and not a hair seemed out of place. Purple eye shadow brightened her face. On most days when she receives visitors, she wears the traditional Tibetan attire of nobility—a long formal dress with a blouse. She sat on a sofa and folded her hands. We discussed at length whether she'd be willing to undergo a series of interviews. She expressed some interest but seemed to mull the political implications. From that initial meeting, it took more than a year to arrange further meetings, and only on condition that I stay away from discussions of her own future or the future of Tibet. Aides made clear that Renji didn't want to venture into political minefields around the sensitive topic of contemporary Tibet.

Many issues could easily entangle Renji. One of them involved her father's reincarnation and a dispute over who now bears his consciousness and centuries-old wisdom. Strolling around Dharamsala, I'd seen many bright green wallboards that deplored the plight of a sweet-faced six-year-old Tibetan boy, calling him "the world's youngest political prisoner." He was a "soul boy" endorsed by the Dalai Lama who, if free, would likely have been enthroned as the Eleventh Panchen Lama. The drama of the boy's discovery and his subsequent disappearance in 1995 is an open sore for Tibetans. As in the disputes over the Karmapa lineage, elements of the clash over the Panchen Lama reincarnation will foreshadow what may happen when the current Dalai Lama passes away. China will manipulate the search for, and eventual proclamation, of his reincarnation, vetting all candidates and ensuring that the one who triumphs is acceptable to the party. Any candidates favored by exiled lamas may well disappear from the face of the Earth.

The photos on the giant wallboards in Dharamsala show an innocent looking Tibetan child with big, trusting eyes. The boy's name is Gedhun Choekyi Nyima. His story began to unfold in early 1989 after the passing of the Tenth Panchen Lama, Renji's father. Within half a year of his demise, a search began for a reincarnation, the transmigration of his consciousness into a new living being. Tibetan Buddhists believe that when senior lamas die, their divine mind stream returns in new living beings, and each successive reincarnation possesses the same consciousness as the previous ones, carrying forward a whole body of wisdom and insight. Thus even "soul boys" who have yet to receive formal religious education are venerated as profoundly holy, carrying the illumination of multiple lifetimes of realized beings returning to Earth. Those selected as reincarnations in the Dalai and Panchen Lama lineages are particularly revered as aspects of the immortal enlightenment of the Buddha himself.

The search for the new Panchen Lama was troubled from the start. The Communist Party set ground rules intended to remove the exiled Dalai Lama from any role in identifying the reincarnation. It agreed to allow senior lamas from the sprawling home monastery of the Panchen Lama, Tashilhunpo, to leave Shigatse and conduct the day-to-day search. But it said Beijing would choose the new lama from the names of the final three candidates. Tapped to lead the search was the abbot of the monastery, a senior monk who had studied in Beijing and enjoyed some trust of the authorities. Unbeknownst to Beijing, the abbot also began a secret correspondence with the Dalai Lama about how to proceed. Pilgrims and monks carried hidden letters back and forth across the Himalayas so that both sides could stay abreast of progress.

The arduous search involved several excursions to holy Lhamo Latso Lake, where the abbot and his team recited mantras and scanned the changing surface waters of the lake with binoculars for telltale auguries that would guide them to the correct child. During the trips, lamas saw visions of a small child with a birthmark and outlines of two Tibetan letters. Armed with the clues, three separate search parties fanned out. Eventually, one senior lama ended up at the doorstep of a home in Nagchu in central Tibet, where a young boy displayed strange markings on his body, including on his wrists, where the previous Panchen Lama had been handcuffed during parts of his lengthy prison term. The child begged to return with the strange monk to Tashilhunpo, leaving his parents and family behind, a traditional sign of a reincarnation. Further investigation convinced the lamas that they had found the "soul boy," and when the Dalai Lama got word of the evidence, he promptly agreed.

On May 14, 1995, the Dalai Lama assembled senior lamas in Dharamsala and announced that the Panchen Lama's "true reincarnation" had been discovered in Nagchu. China responded with anger. Three days later, its agents took the boy and his parents into custody, never to be seen again. Agents also arrested the abbot of Tashilhunpo, sentencing him to a six-year jail term for conspiring with the Dalai Lama and on his eventual release placing him under indefinite house arrest near a military camp. A few months later, the central government proclaimed that another Tibetan boy, the son of two party members, had been found near the same town of Nagchu and was the true reincarnation, creating a situation of dueling Panchen Lamas that would become the template for the officially atheist party seeking to establish itself as the unlikely arbiter of how souls transmigrate.

In a middle-of-the-night ceremony on November 29, senior party members gathered in Lhasa's Jokhang Temple for a quick enthronement of the child. To this day, most ordinary Tibetans view the boy, now grown and in his twenties, as a faux Panchen Lama. In monasteries and temples across the Tibetan highlands, faithful Buddhists continue to venerate photos of the deceased previous Panchen Lama, pulling out images of Beijing's appointed successor only when authorities order them to do so. China acknowledges custody of the missing "soul boy," claiming he "is a perfectly ordinary Tibetan boy, in an excellent state of health, leading a normal, happy life and receiving a good education and cultural upbringing."[1] It refuses to give the whereabouts of their presumed prisoner or his family, claiming it is for their own protection.

Party guardians raised the party-appointed Panchen Lama in a compound in the Beijing suburb of Huairou, separated from his ethnic roots and initially deprived of the specialized religious training in a monastery customary for such a high lama. He later would study in the Kumbum monastery but under close watch of monitors. Cadres increasingly trotted him out for national Buddhist gatherings and to tour Tibetan areas in large convoys of vehicles. As a young man, the lama appeared to grow into his role. But he most likely fears that there is one person who could look into his eyes and determine if he is an impostor. That person is Renji.

As the daughter of the Tenth Panchen Lama, she would sit cradled in her father's lap and listen to his chanting of prayers and mantras. She knows his spirit, the spark of his divinity, and his boundless love for her. If she peered into the appointed reincarnation's eyes and recognized a glimmer of her father's spirit, it would give him an imprimatur that he is indeed the reincarnation. After all, he bears the same consciousness as her father, only in a different physical vessel. Such a declaration would help assuage concerns about China's governance of Tibet. But if she were to say that she sees no flicker of her father in the young man and that she doesn't believe that he's the reincarnation, it could add to the anger, frustration, and resentment that already percolate in Tibet. Will the daughter be permitted to pass judgment? Will she tell the truth of what she knows? With me, she kept her guard shrewdly, saying only that she has yet to gaze deeply into his eyes. But until that action happens, if it is ever allowed to unfold, she understands her strategic value in the drama over the young man who now wears the yellow hat of the Panchen Lama:

"He needs me more than I need him."[2]

IN MY FIRST FORMAL INTERVIEW with Renji at her compound, she agreed to talk about her life while flipping through photo albums. Her father had married her mother after emerging from nearly a decade of imprisonment, and he was yet to be rehabilitated when Renji was born in 1983. But the government returned to him the trappings of power, including the coterie of attendants and the chance to revive friendships with senior party leaders. So Renji grew up in a privileged setting. After her birth, she had three monks and two women who attended to her needs. "I had a person who was my driver, another who was my chef, and my personal 'play with me' person," she recalled. "Whenever I'd go out, there'd be people carrying my silverware." Someone else would trail along carrying a special container for Renji to pee into when the urge struck her.

At a party to celebrate the hundredth day after her birth, she was given another nickname, one by which she is still known among senior party cadres. Deng Yingchao, the widow of former Premier Zhou Enlai, the number 2 to Mao Zedong, picked the name upon seeing how chubby the girl was. She called her "Tuantuan." *Tuan* in Mandarin has two meanings, one of which is "round," and the face of the Panchen Lama's daughter fit the bill. *Tuan* also means "to unify," and the name Tuantuan came to symbolize the hope of party leaders that ethnic minorities would feel unity with the Han Chinese. The name still sticks among older party members who have known Renji since her childhood.

During her early years, the Panchen Lama's compound had as many as fifty or sixty people in residence, including visiting senior lamas, leaders of other religions, relatives, and others. Renji's most intimate times with her father came at dawn. "Every morning, he'd get up at 4:30 or 5 o'clock at the latest to do his morning chanting." After a short period, attendants would wake Renji and bring her into the shrine hall, where she would listen to his chanting. On Saturdays, the Panchen Lama would hold audiences for the public, and throngs of people would show up, crowding the *hutong* outside to the point that the public latrine would be overrun. During warmer weather, the Panchen Lama would take his family up to the Western Hills outside Beijing, where the party allotted him a recreational villa with a menagerie of horses, deer, a bull, monkeys, and dogs. Also living in the Western Hills was the family of Xi Zhongxun, the senior cadre whose son is approaching the top party leadership. Madame Deng, the widow of Zhou

Enlai, was also a regular visitor. Madame Deng was a power in her own right, playing a key role in affairs of the Panchen Lama's family.

Renji quickly slipped into the colloquial English she learned as a teenager in Southern California as she flipped pages of the photo albums. "These are us just chilling," she said, looking at one photo of a picnic. Another photo showed the roomy family Red Flag sedan, a luxury car during the earlier Communist era. Her father loved to drive but was normally under orders to let a chauffeur take the wheel. "There were one or two times that he would drive the car out on the street without telling the government. With my mom, they would just drive down Chang An Street." Early memories included wandering into her father's office to see his desk piled high with stacks of papers. "I used to call it the paper mountain." Next to his desk was a desk for Renji's mom, Li Jie, who acted as his secretary. Their daughter would on occasion wander into the office and see her father giving her mother a lesson in the Tibetan language. The Panchen Lama had learned Mandarin during his decade in prison and had grown quite conversant in it. But Li Jie never fully mastered Tibetan. The two doted on their daughter, celebrating her birthdays with massive cakes. When Renji was old enough to go to the neighborhood kindergarten, nearly a dozen people would accompany her each day. Her father's sudden passing shattered her first year of schooling.

Renji explained how the utterly different worlds of her two parents came to overlap—in a Beijing neighborhood that I considered my own. Ritan Park is one of four city parks along the cardinal points radiating out from the Forbidden City. Ritan means "Temple of the Sun" in Mandarin, and the other parks contain temples to the moon, the Earth, and the heavens. All the parks were places of worship for the imperial court, and Chinese emperors at Ritan Park would make ritual sacrifices on the central altar to the sun god. Nowadays, the park is a small arboretum wedged between a bustling and frenetic business district, a Russian commercial area, and one of two main embassy districts. For years, my daughters and I would regularly go there to see residents practice tai chi, fly kites, sing Beijing opera, and swing around in outdoor dancing classes. In one area of the park, would-be gymnasts practiced on outdoor parallel and uneven bars, while others scampered on an artificial rock-climbing wall, a favored site until a foreigner fell to his death. Mold grew on the rundown miniature golf course, and algae flecked the tiny fishing pond, but the park pulsated with life. At one corner, a journalist colleague had set up a bar in an imitation stone boat moored in a pond, a replica of the stone boat of the late Empress Dowager Cixi at the Summer Palace in another corner of the city. Willows, snow pines, persimmons, and other trees made Ritan Park a serene respite from the city. In springtime, yellow forsythias, white magnolias, and pink cherry trees came forth in exuberant bloom.

One hot July evening in 1978, a portly six-foot-tall man sat on a bench in Ritan Park. He wore a white tank top and trousers, typical male summer attire. Unlike others in the park, the man was not ethnic Han. He was Tibetan, indeed the revered Tenth Panchen Lama. He wasn't there to see the imperial sacrificial altar to the sun. He'd already made his sacrifices, forced from his religious birthright. He'd emerged from a decade in jail, a victim of the tumult of the Cultural Revolution, gaining freedom only after the death of Mao. He longed for a normal life. Oddly enough, he wanted a family. And he sat in Ritan Park waiting for a woman he thought could be a prospective bride. It would have been natural for his mind to reflect back on the torment he'd suffered in the previous years.

Way back in 1966, when the Cultural Revolution kicked off, a unit of pro-Mao zealots who called themselves Red Guards burst into his Beijing compound, tied him up with nylon cord, and subjected him to severe harassment. With Mao's blessing, they were looking to turn the tables on revolutionaries who'd lost their zeal, false socialists aiming to veer China down the capitalist road, and holdouts of the "four olds" of Chinese society (old customs, old culture, old habits, and old ideas). The Tibetan lama was an easy target. "Despite Panchen's repeated demand to be untied, the Red Guards ignored him. They spat on him, pricked his ears and castigated him venomously."[3] Then they took him before a crowd of thousands of people for a public shaming. "They paraded Panchen to please the public. The amplifiers in propaganda vehicles blared out the many crimes they accused the Panchen of [being]: [the] 'head of the traitors,' 'the biggest reactionary serf owner,' 'the biggest reactionary Living Buddha' and 'the biggest parasite and bloodsucker in Tibet."[4] If it hadn't been for the intervention of Premier Zhou Enlai, a close friend, the lama's fate might have come to an earlier end. Zhou ordered the Red Guards not to use violence against the Tibetan, specifically banning them from forcing him to bend over, spread his arms, and pose like a "jet plane" for long periods, but permitting them to berate him.

Amid the upheaval of the ensuing months he holed up in his Beijing compound to escape persecution. It was to no avail. On the night of February 22, 1968, soldiers came to his house and took him away, saying they were acting on orders of a superior. He would be held for nine years and eight months, much of it in solitary confinement. Guards forbade him from receiving visitors, as other prisoners did, and talked to him little. But with the help of a dictionary, and books by Mao, Marx, and Lenin, as well as a magazine with the same name as his beloved sedan, Red Flag, the Panchen Lama learned Mandarin. He also conversed with high-powered fellow prison inmates, who included Wan Li, the deputy mayor of Beijing, and Field Marshal Peng Dehuai, a critic of the Great Leap Forward who had fallen from favor.

Almost a decade later, when the Panchen Lama emerged at 3 PM on October 26, 1977, China was gripped by power struggles. The decade-long nightmare of the Cultural Revolution was over, and Mao had died a year earlier, but China's direction was not yet clear. The Cultural Revolution had inflicted a devastating and incalculable toll on the whole of China, including Tibet and its culture. The feverish young battalions of Red Guards had smashed and razed thousands of monasteries in Tibet. Religion was vilified. And the Panchen Lama left prison unsure what lay in store for the future. Senior leaders did not immediately wipe away the charges that had sent him to prison in the first place, restoring him to public life "but not erasing his sin."[5] By 1978, as the government sought to right the wrongs against those relatively loyal partisans who had suffered long prison terms, it invited the Tibetan and some thirty or forty other freed cadres and high officials on an extended tour of China to see the glories of the revolution. The deputy leader of the group was General Dong Qiwu, a former Nationalist army general who had become a loyal Communist. Most of the members of the group were in their sixties, seventies, and eighties. But the Panchen Lama was not yet forty, and during the sojourn around China he mentioned to a bodyguard who was his constant companion that he wanted to find a wife and start a family.

The bodyguard knew nothing of Buddhism and had no idea who the Tibetan was. On the tour's conclusion in Beijing, the bodyguard mentioned the lama's wish around the household of General Dong. "I met this guy called Panchen during the tour. He's about forty years old, just got out of prison, and wants to get married to a girl, preferably one who is younger and in the military," the soldier said.[6] Li Jie, on hearing the account, took interest, perhaps not for herself but for any of her numerous girlfriends. After all, she was a medical student at the Fourth Military University in Xian, and she and her friends were all considered soldiers. She decided to go with a relative for a face-to-face meeting with the Tibetan in Ritan Park on July 2, 1978, so she could choose whether to make a recommendation to her friends.

"My father thought my mom was the one the . . . bodyguard was introducing as a prospective wife," Renji recalled. "My father was really open and honest about his past. He said he'd been in prison, and basically had nothing at the time. My father didn't have money." And he still hadn't been rehabilitated, so he retained the formal black mark of being "antisocialist." The young medical student took a strong liking to the tank-shirt-clad monk, and they met a few more times before reaching the mutual decision to marry. When she returned to her university, she wrote a letter to the authorities announcing her plans. Her grandfather, who had raised her in the absence of her parents, grew enraged, saying the lama was not suitable, even a disgrace. But she persisted, threatening to begin a hunger strike in protest of the patriarch's opposition. With the intervention of some senior cadres, the marriage went ahead at Beijing's grandest venue, the Great Hall of the People.

Seated between the Panchen Lama and the bride's angry grandfather was Madame Deng, Premier Zhou's widow, who obliged the two to speak to one another and offer toasts. The intervention of the illustrious premier's widow could hardly be ignored, and the grandfather put aside his anger at a marriage that literally wed Han and Tibetan and served the political interests of the party.[7] With the marriage, the Panchen Lama never put on his monk's robes again. He obtained new political posts, including becoming the vice chairman of the National People's Congress, the legislature, in 1980.

The couple did not bear their daughter until nearly four years after their wedding. And Renji's happy childhood with her two parents came to an abrupt end in early 1989. It was then that the household was shaken with the news that the Panchen Lama had fallen grievously ill during a trip back to Tibet. Li Jie rushed to the kindergarten to pluck her daughter from class and head to a private jet at Beijing's airport. Upon arrival in Lhasa, they joined a larger team of government officials headed by a bright young cadre, Wen Jiabao, who would later become premier of China. The group boarded various military helicopters for the flight to Shigatse, site of the Panchen Lama's home monastery.

Renji's voice cracked a bit as she described how she and her mother were taken to separate rooms at the monastery; they saw people swooning in grief, even falling into complete faints. No one told her that her father had already passed away. Instead, she was taken to a chamber, where his body sat upright with a yellow scarf over his face. "I was very excited to see my father, so I ran to my dad, 'Daddy!' But he didn't answer me. So I called him a few times. I realized that something was wrong because my father always answered me because I was this little love daughter." I asked Renji if she shared the Dalai Lama's opinion that her father may have been poisoned. She demurred. "This is a tragedy, so I really don't want to talk about it." She indicated that poor health was likely a factor in his demise. Her father, always large, had ballooned in weight at the time of his death. He also drove himself hard. "He slept about three hours a day maximum, and he was flying all the time. Through my father's life, I've learned that working hard is great, but you have to take care of your health." Her expression offered little insight into her feelings about the death. If proven to be a murder, it would place her in a position of a heroine from Greek tragedy, fealty to a party that tore her family apart. But Renji curtly continued her story.

The shock of the death soon gave way to a battle over the family's belongings. Normally, a Panchen Lama's personal effects and property would revert back to his home monastery, in part for use in the search for his reincarnated spirit boy. Never before had the monastery had to contend with a surviving wife and daughter willing to fight for the assets. At stake was a property valued at about $20 million across the moat from the northwest corner of the Forbidden City that the party had assigned to the Panchen Lama, who had bequeathed it to his wife and daughter. Also in play was the principle that the surviving family deserved to inherit some of the assets. Still, monastery agents came into the house and began marking countless personal objects such as tables, plates, underwear, toys, and dolls with the Chinese character 封—"forbidden to touch." They operated under the slogan "Take every needle and every string back to Tashilhunpo."

As Li Jie carried out the inheritance battle, her daughter remained in elementary school, within walking distance of their residence. Renji soon took up tennis, having a chauffeur take her nearly every day to the Shichahai Sports Training Center, a prestigious nearby facility that routinely trained Olympic athletes. She would spend hours whacking tennis balls, dreaming of turning into a professional tennis player—a passing fancy. Renji was on track to go to Beijing's best junior high school. But her mother had other plans.

Li Jie was advised against traveling outside of China. Leaders feared that she might not return and that she might even join with the Dalai Lama and his exile followers aiming darts at China from afar. But she wanted her daughter to study abroad. She turned to her aunt, who had left China a few years earlier and lived in a house near Coney Island. After arrangements were made, Renji boarded a Northwest Airlines jet to Detroit, then on to LaGuardia Airport in New York, traveling without her mother but with the knowledge of the party, which did not object. The mother ensured that word got out that the Tenth Panchen Lama's daughter was traveling to the States, and when Renji got off the plane, enough interest had been raised that hundreds of Tibetans were there to receive her in the terminal.

But life was not easy at her great aunt's home. Like many new émigrés, the relative had painted a better picture of her life in New York to Renji's mother than facts bore out. The neighborhood was rough. Renji had her own room at her great aunt's house but had to walk to P.S. 128, the Bensonhurst junior high school where she enrolled in the seventh grade. Renji could barely speak English and soon found herself in a tiny clique of the only four Asian kids at the racially diverse school. Her friends were often bullied, so Renji decided to fight back. She was involved in a fair share of scuffles and even recalls getting punched a few times in the jostling before and after school. In her telephone conversations with her mother back in Beijing, she didn't say a word about how rough the school was.

Li Jie soon got permission to travel outside of China and got on a jet to see her daughter. She still couldn't quite comprehend how tough Renji's environment was—until one day she spotted the slash marks on a new leather jacket she'd bought for her daughter in Manhattan, telltale signs of a fight. It didn't take long for Li Jie to pull her daughter from the school and move with her into the Soho Grand Hotel. She began to shop around among some of the most costly and exclusive private schools in the United States, among them Phillips Exeter Academy and Andover in rural New England, but the family deemed them too isolated. Renji and her mother toured private high schools in Boston, San Francisco, and Los Angeles, where an unusual personal contact of the family interceded.

Steven Seagal, the Hollywood action hero, had a long-standing interest in martial arts and Tibetan Buddhism. Indeed, in 1997 a senior Tibetan *rinpoche*, or incarnate lama, Penor Rinpoche, declared his student was a *tulku*, or reincarnated Tibetan lama, himself. The declaration drew disbelieving commentaries, and Penor Rinpoche later clarified what he saw in Seagal: "Some people think that because Steven Seagal is always acting in violent movies, how can he be a true Buddhist? Such movies are for temporary entertainment and do not relate to what is real and important. It is the view of the Great Vehicle of Buddhism that compassionate beings take rebirth in all walks of life to help others. Any life condition can be used to serve beings and thus, from this point of view, it is possible to be both a popular movie star and a *tulku*. There is no inherent contradiction in this possibility."[8]

Seeing himself as a guardian for Renji, Seagal recommended that she attend Southwestern Academy, a private school in San Marino, an upscale area near downtown Los Angeles. A boarding and day school, Southwestern has just a hundred fifty or so students, many of them scions of corporate tycoons, offspring of sheikhs, and children of global jetsetters. Even back then, annual fees were about $32,000. The school required students to wear uniforms, but the jewelry and the sports cars parked out front gave evidence of the social status of the students. Seagal promised to keep a close eye on Renji. Li Jie agreed, and by the spring of 1996 Renji was enrolled in Southwestern. Many of the students were Asian, and she felt at home. Friends there knew of her close connection with Seagal, who hadn't yet fallen into the direct-to-video phase of a movie career in freefall.

"Steven would come pick me up every weekend in his long limousine," Renji recalls. "You see him in the movies as a cold-hearted killer, but he's really not." She spent a lot of time at Seagal's mansion on the winding roads of Bel Air, the posh community that edges up the foothills of the Santa Monica mountains. At the actor's home, Renji learned how to play the electric guitar, picked up a fair version of Valley Girl talk (*like, you know?*), and hung out with movie stars and their children. "He gave me a feeling of home in the States, which I wouldn't have had without him. I really was part of his family." By the time she was old enough to drive, Renji was zipping around Southern California on powerful Suzuki and BMW motorcycles, later graduating to expensive sports cars.

The strongest Communist Party supporter of the family happened to be China's leader, Hu Jintao, who is not only president but also general secretary of the ruling party and head of the military. As a rising star in the party, Hu had paid a courtesy visit to the Tenth Panchen Lama in 1984, meeting his wife as well. A few years later, the Panchen Lama and Li Jie traveled to Guizhou, where Hu had been installed as provincial party secretary, deepening what was to become a long-term friendship. At the time of Renji's father's death in 1989, Hu had been transferred to Tibet as party secretary and again saw the family in a period of grief. Hu, certainly aware of the family's potential role as a bridge between the ethnic Han and Tibetan populations, has been on close terms with Li Jie ever since. It would be easy to assume that the friendship with Hu opened up a spigot of cash from party coffers to the family at the time, but Renji insisted it wasn't true, and an aide said the family had "substantial independent wealth,"[9] although the provenance was never clear to me. Even before Renji was out of high school, she had rented a place in Pasadena and was living off campus. She had found a social milieu that remains part of her life as an adult.

At Southwestern, Renji's favorite subject was political science, and when she looked at where to pursue university studies, she focused on the U.S. capital—the heart of American political life—and settled on American University, which has a leafy campus in northwest Washington, DC. Her arrival at American was somewhat of a letdown. Unlike most students, who savor the initial freedom of living away from parents, Renji chafed at a requirement that all students live on campus their first year. Rather than a comfy pied-à-terre in the capital, she was again stuck in a dorm room. Almost every month, Chinese embassy officials swept her away from the university and took her out to the best restaurants in the city. On weekends, she traveled up to New York City or jetted back to Los Angeles. She attended occasional international conferences on Tibetan issues in Europe or elsewhere. At least twice a year, she flew back to China to visit her mother and relatives.

As her senior year drew to a close, Renji considered her options, among them pursuing graduate studies in political science or international relations. Both Oxford University in England and the School of International and Public Affairs at Columbia University in New York City accepted her. She also mulled getting a job in a big city, or even returning to L.A. to try her hand at acting. "I know directors, movie stars, and all the people there," she said. But then she heard from her mother that President Hu had other plans for her: to return to China and enroll in a PhD program at Tsinghua University, his own alma mater and widely considered the nation's top academy. She heard also that Hu thought it best for her to study finance rather than international relations. Tibet has no finance industry, and few Tibetan scholars are studying such practical fields, she was told, and politicians who understand finance would be in high demand. Her eyes rolled a bit as she related this to me, signaling how rigorous graduate-level finance had been for her. A team of tutors was assigned to increase her understanding of calculus, statistics, and general number crunching.

She returned to Beijing in 2005 to undertake her graduate studies, living once again in a dorm room on the sprawling Tsinghua campus. Tsinghua is in a northwest quadrant of the city housing most of the capital's sixty-odd universities, as well as high-tech companies along Zhongguancun, a traffic corridor known as China's Silicon Valley. Coffee shops, cheap noodle joints, and bookstalls cater to the large student population. When traffic is heavy, it can take an hour to reach the flourishing night scene in Beijing's eastern side. Instead of tooling around in a sports car, Renji found herself on foot or joining the proles riding bikes. She felt deeply out of place in her early classes. Most Tsinghua students look like nerdy would-be engineers, a field in which the university excels. While the buildings are modern, students dress modestly. Every day, Renji would put on makeup and arrange her hair nicely before going to class. In the crowded classrooms, she found other students hesitant to mingle with her.

One of her classmates, Li Guangyong, an ambitious young man from Jiangxi province in China's south, said Renji made a strong impression from the beginning. "Her Mandarin was not so fluent then," he said, adding that she'd just returned from the States. "Most Tsinghua students are from average families. Some of them are rich but not as rich as Renji. She's *rich*," he said, emphasizing the last word.[10]

Upon her return to China, in a sign of her family's growing means, Renji surrounded herself with more aides, including a young former American banker, Christopher Thomas, whom she befriended in Washington. The aides worried that her intense studies at Tsinghua had become too much of a grind, and in 2007 they arranged for her to attend fashion weeks in Milan, Paris, and Hong Kong as a break from her studies. She said she enjoyed the fashion shows but had grown accustomed to her new life and didn't desire to return to watch the latest trends on the catwalks.

After several meetings with Renji, I still didn't get much of a feel for her personal life. Our meetings were always somewhat formal, and I still didn't know much about what she did for enjoyment. I'd asked her once about a Facebook page that had numerous articles and photos of her. One photo showed her canoodling in the lap of a Japanese soccer star. She later said a fan created the page for her.[11] Then an email popped into my mailbox, and it turned out to be an invitation to Renji's twenty-sixth-birthday party. She was celebrating at an elegant private club along Beijing's Fourth Ring Road. As I approached an outdoor reception table, aides scurried about taking gifts to safety because a light rain had begun to fall. Renji was wearing a striking gold brocade Tibetan-style wraparound dress with a vermilion blouse. She greeted me warmly, as did Christopher Thomas, the assistant who's been working as her secretary for half a decade.

I recognized a few fellow journalists, both Chinese and Western. The former chief of staff to the U.S. ambassador was there, alongside a number of young prosperous Chinese and hip-looking foreigners. One young woman introduced herself to me as a member of the royal family from the South Pacific island of Tonga. I chatted with a young Chinese jetsetter who said that he organized fashion events and traveled constantly outside China. Another young Han man handed me a card with an Anglicized name. It didn't define what he did for a living, so I asked. He frowned slightly, indicating that there were many ways to make money in today's China. The entertainment began, including a performer who changed masks effortlessly and quickly. The guests heaped piles of "long life" noodles in Renji's bowl, and she bemoaned the tradition that she was obligated to eat all of them. At one point, a reporter for China Central Television, Ray Chen, recognizable to many Chinese television viewers, grabbed the microphone.

Attendants wheeled out a cart containing a huge and elaborate birthday cake designed as if it were a Tibetan palace, with kiwi slices and other fruit serving as architectural adornments. The icing on top read in both Chinese characters and English, "Happy Birthday Princess." Cameras began to flash. I heard some joshing about what Renji would wish for as she blew out the candles, and her mother blurted out that she'd like a son-in-law. Renji said a few remarks in Mandarin thanking everyone for coming on short notice. She then repeated the remarks in English. Wine flowed freely. I looked around and admired the Chinese version of the beautiful people.

In such a hip crowd, there certainly would be a mix of self-made Chinese and those with *guanxi*, or social ties, because of their family backgrounds. There is little better way to get ahead in China then to be the son or daughter of an influential Communist Party elder or retired military man. The offspring of such leaders are known as "princelings," a term that evokes hereditary monarchies with crown princes waiting to ascend to the throne. It is somewhat derogatory, reflecting the resentment many ordinary Chinese feel toward those who have a fast track to power and wealth. In reality, the sons and daughters of the top leaders in China don't quite have their way paved in such a clear fashion. What they do have are sterling connections that help them build business connections and even empires. Little information slips through heavy media censorship into the public realm about the princelings, and talk about them is taboo except in hushed tones over dinner tables.

Various families of top leaders have carved out niches in industry. The son and daughter of former Premier Li Peng are titans in power generation. President Hu Jintao's eldest son heads a business conglomerate that has won state contracts for airport X-ray scanners. Premier Wen Jiabao's son runs a huge private equity fund investing in China. Others make their way into politics, becoming ministers and mayors of large cities, or climbing even higher. The perception that princelings have parlayed their connections into riches is so pervasive that *People's Daily* carried an article denying that 90 percent of the top hundred wealthy people in China were children of high-level cadres.[12] The article described the claim as inflated but didn't say what the real percentage is. The princelings, who are said in colloquial Mandarin to be "born red," or protected, receive the best education available. They share a similar identity and a shared perspective on China's past, although their political interests aren't necessarily identical. "They are born aristocrats. But since their fathers may be enemies and belong to different factions, they seldom have political interaction," said Zhang Zuhua, a former Communist Youth League official who is now a political commentator. Looking around Renji's birthday party, I couldn't tell who might be a princeling. But I knew that the Princess of Tibet would easily rub elbows with such heirs to wealth and privilege.

AT ONE OF OUR MEETINGS, Renji handed me a promotional DVD and urged me to watch it. She said it would help me understand the legacy she bore as the Tenth Panchen Lama's daughter. The DVD contained images of several of Renji's trips into areas where ethnic Tibetans live and where she was received by crowds of thousands, and even tens of thousands, of faithful Buddhists who see in her a profound reflection of her beloved father's legacy and spirituality. The first time I watched the DVD, it struck me as a self-serving paean to ensure Renji's potentially fragile status as a "princess." Between clips of music and majestic scenes of the Tibetan Plateau, the female narrator spoke on the video in grandiloquent terms of Renji's life path, speaking as if she were Renji herself: "From my birth, society has endowed me with responsibility and a mission, which I consider both my own fate and the purpose of my life in the world." She spoke as if her absent parent were there. "Father, people transfer their longing for you to me, a child who has done nothing for them. When I give *khatas* to them, my heart is like a stormy sea. I am getting closing to you, father—you definitely hear that!" She described her return to China as ordained by fate. "Father, do you know, one day my mother told me that the nation's leaders wish for me to return home? That night, you appeared in my dream singing to me again. I saw tears of happiness in your eyes."[13]

Renji's secretary got in touch with me later and suggested that I should see more videos of her three trips to the Tibetan highlands. On a subsequent visit to her house, we sat before the television and watched video of a trip in 2002, when she spent forty-five days touring the Tibetan Autonomous Region and received tutoring in Shigatse, the city that surrounds the Tashilhunpo monastery. Four years later, she went to the Tibetan region in present-day Sichuan province, and in 2008 she traveled to her father's hometown in what is modern-day Qinghai province. Watching raw footage of the trips, one perceives the enormous longing of Tibetans to see in her a connection to her father. Scenes unfolded of elderly women throwing themselves on the ground. "They are kowtowing to me," she said. "It's touching. It's touching. You feel responsibility, for sure. A lot of old people say, 'Now I can die peacefully.'"

Chinese authorities grew nervous at the intense feelings of Tibetans gathered to catch sight of her. During Renji's 2006 trip to Sichuan province, authorities kept erecting roadblocks. Five days into the trip, it became clear that she wouldn't be able to proceed, so she returned to Beijing. She hoped that her trip would extend for a month or two, but too many people were pouring into villages and along roadsides to get a glimpse of the vehicle in which she traveled. At each settlement, Renji would get out and place a *khata*, the ceremonial scarf symbolizing purity and goodwill, around the neck of each pilgrim. Renji would do this so many times each day that her arms would swell up in pain. Some pilgrims would toss the *khatas* back on Renji's four-wheel-drive vehicle, covering it so deeply in white scarves that it looked as if it had been buried under snow.

In 2008, in the middle of winter, Renji traveled back to Wendu, her father's hometown, for celebrations of what would have been the late Panchen Lama's seventieth birthday. Temperatures in Qinghai province had plummeted, dropping to minus 7 degrees Fahrenheit. Frigid weather didn't stop a massive turnout among Tibetans eager to get a glimpse of her. When she arrived in Wendu, about five hundred motorcyclists were lining the road to greet her. Later, at the temple built in her father's honor, Tibetans blew long horns, and Renji walked under the three-tiered ceremonial yellow umbrella that is usually reserved only for the Dalai Lama or the Panchen Lama. Throngs of senior lamas wearing the crest-shaped high yellow hats of the Gelugpa school greeted her arrival. That short trip occurred only a month before the massive and unprecedented demonstrations among Tibetans that began in Lhasa in mid-March 2008. The unrest left the ruling party in crisis mode, and anyone who suggested that the protests reflected long-festering grievances among Tibetans could be accused of supporting the "Dalai Lama clique" and being a dangerous separatist. I was eager to get Renji's take on the upheaval—one of the most significant events in Tibet in modern times—but she was hesitant to talk about it. At our last meeting a month later, she broached the subject in general terms. She had just come back from a trip to Hong Kong and wore black pants and a purple blouse, the first time I'd seen her in non-Tibetan clothing.

"I love both races. I'm personally half Chinese and half Tibetan myself. So I'm not against either side," she said. "Why March 14 happened was because the majority of people have been emotionally suppressed. When things like this happen, it blows up. So it exploded." She called the subsequent violence and loss of life part of "a very unfortunate event," but said she preferred to look on the positive side—that politicians in Beijing realized that policies toward Tibet should be changed and that just shoveling money into the region won't satisfy festering unhappiness. "The Chinese government has been putting a lot of money in Tibet. That we have to admit. And the Chinese government does think that's the best way—that economic development is the best way for Tibetans—but for Tibetans religion is probably more impor-

tant than the money." She said she believed Beijing politicians were re-
alizing that they must relax their grip on Tibetan cultural and religious
expression. At another point, Renji said she didn't speak out at a key
moment because "it was not very convenient for me. There will be one
day in my life that I have to come up and say stuff, but the time is not
right. I'm a person who believes in timing."

In fact, she's rarely felt the time was right, and her reticence draws
exasperated comments from Tibetan intelligentsia inside and outside
of China. They see her as a sellout to the party and as someone with
little capability to bring change. When I mentioned her name to Lobsang Sangay, the Harvard Law School fellow and one of the exile
movement's brightest lights, he said that she would play "a marginal
role at best." Tsering Woeser, a prominent Tibetan blogger and commentator, also dismissed her as inconsequential on Tibet issues. During her decade in the United States, Renji met numerous times with
the Dalai Lama and says that he gave her great encouragement. "He
cares a great deal about me. . . . He wants me to be the bridge person,
like I want to as well. He thinks I could play a big role for the Tibetans.
He thinks I'm unique." Yet Renji has thrown her lot with the continued rule of the party in China, even if she, like her father, has never
formally become a Communist. Renji strives to attain a leadership
role, perhaps a top post in the National People's Congress as her father had.

In the end, like her father, she may be misperceived. In the final
decade of the Tenth Panchen Lama's life, he maneuvered through
party rule to achieve tangible progress for Tibetans. Even as some exiles loathed him for his cooperation with the party, and as activists at
home labeled him the "fat businessman" for business ventures associated with the Gang-Gyen trading company in Shigatse, he did something exiled Tibetans living outside their homeland have been unable
to do: He brought measurable change. "The Panchen Lama demanded, and in 1987 obtained, a law making Tibetan the official language of the Tibetan Autonomous Region and setting a timetable for
the introduction of Tibetan-medium education from primary school
to university."[14] He helped open a university in Lhasa, funded a school
for reincarnated lamas in Beijing, and began the nonprofit Tibet Development Fund that attracted foreign development aid to the plateau,

the first of its kind. Hard-liners in the party rolled back some of the progress after his death, even as the official notice of the Tenth Panchen Lama's passing hailed him as "a great patriot, noted states-man, a devoted friend of the Communist Party of China, and out-standing leader of Tibetan Buddhism."[15]

The Panchen Lama brought tangible progress while still mouthing party slogans and espousing loyalty to the party leadership.[16] With his achievements obscured by such public praise for the party, it is easy to forget the valor that the Tenth Panchen Lama summoned to submit his "poisoned arrow" critique of policies in Tibet to the highest levels of the party under Mao in 1962. He found that same courage in March 1987—after spending a total of fourteen years under house ar-rest or in prison—to repeat face-to-face to the party's standing com-mittee in the Tibet Autonomous Region why he felt the party had failed the region. Such boldness has been rare in modern China. Ac-cording to a professor at the Jawaharlal Nehru University in New Delhi, "No other leader of a national minority had dared to challenge Communist policies so fundamentally within the PRC since its found-ing in 1949 as the Panchen Lama did in 1962 and 1987."[17]

It is yet to be seen what kind of mettle his daughter has. Many po-tentially distasteful tasks may await her—like the day party cadres may insist that she validate their claimant as the Eleventh Panchen Lama. They would like for her to figuratively embrace the young man, only a few years younger than herself, and declare that he is indeed her father's reincarnation, thus quelling a flashpoint of anger among Tibetans. After all, the party may need to trot out the young man when the Dalai Lama passes away to give an appearance of credibility to its search for a compliant Dalai Lama "reincarnation" loyal to the motherland. In theory, if the government appointed–Panchen Lama did carry the soul and wisdom of past Panchen Lamas, he would have a lot to share with Renji, his own daughter in a past incarnation. The two have met twice on formal occasions but have had no chance to get acquainted. The first time was in Beijing's Great Hall of the People in the 1990s, when both Renji and the boy were not yet teenagers. They met again in Lhasa in 2002 on a more politically charged occa-sion. Renji was already nineteen years old and knew that much rested on whether she recognized her father's spirit in the teenager. Before the encounter, Chinese officials asked her to kowtow to the youth. She refused. Some thirty photographers stood by. She explained that her father never asked that she kowtow to him. "If I kowtowed to him every single time I [saw] him, I'd be on the floor all the time," she said, adding that her father gave her dispensation. She told this to the Chinese officials and asked them to tell the young fellow. "If he's my father's incarnation, he would understand."[18]

But the issue won't go away. Renji shifted hesitantly at my question about the young man, saying she was repeatedly asked what she felt in his presence. Some day, she'll share less formal and longer moments with him, she said, and only then will she provide an answer. Till then, Renji is content to bide her time, seeing potential for incremental change from within the one-party system. She'll await that change from her family villa in Beijing, while on the Tibetan Plateau many Tibetans worry that the course of events hurtles in the wrong direction.

chapter nine

Wolves at the Door

The Communist Party is like the parents to the Tibetan people and
are always considerate about what the children need. The party is
the real Buddha for the Tibetans.

   —Zhang Qingli, party secretary, Tibet Autonomous Region

AT SOME DEEP HOUR OF THE NIGHT, A HARSH AND PERSISTENT
barking awoke me. I lay in my sleeping bag on the floor of a Tibetan
mud-brick home, where I had spent the evening drinking yak butter
tea and hearing stories of nomadic life. In the mountain saddle
around the home, dozens of the family's yaks had folded into the
knee-high grass, bedding down in the frigid autumn air. My host family had two large mastiffs, and from the sound of the frantic barking
outside the house, one of the dogs had gotten loose from his tether
and was warning of an intruder, presumably a wild animal, that was
threatening the yaks. The barking kept on for what seemed like half
an hour, and as I nestled deeper into my sleeping bag, I wondered if
the mastiff would tangle directly with whatever predator might be out
there.

The dogs weren't purebred Tibetan mastiffs, but they seemed close
in size and in ferocious temperament. I'd seen similar dogs outside
nearly every nomadic compound. The mastiffs are one of the most ancient canine breeds. They bear shaggy coats so thick that they can remain outdoors all winter long, giving them an especially formidable
appearance. Nomads keep the dogs not so much for companionship as
for protection. The dogs tenaciously protect yaks and other livestock

185

from predators, particularly the wolves that still wander the Himalayas and central Asian steppes. In the last few years, newly rich Chinese have acquired the somewhat rare purebred Tibetan mastiffs to show off status. Not long ago, a rich Chinese woman shelled out more than $580,000 for an eighteen-month-old female Tibetan mastiff, the most ever paid for a dog. She bought it in Yushu, a city in southeast Qinghai province not far from where I lay, and named it Yangtze Number 2. "Gold has a price, but this Tibetan Mastiff doesn't," the new owner told Chinese media.[1]

Maybe it was my overactive imagination, but as I lay there, I calculated that the two guard dogs barking so wildly had sensed a wolf or two lurking nearby. At some point, the barking faded away, and I fell back to sleep.

Wolves have become a cultural touchstone for both Chinese and Tibetans—for very different reasons. Traditionally, Chinese see the dragon as their cultural icon, symbolizing auspicious good fortune and control over the elements. But a best-selling book published in 2004, *Wolf Totem*, allegorically derided Han Chinese for acting like tame sheep, suggesting that their agrarian civilization had fallen victim a century ago to nomadic Western cultures with wolf blood in their veins. The book suggested that Han Chinese would do better to emulate wolves, and it celebrated fearless Mongolian warriors and nomads who used the fierce wolf as a totemic figure. The book smashed publishing records, selling tens of millions of copies, second only to Mao's Little Red Book. The theme clearly touched a nerve. The Chinese have consistently demonstrated anxiety and sensitivity to perceived slights from the international community. An eloquent summons for the nation to invoke its fierce "inner wolf" held deep appeal. After all, Chinese pupils are inculcated with the history of the country's "Century of Humiliation," a period from the first Opium War (1839–1842) to 1949.

At its onset, the British East India Company could find only one product to offer Chinese traders in exchange for the silk and tea that consumers craved back home—opium from India. The ravages of opium addiction soon weakened the Chinese state, giving way to a succession of unequal treaties with foreign powers. China may have enjoyed a millennium of past glories that included such innovations as silk, paper, porcelain, the compass, gunpowder, and cast iron. But under the grip of opium, the Middle Kingdom quickly sank into helplessness. Even as China has grown strong and self-assured again, it is deeply rankled by past victimization and historic injury. It follows that, eager to resume great stature in the world, Chinese embraced the exhortations in *Wolf Totem* to emulate the aggressive attitude of the West and assume the posture of the marauding wolf.

For their part, Tibetans see in the wolf a symbol of their own helplessness. In modern Tibetan songs, the wolf represents rapacious Chinese preying on Tibetan culture, ending the age-old way of life of the nomadic population. Several contemporary songs cast Tibetans as sheep or deer that wolves hunt relentlessly. One Tibetan singer, Tsebe, is explicit in lyrics. "The wolf attacks the sheep in the dark of night, but don't be sad—day is coming. Winter has come, and the leaves have fallen, but don't be sad. Spring is coming," the singer intones.[2] For the vast number of Tibetan nomads who live in the high grasslands, such lyrics are about their present plight, in which the Chinese government herds them into ever larger towns and cities. The song provides hope of an imminent dawn.

A day earlier I had arrived in a nomadic grassland valley at an elevation of some twelve thousand feet. During a walk the next day, I found the mother of my Tibetan host swinging a ropelike device in her right hand, keeping her yak herd moving along a field. As I approached, I saw that it was a Tibetan sling. She would place a small rock in the pocket of the sling and give it a flick of the wrist; the rock would go firing off at a target, perhaps the broad side of a straying yak. She smiled at my amazement at her dexterity, and came over to show me the sling of woven sheep's wool and yak hair. She put it in my hand and urged me to give it a try. I resisted, fearing I would let the rock fly too soon and send it to an unwanted target, which would probably be her forehead rather than a yak's meaty flank.

Only days before, the extended family had finished the annual autumn return to their winter residence, packing up a black woolen tent that had served as their summer home higher in the mountains and returning to the valley with their scores of yaks. Like many simple nomadic homes, the house had electricity. A single bare fluorescent bulb hung down from a wire strung to the ceiling. In the center of the house was a metal yak-dung stove with three burners. An old television with a DVD player sat in one corner. One of her sons put on a DVD, and we watched a succession of Tibetan singers. The pastoral images were constant—scenic snow-capped mountains, flapping Tibetan prayer flags, nomadic singers walking through mist, and families tending to horses and yaks. I didn't understand the Tibetan lyrics, but my host explained some to me. She and her foreign-born husband had done a comparative study of modern Tibetan music and found that it shone a light on contemporary Tibetan thinking.

Tibetan singers express themselves boldly, sometimes eluding the strict censorship that prevents Tibetan expression in literature, in essays, and on the internet. Even as a number of singers were arrested and interrogated following the 2008 uprising, others continued to write songs and produce their music videos on Tibetan culture and education, protection of the environment, and, of course, romance. A surprising number of songs are political, extolling the Dalai Lama without directly stating his name, voicing a longing for his return. In one typical song—"When Are You Coming?"—the images showed Tibetans preparing for the arrival of a high lama, and the singer, Dandron Tserang, sang the following lyrics:

> It's not so far away,
> I want to go,
> But I can't get there.
> When are you coming?

To most Tibetans, the meaning is clear. The Dalai Lama is just over the Himalayas in India, close yet ever so distant. When lyrics refer to "elder brother" or the "snow lion," which is the fearless and celestial heraldic symbol of Tibet, the reference is clear. The mythical snow lion is commonly pictured with a turquoise mane, so songs about the animal also resonate with Tibetans. "When the snow lion returns," the singers Sonam Dongyal and Tashi intone, "the magnificence of [holy] Mount Kailash will be greater." As my friends had explained to me, the lyric paeans to the Dalai Lama often come from singers in outlying regions of Greater Tibet, where the Dalai Lama has historically wielded no power. In essence, the Chinese repression has increased and broadened reverence for the Dalai Lama as Tibet's undisputed leader. As one of my friends said, had most of the singers been born in the days of the largely independent Tibetan state led by the Dalai Lama in the early part of the twentieth century, they would have dwelled outside its borders. So as they advocate today for the Dalai Lama, it is something their forbearers would likely not have done.[3]

Many Tibetan folk songs touch on more secular matters, such as the lives of the nomads who have lived continuously on the Tibetan Plateau for some four thousand years. Nomadic ways, so bound to the natural environment, are close to the heart of Tibetan identity, reflecting the self-reliance and bravery needed to live at inhospitable altitudes in extreme weather conditions. The region where nomads dwell is generally too high for crop cultivation yet contains vast grasslands for foraging herds, ranging from alpine meadows to semiarid mountain scrub. One of the largest pastoral areas on Earth, the Plateau's ocean of grass extends roughly fifteen hundred miles from east to west and seven hundred fifty miles from north to south. More than a millennium ago, Tibetan leaders thrived by rallying nomadic forces into cavalry troops, giving way to strong nomadic tribal federations. The nomadic forces traveled swiftly on horseback for great distances, carving out an important place in Central Asian history. The nomads still cling to their migratory culture, often moving from dwellings at twelve thousand feet above sea level to higher areas of permafrost as high as sixteen thousand feet, where snowstorms in summer are common.[4]

Among Tibetans, the attachment to livestock, particularly the yak, is profound. The yak provides the milk, butter, cheese, meat, and abundant wool that are at the core of the resilient nomadic culture. Nomads dwell in matted yak-hair tents, burn dried yak dung to stay warm in a land where no firewood is available, sip yak butter tea throughout the day, and use yaks to transport their goods across the rangelands. Yak hides provide leather for daily use. Nomads move their herds regularly to prevent overgrazing of grasses and sedges, strapping their tents on the backs of stronger yaks. Yaks are so valuable Tibetans call them *nor*, or wealth, and the sacred yak dance attests to the spiritual importance the nomads place on the beasts. Indeed, it is hard to imagine Tibetan nomads even existing in the highlands without the rugged and majestic yaks. Some nomads also raise sheep, goats, and horses, species that graze on different grassland plants, buffering against overgrazing and forcing nomads to migrate with their herds to new pastures, not at random but based on precipitation and climatic factors.

Nomads have a keen appreciation of their environment, and in recent years it has earned them new sources of income. During a six-week window each year, the family with whom I stayed goes in search of medicinal caterpillar fungus, a species of rare parasitic fungus that grows and takes over the body of caterpillar larvae. Family members dig and root through the soil in springtime to find the fungus during its short season. The popularity of the fungus, which is said to enhance immunity, boost stamina, and increase sexual performance, has skyrocketed in the last two decades, promoted by Chinese sports trainers who credit it with record-breaking performances by Chinese athletes. It now can fetch up to $900 an ounce, near the price of gold.[5] The fungus, which pokes slightly out of the soil, is not easy to find, and the ability of nomads to harvest it underscores their affinity to the environment and its natural cycles.

The harsh weather that nomads have endured over the centuries is no match, however, for the political gale now buffeting the region, threatening to limit or end the nomadic way of life. Beijing blames nomadism for trapping Tibetans in endemic poverty and for speeding along the collapse from overgrazing of some of the plateau grasslands. Government policy calls for resettling—by force, if necessary—hundreds of thousands of Tibetan nomads into permanent camps, saying it is the only way to restore environmental degradation. When the policy is fully implemented, Beijing expects as much as 80 percent of Tibet's 2.25 million nomads to be resettled in what it calls "permanent housing." Along the roadways that now crisscross the Tibetan Plateau, one can see cookie-cutter rows of simple attached housing or duplexes that face the roads. They are resettlement camps, and they look like the government housing found on military bases or American Indian reservations.

In addition to putting an end to ancient ways of life, the policy is toppling a pillar of Tibetan identity. Beijing argues that the relocations into larger communities facilitate the provision of health care, safe drinking water, and education services to impoverished nomads, many of whom earn less than the equivalent of $500 a year, a fraction of per capita Chinese earnings. Nomads resettled into the camps are given annual stipends usually much greater than their previous income. By placing the nomads in compact communities, it is much more economical to provide social services.

The ostensible reason for the resettlements—grassland degradation—cannot be denied by anyone who travels along major roads in southern Qinghai province. I saw vast stretches of what appeared to be overgrazed grasslands that had turned into what the Chinese call "black soil," desert-like areas that barely sustain life. Mangy patches of exposed sand lie bare next to stubby tufts of grass and what appear to be dark lichen. In other areas, overgrazed fields are still green, but livestock have nibbled the grass down to an inch or so above the soil. Nomads removed from such land are environmental refugees. Economic reforms that deregulated herd size in the 1980s prompted some Tibetan nomads to expand their yak and sheep holdings. That trend, combined with privatization of rangelands and an increase in fencing, proved damaging to some grasslands. Other signs appeared that natural cycles had been disturbed, including an explosion in the population of wild pikas, a rabbit-like creature that burrows into the fragile soil. The burrows become homes for small birds and lizards, and turn up the soil in a way that creates more plant diversity. But some Chinese experts view the pikas only as pests that compete with livestock for forage, and they have promoted government campaigns to poison the creatures in the wild.

Whether nomad-led overgrazing or other factors have caused the collapse of up to a fifth of the Tibetan grasslands is the subject of debate. Tibet exile groups clamor for an independent scientific assessment of the problem, preferably carried out by foreign experts, which has never been done. Han authorities dismiss such demands out of hand, viewing the matter with political as well as environmental criteria and denigrating the nomadic population as unsophisticated and backward. Advocates say the nomadic lifestyle has survived for thousands of years because of a rich knowledge of survival in such a harsh environment. They note that managing multispecies grazing (yak, sheep, horses, and goats) requires frequent migration. They blame grassland degradation on what they call misguided Chinese economic policies over the last several decades rather than nomadic behavior.

An old Tibetan nomad's adage about wolves underscores indigenous wisdom about how to survive in the harsh environment. It says that herders should not attack the lair of a mother wolf and her cubs even if it is near their sheep and yak enclosures. If a mother wolf and her cubs are attacked, the mother will slaughter livestock in retaliation. But if left alone, the mother wolf is unlikely to kill sheep nearby lest it draw attention to her lair. The Himalayan wolves and Tibetan nomads have learned to live with one another, and the adage reflects indigenous wisdom not readily apparent at first glance.

In *Wolf Totem*, a wise Mongolian herder explains to his Han Chinese student that the nomadic lifestyle, rather than livestock herding in ranches that have fenced pastures, makes ecological sense:

> Every seasonal pasture has its separate function. The spring birthing pasture has good grass, but it's short. The livestock would die if a winter snowstorm covered the grass. We can't settle there. There's tall grass on the winter pastureland, but it wouldn't last long if the livestock grazed there through the first three seasons. The summer pasture has to be close to water, or the animals would die of thirst. But those are all in the mountains and the animals would freeze to death in the winter. We move to an autumn pasture for the grass seeds, but would there still be seeds left if the livestock stayed to graze in the spring and summer? Every pasture has many downsides and one advantage. The whole point of nomadic herding is to avoid the downsides and make good use of the advantage. If we settle in one spot, we'll face all the downsides, with no more advantage.[6]

The grasslands have also played host to a battle of wits between the Chinese government and the Dalai Lama over environmental issues. In early 2006, the Dalai Lama told Tibetans who gathered for a Buddhist festival in India that he was "ashamed" of photographs showing Tibetans dressed in traditional robes lined in, or with fringe hems of, the fur of wild lynx, leopard, and fox. "When you go back to your respective places, remember what I had said earlier and never use, sell, or buy wild

animals, their products or derivatives," the Dalai Lama said.[7] Word
spread back to Tibetan areas, particularly Qinghai, and within days Tibetans had set mounds of fur-trimmed clothing on fire. Chinese officials exploded in rage at the broad display of loyalty to the Dalai Lama.
To counter the antifur movement, two party leaders arrived at the
Qinghai provincial television network and mandated that Tibetan
broadcasters add fur trimming to their clothing. "The two of them
came to the television station and gave orders, saying, 'You've got to add
fur linings to your clothes. This is compulsory or else,'" one employee
told Radio Free Asia.[8] Despite the campaign, the antifur movement appears to have had results. I found Tibetans wearing only garments with
fake fur linings during several cold-weather visits to Tibetan areas.

Clearly, the political dimension of Chinese government policies
sometimes outweighs the environmental rationale. Nomads are mobile, and thereby ungovernable, and that is anathema to the ruling
party. By doing away with the nomadic way of life, authorities not only
dilute a distinctive form of Tibetan identity but also weaken any
prospect of Tibetan independence. As far back as in 1998, Qi Jingfa,
the then vice minister of agriculture, was quoted by Xinhua as stating
that it was the Chinese government's policy "to end the nomadic way
of life for all herdsmen by the end of the century."[9] That prediction
only partially came to pass. More recently, Zhang Qingli, the hard-
line Tibetan party chief, admitted that the resettling of Tibetan nomads was due to the need to counter the Dalai Lama's influence.[10]
Zhang also said it was essential for "continuing to carry out major development of west China."[11] Official policy now encourages Tibetan
herders to fence off pastures and switch from subsistence herding to
industrial livestock production, a capitalist progression that emulates
what happened in Western Europe hundreds of years ago. Some nomads are urged to give up their way of life completely and become
shopkeepers. Settlement camps also facilitate surveillance and control
of the nomads, most of whom hold little allegiance to China. Through
the policies, non-Tibetan officials in distant offices can regulate herd
sizes, credit, taxes, land allocation, and even sources of drinking water
for livestock.

For older Tibetans, the resettlement policies are just the latest efforts
at the social engineering that has marked their lives. One morning, my

host brought over a sixty-three-year-old neighbor with a deeply bronzed face and a head still full of mostly black hair. The neighbor, who I'll call Laja, wore shin-high leather work boots, trousers, and an open-neck blue work shirt under a light jacket. We settled down with some tea, and he told me of his early memories, beginning with the disastrous 1958–1960 period known as the Great Leap Forward, when Mao set a target of surpassing Great Britain economically within fifteen years. Seeking to take the nation from a peasant economy to heavy industrialization, Mao pulled hundreds of millions of farmers from the fields to build dams, work on huge construction, and tend to "backyard furnaces," where everything from kitchen knives to bicycles were tossed in to make steel for heavy industry. Zealous followers used coercion on ordinary Chinese under the slogan "achieve more, faster, better."

The disruption of normal agriculture led to "the worst manmade famine ever seen on earth."[12] Western scholars say more than thirty million Chinese died from forced labor and hunger during those years. Laja recalled when soldiers first arrived in his valley: "We abandoned our yaks and just ran away. The Chinese said, 'Don't run!' But some ran away anyway, and the Chinese would shoot them." Laja was barely a teenager when police finally snared his family in the mountains and forced them to a camp, where they were taught songs extolling Mao and made to undergo military-style training. But as the Great Leap Forward wore on, food grew scarce. "We were so hungry we thought we were going to die. We ate grass and mushrooms. All they gave us was a little *tsampa* every day. . . . 1960 was the worst year. That's when the most people died. People couldn't dig graves because they were so weak. So hands and feet of the dead would still be sticking out of the ground." A year or so before my visit, work crews building a road near Banma, a town in the Golok Tibetan Autonomous Prefecture, turned up numerous human skulls, presumably victims of that period, he added.

Then came the decade-long Great Proletarian Cultural Revolution, bringing cataclysmic upheaval to all parts of China. For Tibetans, it meant an end to any public expressions of religion. The ban was so sweeping that Laja and other nomads began to question their own centuries-old beliefs. "Anything related to Buddhism was stopped. No monks were allowed, and we weren't permitted to pray," Laja told me, adding that party cadres haranguing against religion found converts to atheism. Many rural Tibetans replaced their images of Buddha with photos of Mao in their shrines at home. "Sometimes I thought it was true: Religion is a trick. I believed it a bit. They tortured the monks and told us religion is political." Only after the Cultural Revolution ended did older Tibetans begin to teach traditions and religion to youngsters again. "If there had been no old people, maybe we would have changed forever."

Up to then, Laja had escaped government pressure to reduce his small yak herd and take one of the simple homes in a resettlement camp nearby. He said he sees that local grasslands are not as productive as they once were, but he saw ulterior motives behind the government resettlement campaign. "The government is doing this because it wants the land. We won't have any land any more," he said, reflecting a deep cynicism toward government policies that I would hear repeatedly.

At a nearby home made of simple mud-brick walls and wooden beam ceiling, another nomad, a wiry thirty-year-old with a slight moustache, Denpa, explained how his family took up the offer to move to a settlement—only to cheat the government and move back to their simple original mountain dwelling. The offer had been too good to pass up. The two-room settlement home was basically free, and local officials offered an annual stipend of about $880. In exchange, the families had to give up yak raising. Denpa said he and his family grew increasingly miserable in the settlement. While the stipend seemed generous at first, they soon realized that without yaks they even had to buy yak dung for the hearth. "You have to pay for a lot of things. There are many people who are unhappy. They think that living there without their yaks is a hard life," the nomad said. So when another family offered to buy his settlement house for the equivalent of about $3,000, Denpa agreed. No one told the local officials, who believed that Denpa's family was still living there. Luckily, Denpa's family didn't give up its yaks when it moved to the settlement. Instead, an aunt had taken the herd higher into the mountains and kept them out of sight. So when the family moved back into their original dwelling, the yak herd was largely intact. Denpa worried that he would be punished if caught. But he said the resettlement was deeply unpopular. "Tibetans talk to each other and say it's because they [government officials] want to stop Tibetan nomad life. They want all Tibetans to live in the city, and for there to be no more yaks. The Tibetan way of life wouldn't exist without our yaks."

The resettlement policies have already affected significantly more than 1 million of the 2.25 million Tibetan nomads. In late 2009, the Xinhua News Agency said the government had spent nearly $2 billion to help build 226,302 "affordable houses for farmers and herdsmen" in the Tibet Autonomous Region, and that 1.2 million Tibetans had benefited from the government-subsidized "comfortable housing program" since it began in 2006.[13] The resettlements are also affecting Tibetan nomads in other regions. A state news agency report on nomads in Sichuan province said 470,000 Tibetans would "settle down in permanent brick houses" over a four-year period. Like all such state news reports, it did not say if the Tibetan families faced compulsory resettlement. At least 73,000 nomads in Gansu province were targeted for settlements during the latter part of the decade, and in Qinghai some 100,000 nomads were to be resettled in the same period. "To move the herdsmen from pasture lands they have inhabited for generations is not easy," the head of a Tibetan community in Qinghai's Darlag County told Xinhua. "But due to erosion and desertification, more and more people are realizing the benefits of resettling. . . . The government has done a lot to persuade those who are truly reluctant to move."[14]

Even as authorities say "persuasion" is sufficient to get the nomads to give up their traditional way of life, international human rights groups say coercion and involuntary compulsion are the methods more commonly used. They also contend the rationale of protecting the environment obscures the government's own role in harvesting natural resources in Tibet, efforts that leave the land scarred. The Dalai Lama's government-in-exile alleges that forest cover in Tibet has diminished sharply under Chinese administration, falling from 25.2 million hectares in 1959 to 13.5 million hectares in 1985.[15] Other factors appear to weigh heavily on Beijing, particularly political control and the desire to bring a dispersed population of nomads, who have a centuries-old history of banding together in rebellion when they feel threatened, into tighter communities under better surveillance. The

Tibet Autonomous Region's rural population of 2.1 million people comprises thousands of roving nomad groups and hundreds of tiny rural communities. According to the 2000 census, Tibet is dotted with 890 townships, each with an average population of 2,368 people. Another 7,577 villages have an average population of 278 people. The party's premier publication on Tibet carried an article that noted that "certain economists remark that 'it is indeed a waste to construct a village with some only 1,000 or 2,000 people.'"[16]

The nomadic life of rural Tibetans is under threat, but the noose is also tight on well-educated Tibetans in the cities. I got a taste of that when I visited the capital of Qinghai province, Xining, a city forgotten amid the plethora of booming Chinese metropolises. I hadn't given much thought to Xining during my years covering China, knowing it as near an inland sea where there was once an outbreak of avian influenza. Xining, which has several million inhabitants, is a blend of cultures, with majority Han Chinese living side by side with Hui Muslims and Tibetans. In the end, I discovered some magic to Xining during several trips, and the more I visited, the more I would hear that a vibrant Tibetan intelligentsia was clustered around the city.

On my most recent trip, I stayed at a youth hostel popular among international backpackers and began talking to a young Tibetan employee there who volunteered that her parents were writers and that her mother had once been a prominent singer. She arranged for me to visit her mother's restaurant later in the day. I didn't even know the mother's name before arriving but jotted it down during a long evening discussing Tibetan music, blogs, and culture. The mother mentioned to me that she'd been imprisoned for twenty-one days shortly after Tibetan unrest broke out in 2008, but I didn't press for details. When I got back to the hostel, I searched online for further background, typing in her name: Jamyang Kyi. To my astonishment, website after website was listed, including a series of worldwide appeals for her freedom during her jailing. Little had I known that Jamyang Kyi was a very popular Tibetan singer and writer on social and women's issues, and for a brief period in 2006 a visiting scholar at Columbia University in New York City.

I wasn't able to go back and see her for another week or so, but the dots were already coming together, and they cast new light on how

China's state security apparatus worked to contain information and quell dissent among Tibetans. Sometime after the bloody rioting erupted in Lhasa on March 14, 2008, Jamyang Kyi picked up her mobile phone and sent off a short text message to fellow Tibetans around the country. She simply passed on a report that several Tibetans had been killed in unrest in surrounding Qinghai province. Among the recipients of the text was Tsering Woeser, the Tibetan blogger in the capital whose website served as a clearinghouse of information on what was really happening in the countryside. Woeser, as she is known, was a contact of mine in Beijing. She received the message and immediately called the singer to urge her to desist from further messages because state security was monitoring her closely. Jamyang Kyi worried a bit, but nothing happened for more than two weeks.

Then on April 1, plainclothes officers in Xining arrived at her workplace and took her away, first to the Public Security Office, then after a few days to an undisclosed location. During her captivity, she was bound to a chair with rope and interrogated at length. Over the twenty-one days, she was given food only on fourteen of them, she said, and lost a dozen pounds. Under intense pressure to betray her friends during her detention, she later wrote, she contemplated suicide: "One day in the middle of an interrogation, I thought instead of enduring this, it would be better to be killed by a single bullet. My family and relatives would grieve but as for me, I would have to suffer the pain only once. One day when I was in the washroom, out of nowhere, I found myself thinking about the means or methods of taking my own life."[17]

It was then that she remembered the small knife she usually kept in her purse because of bad feelings between Tibetans and Han.

> Ever since the Chinese-Tibetan conflict had flared up, and as result of the government's deliberate propaganda, the Chinese would stare at Tibetans with hatred, whether it be in a bus, the market place or on any public road. Once, when I was walking down the road with my daughter . . . a Chinese kid of about six or seven years old came yelling in front of my daughter and stood blocking her way. This kind of Chinese attitude wasn't an isolated incident that we experienced but rather the common experience of other Tibetans, too.[18]

Luckily, Jamyang Kyi said she couldn't get her hands on the knife. Otherwise, "I would surely have cut the veins of my wrist."[19]

While she languished in detention, security personnel searched her home and confiscated her computer. The arrest kicked up publicity abroad, and Amnesty International as well as other groups immediately issued urgent calls for her release. Several U.S. senators also issued a formal query about her case, describing it as "a textbook example of China's use of detention to intimidate peaceful activists."[20]

When I visited Jamyang Kyi again, she was distraught. She tugged at one of the two necklaces around her neck and looked near tears. Her wavy hair was pulled back in a bun. She wore a crimson woolen sweater that contrasted sharply with the bright turquoise pendant hanging from her neck. As we sat in a private room of her restaurant, I gazed at her and could see why she'd become so popular as a performer. Her eyes were large and expressive, and she had a strong presence. We talked about the restrictions authorities had placed on her after her brief incarceration. She was barred from leaving Xining, she said, and all her telephone and internet communications were monitored. She was not allowed to use the internet at state-owned Qinghai Television, where she has been a writer, news editor, and producer for Tibetan-language programming for some two decades. While in custody, police asked her for all her internet passwords, which she said she provided. "They told me, 'You not only sent the text message, you also looked on forbidden websites and are in contact with Tibetans overseas who support the Dalai clique,'" she said.[21]

A few months before our conversation, she finished writing a hundred-page short book describing her detention and posted it online. She shook her head as we spoke, confessing that making the decision to air her feelings about her arrest was excruciating. "I knew when I wrote the book that it would cause me trouble. I don't know why I did it. It's just that the situation sometimes makes me so angry," she said, looking ineffably sad. She said that before police let her return home, one officer said that her life held the value of a wadded piece of paper that could be cast away. He also issued a warning: "You must love your country." He didn't need to specify that he meant China, not Tibet.[22]

About then, her six-year-old daughter poked her head in the room and whispered to her mother in Tibetan. I sensed the agony Jamyang

Kyi felt at risking prison again while bearing the responsibility for such a young daughter. I thought, fleetingly, of my own two daughters. After her release, police had made regular visits to her restaurant, asking about the identities of images of Buddhist scholars on the walls. Twice, they took down and confiscated photos of Gendun Chopel, an incarnate lama who was one of the leading intellectuals and campaigners for the modernization of Tibet in the first half of the last century. The police also wanted names and profiles of all her employees. We spoke a bit about her older daughter, who was just hitting twenty and wore clothing that seemed more hip-urban than Tibetan, seemingly loosening the ties to her ethnic kin. Jamyang Kyi said she and her Tibetan husband strongly feel the need to instill in fellow Tibetans pride in their own culture. "There are so many Tibetans who already have become Chinese. They speak Chinese. They live in Chinese-style homes," she said.[23]

Before I left, Jamyang Kyi looked at me and said, "We Tibetans are very weak. We cannot fight with the Chinese."[24] Yet my next stop gave me a sense of why Chinese authorities often see Tibetans as far from weak. They may not have weapons, but they have shown skill at using nonviolence as a tool, rallying fortitude tempered by Buddhism and aware that global attention can shed light on their plight. Indeed, over the past decade or so, in one high mountain valley that has been a magnet for followers of Tibetan Buddhism, unarmed Tibetan monks and nuns had the strength to stare down army troops. Religion gave them the courage for such a tactic. Religious sentiment is growing in China, from Buddhism to underground Christian churches. For party leaders, religion isn't bringing peace of mind. It's giving them a holy headache.

chapter ten

Getting Religion

People from China's religious circles often speak of the "golden period" in referring to the religious freedom they fully enjoy today under the protection of the Constitution and relevant laws.

—Ye Xiaowen, head of State Administration of Religious Affairs

THE SERTHAR BUDDHIST ACADEMY SITS IN A TREELESS HIGH-mountain valley in an area of Sichuan province in China's southwest that is predominantly ethnic Tibetan. It is outside the area that China formally considers Tibet but inside the greater region that many Tibetans describe as their natural homeland. The academy began a few decades ago as a remote hermitage with barely a hundred monks practicing meditation in the harsh, barren Larung Valley. Despite the academy's isolation—the nearest city was five hundred miles away over dirt roads—it began to attract hundreds, then thousands of monks and nuns drawn by the fame and brilliance of its founder, revered as a "living Buddha."

When I first caught sight of the settlement clinging to the steep hillsides near the academy, I couldn't help but think of the Gold Rush days of the Klondike. Thousands of simple rustic cabins climbed the slopes as far as the eye could see. The cabins were stained blood red—nearly the same color as the robes of the monks and nuns who dwell in them—and sit one practically atop another. The community was abuzz with noise and movement, a Buddhist boomtown akin to Deadwood or Dawson City, only instead of the clatter of dice and revelry from saloons, one heard the rhythmic chanting of Buddhist monks and the helter-skelter banging from new construction. Monks and nuns walked about along stone and mud pathways and on stairs that led up and down the mountainsides. Some tended to domestic chores, like carrying plastic jerry cans of water to their cabins or toting small logs for building projects. Others walked to or from classes.

I sat down and observed from a perch halfway up a hillside. Power saws and chainsaws droned from construction activity. I heard hammering, the clank of metal against metal, and a few horns beeping. Trucks and tractors inched up the lone road on the other side of the valley. In front of me, two cranes swiveled atop a work site, and several monks appeared to be supervising the construction there. A few minutes later, lower in the valley, several thousand nuns flooded out of wooden buildings at the end of classes. Activity unfolded ceaselessly before my eyes. I had come with a Tibetan companion whose sister was a nun at Serthar. In a recent rainstorm, her hillside cabin had washed away, and two workmen used planes and rip-tooth saws to make planks out of logs to build her new one-room cabin. It was supported by flimsy wooden pillars. After watching for a while, my companion and I decide to venture along the labyrinth of trails and explore the community.

As we walked around, we grew briefly lost, encountering a nun who addressed us in English. I voiced surprise at her language ability, and she invited us to her cabin to converse further. A mattress was on the floor under a window with a panoramic mountain view, and a small personal Buddhist shrine graced a wall. The thirty-three-year-old nun said she was from Taiwan and had spent two years in Serthar, studying alongside more than a thousand other Chinese-speaking monks and nuns at the center. The questions began to pile into my head. I'd never been to a Tibetan Buddhist center with so many ethnic Han Chinese. I wondered what was different here. While clearly some of the Chinese were from Taiwan, Singapore, and Malaysia, many were from the Chinese mainland.

I also began to wonder why I hadn't heard of any unrest at Serthar during the 2008 uprisings. Monasteries with far smaller concentrations of Tibetan monks had erupted in disturbances. About a hundred twenty miles to the east of Serthar, the Kirti Monastery in Aba was a hotbed of protest, with reports of numerous arson attacks and monks killed by police.[1] Nearly a year after the unrest, a monk reportedly walked out of one monastery in Aba while holding a photo of the Dalai Lama and then set himself on fire in a rare self-immolation by a Buddhist monk. Authorities put out the fire, and he survived badly burned.[2] Monasteries all across Sichuan province had experienced high tension, and many remained under military lockdown. A year and a half after the unrest, Beijing still kept Aba off-limits to foreigners, and I deemed it too risky to try to get through police checkpoints along the roads leading there.

Like all nuns at Serthar, the Taiwanese woman kept her hair cropped closely to her scalp. She wore wire-rimmed glasses and had an earnest demeanor, giving thought to each answer amid my torrent of questions. She told me she was a geologist by training but had gotten bored with her career and embarked on a long journey to Mongolia, Southeast Asia, and India, exploring her Buddhist heritage. At Bodhgaya, the site where the Lord Buddha is said to have attained enlightenment, in the north Indian state of Bihar, the Dalai Lama was offering a teaching, which she attended but found impractical for a novitiate. She wanted hands-on meditation training. So she and two Singaporeans traveled to Dharamsala and enrolled in a meditation intensive that convinced her to become a nun. Through the intervention of a teacher, she traveled to Serthar in April 2007, settling down.

She had heard little of the outside world because internet usage was discouraged as a distraction. But events of the region and country at large intruded on contemplation. Anxiety mounted during the period of the Tibetan unrest. Police sealed off the Buddhist settlement and prohibited people from entering and leaving. Telephone calls were blocked. "One afternoon, there were helicopters. Everybody was afraid. You could feel the tension. We heard the army had entered [the town of] Serthar and a few people were killed." Tension also mounted during the period around the 2008 Summer Olympic Games, she said, and the community was again sealed off and international telephone calls blocked.[3]

I would learn later that the Serthar Buddhist Academy and the surrounding community had endured intense pressure from authorities on an erratic but long-term basis. In some ways, its situation was little different from that of underground house churches, Muslim temples, and other religious institutions in China, where a revival of faith is creating a sensitive challenge to a party founded on atheism. Religion is largely antithetical to the interests of the party and remains a shoal around which the party ship must chart a careful course. Yet many Chinese are looking for a moral framework to cling to after years of willy-nilly capitalist growth that have taken a huge toll in environmental pollution and corruption.

As Communist ideology fades, some Chinese feel adrift. When they find religion, it can endow them with concepts at odds with one-party rule and give them strong social networks that allow them to resist coercion. Religious groups, with their tight-knit and effective systems of organization, can carry out some of the same functions as political parties. Therefore, they test citizen loyalty.[4] So party officials have dealt with pan-religious issues with a mixture of accommodation and repression. They vet religious leaders, control the content of religious services, keep a tight rein on money raised by the faithful, and bar most foreign pastors, priests, imams, and lamas. In the case of Chinese Catholics, the party bars them from recognizing the primacy of the pope as the ultimate authority in Catholic matters. The party goes further on Tibetan Buddhism, demonizing the Dalai Lama.

In some areas of China, faith has deep roots, and believers have latitude to practice. In others, the fear that security agents may show up and toss people in jail is palpable. The panorama of religion is still evolving. My own experience was that many Chinese are grateful for rapidly improving standards of living, and this has fed a heartfelt patriotism, and in some cases an ardent nationalism. But it coincides with a spiritual hunger among some who feel cast adrift as the nation races to wealth, casting aside other social values, including the equality once vaunted under Mao. Religious activity is expanding and is allowed to flourish where believers present no challenge to the ruling order under current tightly controlled conditions.

Where matters grow more complicated is when religion mixes with ethnic identity. Both Tibetan Buddhists and Uighur Muslims see their respective religions as a core of their identity. The party is deeply wary of both ethnicities, despite its proclamations of ethnic harmony and unity, and it keeps a lid on their religious practices. Members of both groups say the restrictions symbolize their status as second-class citizens. While the state forces Tibetan monks to take repeated "patriotic education" classes and puts up closed-circuit cameras in Tibetan monasteries, ethnic Han who are Buddhists enjoy relative freedom of religious practice. And Uighur Muslims also face greater strictures than the largest Muslim minority group, the Hui, who number some 8.6 million in China. The Hui are deeply Sinicized, having no distinct language and largely speaking Chinese dialects. Of mixed ethnicity, incorporating Central Asian, Persian, Mongol, and Han roots, they look a lot like Han Chinese and have adopted much of Han culture.

If ethnicity adds a complication to the religious panorama in China, so does the steady trickle of well-educated Han who seek religion. I met several lawyers and professors in Beijing who had turned to Christianity, citing its intellectual appeal, disillusioned by dim prospects for political reform following the June 4, 1989, crackdown on pro-democracy activists. Some Chinese are also seeking out Tibetan Buddhist masters.[5] One *Washington Post* report suggested that a few Tibetan lamas surreptitiously have gathered significant followings in prosperous cities of eastern China, where Han predominate. It quoted one Tibetan monk from Sichuan province saying he had ten thousand followers in various cities, mostly in Beijing, Wuxi in Jiangsu province, and in Shandong province.[6] That made me more curious about the thousand or so Han Chinese monks and nuns present in Serthar. If any problems were to erupt at the academy, and ethnic Han monks were to side with Tibetans, authorities would not be able to simply blame Tibetans as a troublesome minority under the sway of the Dalai Lama and prone to foreign influence. They would have to explain why well-off Han Buddhists from urban areas would find a remote Tibetan Buddhist sanctuary appealing.

In the afternoon, I observed the Taiwanese nun take a class in how to use Photoshop. A laywoman led the class, and a dozen or so Mandarin-speaking Han nuns listened intently. From their accents, I could distinguish that they were from all over the eastern part of China. The Taiwanese nun later said she is often surprised by how many of her fellow Chinese-speaking nuns have PhDs and advanced degrees. She said interest is surging among Chinese, and two Mandarin-speaking lamas at the academy regularly tour large cities in eastern China. "If the government doesn't control this, it will become bigger and bigger," she predicted, adding that some Chinese feel empty despite China's rising levels of prosperity. "Normal people have awareness. They begin to start asking: What is my purpose? What is the aim of my life? Buddhism is there."[7]

The magnetic pull from Serthar began with its charismatic leader, Jigme Phuntsok, who set up the academy in 1980. The lama was said to be the reincarnation of a teacher of a former Dalai Lama and had spent much of the previous two decades in remote mountains, engaged in meditation, teaching small numbers of students, and eluding capture during the decade-long calamity of the Cultural Revolution. After he arrived in a deserted valley near Serthar to set up the academy, fulfilling a prophecy of an earlier *rinpoche* in his lineage, word of his teachings spread, and the number of students spiraled upward. The academy boasted no association with any of the Tibetan sects, teaching doctrines from all the major schools and opening its doors to monks, nuns, scholars, and laypeople. In 1987, the lama and hundreds of his disciples went on pilgrimage to Wutaishan, the holiest of China's four holy Buddhist mountains. Set in Shanxi province near Beijing, amid mountains, ridges, and ravines, Wutaishan is believed to be the earthly abode of the Bodhisattva of Wisdom, Manjushri, and for more than a millennium it had drawn Chinese, Tibetan, Mongol, and Manchu pilgrims alike. During the pilgrimage, Jigme Phuntsok met the Tenth Panchen Lama, who gave his blessing to the Serthar Buddhist Academy, an imprimatur that would draw even more students.

Several trips abroad, first in 1990 to India, where Jigme Phuntsok met the Dalai Lama, and again in 1993, when he offered teachings across Southeast Asia, India, Japan, France, and North America, gave his remote mountain academy an international profile. Displeased party cadres banned him from traveling abroad, citing his meeting with the Dalai Lama. But it was too late. Adherents flocked to Serthar, and financial offerings poured in from overseas. By 1998, the valley surrounding the academy held the huts and cabins of some eight thousand monks and nuns. The lama had built the first major new monastic center from the ground up in modern Tibetan history.

Incensed Chinese authorities ordered him to remove all but a hundred fifty monks from the site, but he refused, saying "forcefully expelling them would be akin to trampling upon the laws guaranteeing religious freedom."[8] A series of visits by senior cadres from Sichuan's United Work Front department and the central government's Religious Affairs Bureau increased the to-and-fro about the academy's dramatic growth. Officials backtracked a bit, saying they would permit a thousand monks and four hundred nuns at the site. But the cadres told the lama they would oversee all religious activities of the institute, appoint its abbot, vet all teachings, implement "patriotic education," and ensure that no ethnic Chinese would come to study at the institute. Tensions came to a head in May and June 2001, when police expelled thousands of nuns from the site after making them sign a document denouncing the Dalai Lama. When demolition activity stopped, at least 1,875 dwellings had been razed. It marked the largest scale religious demolition since the Cultural Revolution ended in 1976. The justification was an "evil cult" law passed in 2000 to crush any group the party's rulers perceived as a major threat.

The demolition, at most, was a temporary measure. While thousands of monks and nuns were forced to leave Serthar in 2001, many climbed over the mountains and returned to the academy later. The population has swollen now to an even higher number. And signs of permanence are emerging. In the center of the valley, I spotted offices of China Mobile and China Unicom, as well as a number of dry goods stores and kiosks selling religious items, books, and perishables. Several years ago, Chinese authorities built a brick fence around the sprawling valley of log homes in an effort to contain growth, declaring that not a single home was to be built outside the fence. The result was that the cabins in the settlement were ever more densely built. Central sanctuaries and multistory teaching halls were growing taller, and new building was constant. Many new residents are ethnic Han.

One of them is the nun whose cabin I was in. She told me to call her Yipeng. We chatted for a bit, and then she suggested I follow her to a special building for Chinese-speaking nuns, where we could have lunch. As we walked, she grew nervous, urging caution lest we be spotted. We climbed to the fourth story of a building that has a large glass-enclosed study hall. Even the roof is glass—it seemed like an oversize greenhouse. The flooring was indoor-outdoor carpeting, and low tables and cushions were placed against each wall. Shades covered some windows. The nun discreetly signaled to a large pink building

nearby. That was the base of the team of Han Chinese security personnel assigned to ensure that no unrest would brew against the state,
she said. The government security agents dressed in civilian clothes
and rushed anywhere there might be trouble, prepared to smother any
religious or ethnic grievances that might spill out of the valley and
spark a larger uprising in Tibetan areas. I peered at the multistory
building but couldn't see through the windows. Some of the religious
personnel are also presumed to be informants for the government.

As I conversed with more monks and nuns, details emerged over
how the community—perhaps the largest concentration of Tibetan
Buddhist clergy anywhere in China—avoided major unrest while disturbances engulfed other Tibetan regions. One nun said senior lamas
in Serthar swung into action to avert demonstrations once they received word of protests elsewhere. "The high lamas told all the monks
and nuns they could not have an uprising. They were told that the
academy would be burned down and all lamas thrown in jail. If it
burned down, it would never open again," a nun told me. The senior
abbot began negotiations to keep soldiers outside Serthar's imposing
central gate, with its long file of *chortens*, or small pagodas, and fluttering prayer flags. Some three hundred troops amassed at the gate,
blocking vehicles from entering. Quietly, lamas told angry monks that
if they wanted to speak their minds, they should temporarily leave the
community and do so in the town of Serthar, about twelve miles away.
A few hundred monks did that, and many were arrested.

It wasn't till I reached a young monk whom I will call Dawa that I
learned a more complete story. Dawa, who is in his mid-twenties,
wore rakish wispy sideburns that jutted down his cheeks, pointing to
his beakish nose. We began to converse while in a public minivan that
is the only way to get around the countryside in that region of northern Sichuan. The autumn chill had turned the leaves of white poplars
in lower valleys a brilliant yellow. We were winding our way along a
rushing river through deeply carved ravines and valleys. The driver
and his assistant were both native Sichuanese, and as usual in that
part of China, the Tibetan and the Han Chinese only exchanged perfunctory greetings. We came through several security checkpoints,
and at each one a policeman would peer in the vehicle. Upon seeing a
Tibetan monk, he'd order us to produce IDs, details of which he'd

note on a clipboard. Without fail, Dawa's robes seemed to set off alarm bells.

It was at one of these checkpoints that Dawa first commented to my companion about the treatment he had received by police when he had briefly left the Serthar settlement during the 2008 troubles to attend to personal business in the town. He was with other monks in a minivan when security agents stopped the vehicle at gunpoint. The police made a point of putting clips in their automatic weapons. One opened the sliding side door and pulled the monks out one at a time, while another aimed a gun at each exiting face, he said. Some of the monks spoke Chinese and protested the poor treatment, inflaming tensions. While such smaller indignities were taking place, a larger confrontation was brewing between the Buddhist institution's leaders and local party and military officials, he said. Local leaders said the soldiers amassed at the gates had announced that they would enter the community and hoist China's red national flag over the entire settlement. "The *rinpoche* told the Chinese that 90 percent of the monks would kill themselves if the soldiers entered and raised the Chinese flag," Dawa said. Even as the abbot sought to forestall a Chinese military incursion, he warned the holy men and women to hold passions in check. "Every day, he tells monks and nuns, 'Don't do bad things. You are monks and nuns. Practice compassion, and be patient. Don't get angry.'"[9]

On hearing this, I reflected on the words of a nun I'd spoken with hours earlier, who gave her name as Garmo. She made a similar remark about religious people at Serthar prepared to die for their beliefs. I'd brushed it off at the time. But I now sensed that Serthar had stayed out of the headlines in 2008 by a whisker. A calamity could well have unfolded, especially if unarmed monks and nuns had begun to take their own lives en masse over a military occupation. Other monks told me such a threat of mass suicide was not idle. Traditionally, Buddhism considers life precious and shuns suicide. Buddhists believe a person who commits suicide is usually depressed and sunk in negativity likely to throw him or her into a lower rebirth, simply postponing suffering for another life and putting off eventual enlightenment. Suicide, however, can also be a political act, and in recent times Buddhist monks have accepted it as such. In March 2008, a

Buddhist monk at the Kirti Monastery in Aba killed himself, leaving behind a note that said in part, "I do not want to live under the Chinese oppression even for a minute, leave aside living for a day."[10]

In reporting on that suicide and one of another monk, the pro-exile news service *Phayul.com* said, "The cases of suicides point to an indication of Tibetan monks being pushed to the extreme limits of endurance and helplessness in the face of oppression and repression by the Chinese authorities in Tibet." An exile rights group tallied seventeen cases of monk and nun suicides and two cases of attempted suicide in a little more than a year following the 2008 unrest, saying that suicide was on the rise in Tibet's monastic community. "The monks and nuns are left with no option but to embrace death since the requisites laid down by the Chinese authority are beyond sanity," the report said. The report cited three principle causes for the suicides. One is the psychological trauma during "patriotic education" in which party cadres insist on the party's oversight of Tibetan Buddhism. The other two factors are the heavy crackdown on monasteries and the government campaign forcing monks to commit what they universally consider blasphemy by denouncing the Dalai Lama.[11]

A monk or nun who refuses to denounce the Dalai Lama can face legal charges of "inciting separatism," which carries a minimum prison term of five years but is frequently much longer. At any given moment, hundreds of the 120,000 monks and nuns in China languish in prison for political crimes. A database kept by a U.S. Congress–sponsored commission tallied 445 monks and nuns in prison on political charges as of early autumn 2009.[12] The database indicates that 1,814 monks and nuns have served, or continue to serve, prison terms for political crimes in the past two decades. Under mandatory "political reeducation" classes at monasteries, monks must affirm that Tibet is an inalienable part of China and in many cases denounce the Dalai Lama in writing or place their thumbprints on a printed denunciation of him. Routine discriminatory treatment against monks, while rising and falling from year to year, includes barring free movement, subjecting them to frequent arbitrary searches and police checks, and making it difficult to obtain a passport. Unlike ordinary Chinese citizens, monks in the Tibet Autonomous Region must seek permission from county-level religious affairs officials to travel within the region to study or teach. Any denial of freedom of movement is tantamount to religious repression, since Tibetan Buddhist monks must visit different monasteries for specialized training by experts in different theological traditions.

History offers many examples of why China's leaders worry about religion. It isn't just the periodic appearance of apocalyptic religious sects like Lightning from the East and the Three Grades of Servants, quasi-Christian groups that have arisen in recent decades. Political rebellion in China has often emerged from religious roots, and the bloodiest example is the Taiping Rebellion in the mid-nineteenth century, when a charismatic Christian convert claiming to be the younger brother of Jesus led an uprising against the corrupt Manchu-led Qing Dynasty, which was weakened by its loss in the First Opium War. The rebellion and an accompanying famine took an astonishing twenty million or so lives before soldiers put it down.

Much more recently, the dramatic rise in the late 1990s of Falun Gong, an exercise and meditation group, stunned senior leaders of the party. They responded with unforgiving force. One morning in April 1999, after a nationwide ban was placed on the group, more than ten thousand Falun Gong practitioners silently lined the streets near Zhongnanhai, the compound near the Forbidden City where party leaders live and work. It marked an extraordinary act of public defiance. It also was the biggest public demonstration since 1989, when idealistic democracy supporters thronged to the area around Beijing's Tiananmen Square, only to face tanks and soldiers before dawn one June morning. The fratricidal bloodshed that followed left the square and the party leadership stained by tragedy, and a death toll in the hundreds. In response to Falun Gong, anxious party leaders cranked up the repression, carrying out a ceaseless campaign to exterminate the group. At its peak, the group claimed to have tens of millions of followers. But by the early 2000s, it had been pushed deep underground.

The Falun Gong unrest showed that while Mao's 1949 Revolution sought to discredit religion, it failed to snuff out the creeds and beliefs prevalent in China and the new ones that would arise. During Mao's reign, most religious institutions were closed or destroyed, and the party promoted atheism. Since Mao's passing, the party has permitted a controlled revival of religious expression, tolerating it as a reality and demanding that it submit to party authority. The State Administration for Religious Affairs oversees religion through a sprawling bureaucracy that leaves most activity subject to party approval. The government permits five religions—Buddhism, Taoism, Islam, and Christianity divided into Protestant and Catholic branches. Atop each faith is an official patriotic group patterned after Leninist mass organizations. The patriotic groups, such as the Three-Self Patriotic Movement (which controls the Protestant church), help dictate content of religious services, recruitment of clergy, development of religious sites, and income and expenditures. All ties with overseas religions are banned, and foreign religious figures are not welcome in China, with only a smattering of exceptions. By 1982, party leaders were confident of their control enough to amend the nation's constitution to protect freedom of religious belief but without giving recourse to those who believed their freedom had been impinged.

Decades later, the party has given no signal that it will adopt broader reforms to protect religious practice. In reality, the party has difficulty simply handling the numbers of those who profess faith. State media routinely put the number of religious believers in China at a hundred million people, or less than 8 percent of the population. Yet even at that level, the numbers are significant. The Muslim population of China, which the government claims is eighteen million, means the nation has more Muslims than Malaysia or Syria.[13] Indeed, it has more Muslims than many Middle Eastern nations. As for Protestant Christians, the growth since the 1949 Revolution has been some twentyfold, with estimates ranging from forty million to seventy million—or nearly as many members as in the Chinese Communist Party. One scholar noted that on any given Sunday, there are likely more Protestants in church in China than in all of Europe.[14] Catholics in China number some ten to twelve million, far more than in Ireland. Estimating the number of Buddhists in China is difficult because there are no congregational membership lists, but tens of millions of people are believed to practice devotion in some measure each year, sometimes mixing Taoism with Buddhism. Moreover, many adherents come from restless minorities, such as the Uighurs

and their proselytism and social service could continue. Order would soon come to China under Mao—but also fierce repression.

For decades following Mao's ascent in China, religion lay moribund. The work of Christian missionaries, in particular, seemed drowned in the sea of history. Mao was determined to exorcise any of the traits of his countrymen that allowed foreigners—merchants, opium dealers, soldiers, and missionaries—to get such a foothold as during the Century of Humiliation. After all, Mao had said days before the formal creation of the People's Republic that "the Chinese people, comprising one quarter of humanity, have now stood up!"[17] Three decades later, all religious venues had been closed or destroyed. The reform and opening-up process that followed Mao's death, however, gave new life to religion, and I was eager to see what remained of the half century of work by Methodist missionaries in Yenping, which was now known as Nanping. For years, I had heard family stories about how my grandfather believed he was at the cutting edge of history bringing Christianity to China, and he was convinced that it would become a Christian nation by the turn of the twenty-first century. What a failed enterprise that was, I had thought to myself.

I jumped on a plane to Fuzhou, the largest city in Fujian, with its huge banyan trees lining the streets. From there, I climbed aboard a train that followed the Min River, passing through the numerous tunnels that pierced the rugged mountains. At first, the area seemed sparsely populated, which surprised me. Most of eastern China is full of villages. After my years of living and traveling in the region, it was a pleasant surprise to see so few dwellings and such thick bamboo groves. Along the river, which was slow moving and broad, maybe fifteen hundred feet across, I saw an occasional two-story dwelling, often with a garden plot containing banana trees. The few boats I saw looked like sampans turned into motorized barges. Some carried grain or gravel. As we got closer to Nanping, the villages became more frequent, and I spotted occasional rice terraces and ponds constructed for fish farming.

The city of Nanping bustled with the toot of horns along streets lined with buildings more than a dozen stories tall. The Min River, tamed by upstream dams, no longer raged in cascades of froth but flowed in a big, muddy stream. The city rises at the confluence of two rivers, the Min and the Jiangxi. The banks rise steeply, and the city pushes back only a few blocks before steep hills block more development. Green-and-yellow taxis cruised the streets. It was hot and steamy. Within half an hour of walking, I felt sweat dripping down the back of my shirt and along my legs. I ducked into a fast-food joint, and the cool air conditioning felt refreshing. I checked into a riverside hotel that belonged to a local paper mill and dropped my bag in a room on the fourteenth floor. I struck out for the Protestant church I knew to still be in the city, the remnant of my grandparents' era. I found a taxi that charged me 5 yuan, far less than a dollar, to take me to the church.

Out the window, I saw a remarkably modern and middle-class city. Many shops sold the latest fashions, including Nike and Nine West shoes. There was a McDonald's and KFC. Large trees shaded the sidewalks. People zipped about on smart scooters and in late-model cars. Men and women in fashionable clothing strolled along. Some ladies carried parasols to block the sun and retain the light skin that is a desired characteristic. When we came upon the Meishan Protestant Church on a steep street, I was awestruck. It was huge. I learned later that the steeple rises a hundred thirty feet, nearly as tall as the adjacent high-rises that dot this city of a quarter million people. I walked up the stairs and heard a chorus of joyful giggles. The bottom floor houses a day care center with more than two hundred small charges.

Before long, I came across the pastor of the church, the Reverend Sun Renfu, an affable man who also goes by the English name of the Reverend Thomas Sun. He clasped my hands upon hearing that my grandfather was Xie Fuhui. Rev. Sun was in his mid-forties, too young to have known my grandparents, but he is familiar with the Chinese names of the few dozen foreign missionaries who served in the city. Busy in a meeting, he asked me to come back in two hours for a vespers worship service. I walked along the streets near the church, and when I returned, the service was already underway. Rev. Sun, who was wearing a microphone, saw me enter, and as I sat quietly among several hundred worshippers a few minutes later, he called my name and asked me to come to his side. He explained who my grandfather was and asked me to say a few words to the congregation. I grew nervous, unused to public speaking in Chinese, and uttered only a few halting sentences about my family history. I turned to Rev. Sun to rescue me yet was touched by the appreciative looks of worshippers seated in the pews.

Later in his office, Rev. Sun poured green tea and recounted the history of the church. By the time foreign Methodist missionaries departed at the onset of the 1949 Revolution, nearly a century after their arrival, the local church seemed to have achieved the longtime goal of running itself without foreign help. But Chinese Christians ran into harassment, and the Cultural Revolution was an insurmountable obstacle. "Church activity completely stopped in Nanping in 1966," he said. "They burned Bibles, and the church was closed. The pastors were detained in ox sheds. They had to wear dunce caps and signs hanging from their chests that read, 'Cow ghost snake spirit' [a popular taunt in the Cultural Revolution], and clean the streets."[18]

Religion didn't die, however. In areas of China, particularly in provinces like Hebei, Henan, Shandong, and Fujian, Christianity revived strongly beginning in the 1980s, and today in some pockets of the nation local authorities have loosened the reins of control. In Nanping in 1980, authorities handed back some church property (but not the formerly Christian hospital and schools) and once again permitted religious activity. Interest in Christianity reawakened. Groups loosely aligned with different Protestant denominations battle today for followers, once again venturing into the realm of providing social services. A state-controlled Catholic Church draws new members, as does a parallel but underground Catholic Church that is loyal to the Vatican. Some of the current religious revival may be a backlash against the secularization of society. Churches certainly offer a refuge for those not happy with the government. But much of the religious revival appears to arise from a heartfelt longing, and in Fujian province believers told me they felt relatively free to practice their faith. Only nowadays, almost no foreigners are present to spread the gospel.

Rev. Sun said that the earlier missionaries, led by pioneer Nathan Sites, the bearded missionary who came up the Min River a hundred forty years ago, prepared the terrain for the flourishing of Christianity. "They laid a good foundation for Nanping," he said. "They brought modern education and modern medicine. They changed many of the

old practices like smoking opium and foot binding and female infanti-
cide. They began to adopt those unwanted girl babies. . . . Most im-
portantly, they brought the gospel. In China, we have traditional
culture, but we don't have unselfish love and forgiveness. There is no
element in Chinese culture of loving your enemy. In China, it is never
too late to take revenge on your enemies, even after ten years."[19]

Like many young men in Nanping, Rev. Sun once worked in the paper mill at a stable and well-paying job. He had developed a strong curiosity about the Bible in high school, seeing many references to it in
the novels of Victor Hugo but never obtaining a copy himself. His
elder sister eventually married a Christian, and her mother-in-law
lent him a Bible, which he studied for over half a year, eventually joining the local Meishan church. Over family opposition, he quit his job
in 1983 to take a seminary course in Fuzhou, eventually opting for two
more years of study at the Nanjing Union Theological Seminary, the
leading seminary in China. As he finished his course, the Nanping
church suffered a major blow: A lunatic killed its pastor. Rev. Sun had
no elder pastor to mentor and guide him as he returned to the church.

Still, the ground was fertile. From two original churches, Rev. Sun
now oversees twenty-six churches around Nanping, working with
two other pastors and three associate pastors. The local Nanping
church now has five thousand members. While Chinese law prohibits
the Meishan church from affiliation with overseas denominations,
Rev. Sun identified himself to me as Methodist and heartily praised
the early Methodist missionaries. He is in close contact with overseas
Chinese Christians, who occasionally come to give lectures and invite
him abroad. "We have the trust of the government. They have never
interfered with my preaching." Indeed, Rev. Sun straddles a line with
the government, acting as local delegate to the state-sponsored body
that oversees Protestantism on behalf of the party, the Three-Self Patriotic Movement named for its goal of "self-governance, self-support,
self-propagation" for the Chinese Protestant church.

Rev. Sun asked a church employee to take me to the home of Su
Baixin, the sprightly nonagenarian daughter of the first Chinese
Christian in Nanping. We walked along alleyways between high-rise
buildings and came to a well-kept single-story house. She knocked on
the door, but no one answered. She knocked harder, and a faint cry

from inside urged us to enter. Ms. Su initially appeared perplexed at the foreigner in her midst but quickly warmed upon seeing a stack of age-stained black-and-white photos I had brought that had been handed down from my grandparents. "This one looks like my father!" she chortled as she peered at a photo of Chinese men with silk skull-caps standing beside a foreign missionary.

Ms. Su described what life was like when she was a child. Nanping had no electricity and no roads. Leprosy abounded. Roving gunmen attacked constantly, siphoning off tribute. Since Nanping was along a main north-south artery for military movements, soldiers would arrive frequently, also demanding services. In many ways, the foreign missionaries lived isolated lives, dwelling in separate compounds and eating different foods. One of the recollections Ms. Su offered was of how one Methodist physician traveled from his home atop one of the seven hills of the city to his workplace. "Every day, he was carried in a sedan chair to the hospital," she said. She said the local Christian church was built by foreigners but was flourishing fine on its own. "We Chinese became the masters," she said. "The church is rich now. It has money of its own. It doesn't rely on the government or the foreigners. The Christians here are helping each other now."[20] That statement would have made my grandparents happy. After lengthy efforts to impose Christianity from abroad, China's religious rebirth is led not by foreigners, like my grandparents, but Chinese, like Rev. Sun.

Over two separate visits to Nanping, I grew to understand how a trusting relationship between local officials and Rev. Sun had given his church significant leeway to operate around the rules. Increasingly, the church was offering an array of social services, just as the early missionaries did, and preaching to the young, despite a series of prohibitions that limit such activities. The State Administration of Religions Affairs strictly controls what Protestant churches can and cannot do. Ministers are not allowed to preach outside their designated areas, nor are they allowed to solicit money from abroad. If churches provide social services, they cannot advertise. After all, it would undercut the perception that the ruling party is the source of all such welfare services. With one of the Meishan leaders at my side, I wandered up a hill to a seven-story building that was shaded by several tall trees. The building was on the site of the former home of

Frederick Bankhardt, a Methodist missionary who was in Yenping at the same time as my grandparents. It was the Nanping Christian Charitable Old People's Home, and rector Weiping Shaw offered me a tour.

He said social services such as the retirement home allow the church "to spread the gospel in a silent way. It is to let more people identify with Christianity. It makes them realize that we are a church of love." We walked along the halls of the home peeking into different rooms to greet the elderly residents. It struck me as tidy, with tender care by the workers, perhaps more so than a retirement home in Florida where I once worked as a teenager. It is little wonder that Fujian officials had already designated the retirement home a "pilot benevolent project." We reached a large room, and I asked about its use. He said it could serve as a worship hall but quickly added that such a use is not yet permitted. "You can't teach the gospel in retirement homes." The rector noted that provincial officials granted the church permission to operate the home in 2001, and construction was finished in 2002. At the time of my visit, fifty-seven elderly people lived there, but the aim was to have a hundred fifty residents. "The pastor knows that the missionaries used to run hospitals, schools, and health clinics here, and he has the intention to do the same. He hopes that we can offer social services like in the past."[21]

The day care center I saw in the church's basement also seemed to bend the rules. Government policy stipulates that no religious indoctrination occur at any school or with anyone under eighteen. Yet the church day care slips some teachings in. "During Christmas, we ask the children to do paper cutting related to religious themes, and the government doesn't mind. We also have shows related to Bible teachings," Director Zheng Jianping said. "Many parents are government officials. They are Communists."[22] But she said that the parents are pleased by the care offered by the school and refrained from making the church stick to the letter of the law. Moreover, strictly speaking, many of the local party officials are atheists in name only, still believing in age-old folk religions, a retired middle school teacher, Xu Jiashan, told me: "Many of them believe in idols and go to temples."[23]

When I returned to Beijing, charges that Chinese companies were exporting shoddy and contaminated goods dominated the foreign newspaper headlines. First it was lead paint in toys, then contaminated pet food. Soon, a scandal over adulterated baby milk powder would send tens of thousands of Chinese tots to the hospital, bringing close to home the erosion of ethics under the savage capitalism of today's China. Something seemed to have changed among Chinese, an anger that the race to wealth had created an often-brutal society where business owners could endanger consumers' lives. I'd already noticed the fading of any ideology linked to communism. When hiring news researchers at my office, I would routinely ask if applicants were party members. Those who said "yes" would say they joined the party only to get a leg up in the job market. Even still, as the party seemed to drift, the survival instincts of its leaders are strong. China has more than 400 million internet users, and when they begin to grumble online, party leaders respond swiftly, even if they have to sacrifice senior cadres. Just a few months earlier, amid uproar about unsafe pharmaceutical products, the government executed the former head of the State Food and Drug Safety Administration for corruption, and the baby milk scandal would also lead to death sentences for two men.

One day about that time, I went to see a premier scholar of contemporary religious experience, Dr. He Guanghu, a wizened man with a gentle air who met me at one of the gates to Renmin University in Beijing, a campus so sprawling that it would have been hard to find his office otherwise. Dr. He's advocacy of religion wasn't so pronounced as to cost him his job. But he was among a group of leading thinkers and scholars who challenged the party over its lack of political reforms. In late 2008, Dr. He was one of the first to sign on to Charter 08, a declaration calling for greater respect for universal values in China, an independent legal system, the end of one-party rule, and respect for freedom of expression. Published on the sixtieth anniversary of the Universal Declaration of Human Rights, the manifesto was a Chinese version modeled on Charter 77, which dissidents in Czechoslovakia signed three decades earlier. Some 303 original signers, including Dr. He, risked arrest and jail. One of the proponents of the charter was Liu Xiaobo, a thoughtful writer who was arrested within hours of the online publication of the charter and later sentenced to eleven years in jail for subversion.

We found our way to Dr. He's office, and I tried to turn the conversation to religion. But first he wanted to speak of corruption and abuses of public power. "Many people talk of the collapse of morality in China. It's like a landslide. It's a vivid description of the situation," he began. Some Chinese blame the problem on the advent of market reforms in the late 1970s, but he rejected that argument, saying market reforms also allowed more discussion of equality, human rights, rule of law, privacy, individual dignity, and free and fair competition. "The corruption spreading in today's China can be ascribed to two primary elements: thievery and lying. We can describe all the phenomenon with those two words. . . . Corruption doesn't come from the market economy. It comes from the lack of rule of law. That's the real major cause of the lack of social morality."[24]

As China veered from the political orthodoxy of Maoism, the lack of a moral framework provided fertile ground for religion, he said, and the state estimates that a hundred million Chinese are religious believers, although the breakdown gets fuzzy when one searches for further data. "We can see a very rapid growth in the numbers of believers in Christianity and Buddhism. More and more officials realized after the 1980s that religion, especially Buddhism and Taoism, would not present difficulties or challenges to the state. On the contrary, Buddhism and some religious doctrines would be helpful in keeping social ethics and stability," he said.[25]

Since shortly after the turn of the century, and coinciding with a rise in mass incidents of social conflict and increasingly uncontrolled pursuit of material prosperity, China's leaders came forth with what they called "putting people first" policies that later evolved into a goal of creating a "harmonious society." By 2006, party officials were publicly stating that they had articulated their goals for social harmony based on religious ideals. "Buddhism's philosophy is also a major reference for China's 'harmonious society' concept," the leader of the State Administration for Religious Affairs, Ye Xiaowen, said during a world Buddhist forum in China that year.[26] But such remarks left doubts over whether the party had turned to religion only to boost a slogan designed to calm those worried about China's rise and to provide a balm for social discontent. "The 'harmonious world' theory . . . will help dispel doubts in the international community about China's

continued development and refute the absurd 'China threat theory,'"
Ye said.[27]

Assessing the number of Buddhists in China is difficult because
Buddhist leaders don't maintain statistics on members, unlike Christianity, which has exact statistics on baptisms. "It's very hard to judge
whether a person is a Buddhist or not. Mr. Wang goes to the temple
once a year. Mr. Ni goes twice a year, and Mr. Li goes three times a
year," Dr. He said. "Many among the pilgrims are just tourists." Even so,
he described Buddhism and Christianity as the two fastest growing religions in China. "There are larger and larger numbers of temples."[28]
The Chinese government claims that now there are more than thirteen
thousand Buddhist temples with about two hundred thousand monks
and nuns in China. Moreover, some seven million Buddhists in China
are not Tibetans but are drawn from other ethnic groups.

The most famous Buddhist of all, of course, is the Dalai Lama. If
one were to count him as a Chinese, as Beijing does, he is the most famous Chinese of our time, far more widely known globally than the
faceless party cadres of the Politburo, better known than such Chinese sports luminaries as the NBA basketball player Yao Ming or the
Hollywood action star Jackie Chan. Countless world leaders treat His
Holiness as a personal friend. When he trots the globe, as he perpetu-
ally does, thousands of people fill arenas and stadiums to hear his
teachings. He may be "just a simple monk," as he likes to call himself,
dressed in no more than a robe with a small bag thrown over his
shoulder. But he has the capacity to make China's leaders deeply un-
settled. They await his death, hoping it will sweep away some of their
troubles in Tibet. But he's not dead yet, and his global appeal seems as
strong as ever.

chapter eleven

A "Simple Buddhist Monk"

If I go back to China, I'll probably be handcuffed right at the airport.

—*The Dalai Lama, speaking to a group of ethnic Chinese at the Waldorf Astoria Hotel in New York City, May 4, 2009*

TRADITION CALLS FOR AN AUDIENCE TO GO SILENT WHEN THE Dalai Lama enters an arena or theater. Usually a host signals that the Dalai Lama is backstage, a frisson ripples through the crowd, and people begin to rise to their feet. A hush ensues. As the Dalai Lama ambles into view, he holds the focus even in extended silence. It is little wonder that Tibetans refer to him simply as Kundun, or "the Presence," because his proximity is palpable and he commands attention. Tibetan monks on the rostrum bow in reverence. Sometimes the Dalai Lama approaches monks he recognizes, clasping their hands warmly, bending to touch his forehead against theirs, and offering murmured greetings. Then he walks to the front of the stage, looking out with his hands clasped together, the quiet interrupted by an explosion of clicks from news photographers at the stage apron. He makes a point of looking down patiently at each photographer, allowing them to get photos of his direct gaze, connecting with a vast unseen audience. After a few more seconds, he makes a slight orchestral gesture with his hand and barks in a stentorian voice, "Sit down!" He chuckles in resonant amusement at the fierceness of his own voice, and walks toward his seat. He prostrates three times toward an image of the Buddha, whom he jokingly calls "my boss." He unties his shoes, leaving his socks on, as he settles into a chair or bench with cushions. He pulls his legs up under him and drapes his crimson robe over his limbs as he adjusts his body to the seat. Sometimes he then puts on a headset microphone. On one occasion, the silent adjustment took minutes, and His Holiness acknowledged the patience of his audience, looking up and saying, "More comfortable, very good. But don't worry. I'm not going into silent meditation here," laughing heartily.

Silence, of course, is not what much of the world wants from the Dalai Lama. They itch to hear him speak. People of every faith and those without faith come for what they hope is sage advice on living in harmony in a fast-paced world in which increased wealth does not correlate with happiness. What he prescribes for them are a few moral principles, many of them common to most religions, for day-to-day life. At its bedrock, the Dalai Lama's system of "secular ethics" calls for humans to strive for greater levels of kindness, compassion, tolerance, and self-restraint. He describes compassion and affection as human traits crucial to the health of humankind and the planet. No one starts out evil from birth, he says. Beginning with the kindness shown by mothers, children can grow into adults with deeper levels of kindness, including altruism, a trait as important as intelligence. The world is interconnected, and humans must nurture the happiness of those around them, radiating from family outward, to find true happiness themselves. Treat the globe as part of yourself, he tells listeners, because your future is also dependent on the rest of the world. It is a message that resonates in both the developed and the less developed worlds. As the Dalai Lama heads off nearly every month to some corner of the globe, attracting thousands of people to theaters, arenas, and even sports stadiums to hear his talks, his core message contains only a tangential reference to his own religion or his own homeland. In reality, in his final years, the Dalai Lama's humanistic views and global stature transcend religion and the issue of Tibet.

To the consternation of China's ruling party, the Dalai Lama is arguably the most widely known person in the world today born within contemporary China's borders. It is no small irony that the party that helped push the Dalai Lama into exile is responsible for his renown. If he had not fled Tibet, he would not have been forced to lobby for Tibet in foreign capitals. As it is, the Dalai Lama usually visits Europe,

North America, Australia, and Japan once or twice a year, and sometimes more. In recent years, he's also visited far-flung places like Nige-
ria, Jordan, Slovenia, Chile, and Peru. On his personal website is a
registry of dignitaries with whom he's met. For one recent five-year
period, the list was seemingly endless, numbering nearly two hundred
presidents, prime ministers, kings and queens, senior parliamentarians, retired politicians, popes, chief rabbis, and imams as well as a
healthy listing of top scientists, fellow Nobel laureates, movie stars,
and famous entertainers.[1] He has not noticeably slowed with advancing age.

Exile has forced on the Dalai Lama vast exposure to the modern
world. It forged an outlook broader than his own religious tradition
and made him a figure of larger dimensions. In North America and
Europe, talks by the Dalai Lama can draw enormous crowds. At one
free event in the East Meadow of New York's Central Park in 2003,
some sixty-five thousand people poured out to hear him. At another
more recent event in Seattle, in which he appeared along with fellow
Nobel Peace Prize laureate Desmond Tutu, a roughly equal number
came. Tutu later expressed awe at the Dalai Lama's drawing power:
"Can you imagine, 70,000 people came out for someone who can't
even speak English properly?"[2]

His supporters hail the Fourteenth Dalai Lama as a universal moral
figure on a par with such luminaries as Mahatma Gandhi, whose nonviolent resistance led to India's independence from Britain, and Nelson Mandela, who overturned apartheid in South Africa and came to
epitomize the essential dignity of all races. In the same league is Martin Luther King Jr. Like Mandela and King, both fellow Nobel Peace
Prize winners, the Dalai Lama is committed to nonviolence as a tool
for change and espouses social equality as a necessary step toward
genuine social harmony and peace. His battle to win greater freedom
for Tibetans under China's yoke has given the Dalai Lama a distinct
political hue. Like another former religious leader, Pope John Paul II,
the Polish prelate who helped bring down Communist rule in Eastern
Europe before his death in 2005, the Dalai Lama is a strong critic of
authoritarian one-party government. He ridicules Chinese leaders'
dismissal of him as a "devil" and a "beast" looking to break apart the
Chinese motherland. "Do you see my horns?" he often asks crowds,

chuckling and holding up his index fingers to simulate horns on his tonsured, balding pate.

The idea that the Dalai Lama embodies a cartoonish evil is so dissonant that the line usually draws laughter. In reality, he is a figure of grace and humility. While savvy about the political consequences of his actions, I found him straightforward about his aims. A sharp wit allows him to play with the image of himself as a devilish figure. Once at a news conference in Tokyo, a British reporter raised whether the Fourteenth Dalai Lama would reincarnate after his death. "You've said you may not return. My question to you is, where are you going to go?" "To hell!" the Dalai Lama responded without missing a beat. He went on to recount a daily prayer in which he pledged to help any sentient being who was suffering. If there are sentient beings in hell, he said in what he described as a half joke, "I'm ready to go there. If not much work, then I go to heaven."[3]

Business tycoons seeking to find favor with China sometimes speak ill of the Dalai Lama. The most renowned case involved Rupert Murdoch, the Australian-born billionaire media tycoon, who told *Vanity Fair* magazine in 1999 that the Dalai Lama is "a very political old monk shuffling around in Gucci shoes." At the time, Murdoch was seeking Beijing's green light for his satellite television interests. Murdoch's hopes of big profits in China eluded him, despite his flattery of China's leaders and his efforts to cultivate business ties with their children.[4] His jab at the Tibetan leader seemed wide of the mark, especially when it came to His Holiness's shoes. When I sat before the Dalai Lama in an interview, I couldn't help but look at his shoes, which were conventional lace-up walking shoes, neither fashionable nor noteworthy. And when, on a wintry day in February 2010, with snow piled up outside the White House, the Dalai Lama showed up for a meeting with President Barack Obama, he wore flip-flops instead of shoes, a sly rebuttal to Murdoch. The BBC headlined the visit "Flip-flop diplomacy with the Dalai Lama."

For all his fame, the Dalai Lama remains modest and humble, exhibiting consideration and caring. His charms certainly rubbed off on me, and I am neither a Buddhist nor one of his followers. When I sat before him, I tried to sense whether I was in the presence of an illuminated being. After all, Tibetans consider him an emanation of the

Buddha of Compassion. In the end, I simply noticed intense personal warmth. He listened carefully to questions and went far beyond the allotted time. And what left the greatest impression was the moment for the perfunctory photo when the interview ended. The Dalai Lama reached over and grabbed my hand, pulling me closer. He used his other hand to embrace my forearm as if it were valuable treasure. The act of taking a photo, done tens of thousands of times before, was an act of intimacy and human communion.

Those who have observed him for decades say the Dalai Lama gives equal treatment to nearly everyone. "When he goes to the White House, he'll shake the hand of every waiter and bodyguard as well as the president," the writer Pico Iyer said during a town hall meeting with the Dalai Lama.[5] I had already noticed that the Dalai Lama seemed to have a relationship with members of the State Department Diplomatic Security Service detail assigned to protect him, several of whom were veterans of his trips. Matthieu Ricard, a French monk and translator for the Dalai Lama, also noted his habit of greeting those who are part of the invisible landscape: "How often have I seen him, just after having bid goodbye to a president or a minister, go and shake hands with the doorman in his box, or with the telephone operator behind her glass window."[6]

Invitations pour into the Dalai Lama's office to attend conferences, charity events, universities, and other venues, and his schedule is filled at least a year out. His office turns down most invitations. During a two-week trip to the United States in the late spring of 2009, on which I tailed along, the Dalai Lama spoke at intimate events with a few hundred supporters, in large arenas and theaters with several thousand people, and once at a massive football stadium, where tickets went for as much as $117.50 each. His schedule was packed, free only a few days for a stop at the Mayo Clinic in Rochester, Minnesota, for a health checkup. A few of his talks were esoteric teachings for Buddhist practitioners, and the rest were aimed at non-Buddhists, even nonbelievers. The talks carried names like "Peace Through Compassion," "Ethics for Our Time," "Educating the Heart," "The Path to Peace and Happiness," and "Ethics and Enlightened Leadership." From the first talk, it was clear that the Dalai Lama is a man of stories. He almost never refers to notes, speaking extemporaneously. His anecdotes are usually personal, drawn from childhood or life in exile, and sometimes belie his image as a holy man unruffled by normal emotions.

A typical story touches on the small parrot the Dalai Lama had as a youth. One of his attendants would feed nuts to the bird when he passed through. The parrot would hear his footsteps and perk up. When the monk fed him, the bird would show delight. The Dalai Lama grew jealous, selfishly wanting the parrot to show affection to him as the rightful master of the bird. He began to feed the parrot nuts as well, but the parrot would only peck at him aggressively. Eventually, the Dalai Lama says he lost his temper and took a stick and hit the parrot, and the relationship only got worse, with no hope of reconciliation. In telling the story, the Dalai Lama says the experience taught him that anger is self-defeating. Even simple animals appreciate genuine affection and can sense if a person is tricking them. "They know," he says.

In Santa Barbara, California, people were itching to put their concerns to the Dalai Lama—big questions about the meaning of life and smaller questions about humanistic concerns. They see him as Mr. Answer Man, the omniscient Himalayan sage, and take him far more seriously then he takes himself. Most of the Dalai Lama's public talks conclude with a session of questions and answers. That was the case in the seaside city, where the Dalai Lama spoke in the basketball arena of the local campus of the University of California. Some five thousand people came to each of two talks. At the afternoon session, the Dalai Lama warned listeners: "I'm nothing special. I'm just another human being, just like you. When you listen to my talk, just listen to another human being. . . . If the audience considers the Dalai Lama very special, then my talk is useless."[7]

Many of the questions were heartfelt, although a few reflected concerns of the place and the generation. As the morning session drew to a close, a student asked the Dalai Lama his thoughts about the use of LSD and other hallucinogens to explore consciousness. "Of course, I personally have no such experience," the Dalai Lama began. He advised against taking drugs in search of new experiences. "Why do we need additional illusory experiences? Should not rely on external substances. Should try to concentrate on natural quality of mind. That's much better."[8]

A few days later, the people waiting in lines outside the Greek The-ater in the hills above the campus of UC Berkeley chatted in a festive mood. Security personnel and attendants were exaggeratedly polite to the ticket holders. "How's your day been so far?" a burly black-suited security guard asked me as he moved a security wand over my body in search of metal. Rather than students, most in the crowd seemed to be leisure-class Californians. Many of the men wore trim beards, small ponytails, and Hawaiian shirts. The women wore turquoise jew-elry and beads, with some draped in silk scarves or toting suede jack-ets with fringe. Among those introducing the Dalai Lama was Richard Blum, then-chair of the Board of Regents of the University of Califor-nia system. Blum, the husband of California's senior U.S. senator, Di-anne Feinstein, interjected a strong pro-Tibet tone to the event, criticizing China's leaders for their policies. "If they want to become a great nation, they need to become a moral nation, and what goes on in Tibet is simply not moral."[9]

Typically, the Dalai Lama did not bring up Tibet or China, leaving that to others. Rather, he spoke about compassion and its biological basis among mammal mothers showing extreme care toward off-spring. He brought up his childhood and his "illiterate, uneducated, but very, very kind" mother, and how she used to dote on him. "What-ever she had in the kitchen, she immediately shared," he said. During the day, she would hoist him gently on her back while doing chores around their rural Tibetan home. Strapped to her back, he would yank her left or right ear to indicate the direction he wanted to go. A mother's kindness absorbs such pranks, the Dalai Lama said, and is the seed of compassion, which brings energy and action. "Compas-sion is my one important daily practice," he said. Another story rolled out. The Dalai Lama related how on a transoceanic flight, he shared a cabin with the parents of two crying children. For three hours, the fa-ther helped the mother tend to the wailing kids. "After three hours, the father doesn't care. Next morning, the mother's eyes were very red, completely exhausted." The Dalai Lama told the story to illustrate how mothers go to great lengths to tend to their children rather than to chastise the father.[10]

The Dalai Lama attended a charity breakfast titled "The Joy of Giv-ing" the next day at a luxury San Francisco hotel. Wealthy society matrons filled the Ritz Carlton Hotel ballroom, quaffing sparkling wine and dining on an exquisite breakfast, as they heard how the Dalai Lama would go to a soup kitchen later in the day to serve lunch. Tom Nazario, a professor at the University of San Francisco Law School and a longtime supporter of the Dalai Lama, related how the soup kitchen visit came about. Two years earlier, he had suggested to the Dalai Lama that he spent too much time with America's rich and should visit the homeless and the hungry as well. "When I said this to him, he said, 'Let's go today.' I said, 'You can't just do it like that. There's security, and the [bomb-sniffing] dogs have to go through the place.' I found myself having an argument with the Dalai Lama. One of the things he likes about Westerners is that we argue with him."[11]

The Tibetan leader immediately launched into a discussion on the nature of giving. "Taking care of our community is the best way to take care of ourselves. You get immense inner satisfaction and you get fulfillment [by] sincerely giving, but taking care without calculation [or] thinking, 'How much do I get?'" He discussed altruism and noted that Buddhism extensively discusses how and when to give. Then he paused. "I don't want to go into details. You may get bored. I won't give lecture on Buddhism."[12] His remarks remained general.

Only a few days into his tour and the Dalai Lama had already attended eight public events and held several private audiences as well. He seemed indefatigable, using energy drawn from a disciplined monastic routine. The Dalai Lama awakens every morning at 3:30 AM whether he is on the road or at home, aides say. As soon as he rises, he begins his morning prayers and meditation. He also does some exercise. When he's at his personal residence in Dharamsala, especially during the rainy season, he may exercise indoors on a treadmill. Otherwise, he will walk outdoors. By dawn, the Dalai Lama sits down to a hearty breakfast, usually bread, jam, fruit, and tea. In total, he'll do four hours of prayers and meditation each morning, and then read Buddhist scriptures. Sometime around noon, he'll have lunch. While in Dharamsala, at 12:30 or 1 PM, he goes to his office and remains for three hours of audiences and personal meetings. Sometime after 4, he returns to his personal residence. At 5:30 or so, he'll have tea and perhaps a biscuit, shunning an evening meal. He prepares for bed by 8 or 8:30 each evening. The routine rarely varies whether the Dalai Lama is in India or on the road. When he travels, as soon as he hits a new time zone, he adjusts his schedule accordingly. His aides know to avoid evening events.

Until the early 1990s, the Dalai Lama never flew anything but economy class. These days, he'll occasionally accept a free flight on the private jet of a wealthy supporter, but more commonly he continues to fly on commercial airlines, business class rather than first class. "First class too much luxury. Too much drink. I'm a Buddhist monk," the Dalai Lama had said in Berkeley.[13] "I've traveled with him, I think, first class two times, and that was because Lufthansa insisted," said his personal assistant, Tenzin Taklha, referring to the German airline.[14]

He takes little with him, although a small crimson bag is almost always slung over his shoulder. Inside, Taklha said, are some sweets, napkins, pens, a visor for the sun, and other small items. The Dalai Lama frequently voices admiration for scientific advances and the responsible use of technology but does not use a computer. Nor does he use a mobile telephone. His aides opened a Twitter account for him, and maintain www.dalailama.com as his official website, with his schedule and the recordings of his speeches and talks. The Dalai Lama routinely travels with a delegation of half a dozen people comprising a translator, two attendants, a personal secretary, and two or three bodyguards. Most countries where he visits provide additional security. In the United States, the State Department gives him the protection accorded a top-level visiting foreign dignitary.

On a later stop in Cambridge, Massachusetts, security aides to the Dalai Lama were alert to small protests from mainland Chinese students, but none turned out at the Memorial Church near the center of Harvard University. It was easy to see why. Some of the leading academic lights of Harvard arrived for his talk, giving him the imprimatur of the most prestigious university in America. No mainland Chinese student, no matter how loyal to the ruling party, dared go against the collective view of major Harvard dons. The Dalai Lama often speaks of the promotion of human secular values and religious harmony as two of his commitments in life, saying they are outgrowths of the essential unity of humankind. As he looked around the church hall, the Dalai Lama began: "Differences of race, differences of color, differences of religion, differences of age—but fundamentally no differences. Mentally, emotionally, psychologically, we are the same." All people have similar potential. He suggested that humans should do away with thinking of "us" and "them," of friends and enemies. Nationalism is useless, and so is resentment of historical injustices. "We are the same human beings. No one wants war. No one wants suffering. Work together." He said that material wealth does not bring inner joy. "Some poor people are very happy persons. That shows that happiness and joyfulness come from inner attitude," he said. The Dalai Lama then told the tale of encountering a monk who had spent nearly two decades in China's prisons, finally to escape to India. On relating the experience to the Dalai Lama, the monk said he faced "great danger" in prison. The Dalai Lama asked why. The monk responded that he faced "great danger of losing my compassion" for his Chinese jailers.[15]

A different event in the Boston area brought out some of the sharpest thinkers in the fields of neurology, psychiatry, and mental health and the study of altruism. They gathered in a cavernous ballroom of a posh Boston hotel where a Harvard Medical School conference unfolded with the tepid title of "Meditation and Psychotherapy: Cultivating Compassion and Wisdom." Alongside me were a thousand psychotherapists and medical professionals. The crowd stretched so far back that huge screens had been set up at intervals along the sides of the ballroom so that people could see and hear the Dalai Lama engage in a dialogue with experts on the dais. Many experts asked questions, and some voiced their own inner conflicts over how to deal honestly with psychotic patients. A Boston psychiatrist said that some of her patients heard cruel voices or claimed they were being punished for crimes they didn't commit. Medical professionals routinely tell these psychotics to take their medications and wait for their lives to get better. But she said the illnesses sometimes worsen and medicines don't help, presenting a dilemma to caregivers. "What do we say to them and not lie?" she asked. The room grew still, awaiting his response.

"The precise answer to that question," the Dalai Lama said slowly, "is I [clap] don't [clap] know."[16]

He spoke anyway, seeming to savor the complex moral and ethical issues underlying the question, relating anecdotes that hit on broader points of serving others. He told of his own profound sense of loss, even grief, at being forced into exile from Tibet in March 1959. As the towering Potala Palace faded from view, and his caravan headed over the Himalayas, the Dalai Lama said his senior tutor counseled him against being overcome with sadness and to look at the matter from different perspectives. Focusing on the negative was neither sensible nor pragmatic. From one angle, the tutor said, the loss of his country would create new opportunities. Sure enough, with his forced exile new horizons opened, and he became a globe-trotting figure. "If I still in Lhasa," he said in typically fractured but comprehensible English, "I not participate here in this discussion. . . . If I'm considered most holy person in Potala, waste of time." The Dalai Lama then touched on the need to act resolutely when passing through difficulties. At the time of the conference, recession gripped the United States and major world economies, and the Dalai Lama said such crises should coax people to reevaluate the essence of their lives. Tragic circumstances or major difficulties can strengthen and temper individuals, he said, adding, "It's like how fire makes an earthen jar stronger."[17]

The audience contained major figures in the world of psychiatry, and some wanted not only answers from the Dalai Lama but spiritual shortcuts. During a panel discussion, one participant turned to the Dalai Lama and asked, "Could you lead us in a meditation?" The Dalai Lama hesitated for a moment and began talking about how to maintain a calm mental attitude. Then he responded directly: "Some of you may want just one simple meditation, 100 percent effective. Impossible." Tibetan Buddhists practice thousands of different meditations for all kinds of purposes, he said. "Even myself, after sixty years of practice, still not adequate," he added, breaking into a chuckle.[18]

No matter how deeply participants delved into science, the Dalai Lama listened intently, the result of a lifelong interest since shortly after lamas plucked him from Taktser, a tiny wheat- and barley-growing hamlet in northeastern Tibet, claiming he was the reincarnation of the Thirteenth Dalai Lama. His father was the headman of the village, and the family was relatively well off, but life was still harsh. The boy's mother bore sixteen children, and only the future Dalai Lama and six others survived their childhood. The family ceded the two-year-old boy to the high lamas after he passed unambiguous tests of recognition of the personal possessions of the previous Dalai Lama.

Once he was installed in Lhasa, tutors ensured that the young Dalai Lama devoted his time to religious study and meditation. Engaged in a solitary life within the towering thirteen-story Potala Palace, the boy king would look longingly through a telescope at children playing on the dirt lanes of Lhasa far below. The telescope and other devices, including a movie projector, became his prized possessions and nurtured his interest in science. "When I was small, kind people who knew of this interest sometimes sent me mechanical toys, such as cars and boats and airplanes. But I was never content to play with them for long—I always had to take them to pieces to see how they worked. Usually I managed to put them together again, though sometimes, as might be expected, there were disasters," he wrote in his autobiography.[19]

His curiosity opened the door for a German adventure seeker and fugitive residing in Lhasa, Heinrich Harrer, to serve as his Western tutor on matters scientific. Harrer later penned the autobiographical *Seven Years in Tibet*, recalling the voracious appetite of the young Dalai Lama for information:

> It seemed as if a dam had burst, so urgent and continuous was the flood of questions which he put to me. I was astounded to see how much disconnected knowledge he had acquired out of books and newspapers. . . . He knew how to distinguish between different types of aeroplanes, automobiles and tanks. The names of personages like Churchill, Eisenhower, and Molotov were familiar to him, but as he had nobody to put questions to, he often did not know how persons and events were connected with each other.[20]

This early interest augured a lifelong fascination with history and science. The young lama pored over atlases, took apart and reconstructed a wristwatch, and managed to put one of three old cars carried into Tibet, a 1931 Dodge, in working order.

In adulthood, following his flight to exile, the Dalai Lama's fame grew, allowing him to sprinkle in meetings with scientists among his activities. "World-class scientists have generously coached me in subatomic physics, cosmology, psychology [and] biology," he wrote in a *New York Times* op-ed in 2005. By the mid-1980s, he'd grown particularly interested in neuroscience and its explanation about the activities of the brain, seeing similarities between the scientific empirical approach and the Buddhist exploration of the mind. It was then that he joined in the founding of the Mind & Life Institute, which brings together Buddhist meditation masters and top scientists studying functions of the brain, physics, and cosmology. Meeting once or twice a year in relaxed settings, usually with the presence of the Dalai Lama, the eclectic group of scientists and contemplatives discusses subjects like the nature of compassion, brain plasticity, altruism, dying, and mind-body relationships.

One of the founders of the group, psychologist and science journalist Daniel Goleman, recalled how at one of the early meetings, the Dalai Lama and scientists debated the role of emotional responses, like anger, anxiety, fear, and joy. The scientists explained that emotions have an evolutionary function with great survival value, although when distressing feelings are heightened, they can trigger people to do harm to themselves or others. "The Dalai Lama said, 'That's interesting but I look at it a different way.' He said, 'I think of a destructive emotion as any emotional state that destroys your inner balance, that upsets your inner equilibrium and skews your perception of reality.' It was a much more subtle standard, and that created a very interesting discussion over five days," Goleman recalled. As a result of the meeting, scientists agreed to study the brain activity of what Goleman described as "Olympic-level meditators" who had decades of experience. At brain imaging labs in the West, the meditators had their brains studied while they did different practices, and scientists were astounded at the brain configurations they saw. "These are different brains," Goleman said. "For example, the left prefrontal cortex just behind the forehead is the center of positive emotions, or a key part of the circuitry for that. And when these monks meditate on compassion, it lights up. It activates to levels never seen in ordinary life."[21]

For anyone familiar with Tibetan mystic practices, such phenomenon may not seem unusual. Tibetan lore is replete with tales of supernatural saints and mystics. Early Western travelers to Tibet reported seeing monks running and leaping faster than a horse, traveling up to two hundred miles a day. The gravity-defying monks, known as *lung-gom-pa*, a name that derives from "wind meditation," appeared to be bounding across the landscape in a trance. Alexandra David-Neel, the

French explorer, described the moment she spotted one of them: "The man did not run. He seemed to lift himself from the ground, proceeding by leaps. It looked as if he had been endowed with the elasticity of a ball and rebounded each time his feet touched the ground. His steps had the regularity of a pendulum. . . . My servants dismounted and bowed their heads to the ground as the lama passed before us, but he went his way apparently unaware of our presence."

Tibetan oracles in trances are said to bend hard iron swords in half or twist them into spirals. Even in modern times, travelers to Tibet report seeing monks practicing *g tum-mo*, or the raising of the inner fire, in which they generate such intense body heat that they can cast aside all their garments while sitting on a snow bank, or dry icy sheets dipped into frigid Himalayan lakes on their bodies. The practice has even attracted the attention of Harvard Medical School researchers. One of them, Herbert Benson, said, "Buddhists feel the reality we live in is not the ultimate one. There's another reality we can tap into that's unaffected by our emotions, by our everyday world. Buddhists believe this state of mind can be achieved by doing good for others and by meditation. The heat they generate during the process is just a by-product of *g tum-mo* meditation."[22]

The Dalai Lama publicly downplays talk of any personal mystical powers, especially when it comes to healing people. He said repeatedly he has no such ability, or he wouldn't have entered the hospital in 2008 suffering from gallbladder problems. "That proves scientifically the Dalai Lama has no healing power," he told a multitude in Los Angeles.[23] The Dalai Lama urged skepticism of so-called healers, saying that a compassionate heart is the only healing energy one can have. While dismissing healing claims, the Dalai Lama does talk about unusual physical phenomena among high Tibetan lamas, unexplainable by modern science. He regularly brought up the death of senior lamas and said their bodies did not always decay normally. "My own senior tutor, after death, for thirty days his body remained fresh," he said at the talk in Santa Barbara. Neuroscientists observing the body of a senior lama at Ganden Monastery after his death found some electrical signals coming from his brain weeks later, he added. "We believe that that person's subtle mind still in the body."[24]

The Dalai Lama's interest in matters outside the traditional purview of Tibetan Buddhism—such as science, nuclear conflict, and environmental degradation—has led him to friendship with a broad spectrum of influential people. These contacts, away from the focus of the media, have been instrumental in giving the Dalai Lama large support in academia and among environmental and conflict resolution groups worldwide. Add in the politicians and world leaders, and the Dalai Lama enjoys an extraordinary network around the globe. Important people listen to his views. Near the end of his life, the Fourteenth Dalai Lama may not have brought tangible change to Tibetans under China's control. And some critics contend that he has made political mistakes in talks with China. A few argue that he should not have laid claim to Greater Tibet, instead accepting to negotiate for greater freedoms in the lesser area that China calls the Tibet Autonomous Region. Others say the Dalai Lama should have campaigned on an anticolonial platform instead of accepting China's sovereignty over Tibet. Even if those arguments have merit, it is unlikely that the status quo of the Tibetan Plateau today would be different.

In assessing his own legacy, the Fourteenth Dalai Lama likes to say he's been neither the best Dalai Lama in the lineage nor the worst. But in reality, it's hard to imagine how a Tibetan leader could have risen more suitably to the times and challenges. As Dalai Lama, Tenzin Gyatso has harnessed the reach of Hollywood, appealed to vast audiences around the world with a unique global message of harmony, and elevated awareness of the plight of Tibetans. When the Dalai Lama passes on, his people will lose an exceptional asset. If a Fifteenth Dalai Lama emerges, the likelihood seems slim that the person would embody such charisma and capture such global attention.

A stop in New York City was one of the last on the Dalai Lama's two-week trip, and it included a private meeting to reach out to overseas Han Chinese and discuss Tibet with them. Such meetings have not always gone smoothly. I'd heard the Dalai Lama describe how he'd met with several Han university students in Rochester, Minnesota, just weeks after the 2008 Lhasa riot. Several of the students were so angry that the Dalai Lama said he was thankful a large table separated them so they could not reach over and slap him. "Too emotional," he said. In midtown Manhattan, I sat in the back of a room in the Waldorf Astoria Hotel for a meeting he had organized with ethnic Chinese from up and down the Atlantic seaboard. I quickly discovered that many of the hundred or so Chinese in the room were democracy activists opposed to the ruling party in China, and thus friendly to the Dalai Lama. A Chinese graduate student who had driven up from Maryland sat next to me. He said he supported the Dalai Lama's efforts to negotiate with China but that the talks would lead nowhere. We chatted for a while, and he seemed a tad nervous, asking me not to write down his name. He said pro-Beijing nationalists studying at universities in the United States could persecute him and his family back on the mainland. "If the Chinese community in Maryland knew that I was here, there would be trouble. They may sniff me out."[25]

Such fears weren't without merit. After the Tibet protests in 2008, a Chinese freshman at Duke University in North Carolina, Grace Wang, tried to mediate between pro-Tibet and pro-China protesters on campus. Her actions enraged some pro-China forces, and they branded her a "race traitor." Back in China, online activists formed a digital vigilante mob, which Mandarin speakers call a "human flesh search engine," trying to dig out details of Grace Wang's private life, including her mother's address in the port city of Qingdao. They succeeded, and several took matters further. They dumped feces on the mother's doorstep and forced her into hiding.[26] The daughter suffered a nervous collapse.

The Dalai Lama walked into the room, and most everyone in attendance stood up. He offered a few words in rudimentary Mandarin, which he doesn't speak well, and switched to English. He offered a quick history lesson, talking about a six-month trip he made from Lhasa to Beijing in late 1954 to meet Mao Zedong and other senior leaders, who sought his support. He was deeply apprehensive about the trip but found himself sympathizing with Mao's socialist aims. "While I was in Peking, I expressed that I wanted to join the Communist Party. So much attraction," he told the group. He said he returned to Lhasa "full of confidence, full of hope," only to have those hopes dashed in later years, when Mao's "nice words" did not match on the ground practice, coming to a head in March 1959.[27]

By then, thousands of bedraggled Tibetan refugees from the eastern region of Kham had poured into the plains near Lhasa in despair

over military repression. On March 1, 1959, two junior Chinese officers arrived at the main Jokhang temple of Lhasa to ask the Dalai
Lama to accompany top officers to a theatrical show. The invitation
aroused misgivings among the Dalai Lama's top advisers, a suspicion
that deepened days later when they were told he was to come to the
military camp for the show without his customary retinue of twenty-
five Tibetan soldiers. The suspicions soon filtered out to ordinary
people, who believed that China was laying a trap, and some thirty
thousand deeply agitated Tibetans streamed around the Dalai Lama's
summer palace shouting, "The Chinese must go! Leave Tibet to the
Tibetans!" On March 17, two shells landed near the summer palace,
heightening panic that the Chinese troops were preparing to take the
compound. That night, the Dalai Lama, dressed as a soldier with a rifle slung over his shoulder, slunk out of the palace to join a group of
high lamas bound for a Himalayan pass that would take them to India.
The ruse worked, and *Time* published the news a month later with the
headline, "The Escape that Rocked the Reds."

The Dalai Lama told the gathering in the Waldorf Astoria that government propaganda had cast him as anti-Chinese, which was not
true. "Wherever I go, [there are] demonstrations from Chinese community, mainly students. Some of them really showing anger," he said,
adding that the Communist Party appeared to sponsor some of the
protests. He said that international pressure would not bring a lasting
solution to the Tibet issue. Rather, it is a matter for Tibetans and Chinese to work out. "Tibetan problem must solve between Han brothers
and sisters and we Tibetans. No other way," he said. The problem, he
added, is that Beijing misinforms about conditions in Tibet and alleges that Tibetans are happy. The only way to lift the propaganda veil
is to visit Tibet and see for oneself, which he urged the assembled Han
Chinese to do. "Please, you must study upon reality. If there is no
problem, if 60, 70 percent of Tibetans are happy, no problem. If things
are good, we have nothing to complain [about]." If that were the case,
he said he would owe an apology to the ruling party.[28]

I'd heard the Dalai Lama make similar remarks at several earlier
talks. At various times, he poked fun at the ruling party's authoritarian
ways and hybrid theories taking it away from socialism. "Communist
Party [is] without Communist ideology. Just capitalist. Very strange." He

made light of the habit of China's leaders to say they hew to "scientific development." "They always say, 'scientific, scientific, scientific,' but there's nothing scientific there." He called modern China a "confused state" and would say it is time for the Communist Party, after six decades in power, to retire.[29]

But I found the Dalai Lama to oscillate between a conviction—as he voiced to me directly—that the Communist Party will not hang on to power much longer and an acknowledgment that rapid change might bring chaos. At the New York session, he expressed hope for gradual change. "If China becomes an open society, it will become really great. We hope that China gradually becomes a free country, not quickly like Russia," he said. Yet at one point, the Dalai Lama seemed to take an extraordinarily long view, urging the psychotherapists gathered in Boston not to lose confidence even if their goals are not attainable in a single lifetime: "One Tibetan master said, even what may seem impossible to achieve in a hundred years, later on seems achievable."[30]

Within China, the party portrays itself as stronger than ever, on a steady course toward becoming a global counterweight to the United States. Ordinary citizens voice optimism about the future, and party officials sound increasingly self-assured. In reality, a quiver of paranoia runs through the party. Potential social problems abound. They include a quickly aging population, gender imbalances, internal migration, a faulty pension system, the threat of infectious disease outbreaks, and a yawning urban-rural income gap. Despite these problems, officials portray the Middle Kingdom as stable, and they cover up crackdowns on dissent, even denying minimal opposition.

The performance artist and painter Ai Weiwei, who has become a prominent social analyst, said serious flaws undermine China's political system. "China is like a runner sprinting very fast but it has a heart condition," he told one newspaper.[31] Party leaders certainly keep their heart medicine at hand, trying to avoid the doomsayers' predictions of social implosion. With so many potential land mines in their path, they are determined that Tibet does not cause further problems. So they act to impede the Dalai Lama's every step. Chinese agents penetrate his computer systems, cajole and bully his foreign hosts, and try to sow discord among his followers.

chapter twelve

Thwarting the Dalai Lama

The small countries appease China due to fear, the bigger countries appease China due to greed. . . . The human rights and democracy is not important. The market is more important.

—*Samdhong Rinpoche, prime minister of the Tibetan government-in-exile, speaking in Melbourne, Australia, December, 8, 2009*

ON A MAGNIFICENT COASTAL RIDGE OVERLOOKING THE PACIFIC Ocean north of San Francisco, a copper-plated Tibetan stupa juts 113 feet into the air, a beacon of Buddhism shimmering majestically in the afternoon sunlight. Built three decades ago, it was the first large-scale stupa erected anywhere in America. The huge dome-shaped shrine towers into the sky at the Odiyan Tibetan Buddhist Center, built by followers of Tarthang Tulku, a Tibetan lama who came to the States in 1975. His center in the Sonoma hills includes an eleven-story temple, and when pilgrims make a circuit to spin the twelve hundred copper prayer wheels, their noise fills the air with a holy hum. Those driving along the rugged California coast would hardly find the thousand-acre temple complex out of place. After all, the hills are dotted with Buddhist monasteries, meditation halls, dharma centers, and retreats. Buddhism is chic in California.

The state is probably more hospitable toward Buddhism than any place in the West, a result of the nineteenth-century immigration of Japanese and Chinese laborers who brought the Asian religion with them. Roughly half the estimated 1.5 million practicing Buddhists in the United States reside in California, and about two-thirds of them

243

are immigrants from places like Vietnam, Cambodia, Thailand, Taiwan, and China. Art museums in Los Angeles and the San Francisco Bay Area maintain large collections of Buddhist art. And universities house significant faculties focusing on Buddhism. Indeed, the University of California at Los Angeles has more academics dedicated to Buddhist Studies than any other university in the Western world.[1] Only about a thousand of the seven thousand Tibetans believed to reside in the United States live in California, but their culture and religion hold an outsize importance. Proof of that is the surging number of Hollywood stars who embrace Tibetan Buddhism, and the large crowds that eagerly snap up tickets to see the Dalai Lama every time he visits the state.

Given such a conducive environment, it may be a surprise what happened in 2009 in Sacramento, the state capital, when the state assembly considered a resolution in support of the Tibetan struggle for self-determination. The rejection of the resolution is instructive about the changing dynamics of the Tibet issue, the growing influence of an economically mighty China, and the kinds of tactics China employs when it comes to its core interest in Tibet. The sponsor of the proposed resolution was Sam Blakeslee, a Republican from the coastal city of San Luis Obispo who holds a PhD in geophysics from the University of California at Santa Barbara. I traveled to Sacramento to find out firsthand what occurred, and drove about an hour from the Bay Area across California's expansive, fertile Central Valley to the state capital.

Sacramento is not a huge metropolis, ranking only seventh largest among the state's cities. Nearly two centuries ago, its importance was greater. Sacramento boomed during the California Gold Rush in the mid-nineteenth century, and was a key terminus for wagon trains, riverboats, and the transcontinental railway. Tens of thousands of Chinese migrant workers traveled across the Pacific to toil in labor gangs on railway construction. Sacramento once had a thriving Chinatown. I arrived a bit early for my appointment with the legislator, so I strolled down to I Street, where Chinatown once existed. I counted two Chinese restaurants, but one appeared to have gone out of business and was not open. After surviving decades of oppression under the Chinese Exclusion Act, which barred Chinese from becoming permanent residents and kept Chinese men from bringing wives and family members from their homeland, the immigrants could not live normally until the act's repeal in 1943. In subsequent decades, Chinese immigrants integrated more easily into American life, moving out of Chinatown and into the suburbs. Little is left of Sacramento's Chinatown today, although Chinese surnames dot the phonebook.

After lunch, I walked down to the imposing state capitol, built a century and a half ago in a classical revival style reminiscent of the U.S. Capitol in Washington. It was a sunny spring day close to the end of the school year, and several busloads of school children stood excitedly in line for a tour of the building. I didn't at first grasp why the kids seemed so animated until I looked down a hallway blocked off by khaki-uniformed state troopers wearing flat-brimmed hats. There in the hallway, outside a huge set of wooden doors, stood a bronze statue of a grizzly bear, the state symbol. Overhead in gold letters it said, "Arnold Schwarzenegger." In case anyone wasn't aware that the Hollywood action hero had become the state's leader, a separate sign noted that it was the office of Governor Arnold Schwarzenegger. I fought my way through the crowds of school kids, lobbyists, and legislative staffers to Assemblyman Blakeslee's office, which at the time was on the fifth floor.

I knew that Blakeslee had an unusual reason for thrusting himself into the Tibet issue. Back in 1998, his son, David, had graduated from high school and traveled to India for six months. Blakeslee, who had raised David as a single parent, adored his son, and was in his own words "worried silly" about his welfare in India. "Our relationship had been a particularly close one. Even during the difficult high school years, we stayed close. In the evenings, we would listen to music, shoot pool, play chess, watch the tube, and debate everything under the sun. His absence, and silence, had made the past six months unbearable," Blakeslee wrote in a newspaper commentary at the time.[2] So when his son finally got in contact and suggested that the father fly to Dharamsala, where he was doing volunteer work, Blakeslee quickly hopped on a plane for the long journey. "Forty-four hours after leaving San Luis Obispo, I found myself fighting back tears as I embraced my little boy—a boy sporting a beard and a far-away look in his eyes that belied his tender years." Blakeslee's son had been volunteering at the Tibetan Children's Village in Dharamsala, and over the next three weeks, as father and son explored northern India, Blakeslee got a solid dose of how the world looks through the eyes of local Tibetan exiles and his son.

Blakeslee maintained his interest in Tibet after taking over his family's investment firm, then getting elected on the Republican slate to the state assembly in 2004. While such a post may seem insignificant on a national scale, it's nothing to sneeze at either. California, were it a country, would have the eighth largest economy of any nation around the globe. The lack of religious freedom and self-determination in Tibet particularly irked Blakeslee, and it is an issue that also riles some of his fellow Republicans. In the spring of 2008, he grew disturbed by reports of a Chinese crackdown following unrest in Tibet, and he asked staff members to research resolutions on Tibet approved in other states and cities around the United States. They quickly found twenty or so such resolutions and cobbled together their own version. While the proposal was rewritten on the way to a vote, removing such terms as "cultural genocide," and given to another assembly member to sponsor, it still noted that the Dalai Lama "has received worldwide recognition and praise for his leadership in seeking nonviolent solutions to international problems." The resolution established March 10 as "'Dalai Lama and Tibet Awareness Day' to educate Californians about the teachings of the Dalai Lama and his efforts to preserve the Tibetan culture." After passage, Blakeslee issued a statement hailing the resolution and concluding, "We stand with the Dalai Lama in opposition to the brutal oppression of Tibetan people." The resolution sailed through on a voice vote.

Blakeslee, who has an easygoing manner with little inclination for formalities, invited me into his office and explained what happened in early 2009 when he took the same resolution and rewrote it to note that the year marked the significant fiftieth anniversary of the Dalai Lama's flight into exile. He submitted it to the state assembly, figuring it would pass easily. After all, new breezes were blowing from Washington, where Barack Obama had taken over the White House. But Blakeslee said he miscalculated the resolve of the Chinese government to block the resolution. "I began hearing from other legislators that the Chinese consulate was interacting with them, making calls, showing up at their offices." As part of what appeared to be a coordinated campaign, a wealthy Chinese-American donor from Southern California also made the rounds of the State Capitol with a loose-leaf binder containing gruesome photos of what he claimed were torture victims of the theocratic regime the Dalai Lama headed before his flight into exile. The donor argued vehemently that the Dalai Lama was guilty of crimes against humanity and the people of Tibet were fortunate to be liberated by Chinese armed forces. Several legislators paid a lot of attention, given the donor's clockwork largesse at election time. A few days later, two diplomats from the Chinese consulate in San Francisco arrived at his office, making similar arguments. "They were very polished, very determined to express their opinion. At the end of the conversation, they asked me to reconsider moving forward with the bill. . . . They talked about desiring good relations, which is perhaps code for, 'You criticize us at your own risk.'" Blakeslee said other assembly members began telling him the Chinese diplomats were visiting them as well—and even inviting them to lavish banquets at the San Francisco home of Gao Zhansheng, the seasoned consul general who holds a Foreign Ministry rank equivalent to an ambassador, and getting invitations to travel to China at low cost.

Around that time, Gao sent a four-page letter to all the members of the state assembly explaining that the arrival of Chinese troops in Tibet marked a "peaceful liberation" that ended the "darkest slavery in human history" under the Dalai Lama. "I sincerely hope you understand the fact that for more than 700 years the central government of China has continuously exercised sovereignty over Tibet, and Tibet has never been an independent state. No government of any country in the world has ever recognized Tibet as an independent state. There's no 'invasion' or 'occupation' at all."[3] Gao's letter also noted that California exported $11.3 billion in products and services to China in 2008, higher than any other U.S. state.

Attached to Gao's letter was a three-page document titled "Backgrounder: Historical Facts of Tibet." It gave a one-sided view of the often-complex details of the China-Tibet relationship, casting Beijing's sovereignty over Lhasa as a matter of historical record, beyond dispute, and portraying Tibetan religious leaders as unremittingly hostile to their own people. "Even in the first half of the 20th century,

Tibet remained a feudal serfdom under theocracy, one even darker and more backward than medieval Europe." The ecclesiastical elite, comprising less than 5 percent of the population, practiced "extremely savage punishments, including gouging out eyes, cutting off ears, tongues, hands and feet, pulling out tendons, throwing people into rivers or off cliffs."

The letter and the pavement-pounding diplomats marked an unusual lobbying campaign within the state capitol. Nearly all large companies and foreign governments with interests in an issue before the state legislature hire professional lobbyists. So seeing the briefcase-toting Chinese diplomats—representatives of a one-party Communist state, no less—walking the halls of the state assembly was quite rare. But it worked. Legislators supportive of China's position sent the bill back to committee for "further study," a move that condemned it to languish with no further action. Buddhism may be hip in California, but legislators knew that the Chinese keep tally of who criticizes them, and would make sure of an economic payback down the road.

Still fuming over the fate of the proposal, Blakeslee got a call from a fellow Republican assembly member, Chuck Devore, who summoned him to come to his office, where an FBI agent was briefing him on computer security concerns related to China. The agent told the assembly members that because they were supporters of the resolution, Chinese security agents would likely try to hack their office computer systems. "As we sat with the FBI agent, he described the sorts of things you, I, could expect. They use very sophisticated worms and other agents to log keystrokes, to turn on and off cameras in your computer, to capture your emails. He said, 'There's a very high likelihood you've already been penetrated.'" Blakeslee said the briefing left him feeling anxious. A few months later, the whole of the Tibetan government-in-exile would begin to feel anxious over computer security as well.

Around the same time as the FBI agent's visit, a letter arrived at Blakeslee's office from a retired California Supreme Court justice, William P. Clark, a resident of Blakeslee's district who was a former top aide and national security advisor to President Ronald Reagan. Clark said he'd reviewed the details of the Chinese lobbying effort on the proposed resolution and that he couldn't recall "any case of for-eign consular officials lobbying at our state level in such a blatant and aggressive way." He described the lobbying campaign as not only ir-regular but inappropriate. He went on:

> The fact that such actions occur in relation to a resolution recognizing the 50th anniversary of the flight of the Tibetan religious leader in the aftermath of an unprovoked invasion by the armed forces of Commu-nist China is not merely ironic, but indeed tragic. As your resolution correctly details, the United Nations General Assembly has on three separate occasions passed resolutions calling for the cessation of prac-tices that deprive the Tibetan people of their fundamental human rights and freedoms, including the right to self-determination. That consular officials of the Chinese Communist government would utilize the freedoms and liberties afforded them by the governments of the United States and the state of California to seek the defeat of a resolu-tion advocating the same freedoms for the occupied and oppressed people of Tibet is unfortunate.
>
> My thoughts on this circumstance may be emphasized by asking the following question: Would consular staff of the United States ever be allowed to walk the halls of any Chinese provincial government to lobby Chinese state officials to cast a vote in support of or in opposi-tion to any measure related to the issue of human rights? To ask the question is to answer it.[4]

Resolutions demanding China reduce its chokehold on Tibet have been a dime a dozen within Congress, various state legislatures, and even city councils in recent years. At the time China was wrestling to bottle up the proposed resolution in Sacramento, the U.S. House of Representatives passed a resolution 422–1 calling on China to end re-pression in Tibet and urging the Obama administration to press Bei-jing to respect the human rights of Tibetans. Cosponsors of the House resolution included conservative Republicans, like Ileana Ros-Lehti-nen of Florida and Frank Wolf of Virginia, as well as liberal Democrats such as James McGovern of Massachusetts and Jan Schakowsky of Illi-nois. So naturally one might ask: Why did Chinese diplomats expend such energy battling the California proposal while doing little against a larger resolution on Capitol Hill? The answer seems to be that China knows it isn't strong enough to quell such a vote in Washington, DC, where lobbying restrictions are more stringent and a public anti–Dalai Lama campaign might prove counterproductive. So it limited itself to declaring after the fact its "strong dissatisfaction and resolute opposition" to the U.S. House meddling in China's affairs. And it may not care as much about, or have the diplomatic manpower to thwart, successful drives to approve Tibet resolutions in other states. Legislatures in Vermont and Wisconsin both approved resolutions in 2009 condemning human rights violations in Tibet. But state resolutions have moderated sharply in tone in the past decade, no longer condemning China's invasion of the "independent country" of Tibet in 1950, as New Hampshire legislators did in 2001, or lambasting China's "acts of genocide" in Tibet, as New Mexican lawmakers did in 1999.

It is not just politicians who receive strong lobbying over Tibet issues. University presidents are also subject to an occasional blitz. When China can exert its influence to throw roadblocks before potential visits by the Dalai Lama to the United States, it does so. Shortly before the Tibetan leader made a stop in Washington state in April 2008, the president of the University of Washington, Mark A. Emmert, got a polite letter from Gao, the San Francisco consul general, noting that one of the Dalai Lama's events was scheduled for a venue on campus. "It is my sincere hope that you and your colleagues will refrain from meeting with the Dalai, attending any functions held for him and providing any venue for his activities," Gao wrote. The letter asserted that the Dalai Lama "is not a religious figure only, but also a political figure in exile engaged in activities of splitting Tibet from China." The letter contained no direct suggestion that China would block exchange programs or other collaborations between the University of Washington system and Chinese universities, but concerns about those potential steps are latent. All academic leaders know it is important to attract bright mainland scholars and expand U.S.-run programs on the mainland. Prior to the Dalai Lama's appearance at the Massachusetts Institute of Technology in May 2009, aides to the Tibetan leader say the university received veiled indications that the visit would bring a cost to MIT, with China nixing future collaborations or otherwise exacting a price.

Such pressure on universities has sometimes been more explicit outside the United States. London Metropolitan University, which has a fairly large contingent of students from mainland China, awarded the Dalai Lama an honorary doctorate in May 2008 for his role in "promoting peace globally as well as for his inspirational spiritual guidance and leadership." Angered by the degree, Chinese students went on the internet to demand a boycott of the university. Chinese diplomats in London then demanded an explanation from the chancellor's office. After the meeting, the English-language *China Daily* reported that the university regretted its actions and that Vice Chancellor Brian Roper said that awarding the honorary degree was an ill-considered move. The *China Daily* story suggested that the university would suffer for its actions. "Many study abroad agencies in China have reportedly boycotted the university, advising students who wish to study in Britain not to attend the school. 'We would not recommend our students to study at universities that support "Tibetan independence" and are not friendly to China,' a worker at a study abroad agency in Beijing said in an interview with the Global Times," the *China Daily* story said.[5]

Two days later, the university issued a statement saying it had not apologized for the honorary degree and would not retract the award. It acknowledged that the vice chancellor had met with Chinese diplomats but said he had "expressed regret at any unhappiness that had been caused to Chinese people by the recent award. . . . It was not the university's intention to cause any such unhappiness."[6] Still, British universities have grown accustomed to the revenue flow from cash-paying Chinese students, some fifty thousand of whom were studying in Britain at the time of the incident. The incident had repercussions as far away as Australia, where the University of Tasmania cancelled the awarding of an honorary doctorate to the Dalai Lama during his visit at the end of 2009. The university collects some $26 million a year in tuition payments from Chinese students and had received a visit from concerned Chinese officials.[7]

China has been particularly forceful that European countries must yank the welcome mat they seem inclined to extend for the Dalai Lama. Nations that dismiss the warnings find reprisals in the form of cancelled summits, delayed trade deals, and other actions. But more often, countries listen to, and heed, Chinese mandates. In 2007, China warned Belgium to cancel the Dalai Lama's long-planned visit to Brussels to meet with European parliamentarians and activist groups supporting Tibet. In the balance, China said, was a pending Belgian trade mission headed by the nation's crown prince. Belgium acquiesced, and the Dalai Lama issued a statement of understanding. "The Belgian government shared with me their predicament on account of pressure from the People's Republic of China," the statement said. "Having considered the situation, I have decided not to visit Brussels this time."[8]

The next year was particularly trying for Sino-European relations, and once again at front and center was the Tibet issue. Some Europeans grew so frustrated that they accused China of arm-twisting and intimidation. The nadir came when China stunned European capitals by canceling an annual summit with presidents of all the EU nations because French President Nicolas Sarkozy was scheduled to receive the Dalai Lama in Gdansk, Poland, shortly afterward. The annual summits are important for both sides. The EU is China's largest trade partner, and at the time of the cancellation trade volumes between the two sides were surpassing $400 billion a year. On hearing of Beijing's cancellation, analysts in Brussels voiced indignation. "China's bully-boy tactics of trying to dictate who European leaders can and cannot meet are completely unacceptable and Europe should stand firm in defending President Sarkozy's decision to see the Dalai Lama in Poland," sputtered John Fox, a former British diplomat in Beijing who had moved over to the European Council on Foreign Relations, a think tank. Others howled in chorus. "Communist bullying tactics of this kind will not work in Europe," said Graham Watson, a member of the European Parliament and leader of the Alliance of Liberals and Democrats in Europe.[9]

For their part, many ordinary Chinese hailed their government for finally doling out what they considered well-deserved punishment to the Europeans. They still cringed over the loss of face China endured in the spring run-up to the Beijing Summer Olympic Games, when a global torch relay was constantly interrupted by protests. If their anger had a human dimension, it was that of Jin Jing, a sweet-faced Paralympic fencer who was a torchbearer during the Paris leg of the torch relay. Jin had lost her right leg to a tumor at the age of nine and competed from a wheelchair, overcoming adversity and winning a coveted spot among the twenty thousand torchbearers around the world. Jin had woken up that chilly morning of the Paris leg with one thought on her mind: Don't blow it. Unruly protesters had already tried to disrupt the torch relay in San Francisco and London, and Jin had received a text message from a friend suggesting that she be extra careful against attackers trying to grab the torch. So she jettisoned the original plan to place the silver and maroon torch on a special support device connected to her wheelchair. Instead, she would clutch it with all her might in her two hands.[10] Almost immediately upon receiving the torch from the second bearer, Jin spotted several attackers breaking through a security cordon and lunging at her. She gripped the torch, desperately twisting her body to turn her back on the assailants. Security agents rushed in to pull the attackers away, but not before they scratched her chin and bruised her shoulder. One pulled her hair. Even so, she'd kept a firm grasp on the burning torch. It seemed like a small triumph, but the moment was caught on film and transmitted back to China. To her countrymen, her actions were nothing short of heroic, a defense of the motherland.

Barely a few hours passed before supporters dubbed Jin the "smiling angel in a wheelchair." Angry bloggers and internet users decried the failure by French police to protect the torchbearers. An assault on the torch, many Chinese felt, was an assault on their nation. And the only suitable response for such contempt was for Chinese to let the flame of patriotism burn brighter and wave the red flag with more vigor. If that meant outshouting the pro-Tibetan protesters at rallies, so be it. Chinese would shout their anger louder. Foreseeing trouble from pro-Tibetan groups when the torch relay was to hit Canberra, the Australian capital, Chinese student groups allegedly backed by the Chinese embassy arranged for busload after busload of Chinese nationals to arrive along the torch route, some of them carrying walkie-talkies. Some ten thousand China supporters showed up, many carrying large flags and chanting, "One China" in a fervent outpouring of nationalism that overwhelmed the pro-Tibetan protesters.[11] In many ways the event tilted the prism, casting light from a new angle to show a stronger and more angry China flexing its muscles and placating surging nationalist sentiments. Indeed, at times the one-party state seemed behind the curve of domestic public opinion, acting forcefully only when it became apparent that showing strength was crucial for regime survival.

Australia, a nation thriving on exports of raw materials to feed China's manufacturing boom, is another case study on how Chinese diplomats are upping their game to warn politicians off touchy issues like Tibet. One target has been Michael Danby, a portly Labor member of Parliament with a long-standing interest in Tibetans. When Danby made it known in February 2009 that he would attend a commemorative event marking the fiftieth anniversary of the Dalai Lama's flight into exile, China's ambassador to Canberra promptly wrote him a letter suggesting that he not go. "The rally on 10 March will be another act of 'Tibetan independence' groups to pursue 'Tibetan independence,' tarnish the image of the Chinese government and impair Chinese-Australian relations," Ambassador Zhang Junsai wrote to Danby. "Obviously, your attendance will be inconsistent with what you have said and will inevitably be utilized by 'Tibetan independence' groups. I hope you will give careful consideration to this and refrain from attending the 'Tibetan independence' activity on 10 March." Danby ignored the letter and attended the event, saying that "no self-respecting MP would listen to a letter like this." Australian Foreign Minister Stephen Smith jumped in, declaring that ambassadors of foreign countries are not entitled "to somehow seek to direct an elected official or an elected Member of Parliament about how he or she might conduct himself or herself."

By coincidence, I happened to run into Danby a few months later in Dharamsala, where he'd arrived as head of an unofficial delegation of six Australian legislators from the Labor, Liberal, and Green parties, covering the gamut of the nation's political spectrum. They had come to see the Dalai Lama and other officials of the government-in-exile. Danby, who has a thick mop of white hair and wears glasses with translucent rims, told me that Chinese diplomats had tried to curtail the legislators' six-day visit to India. At a news conference that same day, Danby and his fellow legislators were in high dudgeon over China's efforts to halt their trip. Most vociferous on the issue was Peter Slipper, a lawyer from the center-right Liberal Party, who suggested that the public Chinese pressure had backfired, making some Australians uneasy that Beijing was telling their legislators what to do. "When such a thuggish or bizarre or outlandish, outrageous demand comes from Chinese authorities that we ought not to dare to visit one of the world's living treasures in Dharamsala, ordinary decent Australian people say there's something seriously wrong with the approach of the Chinese Embassy and the Chinese government," Slipper said.[12]

But for every place where China's tactics may not go smoothly, such as in Australia, there are other countries where it is working. For example, Costa Rican President Oscar Arias asked the Dalai Lama, a fellow Nobel Peace Prize winner and the spiritual leader of Tibet, to cancel a planned private visit to San Jose in August 2008. Arias cited "scheduling problems," but it was clear that he knew that a visit by the Dalai Lama would have sacrificed Costa Rica's chance to host Chinese President Hu Jintao later that year. Moreover, Costa Rica had only a year earlier broken diplomatic relations with Taiwan after nearly six decades and opened an embassy in Beijing.

China's immediate neighbors are yet more inclined to defer to Beijing on Tibet. Both Russia and South Korea have prohibited the Dalai Lama from even transiting their countries in order not to offend Beijing. Nepal is home to the second-largest community of Tibetan exiles in the world. Long under heavy influence from its southern neighbor, India, landlocked Nepal more recently is increasingly deferring to China to its north. Chinese security officials regularly operate in Nepal in search of Tibetans, and at their behest Nepalese police increasingly have low tolerance for protests by anti-Chinese Tibetan exiles.[13] Under prodding from China, another southern neighbor, Bangladesh, is also ensuring that pro-Tibetan voices are muffled. Police blocked a photo exhibition of Tibetans in exile in late 2009, saying they were acting at the request of two officers from the Chinese embassy in Dhaka.[14]

In a demonstration of China's growing clout in Africa, the Dalai Lama was refused a visa by Pretoria to attend a peace conference in South Africa for Nobel laureates in early 2009. The Dalai Lama's presence in the nation "would not be in the best interests of South Africa at this time," a government spokesman said. The conference was linked to the 2010 Football World Cup and was to discuss the role of soccer in fighting racism and xenophobia. When word leaked that the

Dalai Lama was not welcome, Archbishop Desmond Tutu and former South African President F. W. de Klerk raised a howl of protest, and Tutu told the BBC that the government was "shamelessly succumbing to Chinese pressure." South Africa prides itself as a beacon of human rights and democracy on the continent, but as in other parts of the world the growing importance of trade with China is trumping such concerns.[15]

Criticism of China's strong-arm diplomatic tactics might seem hypocritical, especially coming from a nation like the United States with a history of covert and overt pressure to topple and install regimes in places like Latin America, the Middle East, and Africa. But that was before news broke of GhostNet, which appears to illustrate China's penchant for its own covert shenanigans. GhostNet is the codename for an investigation undertaken by a "brain trust" of computer security researchers based in Toronto, Canada, and Cambridge, England. The high-tech internet ghostbusters discovered a network of hackers, linked to servers in China, that had covertly gained control of some thirteen hundred computers worldwide in foreign ministries, embassies, news media, and international organizations, particularly the international offices of the Dalai Lama in Dharamsala and around the globe. The discovery did more than alarm the Tibet movement and jar the offices of the Dalai Lama, where aides surmised that supporters in Tibet might be in danger of arrest or worse. It marked the latest skirmish in what computer security officials say is the way global information warfare may be conducted in the future.

The search for ghosts began simply enough. Techies in the tiny IT office in the back of the quaint yellow hilltop complex where the Dalai Lama maintains his personal offices began to suspect in 2008 that there were gaping holes in the cyber walls around His Holiness. They believed hackers were snooping around in their mail servers. Moreover, the private office had sent an email to a foreign diplomat to arrange a meeting with the Dalai Lama, but before the secretary could follow up with a phone call, the diplomat's office was contacted by the Chinese government and warned not to attend the meeting. Worried by the breaches, the techies called the Asian office of the OpenNet Initiative, a collaborative effort linking top internet researchers at the universities of Toronto, Harvard, Cambridge, and Oxford. ONI focuses mainly on internet filtering and surveillance practices done by repressive governments. The ONI Asian office, in turn, contacted researchers in England. One, an Indian, Shishir Nagaraja, was based at Cambridge, and the second, London-based Greg Walton, was the Initiative's chief investigator in Asia and had been in contact with the Dalai Lama's office before. One of the tech sleuths headed for Dharamsala, toting programs and gear to monitor incoming and outgoing traffic from the Dalai Lama's networks. Working fourteen-hour days, Nagaraja employed a commercial program, WireShark, to watch for suspicious activity. Suddenly he saw it. Hackers were instructing malicious code to pull a certain file from the network computers.

The researchers isolated the code, or worm, and found that it attached itself to Microsoft Word documents and Adobe PDF files and kept spreading with the documents as they were passed along to new computers, allowing hackers to seize control of a spreading network. They dubbed the worm GhOst RAT, later adding the name GhostNet to the entire network of hacking. Keeping an eye on the data traffic, they soon discovered something else: The offices use a web-hosting and email service provided by a California company, but a look at server logs revealed a number of successful logins from IP addresses that belonged to Chinese and Hong Kong internet service providers, which had no association with anyone in the Dharamsala offices. With a little more legwork, they discovered that some of the traffic was coming from China's Xinjiang Uighur Autonomous Region, "where police and intelligence units dealing with Tibetan independence campaigners are based."[16] After five days, the researchers returned to England to analyze further the data they captured.

Dissecting the digital worm, the research team slowly discovered GhOst RAT's extraordinary ability to give a hacker complete control of an infected computer. "It could view all the files on the computer. It could take snapshots of the desktop. It could remove files from the system manager. It could turn on web cameras. It could open up audio files. So essentially [it could] use the infected computers as eavesdropping equipment," said Ronald J. Deibert, a member of the GhostNet team and a professor of the Citizen Lab at the Munk Centre for International Studies at the University of Toronto.[17] It was as if the Dalai Lama's computer systems took on a life of their own, with unseen masters distantly pulling strings. One monk claimed he watched in astonished silence as the worm opened his Outlook Express and began sending infected attachments to others.[18] It was worse than if a spy or two had penetrated the office. Wherever a computer sat, which was everywhere, a likely foe of the Dalai Lama appeared to have complete information awareness. Even the most sensitive strategy discussions had fallen into the wrong hands. "We actually witnessed the negotiating positions of the Tibetan government-in-exile being extracted from computers as we were running network monitoring devices," Deibert said.

Lives were literally at stake. The IT system held sensitive information about Tibetan refugees arriving over the Himalayas, what they said about conditions back home, where they lived before they left, and where they live now in India. Presumably, the computers also held confidential information about pending overseas trips by the Dalai Lama, debriefing reports on past negotiations with China, analysis of the future of the Tibet issue, and a series of other confidential matters. As the magnitude of the cyber espionage became apparent, one of the researchers concluded: "Few organizations outside the defense and intelligence sector could withstand such an attack."[19] The cyber-espionage investigation dragged on for ten months as researchers looked for the extent of infected computers.

One day they got a lucky break. They discovered that several of the control servers for the GhOst RAT worm were not password-protected. The servers, connected to network addresses in China, listed every computer infected with the worm, showed how to issue commands to those computers, and informed operators about which commands were pending and which have been completed. The sleuths mounted a sting. They set up a "honey pot" computer and infected it with GhOst RAT, watching while the hackers extracted information. Of six control servers, five were in China.[20] And they began to find the locations of infected computers, which included the Asian Development Bank headquartered in Manila, the offices of the Associated Press in Britain, the German embassy in Canberra, the Indian embassy in Washington, and the Secretariat of ASEAN (Association of Southeast Asian Nations). The researchers also found infected computers in the offices of the Dalai Lama's personal envoys in New

York City and London, as well as seven infected computers belonging to the International Campaign for Tibet, the global movement in support of the Dalai Lama that is closely linked to him.

GhostNet researchers officially remained circumspect about blaming the Chinese state directly. The fifty-three-page report, *Tracking GhostNet: Investigating a Cyber Espionage Network*, which broke the news in March 2009, charitably noted that the Trojan worm could have emerged from the burgeoning population of Chinese internet users and that maybe it wasn't a deliberate or targeted intelligence gathering operation. Deibert, one of the lead investigators, was less cautious when a Canadian journalist interviewed him for a podcast: "The attacker logged in from IP addresses which were located on Hainan Island, which is the home of the main signals intelligence facility of the People's Liberation Army. You know, it's not a smoking gun but it points pretty heavily toward China."[21]

Indeed, the Lingshui electronic signals intelligence facility on the southeastern coast of Hainan Island is said to be home to more than one thousand analysts of the Third Technical Department of the PLA. The complex is used to intercept international satellite communications. Nagaraja, the Indian researcher who first went to Dharamsala to monitor network traffic, also laid blame at China's door, saying the cyber espionage was the work of "agents of the Chinese government." The twelve-page report he coauthored for Cambridge University, which carried the catchy title *Snooping Dragon*, described the espionage as "a targeted surveillance attack designed to collect actionable intelligence for use by the police and security services of a repressive state, with potentially fatal consequences for those exposed."[22] For its part, Beijing reacted indignantly, using scary with-us-or-against-us language that carried no hint of nuance. "China pays great attention to computer network security and resolutely opposes and fights any criminal activity harmful to computer networks, such as hacking," said Foreign Ministry spokesman Qin Gang. "Some people outside China now are bent on fabricating lies about so-called Chinese computer spies. Their attempt to tarnish China with such lies is doomed to failure."[23]

Several months had passed since the initial GhostNet report when I dropped into the IT office for the Dalai Lama. An American and a

Tibetan technician explained in general terms how the compound had upgraded security. Servers had been replaced, and there were now two levels of computers. Some computers were connected to the internet and the outside world, passing through a beefed up firewall. For more sensitive work, other computers had no access to the internet at all. Since those computers can't access email, the chance that they might pass along documents infected with a virus or worm is substantially reduced. When the aides to His Holiness need to share documents, they use secure USB thumb drives that are protected every night under lock and key.

The human fallout from GhostNet was still apparent in Dharamsala, though, and activists were buzzing about what happened to a young Tibetan exile from the Drewla Initiative Project. Drewla was set up in 2005 as an online outreach program to make contact with Chinese citizens over the internet. Tibetans fluent in Chinese use computers in the project's offices in Dharamsala to log onto forums and other websites to chat with people on the mainland. The purpose is to teach Chinese how to circumvent the censorship imposed by China, raise awareness of Tibet issues, and talk about the Dalai Lama's teachings. Because of the heavy online presence of employees of Drewla, which means "connection" in Tibetan, the GhostNet researchers began to monitor several of their computers and found them to be infected. The worm seemed to explain what happened to one of Drewla's volunteers while the researchers were doing the monitoring. After two years work at Drewla, she decided to return to Tibet. Upon reaching the Nepal-Tibetan border, she was arrested and taken to an interrogation facility for two months of isolation, where Chinese agents asked about her job in Dharamsala. She insisted that she was only studying and not involved in politics. The agents then pulled out a dossier containing complete transcripts of her internet chats over the years. They said they were monitoring the Drewla outreach and warned her and her colleagues to stay away from Tibet.

CHINA HAS ALSO GAINED GROUND from centuries-old rifts within Tibetan Buddhism, which has allowed it to stir dissension among Tibetans. It is a political chess match with a brutal—and even bloody—aspect, one that involves the nighttime stabbing of monks, a ferocious deity, and a lawsuit that accuses the Dalai Lama of religious intolerance. The dispute has polarized Buddhists and given China the opportunity to portray the Dalai Lama as a hypocrite on freedom of religion to undermine his credibility.

The dispute revolves around Dorje Shugden, a deity that made its first appearance nearly four centuries ago and is seen as either a wrathful demon or a protecting savior. Until a few decades ago, Shugden worship was far from widespread. But as fundamentalist sects have arisen in Christianity, the aggressively sectarian Shugden worshipers say they are protecting the purity of the Gelugpa tradition, shunning the other three major traditions. The dispute has rippled around the world, largely because of a dissident Tibetan lama living in England with a large Western following, and given rise to Shugden worshipers following the Dalai Lama to New York, London, Oxford, Nuremberg, and other cities carrying placards that say, "Dalai Lama, Stop Lying!"

In July 2008, Sixth Avenue in midtown Manhattan had to be shut down for twenty minutes while police cleared out pro- and anti-Shugden protesters, some of whom were throwing objects and spitting at each other. Pro-Shugden forces render the Dalai Lama in terms that would be unrecognizable to many outside the Tibetan community—calling him a tyrant and a power-hungry religious dictator. Curiously, the Dalai Lama himself once worshiped Dorje Shugden. His junior tutor, Trijang Rinpoche, propitiated the deity and promoted the practice, and privately introduced the Dalai Lama to it in 1950 in Dromo on the southern border, where they had retreated on the arrival of Chinese troops into Tibet. At the time, Trijang Rinpoche encouraged the practice in Gelugpa monasteries. To fully understand the dispute, which has pit monk against monk, one must delve into baroque aspects of Tibetan Buddhism. A brief history will help shed light on the murky issue.

The deity has its origins in the seventeenth century. Different legends exist, but several coincide that Tulku Drapga Gyaltsen, a strong contender to become the Fifth Dalai Lama, later clashed with the boy who was chosen, and one version says he ended up foully murdered, coming back to roam Tibet as a dangerous "hungry ghost" imbued with powers because of his religious training. Instead of seeking personal revenge, however, the spirit, Dorje Shugden, put his efforts into the righteous task of enforcing doctrinal purity.[24] The deity is some-times depicted as a black-faced demon wearing a necklace of human heads, symbols of conquered vices. He rides a snow lion through a sea of blood, an omniscient third eye peers from his forehead, and a mongoose clasps his arm, indicating his power to grant wealth to his followers. Some scholars say Shugden worship may grow with the rise of a powerful Dalai Lama, a natural reaction of conservatives in the Gelugpa hierarchy that see their power eclipsed.

In more recent times, friction arose between another strong Dalai Lama, the Thirteenth, and a great and influential lama, Phabongka Rinpoche, who was the main teacher of the current Dalai Lama's two principal tutors. The Thirteenth Dalai Lama considered Shugden a minor deity, not an enlightened being, and pressured Phabongka to stop disseminating Shugden worship. Phabongka conceded to the Thirteenth Dalai Lama, not promoting Shugden any more. However, his pledge seems not to have extended to his followers nor to have bound him once the Thirteenth Dalai Lama died. The sect spread wider as a revivalist movement, and Shugden followers soon saw themselves as protecting the order from doctrinal contamination. They decried a trend toward bringing in teachings from other traditions, telling followers that they faced misfortune or even death if they incorporated practices from Nyingma or other schools. They saw themselves as last-ditch guardians of the faith.

It wasn't until nearly two decades after his own initiation that the current Dalai Lama voiced concerns about Shugden worship. He faced the dilemma of many liberals: Do you tolerate the religiously intolerant, those who are fiercely sectarian? In the 1970s, after a high lama published a book on Shugden that claimed the vengeful deity had killed or tortured dozens of Gelugpa members for bringing eclectic traditions to their religious practice, the fear and awe that many Gelugpa Buddhists felt for the deity grew. Following a series of dreams that he took for premonitions, and deep research of his own, the Dalai Lama ordered Shugden statues taken out of chapels at reestablished Tibetan monasteries in southern India, particularly from the main hall of Ganden Monastery, which is the headquarters of the Gelugpa tradition. He requested that monks there not propitiate Shugden in public. If they wanted to worship the deity, he asked them to do so discreetly.

In 1996, the Dalai Lama went further, telling monks ahead of a special initiation not to participate unless they abandoned the worship of Dorje Shugden. He cited prognostications by the Tibetan state oracle, Nechung, who entered a trance and advised him that the deity was a threat to his personal safety and the future of Tibet. He voiced the view that worshiping Shugden corrupts pure Buddhist tradition and that the strong sectarianism attached to the practice is harmful to the unity of Tibetans, particularly at a time of crisis with China. Since then, hundreds of monks and nuns in southern India have been thrown out of Tibetan Buddhist monasteries or sent to isolated cells. In Tibet, followers of the Dalai Lama have clashed with others as they tried to tear down Shugden statues. The clashes have been encouraged by Chinese authorities, who have seen an opportunity to get at the Dalai Lama by giving support to the Shugden side.

Hardening the debate was a particularly savage act. On the chilly night of February 4, 1997, assailants wielding knives entered the Institute of Buddhist Dialectics just a few hundred yards from the Dalai Lama's hillside residence in Dharamsala. They found the room of its director, Lobsang Gyatso, and stabbed him repeatedly in the stomach and the eyes. The cell walls of the seventy-year-old monk were splattered with blood, attesting to the savage, ritualistic nature of the attack. Two of his young monk attendants were also stabbed, each one fifteen to eighteen times, and died hours later. Police formally questioned five Shugden followers. But there were no witnesses who saw the assailants enter the room and carry out the attack, so the five were eventually released and are believed to have returned to Chinese protection in a Shugden-supporting region of Tibet.

Following the murder, Robert Thurman, a Columbia University Buddhist scholar (who is also the father of Hollywood actress Uma Thurman), cast the finger on the Shugden sect and described adherents as "the Taliban of Tibetan Buddhism," referring to the fundamentalist Islamic militia in Afghanistan. A decade later, acting on behalf of the Indian police, Interpol issued formal requests asking China to arrest Lobsang Chodak and Tenzin Chozin for involvement in the slayings.

Both men are believed to have arrived in India from China only four days before the murders. A taxi driver who took them from New Delhi to Dharamsala was the key witness. The men are reported to be members of the Dorje Shugden Devotees' Charitable and Religious Society.[25] As of this writing, Beijing has not complied with the request.

The murders offered fertile ground for the belief among some Tibetans that China was using the Shugden sect to sow discord. "It is very clear that now people who are perpetrating Shugden are very close to the PRC leadership," said Samdhong Rinpoche, the government-in-exile's prime minister.[26] In recent years, the Dalai Lama has denounced the Shugden practice as "just spirit worship" and labeled it an "evil" sect. At a teaching for Buddhists in southern India in early 2008, he urged new momentum for a purge of Shugden followers: "Recently monasteries have fearlessly expelled Shugden monks where needed. I fully support their actions. I praise them. If monasteries find taking this action hard, tell them the Dalai Lama is responsible for this. Shugden followers have resorted to killing and beating people. They start fires, and tell endless lies. This is how the Shugden behave. It is no good."[27]

At Ganden Monastery in southern India, lamas ordered construction of a nine-foot wall to segregate followers of the "demon" deity from the rest of the monks. The wall is now as impenetrable as any separating Israel from the West Bank. Throughout India and Nepal, loyalists to the Dalai Lama largely shun the Shugden followers. In the larger Tibetan settlements, they have placed "name and shame" posters identifying the deity's proponents and their family members. Some stores and restaurants bear signs saying, "No Shugden worshipers allowed." Shugden followers complain of religious apartheid, a charge that supporters of the Dalai Lama refute, saying followers of Shugden are free to worship the deity—just not in Gelugpa religious facilities. In the West, the devotees do not bear such a stigma. The largest following has its headquarters in Britain, where Kelsang Gyatso, the dissident Tibetan lama, has built the New Kadampa Tradition into a fast-growing sect with some eleven hundred residential centers and branches scattered in Australia, Malaysia, Brazil, Mexico, and the United States and around Europe.

Curious about the phenomenon, I wandered into the warren of alleys in the Tibetan zone of New Delhi, called Majnu Katila, where I
had heard that Shugden followers had a temple. The zone, north of
Old Delhi's Red Fort, sits between a large highway and the Yamuna
River. Driving past, one can easily miss it unless one spots the simple
yellow Tibetan-style arches that announce "Tibetan Refugee Colony."
The colony is no more than a few blocks deep, comprising a series of
labyrinthine dirt alleys that get narrower as one enters further, to the
point where one can touch both walls easily. No cars or rickshaws are
allowed in the colony, so it is a relative island of calm compared to
chaotic, noisy, and crowded New Delhi. Along the alleys, Buddhist
bookstores, Tibetan *thangka* galleries, cheap hostels, and small food
stalls with names like "Little Lhasa" tend to visitors. Vendors sell porridge and *momos*, the Tibetan version of Chinese steamed dumplings
filled with mutton. Litter lies uncollected in the alleys, and some of
Delhi's filth has seeped in. Even in the shade of the alleys, the Delhi
heat is oppressive, and Tibetans used to the chill of the high Himalayas look distinctly out of place. Monks chatting on cell phones
look overdressed in their robes in the heat, and I found I pitied them
even as sweat dripped down my body.

The day of my visit coincided with the Dalai Lama's seventy-fourth
birthday, and a holiday ambience prevailed. Loudspeakers everywhere
blared out the proceedings of a district-wide celebration, and hundreds of people crowded near a central temple. The Tibetan residents
smiled warmly. Yet when I asked Tibetans where to find the Shugden
headquarters, I quickly felt that I was breaking a taboo by even mentioning the name. Usually, a short pause ensued as they sized me up
and pondered how to respond. The colony was tiny, yet several
shrugged their shoulders and said they didn't know. Finally, with the
help of a boy, barely a teenager, who agreed to lead me after pondering for quite a while, I found myself in front of a narrow, multistory
building. It was the office of the Dorje Shugden Devotees' Charitable
and Religious Office. As soon as I walked in, someone shut the door
behind me, and I was led up narrow stairs to a second-floor waiting
room. I heard several people consulting over what to do with me. Finally, a young Tibetan with short-cropped hair came out. He told me

he was late for an appointment but that we could talk in the taxi if I took him to central Delhi.

As we climbed into the Ambassador sedan, the young man identified himself by a sole name, Tustrim, and affirmed that Shugden followers were persecuted illegally by the Dalai Lama and treated as if they were too ignorant to discern the nature of the deity they revere. "It is discrimination. If it's evil or not, we know that. We're not stupid. We know how to distinguish between right and wrong. . . . Our society has sent so many petitions, so many clarifications, asking to speak to the Dalai Lama, and all the petitions are rejected." He recounted how the government-in-exile makes employees affirm that they are not Shugden followers and forces refugees in settlements in South Asia to renounce the deity in order to get identity cards, essential for travel and other procedures. "We Shugden followers are Tibetan, but we don't have any place in Tibetan Buddhism."

Tustrim's aggrieved, almost helpless tone contrasted with the aggressive style of his group, which fired a portentous legal shot across the bow of the Tibetan exile movement. In May 2008, the group filed a lawsuit before the High Court of Delhi asking judges for protection against harassment by the Dalai Lama and his exile government. The suit urged the court to punish the Tibetan leader "for inciting communal and religious hatred"—a serious crime in a nation that has seen its share of religious violence over the decades. It charged that Shugden worshipers were ostracized socially in defiance of both the Indian and the Tibetan exile constitutions, which enshrine freedom of religion. The suit went beyond religious discrimination, seeking to bring down the government-in-exile altogether. The litigants asked judges to determine if "it is permissible to run a foreign government from the territory of India, which acts as a parallel government, and which administers its own code of justice, has its own parliament, executive and court systems, and has its own departments of Home, Security and External Affairs?"[28] A High Court justice rejected the appeal in April 2010, ruling that India does not formally recognize the Tibetan government-in-exile. The ruling also noted jurisdictional problems, saying that a state court would have to decide on issues of whether the rights had been infringed of individual Shugden followers in Karnataka in the south. The ruling left the door open for further suits, leaving in limbo whether further legal challenges would try to smudge the image of the god-king.

Such legal challenges put the Tibetan leader in a curious situation. He accuses China of repressing religious freedom in Tibet while a religious sect in turn accuses him of persecution. The lingering suspicion of followers of the Dalai Lama is that Beijing's hand and money were behind both the failed lawsuit and the resurgence of the Shugden cult. It is largely beyond dispute that Chinese authorities have provided money to Tibetan Buddhists to erect Shugden statues in monasteries in Tibetan areas and have promoted Shugden belief abroad among Tibetan exiles, part of a strategy to weaken and undercut an enemy. In the run-up to the Olympic Games, another seemingly well-funded Shugden group popped up, the Western Shugden Society, which produces slick pamphlets and webpages that call the Dalai Lama a "21st Century Buddhist Dictator."[29] The lama behind the lawsuit, the self-proclaimed Kundeling Rinpoche, also known as Lobsang Yeshe, is ethnically Han-Tibetan and acknowledges his sympathy with China's administration of Tibet, saying the region is better off under Beijing than it would be under the Dalai Lama. He has defended China's treatment of Tibetans during the Cultural Revolution and is a regular traveler from his base in southern India to China. Dharamsala officials say he is a paid agent of the Chinese government, a charge he dismisses.

Back in Dharamsala, I wandered into the offices of Karma Rinchen, who is the deputy head of security for the government-in-exile, to speak about the Shugden dispute. As we launched into a discussion, he pulled out a stack of photos that illustrated the close ties between Shugden proponents and the Chinese government. One showed a principal Shugden backer, Gangchen Lama, who lives in Katmandu, attending a reception at the Chinese embassy in Nepal. He handed me a paper marked "confidential." It claimed that the lama's close associates in Lhasa had won ownership of a large plot of land in Lhasa and a big hotel along the Nepalese border. It also alleged a series of meetings between the principal Shugden backers in India and Nepal and Chinese diplomatic and intelligence officers in various cities around Asia, including Hong Kong. Other photos showed Shugden protesters shoulder-to-shoulder with Chinese nationalists during a visit by the Dalai Lama to various cities around the United States in 2008. Increasingly, as the

Dalai Lama travels to Europe and North America, his security detail focuses as much on possible violence from Shugden followers as from other sources, including nationalist Chinese citizens who heed Beijing's view that the Dalai Lama is head of a criminal clique.

The conflict embroiling Shugden followers and the Tibetan government-in-exile has coincided more recently with a new phenomenon: A steady trickle of youthful Shugden adherents from Tibet arrive in Dharamsala, practically at the Dalai Lama's doorstep, claiming to seek monastic education. When a group of sixteen such teenagers, ranging in age from thirteen to eighteen, showed up at summer's end in 2008, their presence at the Tibet Reception Center, where refugees are housed, produced what police described as "law and order problems." Rinchen, the security official, told me the youths had come from Tibetan areas of China, spending two months undergoing training at a Shugden center in Nepal, then arriving in Dharamsala with the intent of raising social frictions. When they were asked to leave Dharamsala, they adamantly refused. Police later ordered their deportation back to Tibet.

China's efforts to obstruct and weaken the Dalai Lama's movement go largely unnoticed in the West, where sympathetic media coverage of the Tibetan leader focuses on his charisma and his feel-good exhortations on global issues and human compassion. Less attention is paid to the multipronged and often-subterranean battle to ensure that China's dominion over Tibet becomes an immoveable fact of life. China knows it has lost the battle in the West for public opinion. The movie stars and rock singers on the Dalai Lama's elbow attest to that. But in the end, glowing media coverage may not triumph over the groundswell of corporate interest in profiting from China's spectacular rise. No matter how many legislators rally to enact resolutions, no president dares risk the wrath of China and his or her own business community and recognize the Dalai Lama's exile government. The game is not over yet. But the corporate world is largely putting its money on the continued rule of the Chinese Communist Party, and the movie stars standing by the Dalai Lama's side are not turning back a rising tide.

chapter thirteen

Hollywood Versus Wal-Mart

I want our friends in Beijing to know that while occasionally we
look like a divided country, we are all united . . . in making this plea:
Let this man of peace visit Beijing.

—*U.S. Representative Tom Lantos, speaking at the Congressional
Gold Medal ceremony for the Dalai Lama, October 2007*

THE DALAI LAMA HAS SOME POWERFUL PLAYERS ON HIS SIDE FROM
Hollywood and the entertainment industry; they include A-list actors,
directors, producers, singers, composers, and rock bands. The celebrities
bring glamour, and they have time and again shown they can mobilize
global awareness on behalf of the Free Tibet movement. Some
actors, seeking to shed their images as narcissists in the superficial
world of Hollywood, flock to the side of the cuddly, impish Dalai Lama
and take up Tibetan Buddhism. As a religion, it does not make the
kind of cultish demands imposed by the Church of Scientology, a spiritual
sect that recruits heavily in Hollywood. Tibetan Buddhism seems
as benign as yoga, if not deeper. In turn, the Dalai Lama, savvy to the
political power of celebrity, actively woos entertainers, making time
for them at his enclave in India and providing special audiences when
he travels to the United States and Europe.

The Free Tibet movement took off in the 1990s. A series of Tibetan
Freedom Concerts raised awareness of China's repression. The first of
the concerts, a two-day show in San Francisco's Golden Gate Park in
June 1996, drew some hundred thousand people to see the Red Hot
Chili Peppers, Smashing Pumpkins, Rage Against the Machine, the

269

Beastie Boys, and other bands, and became one of the largest benefit concerts of modern times. Subsequent concerts were staged in New York and Washington in 1997 and 1998, and rural Wisconsin, Sydney, and Tokyo in 1999, pulling in such bands as U2, the Foo Fighters, Sonic Youth, Pearl Jam, and R.E.M. Like the Live Aid and Artists Against Apartheid concerts of the previous decade, the concerts inspired young people and spurred the worldwide growth of Students for a Free Tibet, a group advocating total independence for Tibet.

The late 1990s also saw several films, chief among them *Seven Years in Tibet*, starring Brad Pitt, and the Martin Scorcese–directed *Kundun*, about the Dalai Lama's early life. By the end of the decade, the Tibet issue was hot, and Adam Yauch, a bassist for the Beastie Boys who was instrumental in organizing the freedom concerts, enthused that "the more that we can raise this awareness, the more chance there is that our corporations and government will be forced to act in the interest of humanity."[1] Yauch saw that foreign conglomerates racing to get a piece of the China market would become a lever on the Tibet issue if their interests aligned with the Hollywood icons. But that was a tall order. Cultural artists said they spoke for the conscience of humanity on Tibet, while corporations said they spoke for consumers' wallets and the appetite for inexpensive Chinese-made goods. In the end, the Tibet issue would become a battle of Hollywood versus Wal-Mart.

By the end of the decade, the Dalai Lama was the world's most well-known Buddhist—and his celebrity followers, chief among them the squinty-eyed actor Richard Gere, constantly promoted the Tibet cause. Gere's interest was not the passing fancy of a Hollywood star adopting a religion du jour. He has been a committed Buddhist supporter of Tibet for over two decades, first coming to the public's attention on the issue during the 1993 Academy Awards ceremony. Departing from a script, he used his thirty seconds as presenter for the best art direction Oscar to denounce China for its "horrendous, horrendous human-rights situation." He appealed to China's then paramount leader, Deng Xiaoping, to "take his troops and take the Chinese away from Tibet and allow people to live as free independent people again." The sober outburst led the Academy to informally ban Gere as a presenter. Since then, Gere has grown more devoted to

Tibet, setting up his own charitable foundation, chairing the International Campaign for Tibet on behalf of the Dalai Lama, and camping out in Dharamsala for meetings with the Tibetan god-king, whom he considers his spiritual teacher.

I saw Gere in person on a brisk night in December 2009, when an eclectic mix of retired tycoons, socialites, mountaineers, monks in maroon robes, and social benefactors poured into a ballroom at the Westin St. Francis Hotel on San Francisco's Union Square. They arrived for a fund-raising dinner put on by the American Himalayan Foundation, a nonprofit group that supports Tibetans, Sherpas, and other Himalayan people. Tibetan prayer flags festooned the ballroom, and brilliant photographs of the Himalayas filled two huge screens on either side of the dais. The annual tribute dinner routinely draws Hollywood stars. The Dalai Lama attended one of the tribute dinners, and so did actors Harrison Ford, Sharon Stone, Steven Seagal, and Shirley MacLaine.

On the night I attended, the two men being honored were Gere and Lodi Gyari, the moon-faced longtime envoy of the Dalai Lama to Washington. Women seemed to predominate in the ballroom, and the Foundation's chair, Richard Blum, a financier and the husband of Sen. Dianne Feinstein, quipped that they had flocked to see Gere, who in his early sixties retains his trim, combustible look and dangerous charm.

Many celebrities have joined the Tibet bandwagon over the past two decades, including actors Pierce Brosnan, Dennis Quaid, Goldie Hawn, and Keanu Reaves. Directors Martin Scorcese and Oliver Stone are avid supporters of the Tibet cause, as is composer Philip Glass. Among musicians who are declared Buddhists or supporters of the Dalai Lama are Paul Simon, Sting, and Michael Stipe. But none display quite the earnestness and depth of conviction of Gere, who tends to hyperbolize when speaking about the plight of Tibetans. He did so on the night of the tribute. For Gere, the Tibet cause goes beyond salvaging a culture and a religious practice that, like a rare tropical jungle orchid, is endangered. Rather, it is something deeper. "This is not just about Tibet," Gere said from the podium, leaning forward and speaking slowly. "When His Holiness talks about Tibet, it's in the general sense most of the time. Tibet is an idea. It's an emotional, spiritual concept that's deep inside of all of us. 'Tibet' is the easiest form we've got to grab on to that concept, that yearning inside of us . . . to know that there is a way that we can live, where we can deeply respect each other and care for each other and be there for each other."[2]

Gere is in his fourth decade as a Hollywood heartthrob. The world got its first glimpse of him in the 1977 movie *Looking for Mr. Goodbar*, but he didn't break out until he played the boy toy starring role in *American Gigolo* in 1980. His status grew with the 1982 film *An Officer and a Gentlemen*. His career went through several ups and downs, morphing from sensual bad boy to mature smirking heartthrob, rising again in 1990, when he teamed with Julia Roberts in the smash romantic comedy *Pretty Woman*, and catching fire anew in the 2002 hit *Chicago*, for which he had to sweat through five months of training to prepare for a tap dance scene. "No, I can't dance, and I certainly don't dance as well as I look in the movies," he said at the time. "I worked for a long time, and I had a very smart teacher."[3]

In reality, Gere was depressive in his early career, reportedly checking himself into a New York psychiatric clinic at the age of twenty-one. "Like most young men, I was not particularly happy. I don't know if I was suicidal, but was pretty unhappy, and I had questions like, 'Why anything?'"[4] By age twenty-four, Gere was dabbling in Zen and beginning to practice meditation seriously. He traveled to Nepal after the success of his first movie, and by the time he was thirty or so, he had the opportunity to meet the Dalai Lama.

"I had been a Zen student for five or six years before I met His Holiness in India. We started out with a little small talk and then he said, 'Oh, so you're an actor?' He thought about that a second, and then he said, 'So when you do this acting and you're angry, are you really angry? When you're acting sad, are you really sad? When you cry, are you really crying?' I gave him some kind of actor answer, like it was more effective if you really believed in the emotion that you were portraying. He looked deeply into my eyes and just started laughing. Hysterically. He was laughing at the idea that I would believe emotions are real, that I would work very hard to believe in anger and hatred and sadness and pain and suffering. . . . It completely changed my life the first time I was in the presence of His Holiness. No question about it."[5]

Gere is a regular visitor to McLeod Ganj in India, where he has gone for individual instruction from Buddhist teachers, for meetings with the Dalai Lama, and to oversee charitable works. Once when I checked into the Chonor House, a charming eleven-room guesthouse run by the Dalai Lama–founded Norbulingka Institute, they asked if I wanted to stay in the room often occupied by Gere. I said yes. The third floor room has huge murals of Tibetan life and a big woolen rug with a tiger spreading its paws. Down the hill toward the Dalai Lama's offices, a small billboard lists Gere as one of the donors for a sewage system in McLeod Ganj.

Curiously, despite his outburst at the 1993 Academy Awards, Gere was invited by Beijing to go to China, and he recounted at the dinner his surprise at the invitation. The call came from a man representing China's version of its own Academy Awards, and Gere said he thought it was a prank. "The guy is obviously going to kill me, so I just ignored it. They kept calling repeatedly." He said he checked it out with friends in government (he said "the CIA," although I couldn't tell if he was serious or joking), and they confirmed that it was a legitimate invitation. Gere said he kept adding conditions to his participation, first declaring that he would only go to China if he could also go to Tibet, then demanding that his Buddhist teacher be allowed to accompany him. The Chinese agreed. "We did get to Tibet, and we had one of the most extraordinary times. It was so dense that every moment of that is still extraordinarily alive in me."[6]

Gere said one day he met with two nuns, one of whom revealed to him that the two had just been freed from prison, where they had been raped and abused. "When she finished telling the story, tears were streaming down my face. I said, 'How could you ever forgive your torturers?' and she looked at me with one of those very deep breaths and open gazes and said, 'It's so much bigger than them, and I can't be angry with them.'"[7]

Gere spends a large amount of time on Tibet issues. In one three-month period in late 2009, he traveled to Washington to catch up with the Dalai Lama, who was in town, and to take part in an annual conference put on by the Mind & Life Institute, which brings together leading scientists and Buddhists. A few weeks later, he flew to Rome for a global interparliamentary event on Tibet. Then in December, he turned up in San Francisco for the tribute dinner. I had been seeking a face-to-face interview with Gere for more than six months at the time of the tribute. But it was to no avail, and I couldn't help thinking he was more careful about his image and more difficult to see than even the Dalai Lama himself. His assistant asked me for a comprehensive list of my questions, a list of all the people I'd interviewed on Tibetan matters, a résumé, and a pledge to "share the text prepublication." I dutifully responded positively to all her requests and at one point was ready to board a transoceanic flight to meet him for half an hour, when she sent a short email that said in part, "Unfortunately, we cannot make this happen during the Washington visit. My apologies. I've given it the best try I can and we simply cannot get the time."[8]

If Gere was wary of letting a journalist probe his involvement on Tibet issues and views on China, he probably had ample reason, given the increasingly potent reaction from China on movie stars who mouth off about Tibet. Foremost is the case of actress Sharon Stone, the leggy star of such films as *Basic Instinct*. Following a devastating earthquake in China's Sichuan province in May 2008, killing some eighty thousand people, Stone was snagged by a journalist at the Cannes Film Festival and asked about the earthquake, which came nearly two months after repression of unrest in Tibet. "Well you know it was very interesting because at first, you know, I am not happy about the ways the Chinese were treating the Tibetans because I don't think anyone should be unkind to anyone else. And so I have been very concerned about how to think and what to do about that because I don't like *that*. And I had been this, you know, concerned about, oh how should we deal with the Olympics because they are not being nice to the Dalai Lama, who is a good friend of mine. And all these earthquake and stuff happened and I thought: Is that karma . . . when you are not nice that bad things happen to you?"[9]

Her off-the-cuff remarks brought a harsh and furious response in China. The video of her remarks went viral, with Chinese subtitles. Internet users called her "dirty swine," "whore," and worse, threatening to stone her if she set foot in China. The state-owned Xinhua News Agency declared her "public enemy of all mankind."[10] The French luxury goods group Christian Dior, for whom Stone modeled, posted an apology. "We absolutely disagree with her hasty comments and we are also deeply sorry about them," the Dior statement said. It then added what it said was a personal apology from Stone: "My erroneous words and deeds angered and saddened the Chinese people, and I sincerely apologize for this. I'm willing to participate in any earthquake relief activity and to do my utmost to help Chinese people affected by the disaster." Stone later denied making the apology, saying "I'm not going to apologize. I'm certainly not going to apologize for something that isn't real and true—not for face creams."[11] But it was too late, and Dior pulled all Stone's images from its advertising in China and said it would never use them again in the Middle Kingdom.

China had also reacted fiercely to criticism from another celebrity a few months earlier. When the Icelandic rock star Bjork performed to a sold-out crowd in Shanghai, she concluded her concert with an encore performance of "Declare Independence"—a rousing anthem containing such lyrics as "Raise your flag!" Just before walking off stage, Bjork yelled to the crowd in English: "Tibet! Tibet!" While the remark wasn't immediately reported in the state media, word got out on the internet, and Chinese fans voiced disappointment and even rage. "If she really did this, then this woman really makes people throw up," one person wrote on the website *sina.com*.

The Ministry of Culture said afterward that it would enhance scrutiny of foreign artistic acts coming to China to prevent similar incidents. Bjork's "political show has not only broken Chinese laws and regulations and hurt the feelings of Chinese people, but also went against the professional code of an artist," the ministry said.[12] Keeping its promise, the ministry barred the English rock band Oasis from performing in China in April 2009, and the band said the decision "left both Oasis and the promoters bewildered."[13] It shouldn't have. Lead songwriter Noel Gallagher of Oasis played at a Tibetan Freedom Concert in New York City twelve years earlier.

WHILE SOME ACTORS AND MUSICIANS are now watching their p's and q's, keeping an eye on the China market, the Dalai Lama is having none of it. He routinely seems to say what he believes, on China and other matters, and behaves in refreshing ways that perhaps break unwritten rules of protocol for holy figures. I've seen him repeatedly put on goofy sun visors when speaking in stadiums, or don strange hats. When he spots a friendly face with a long beard, it is not uncommon for him to grasp the beard with one hand and give it a waggle. On a trip to the United States, he spotted a young reporter with a lip ring. It was outside the National Civil Rights Museum in Memphis, Tennessee, and the Dalai Lama had just finished answering questions from the public. "After the Q&A, he was leaving the auditorium and everyone was reaching out to him," reporter Bianca Phillips said. "He stopped at me and said, 'Ooooh,' and he reached out and jiggled my lip ring. He kind of laughed to himself and then he walked on."[14]

Even when confronted with culturally confusing situations, the Dalai Lama takes them in good humor, generating headlines because of it. On the same trip, Memphis Mayor Myron Lowery received a *khata* from the Dalai Lama, then caught his attention by saying, "Here, we also have a tradition. You ball your fist like this." He then slowly moved his arm and gave the surprised Dalai Lama a fist-bump, touching fists gently with him rather than clasping hands. "They say you've got a sense of humor? I've always wanted to say, 'Hello, Dolly!'" Lowery said, as he gave the Tibetan another fist-bump. Chuckling but looking slightly perplexed, the Dalai Lama torqued his arm upward, unaware of how to do a fist-bump, and only vaguely aware that this symbol of violence had been converted into a contemporary sign of friendship. Amid some media criticism that the mayor was being disrespectful to the Dalai Lama, Lowery later defended himself. "I greeted him this way because I'm a down to earth guy, who was raised by a single mother with four sons in public housing," Lowery said. "I know His Holiness is always happy to participate in local customs, however obscure. He is about peace and harmony, and a fist bump is just another expression of warm friendship that he again returned to me before he left."[15] Whatever the Dalai Lama said over the next day or so was eclipsed by headlines that varied on the theme of, "Memphis mayor fist-bumps the Dalai Lama."

The unfailing good cheer of the Dalai Lama, and his seemingly shatterproof image of kindness and integrity have allowed him to overcome what some might consider blemishes on his reputation. One example is his friendship with Heinrich Harrer, an Austrian mountaineer and former Nazi SS sergeant who escaped internment in India and made his way to Lhasa in 1946. Harrer became a friend of the Dalai Lama, who was eleven years old at the time, after the boy spotted him with his telescope from the heights of the Potala Palace as he walked around the streets of Lhasa. Harrer stayed in Lhasa nearly seven years, serving some of the time as a tutor of the young Dalai Lama in English and geography, drawing worldwide attention to China's takeover of the mountain realm in his subsequent book *Seven Years in Tibet*. Aides to the Tibetan leader dismissed concerns about Harrer's past, saying he had mobilized concern and sympathy for Tibet worldwide later in his life.

Another example was the acquaintance of the Dalai Lama with Shoko Asahara, later known as the "doomsday guru," Japanese leader of the Aum Shinrikyo sect. The nearly blind Japanese spiritualist was born into a poor family of tatami makers and later attended a school for the blind. On return from a trip to India in 1987, during which he met the Dalai Lama, he declared himself enlightened, fighting on behalf of his group with the Japanese government for status as a religious organization. Dalai Lama supporters interceded on his behalf, and the status was obtained in 1989. In gratitude, Asahara sent $100,000 to Dharamsala to help Tibetan refugees. As the Japanese guru gained more adherents, often exhibiting messianic tendencies, his group's relations with Dharamsala frayed. On March 20, 1995, members of the group used the nerve gas sarin in an attack on the Tokyo subway system. The attack killed twelve commuters, and injured some fifty-five hundred others. The goal of the attack was to destroy Tokyo and allow Asahara to rule Japan. He was later convicted and sentenced to death by hanging.

The Dalai Lama later said his error was proof that he is not a "living Buddha."[16] Such occasional relationships are perhaps inevitable, given the enormous number of people with whom the Dalai Lama has contact and his propensity to give everyone the benefit of the doubt. The Dalai Lama is also not one to back away from a friendship with the changing mood of the times. I'd heard him on several occasions extol his friendship with George W. Bush before crowds who undoubtedly did not share his warm feelings toward the former president.

Other less well-known aspects of the Dalai Lama might surprise the casual supporter. For one, unlike many Buddhists around the world, who revere all living things and practice vegetarianism, the Dalai Lama is a moderate meat eater. Most Tibetans living on the high Plateau eat meat because few vegetables grow in the harsh climate.

The Dalai Lama experimented with vegetarianism in the early 1960s after his arrival in India but said he followed the advice of physicians to return to moderate meat consumption after he developed liver damage from a slight case of hepatitis B. Decades later, he said he only consumed meat every other day, then by 2004 only when he was traveling, lauding the vegetarian diet as good for the planet. Still, some of those who saw him consume meat voiced surprise. During a stop in Milwaukee, Wisconsin, in May 2007, a chef said she planned a vegetarian feast for a fundraiser that His Holiness would attend but was instructed to include meat. So the menu included a cured fish appetizer, soup with a chicken base, stuffed pheasant breast, and a slow-cooked veal roast. The Dalai Lama ate with gusto. "He chowed down," chef Sandy D'Amato told a local newspaper.[17] A vegetarian American Buddhist wrote in disgust to the Dalai Lama after the event, publicly chiding him for "continuing to eat the flesh of murdered mother beings."[18]

The Dalai Lama's views on homosexuality have also distressed some of his supporters. In 1997, he told Buddhist supporters in San Francisco that gay sex, from a Buddhist point of view, is considered sexual misconduct. In fact, Tibetan Buddhism proscribes homosexual sex and heterosexual sex through orifices other than the vagina, including masturbation or other sexual activity with the hand. He later clarified that he advocates respect, tolerance, and compassion for gays, who should enjoy equal rights as others.[19]

Such potentially negative stuff doesn't stick, and it's partly because the Dalai Lama has become a pop culture icon, mentioned in movies and appearing in advertising, held up as an epitome of peace and spiritual grace. In *Caddyshack*, the 1980 film comedy, Bill Murray's character Carl Spackler recounts how he wound up as a golf caddy in Tibet for the Dalai Lama—and got a holy promise in lieu of a tip. "So we finish the eighteenth, and he's gonna stiff me. And I say, 'Hey, Lama, hey, how about a little something, you know, for the effort, you know.' And he says, 'Oh, uh, there won't be any money, but when you die, on your deathbed, you will receive total consciousness.' So I got that goin' for me, which is nice," Spackler says. Advertisers have profited from the Tibetan leader's beatific, enlightened image. As part of its five-year Think Different ad campaign begun in 1997, Apple helped restore its reputation as an innovative company by pasting up images of the Dalai Lama on billboards and in magazine ads, along with images of Thomas Edison, Albert Einstein, and other luminaries. Mentions of the Dalai Lama find their way into television programs. In an episode of the sitcom *Frasier*, the main character criticizes his manager for unethical tactics, and she snaps back, "If you wanted an ethical agent, you should have hired the Dalai Lama!" The Dalai Lama found his way into an episode of *The Simpsons* in its fifteenth season, when Homer Simpson, dressed as the superhero Pie Man, prepares to throw a pie in the face of the Tibetan leader at the behest of his boss, who says "all his talk of peace and love is honking off my Red Chinese masters." Homer Simpson eventually desists.

THE DALAI LAMA HAS BEEN CLEVER at harnessing both the power of celebrity and political power to the Free Tibet movement. More than two decades after he won the Nobel Prize, the movement has become a formidable force in a number of capitals in Europe and North America. To better understand how that rise occurred, I scheduled an appointment with Lodi Gyari, the Tibetan envoy honored with Richard Gere in San Francisco.

Gyari is the Dalai Lama's most trusted adviser on foreign affairs and his lead negotiator with the Chinese government. He operates from the Washington office of the International Campaign for Tibet. The campaign, a global nonprofit advocacy group begun in 1988, operates from an attractive four-story brownstone painted mustard and wine red on a side street off of Connecticut Avenue in Washington, DC. It is a neighborhood occupied by elegant restaurants, law firms, think tanks, banks, and lobbying concerns. Like much of the building, Gyari's office is decorated simply. A few Tibetan carpets grace the floor, and modest wooden office furniture fills the room. No curtains block the sun's rays through the two bay windows facing south. Gyari wore gray trousers, an elegant pink shirt, and a brown herringbone sport coat with a Tibet pin in the lapel. He took his glasses off and put them back on repeatedly during our conversation. The photos on bookcases and on one wall were mostly of the Dalai Lama and other Tibetan leaders, not of his wife and six children.

Gyari is widely credited around Washington as a sharp-witted and honest envoy, winning the trust of those in a position to offer good advice. His talent as a diplomat has coincided with the growing awareness of Tibet generated by Hollywood, and one can chart the rise in Gyari's clout through the years with his increased access across the Washington bureaucracy. Today, although no country recognizes the Tibetan exile government, Gyari is treated as if he were the ambassador of a middle-size power. In a sign of the trust in him, the FBI periodically sweeps his Washington office for bugs presumably placed by the Chinese and offers other security advice. In the early years, though, such gestures were rare, and access was minimal.

When Gyari accompanied the Dalai Lama on his first visit to Washington, it was the late 1970s, Jimmy Carter was in the White House, and the Oval Office declined a meeting with the Tibetan leader. The Dalai Lama even had trouble getting a visa to enter the United States. When Gyari relocated to Washington as a permanent representative during the Reagan administration in the 1980s, it still wasn't easy. Any meetings were only with junior-level officials, and they always were wary of compromising the "one-China policy" by which Washington recognized Beijing's position that it was the sole legitimate government of mainland China (including Tibet), Hong Kong, and Taiwan. The low-level officials refused to meet in their own offices, insisting on going out to the street. "We'd meet at the most sort of funkiest places, you know, not even the kind of decent hotel or restaurant—very small funky coffee shops. Compare that with the current situation, and to use a Chinese term, the change is earth-shattering," Gyari recalled.[20] The change was slow. Even years after his arrival, Gyari would have to stand in line at the State Department and present his ID, waiting for a guide to see him to his appointment. He couldn't even go to Capitol Hill without a State Department escort.

Throughout the two terms of the Reagan presidency, a White House meeting for the Dalai Lama could not be arranged. The first such meeting was with President George H. W. Bush, and while the encounter was cordial and warm it was nothing like the love-ins a decade or so later with his son. "The senior Bush did not show the kind of interest that his son took. . . . For him, the China relation was very important for the United States, and I think he . . . saw that compared to the importance of the China issue, Tibet was insignificant."[21] Senior advisers to the elder Bush saw Tibet as an irritant in Sino-U.S.

relations, already soured by the 1989 Tiananmen uprising. But the president saw the Tibetan for thirty minutes in the White House just three days before the Dalai Lama spoke to a receptive gathering of legislators in the Capitol, an event arranged by the Speaker of the House and the Senate majority leader, both Democrats.[22]

It wasn't until the White House had a new occupant, the saxophone-playing former governor of Arkansas who hobnobbed with the Hollywood set, that the Dalai Lama's profile (and Gyari's status) began a sharp ascent in Washington. The Dalai Lama now had the Nobel distinction, and legislators on Capitol Hill treated him as a global dignitary worthy of a grand reception, in part to show their pique with China's one-party system. "It was not the kind of instant rapport, which took time, but gradually it became a very warm friendship both with President Clinton and also I must say with Hillary. In fact, Hillary in some ways had more of a heart connection. She actually even hosted His Holiness for a meal. I remember vividly because this was soon after her trip to China for the world women's conference [in 1995]," Gyari said. During that trip, Hillary Clinton also toured Mongolia, where she saw photographs of the Dalai Lama in nearly every nomad's tent. She brought it up at the meal. "I remember her saying, 'Your Holiness, I did not know that you are such a popular figure in Mongolia. If you run for any office there, most likely none of the present politicians would have a hope.' And His Holiness said, 'Yes, that's true.' . . . Every time His Holiness would meet with the president, she would make an effort to join."[23]

The Dalai Lama already had an established relationship with Vice President Al Gore from when he was a U.S. senator, and the ties warmed further when the two met in Rio de Janeiro at the 1992 Earth Summit. Gore served as the pretext for meetings with Clinton, who initially was reticent to meet one-on-one with the Dalai Lama on the advice of his China experts. "Two of the meetings were initially 'drop by.' We'd go to meet with Al Gore, and Clinton would come and join them." After those drop-bys in 1993 and 1994, the Senate passed a unanimous resolution in 1995 urging Clinton to meet with the Dalai Lama one-on-one in the White House, but again he preferred to enter a prearranged meeting between the Tibetan and Gore. In 1998, Clinton spent thirty minutes with the Dalai Lama at the White House, but the meeting was on the calendar as hosted by Hillary Clinton, keeping it at an informal level.

Perhaps surprisingly, given that Democratic lawmakers had pressed hardest to open doors for the Dalai Lama, it was Republican President George W. Bush who developed the warmest relations with him. Months after coming to office in 2001, Bush invited the Dalai Lama to the White House residence, and the Tibetan later said the meeting was like "when two old friends" get together.[24] Years later, when the Bush presidency was mired in two unpopular wars, the Dalai Lama maintained his public praise of the former U.S. leader: "To be honest, some of his policies have been a disaster, but as a person I love him. He is open, very truthful. At the first meeting, we were very close." Gyari said the affection was sincere. "From the very first meeting, there was instant chemistry between the two." Gyari said Bush must have spoken of the meetings in 2001 and 2003 to his wife, Laura Bush, because she expressed a desire to meet the Tibetan holy man. Gyari described the First Lady as "a very, very warm person, an exceptionally warm person," and said she'd already shown interest in certain global issues such as in Afghanistan and Myanmar. Laura Bush grew so interested in the Tibet issue that she invited Lodi Gyari to a private lunch at the White House near the end of the second Bush term. "She indicated that she herself would like to be active on the Tibet issue," he said later, suggesting that the couple would be "of great value to Tibet" postpresidency. Laura Bush later mentioned the Dalai Lama in her memoir, calling him a "dear and gentle man whose example is an inspiration. . . . George believes that acknowledging the Dalai Lama is a special American responsibility. The world looks to the United States for leadership, and if we do not stand up for freedom, who will."[25]

Despite the personal warmth during the Bush term, occupants of the White House have generally shown goodwill toward the Dalai Lama behind closed doors, unlike the open-armed embrace given him at the U.S. Capitol. Indeed, for nearly two decades U.S. legislators have followed a different, far friendlier foreign policy toward Tibet than the White House, even declaring in a concurrent Congressional resolution in 1991 that Tibet and ethnic Tibetan areas of Qinghai, Gansu, Sichuan, and Yunnan provinces constitute "an occupied country . . . whose true representatives are the Dalai Lama and the Tibetan

Government in exile." Elected members of Congress, responding more directly to public sentiment, felt greater sympathy to the Tibet issue, while the occupant of the White House listened attentively to corporate and trade interests. Presidents have tended to foster better relations with China, where U.S. corporations hoped to profit, keeping the Tibet issue secondary. But slowly, Congress used its power to force executive branches to give Tibet special treatment.

In 1994, Congress passed a Foreign Relations Authorization Act that obligated all future executive branch reports to Congress to list Tibet alphabetically under its own state heading. In subsequent years, Congress made further demands on the executive branch, ordering it to seek to station a Tibetan-speaking U.S. diplomat in Lhasa, query China on a semiannual basis about Tibetan political prisoners, and install a senior official as a high-level "special coordinator for Tibet issues" at the State Department. Funding for programs to tend to Tibetan exiles was assured. By the turn of the century, U.S. legislators ditched language that labeled Tibet as an "occupied country," but annual nonbinding resolutions urged the White House to press China to conduct meaningful negotiations with the Dalai Lama about Tibet's future and monitor political and religious repression in Tibet.

Still, as China's rise as a global player gathered greater momentum, the chasm only grew between the highfalutin rhetoric of Capitol Hill in support of the Dalai Lama and the Realpolitik policies of a White House eager to win Chinese support on issues ranging from Iraq and North Korea to global warming. The chasm was only one of many fault lines that seemed to favor China's status quo iron grip on Tibet. Other fault lines included the failure of various aggrieved minorities, religious freedom advocates, and pro-democracy forces to unite in a common approach to challenge Beijing. A third crevasse separated the harsh world of Tibetans living under China's thumb, largely unaware of the actions of a muscular global Tibetan movement overseas, powered by a potent media machine and the worldwide fame of the Dalai Lama.

For one brief day in Washington, the differing fault lines seemed to melt away in a moving moment of solidarity and goodwill with the Dalai Lama. Democratic and Republican legislators—at each others' throats on many domestic and international issues—joined together on October 17, 2007, to award the Dalai Lama the highest U.S. government civilian honor, the Congressional Gold Medal. Few other world leaders have been so honored. Mother Teresa, Pope John Paul II, Nelson Mandela, and Tony Blair are among those who have. President George W. Bush, his wife, and the two highest-ranking members of the U.S. Congress presented the medal in a ceremony that marked the first time a U.S. president had appeared in public with the Dalai Lama. They did so in the Rotunda, the majestic central hall of the Capitol and symbolic heart of legislative power. Outside on the Capitol lawn, nearly ten thousand Tibet supporters watched on giant screens as the ceremony unfolded inside, where high-powered legislators, cabinet members, Nobel laureates, celebrities, and clergy of many religious affiliations, including Tibetan monks, sat in the audience. A flag-bearing Marine Corps honor guard added to the sense that the ceremony was an expression of the highest levels of state.

At the ceremony, one of the first to speak was Elie Wiesel, the Holocaust survivor and fellow Nobel Peace Prize laureate. "Admired by millions all over the world, true to his tradition and open to all others, forever ready to listen and willing to learn, His Holiness the Dalai Lama is a man of profound spiritual conviction who believes that like all people his own in Tibet have the right to live a sovereign religious and cultural life. This is a right that must never be deprived from anyone," Wiesel said to a standing ovation.[26] The clapping resounded in the Rotunda, a stately room ninety-six feet across with a soaring canopy that extends a hundred eighty feet overhead. The walls embody the history of the nation. Friezes below the dome windows depict scenes from American history, and at a lower level large oil paintings feature scenes like the embarkation of pilgrims to the New World, the 1776 signing of the Declaration of Independence, and the surrender of Lord Cornwallis, signaling the coming end of the Revolutionary War.

As Wiesel finished speaking, House Speaker Nancy Pelosi, seated on one side of the Dalai Lama while President Bush sat on the other, wiped away a tear. Pelosi, a Democrat, invoked the history of the moment in recalling that President Franklin Roosevelt had sent the very young Dalai Lama, who enjoyed the sciences and mechanics, a watch showing the phases of the moon and the days of the week. "The Dalai

Lama described the watch as magnificent and even took it with him when he fled Tibet in 1959," Pelosi said. "President Roosevelt gave the Dalai Lama a gold watch. Today, President Bush will give him the Congressional Gold Medal."[27]

Speaking that day were liberal Democrats from California, an anti-communist Cuban-American Republican from Miami, and a conservative senior senator from Kentucky. Reaching across the aisle, they hailed the Dalai Lama as a peacemaker who transcended his religious tradition. Rep. Tom Lantos, a Jewish Hungarian Holocaust survivor, who died a few months after the ceremony, acclaimed the Tibetan leader as a global moral leader: "At a moment in world history when nothing is in as short supply as moral authority, this humble Buddhist monk has an inexhaustible supply." Lantos said Democrats and Republicans were united in urging China to permit the Dalai Lama to travel to Beijing to present his case for Tibetans. Sen. Mitch Mc-Connell, leader of the Republican bench in the Senate, recalled the longstanding sentiment on Capitol Hill demanding that China grant Tibetans greater freedom and protection of their heritage:

> Congress has expressed this view in 16 resolutions since 2001. We've delivered funds to preserve the Tibetan culture and to help refugees who've escaped through the mountains to India and to Nepal. We've educated some of these refugees at U.S. schools through the Tibet Fulbright Program. And we broadcast a message of hope across Tibet through the Voice of America and Radio Free Asia. Again and again, we've reached out in solidarity to the Dalai Lama and the Tibetan people, and the Chinese government needs to know that we will continue to do so. The U.S. Congress stands with Tibet.[28]

The venue provided the Dalai Lama with one of his most important political platforms ever. And it was one of the rare occasions on which he relied on a printed speech rather than speaking extemporaneously, certain that his words would ricochet to multiple audiences around the world and to his own people inside modern-day China. He told the legislators that the award would "bring great joy and encouragement" to Tibetans. Turning to the issue of negotiations with China, he said the achievement of broader autonomy for Tibet would not be a stepping-stone toward full independence, as Beijing argued. Rather, Tibet needs to be linked to China's stronger economic growth to prosper and is sincere in seeking to remain under China's umbrella. But he also exhorted Beijing to examine the reasons for simmering tensions in Tibet: "Let me take this opportunity to once again appeal to the Chinese leadership to recognize the genuine grievances and deep resentments of the Tibetan people inside Tibet, and to have the courage and wisdom to address these problems realistically in the spirit of reconciliation."[29]

The medal ceremony lasted less than an hour, and to the other-worldly sonorous sound of Tibetan long horns the Dalai Lama walked arm in arm with Pelosi to the front steps of the Capitol to greet the thousands of people assembled. Pelosi told the crowd that the ceremony inside the Rotunda was aimed partly at Beijing. "The United States was sending a very clear message, a very clear signal, to the People's Republic of China that we want them to receive His Holiness in Beijing for substantive talks," she said.[30]

More than two years later, at the tribute dinner in San Francisco, Gere brought up the congressional medal ceremony, saying it "was kind of a recapturing of possibilities." His talk was relentlessly positive, yet at one point at the end of his speech he segued into what I took to thinking of as the "Hail Mary" strategy of Tibetan activists. The strategy entails keeping one's fingers crossed that China's political system will implode, permitting Tibet to exert itself and gain autonomy, perhaps like that of Hong Kong. "There's so much more to be done," Gere said, "even when China changes radically. And that is going to happen. History tells us that it will change radically. Therefore the state . . . and the lives of Tibetans [are] going to change. But we've got to keep the Tibetans alive until that happens. We need education; we need health; we need all the things that refugee communities need."[31]

It was the second time during the evening that I had heard the suggestion that the viable hope for exile Tibetans, and by extension all Tibetans, is to ride it out until radical change comes to China. Sitting across from me at my table in the vast ballroom was a well-dressed, middle-aged gentleman with an Old World accent that I couldn't immediately place. As we feasted on glazed salmon during the dinner, a

Berkeley psychologist sitting beside me, Danny Goldstine, heard that I was writing a book about Tibet and suggested I move to an empty chair across the table next to the European, who later identified himself as Michael C. van Walt, a lawyer from the Netherlands who had spent more than two decades as a legal consultant for the Dalai Lama. During the 1990s, van Walt was general secretary of the Unrepresented Nations and Peoples Organization (UNPO), an advocacy group representing scores of ethnic groups and peoples with no representation in the United Nations and other international groups. I knew that Tibetan exiles worked extensively with UNPO.

As I introduced myself to van Walt and noted my pessimistic outlook on any greater autonomy for Tibet, he immediately demurred, bringing up the case of East Timor, with which he had intimate familiarity. A former colony of Portugal, East Timor declared independence in late 1975, only to be invaded and occupied by Indonesian troops and declared a province within the Indonesian archipelago a year later. Indonesia resisted all attempts by the Timorese for freedom.

But a series of sudden, unforeseen events rocked Indonesia in the late 1990s, and East Timorese independence advocates took advantage of the opening. The East Asian financial crisis of 1997–1998 hit Indonesia harder than anywhere else in Southeast Asia and loosened General Suharto's grip as the nation's strongman leader. As huge forest fires and severe drought brought further calamity, Suharto faced protests and street riots when he won reelection in early 1998. He agreed to step down in May that year. A weak leader, interim President B. J. Habibie acceded to pressure from Washington and Lisbon to allow East Timor to hold a UN-supervised referendum on independence, which separatists won by a landslide. Amid ongoing political instability in Indonesia, East Timor's proclaimed independence was recognized in the United Nations in 2002. As an adviser to the nascent Timorese government, van Walt helped review the draft constitution and set up the Foreign Ministry.

"Look at East Timor," he told me during the dinner. "Once there was a change in Indonesia, they were ready." That was the best hope for Tibetan exile leaders, he added. Tibetan exile leaders must engage China in negotiations, even when the talks go nowhere. But as they do so, they should prepare tactics for quick action when radical political change comes to China. A boisterous charity auction at the tribute dinner prevented us from talking further. But I mulled the implications of what he said. Given the history of the fall of the Berlin Wall, it isn't hard to imagine a crumbling or even sudden collapse of one-party rule in China. Already bookstores hold volumes like the 2001 title *The Coming Collapse of China*. But such predictions seemed a fool's game. The timescale for "coming" could be quite distant, and things might be different this time around.

Few pundits predicted how quickly the Soviet Union and Eastern Europe would come apart in 1989. Equally few foresaw that China could sustain its dramatic economic rise over three decades. China began the century with economic output of $1.1 trillion. It finished its first decade of the century with output of nearly $5 trillion. I saw the growth every day once I left my office in China, observing people in the streets. At the beginning of the decade, some 48 million mobile phones were in use in the country. By decade's end, there were 739 million mobile phone users, or more than half the total population.[32] A dose of wishful thinking appeared to be at play in the doomsday predictions for China's Communist Party, perhaps partly from the discomfort at the Middle Kingdom's newfound strength and role as banker to Western nations. After all, China's holdings of U.S. Treasury bonds approached $1 trillion, giving it significant leverage as the holder of the mortgage on the U.S. future. China's rise is far from over.

In reality, the goodwill of the Congressional Gold Medal ceremony for the Dalai Lama was a temporary mirage, having symbolic importance but unlikely to shift U.S. policy. Tibet is a sideshow to complex, multifaceted Sino-U.S. relations on which key issues that affect the two countries, and even the world, completely rest, such as efforts to fight global warming. Like a struggling mountaineer, Tibet could fall into multiple crevasses on the slopes. One crevasse might be figuratively labeled the "Wal-Mart fissure." While legislators indicate they speak for the conscience of Americans in supporting the Dalai Lama, and celebrities clamor on behalf of Tibet, the White House speaks for the major U.S. corporations with huge investments in China, like Wal-Mart, the world's biggest retailer and number 2 on the list of Fortune 500 corporations. Wal-Mart imports about 70 percent of its products from China. In 2007, Wal-Mart alone imported $32 billion from

China, and today it accounts for between 10 and 15 percent of all U.S. imports from China. If Wal-Mart were its own country, in 2008 it would have ranked as the eighth largest importer of Chinese goods, ahead of Russia and India.[33] With its control over suppliers, Wal-Mart provides consumers with too-cheap-to-beat prices. Westerners might adore the Dalai Lama, but many love their high-paying jobs and their cheap Chinese-made products more. In essence, Wal-Mart has trumped the Dalai Lama. And as long as that is the case, elected leaders of government are likely to allow good relations with China to outweigh concerns about religious freedom and Tibet. Even Tibetan exiles have largely ignored half-hearted calls to boycott Chinese-made goods.

In a small way, even while it is vastly outgunned by pro-China business interests, the Tibet movement has grown institutionally stronger. A shoestring outfit during the late 1980s and early 1990s, the International Campaign for Tibet had barely eleven employees on its staff in 1999. By 2008, the group employed thirty staff; maintained offices in Berlin, Amsterdam, and Brussels as well as Washington; and received $5.3 million in contributions. One large donor had given the group around $2 million, enough to buy its imposing offices in Washington, DC. The group's skilled lobbyists were helping shape resolutions on Capitol Hill, funnel information to the media, and provide a steady stream of reports about conditions inside Tibet.

Still, in the broader community of Tibetan activists and on the ground on the Plateau, a measure of unreality has set in. Young activists abroad carry out stunts to garner headlines, making their fundraising easier but ignoring the fact that it has no impact on Tibetans under Chinese rule. One day in June 2006, I got word that I should go to the main Beijing railway station to witness an action by Students for a Free Tibet. The protest was to coincide with the inauguration of the new railway line linking Beijing to Lhasa. I mingled outside the station with a few colleagues when we saw two Westerners suddenly move out on a ledge on the main railway building and unfurl a banner. It read: "China's Tibet Railway: Designed to Destroy."

I had mixed feelings about the incident and ended up writing a blog item, noting that none of the activists were even Tibetan. "Their banner was in English, not Chinese or Tibetan, and few people in front of the train station took notice or were able to read the banner," I wrote. "So without complicit Western media to document the event, it would have gone unnoticed. Is this unfurling of a banner news, or is it not?" In hindsight, it seemed, as one astute person commented on the blog afterward, "street theater without content. Of course, this in itself can be a meta-story about why people pursue this apparently pointless approach."[34] Another reader wrote in to say that other kinds of culture are being destroyed all over China, but Westerners only seem to care about Tibet. "Maybe if the other 1.3 billion people in China thought Tibetan activists gave a crap about them too, they might listen to what they say once in a while."[35]

As I pondered Tibet's future, my thoughts harkened back to the Dalai Lama's bet that he would live longer than the Chinese Communist Party. Maybe his wager will pan out. But the prediction reflects the essential failure of other options. No amount of Hollywood celebrity chatter about His Holiness has weakened China's chokehold on Tibet. In the end, Tibetans hope that they are more robust than a Chinese political system with fundamental flaws that may someday cause it to crumble. It is a wager that may go wrong. And in the interim, Tibetans on the Plateau, hearing of certain events abroad, such as when the U.S. president meets with the Dalai Lama, can tragically misinterpret such events as solid support and take to the streets in protest only to be severely repressed.[36] Tibetans at home are only dimly aware of the Freedom Concerts, street actions, and elements of the overseas campaigns on their behalf. I had made a habit of asking them about it. My questions brought approving nods and signals of appreciation. But most Tibetans know no details. Hardly any I ever met had ever heard of Richard Gere. I would continually ask about the man known in Mandarin as Li-cha Ji-er and find puzzled looks. Invariably, the Tibetans would turn the conversation to one topic: When will the Dalai Lama return to Tibet? Some would even ask, Will he return this year? I rarely had the heart to disrupt their delusional dreams: China's leaders will never permit the Dalai Lama to return to Tibet. He may well pass to the "heavenly fields" without ever setting foot again in Tibet, denying the chance for his devoted followers to lay eyes on their god-king.

epilogue

China's "Totally Correct" Policies

It is impossible for the West to cooperate with China unless it develops an objective and unbiased stance on Tibet.
  —People's Daily *commentary, March 5, 2009*

TO HEAR GOVERNMENT SPOKESPERSONS TELL IT, INTERNET censorship does not exist in China. Nor is the peace-loving People's Liberation Army building up its strength at a particularly fast pace. China's society is stable, inherently democratic, and a multiethnic quilt in which religious freedom and social harmony prevail. The nation's foreign policy is pragmatic, yet the nation has no real leverage over its troublesome neighbor, North Korea. Such blatant mistruths are part of the manufactured reality that the one-party state creates as it exerts control over China. Occasionally, though, a spokesperson will come up with a new whopper, a claim of such prodigiously false dimensions that even experienced China hands sit up and take note.

That happened one day in early 2010. Chinese courts had just upheld an extraordinary eleven-year prison sentence for Liu Xiaobo, a tart-tongued dissident with a penchant for needling the party. I had interviewed Liu many times. Every time I saw him, I would walk out smiling, appreciating his ability to unravel the inner logic of the party. A literature professor by training, Liu used an acute ability at deconstruction to explain the party's subterfuges, and his amused irony made his analyses especially engaging. Liu wore rimless glasses and usually kept his hair tightly cropped. His teeth were stained from a heavy smoking habit. He always asked me to buy him a pack of cigarettes at the teahouse where we would meet, and I was happy to oblige. He could smoke all he wanted—as long as he kept talking. Then in late 2008, Liu overstepped the subtle red line drawn by the party, taking action that it saw as a threat to its grip on power. He led a small group of dissidents in devising a pro-democracy manifesto that they called Charter 08, which demanded a guarantee of basic civil rights. Word of the charter drive, which would eventually gather thousands of signatures, reached the public security bureau, and officers came to arrest him. After a closed-door trial, judges gave Liu his harsh sentence for "inciting subversion of state power." His defense was not allowed to present evidence. On Feb. 11, 2010, a court upheld the lengthy prison sentence.[1]

Later the same day, the spokesman for the Ministry of Foreign Affairs, Ma Zhaoxu, a polished and suave figure, was asked at a press briefing what signal Liu's sentence sent to political dissidents in China. "There are no dissidents in China," Ma said, without betraying any discomfort at making such an extraordinary claim.

When word got out of Ma's assertion, another of the myriad dissidents in China, Ai Weiwei, quickly went into action. The artist and commentator wrote a message to his followers on the Twitter microblogging service, suggesting a multilayered meaning to Ma's statement.[2] The subtext, he wrote, was the following:

1. Dissidents are criminals.
2. Only criminals have dissident ideas.
3. The distinction between criminals and noncriminals is whether they have dissident views.
4. If you think China has dissidents, you're a criminal.
5. The reason China has no dissidents is because they have already become criminals.
6. Does anyone have a dissenting view about what I've said?

Ai Weiwei's father is one of China's most prominent modern poets, a man admired by Mao even though the party banished him for years to the western desert. Ai himself is a pioneer in the contemporary art scene. Perhaps because of all of this, security agents didn't detain him. China's internet-blocking software, known as the Great Firewall, denies access to Twitter, and the fact that not many Chinese saw Ai's sardonic commentary might have saved him. Still, tens of thousands of Chinese use commonly available technology, such as virtual private networks or proxy servers, to leap past the Great Firewall and access banned services like Twitter and YouTube. Indeed, Ma's claim and Ai's sarcastic response embody some of the paradoxical trends in China, developments that make predictions about the Middle Kingdom— and Tibet—far from certain.

Since the "color revolutions" against authoritarian rule spread across the Caucasus and Central Asia, and in the wake of widespread ethnic unrest in Tibet in 2008 and Xinjiang in 2009, the party has tightened its repressive measures. Yet the sheer number of internet users has exploded, multiplying nearly fourfold in four years to more than four hundred million. Public debate occurs on a surprising range of topics, and censors race to keep atop sensitive issues and delete some topics even as party leaders from the highest echelons to the county level constantly take the temperature of public opinion and respond to it. In some ways, a nascent participatory system is emerging, although far from a democratic one.

The shifting boundaries of debate are often linguistic and never more so than on Tibet. The party has named the main English-language magazine about the region *China's Tibet*, and the possessive phrase is common in state news reports, sounding as unnecessary as saying America's Florida, Canada's Yukon, or India's Karnataka state. Since unrest in 2008, official foreign policy has entailed requiring foreign leaders visiting China to take a verbal stand on Tibet. It doesn't matter whether foreigners agree in their hearts or not, party leaders want to hear them say Tibet is an integral part of China, as if uttering the statement actually makes it so. The verbal stand has become a basic requirement of winning China's cooperation. The diplomacy is a variation of the Nike ad "Just Say It," and it reflects the antithetical strains of China's growing self-assuredness and its insecurity.

China's leaders know that after more than six decades of strict military control of Tibet, and billions of dollars in investment and subsidies, they have failed to integrate Tibet into China's fabric. They feel the palpable alienation of Tibetans from their rule, and they fear that Beijing's hold on the geostrategic region may be tenuous. It's not only

Tibet. Social stability faces challenges from multiple sources of in-equality and disapproval of one policy or another every week, testing the party's legitimacy and grip on power. By one measure, the num-ber of "mass incidents" of unrest increased from 8,709 in 1993 to 90,000 in 2006, and has exceeded that number through 2009.[3] It is one of the paradoxes of modern China that its leaders have much to be confident about yet exhibit such a state of jitters over the nation's stability and the future of Tibet. Their insistence on having foreigners assure them that Tibet is a part of China has the odor of a compulsive neurotic whose anxiety is slightly repellent but nearly beyond his or her control.

The party's mistrust of Tibetans continually finds new outlets. Most recently, printing and copy shops in Lhasa have been required to record customers' identities for fear that photocopying documents in Tibetan could be a channel for unrest. In putting forward the regu-lation, the party indicated how it views Tibetan language documents as potentially incendiary and destabilizing. The *New York Times* quoted a Han Chinese print shop operator in Lhasa who said that her husband had been summoned to a meeting about the new require-ments. "You know sometimes people print documents in the Tibetan language, which we don't understand," the woman told the *Times*. "These might be illegal pamphlets."[4]

Yet no matter how worried party leaders may be about Tibet, their public posture reflects no indecision or internal debate. After a top-level forum in early 2010 to design strategy toward Tibet in the decade ahead, an event held periodically, the state media hailed the party's policies as unerring. "The Communist Party of China (CPC) Central Committee's policies towards Tibet in the new era were to-tally correct, suiting to national condition, Tibet's actual conditions and the fundamental interests of people of all ethnic groups in Tibet," Xinhua said in its news story.[5] The results of the forum coincided with other policy measures that illustrate Beijing's goal of developing Tibet and inexorably subsuming it, indeed, giving it more "Chinese characteristics" and fewer "Tibetan traits."

In a nutshell, party leaders at the Fifth Forum on Tibet planned how to throw more money at the Plateau to weaken potential for ethnic unrest and take it out of the international spotlight. Tibet policy is "vital to ethnic unity, social stability and national security, as well as a favorable international environment," President Hu said from the dais.[6] Next to him sat Premier Wen and seven other members of the Standing Committee of the Political Bureau of the party's Central Committee, or top body. The elders, all (except Wen) with dyed jet-black hair, ordered "leapfrog development" for the Tibet Autonomous Region and embraced Hu's goal to narrow the income gap between rural Tibetan farmers and herders and the national average by 2015, and to close the gap by the end of the decade. The roads, railways, and airports of the Tibetan region must be "completely improved." In a concession to Tibetans calling for an end to piecemeal policies toward Tibetan areas, Hu ordered policy coordination across all areas where Tibetans dwell, not just for the half that is the Tibetan Autonomous Region.

The goals sound laudable. Yet gathering less attention were policy targets to swarm Tibet in the years ahead with Chinese tourists, utterly disregarding Tibetan complaints that they have no say in policies that affect their struggle to hang on to their culture. But that may be precisely the point. Tourism authorities plan to nearly quadruple arrivals to Tibet (almost all domestic tourists) to twenty million by 2020, and they identified seven scenic areas where travelers will be funneled. Development plans include a new railway from Chengdu, the thriving capital of teeming Sichuan province, to Lhasa. The 1,012-mile-long railway will put Sichuan province, with its population of eighty-seven million people, only a short train ride away from Lhasa. As it is now, poor Sichuan migrants endure an axle-breaking journey by bus of three days from Chengdu to reach Lhasa. The new railway will be designed for speeds of 200 kilometers per hour (124 miles per hour) and will take only about eight hours to reach Lhasa.[7] The tourism reports made me think of the perennial fear of China's Southeast Asian neighbors that its colossal size could send them floating off to sea. Cambodia's strongman leader Hun Sen voiced those fears in 2007. "China is a very big country with 1.3 billion people. If the Chinese all urinated at once, they would cause a great flood," he reportedly said.[8]

With development plans like new railways afoot, it is little wonder that some Tibetans see themselves in a race against the clock. The

Dalai Lama tells Tibetans to remain optimistic because the Communist Party's hold on power will not be eternal. He may be right. Authoritarian states often seem impervious to change, and then sweeping change arrives in dramatic fashion. Party leaders are dead set on avoiding that fate in China, and their resolution is matched only by the tenacity of the citizenry to improve their lot. I saw it in the endless factories of the Pearl River Delta and the bustle of commerce in its cities. I also saw it in the tense faces of parents delivering their high school seniors each June to the venues for administering the dreaded *gaokao,* the annual entrance exams that determine placement in universities. I even saw it in our younger daughter's experience at a Chinese elementary school in Beijing. The pressure to excel was so great that she would fuss by Saturday morning about homework that wasn't due until Monday. China today is a churning blend of ambition, sublimated desire, pride over growing national strength, and anger at official corruption.

Much about the Chinese Communist Party's authoritarianism I grew to abhor. I had spent time in authoritarian states of both the political left (Cuba) and the right (Chile under General Augusto Pinochet), and I had little stomach for those harder edges. Even so, I had met many officials in China whose competence was apparent. And the economic achievements of the past three decades have been an unparalleled feat. I harkened back to a conversation I once had with Richard Baum, a China scholar from the University of California, Los Angeles, who spent part of 2005 teaching in Beijing. Despite widespread corruption in the lower ranks of the ruling party, he said, its senior leaders are a skilled lot. "I'd be willing to put up the top twenty leaders in China any day against their counterparts in the U.S. in terms of competence."[9]

The future of China—and of Tibet—depends on how well the party can satisfy citizens accustomed to constant improvement in their daily lives. How long party elders can continue to plot a successful course is hard to predict. Forecasting China's future has become a major cottage industry. The brightest Sinologists always admit the complexity of the challenge and say they can only game out potential scenarios. In one exercise in the autumn of 2009, a group of widely known China analysts from several continents came up with three possible scenarios for what China would be like in 2020.[10] They labeled one scenario "fragmentation," and it foresaw escalating social demands that chip away at the party's legitimacy. When economic growth slows sharply, central authorities become overwhelmed by demands from entrepreneurs and emerging civil society groups. Adding to their woes, a major natural disaster coincides with an international crisis. The party is unable to respond and begins to break apart.

Under a vastly different "strong state" scenario, the party's leading lights sustain high economic growth all decade. The party remains firmly in control, using technology extensively to resolve problems and to suppress dissent. A massive video surveillance system takes shape to ensure public order. A higher level of transparency reduces corruption, and improved government leads to effective campaigns to clean up the environment. China reaches 2020 with a stronger economy, a highly autocratic system, but a populace satisfied with better living conditions. Under a third scenario, "partial democracy," the party retains great political power but only after opening up the political system because of its failure to meet rising economic expectations and combat corruption. The party elite allows factional politics, hanging on to single-party rule but permitting power centers with real clout to form. By 2020, the party institutionalizes checks and balances, broadens participation, and placates critics of China around the world.

One of the tragic ironies for many Tibetans is that no matter what scenario unfolds in China, the Fourteenth Dalai Lama will likely only be a distant observer to events there. He has created a large following around the world, grabbing headlines and harnessing powerful cultural forces in the West for the cause of Tibet. But China's censors have ensured that he has almost no way of communicating with ordinary Chinese. Like the rest of the world, the Dalai Lama will watch keenly events in China, able only to make symbolic gestures to ordinary Chinese, only rarely able to pierce China's Great Firewall.

Occasionally, his efforts succeed. That happened in May 2010 with the help of Wang Lixiong, the Chinese writer who is the husband of Tsering Woeser, the prominent Tibetan blogger in Beijing. Wang, an ethnic Han dissident intellectual and a recent convert to Tibetan Buddhism, came up with the idea of holding an uncensored dialogue between the Dalai Lama and Chinese internet users. Ordinary Chinese never get to ask questions of their leaders, adding to the idea's novelty. Wang used Twitter for the hour-long Q&A. For four days before the scheduled dialogue, Wang asked Chinese Twitter users to post questions for the Dalai Lama. Using another web-based tool, some twelve thousand viewers voted on which questions were the best among 282 submitted. At the appointed hour, the Dalai Lama, who was visiting the United States at the time, answered the most popular questions.

The top-ranked questions were heartfelt and addressed a range of issues. Questioners wanted to know how the Dalai Lama felt about Chinese troops in Tibet and what kind of political system he'd like to see there. They asked whether Han migrants already in Tibet would be allowed to stay if Tibetans had greater say, and they wanted to know whether a succession struggle would occur after his passing. In all, eight questions were posed, and the Dalai Lama's answers largely tracked what he'd said on numerous public occasions.

On Chinese troops in Tibet, the Dalai Lama said he'd once called for an army-free "zone of peace" in Tibet. "But this was little more than a distant ideal. The whole world, actually, holds this kind of ideal. So there truly is nothing to worry about." The Dalai Lama was terse in addressing Tibet's future political system, saying that Tibetans living in Tibet would decide, although exile society has "already achieved democratization in its social system." He suggested that the Tibetan Plateau could not endure a huge number of ethnic Han, noting that in recent times the Han population has grown in some districts to the point it puts Tibetan culture at peril. "The crucial question is whether Tibet will become like Inner Mongolia, where Mongols have now become a minority. When this happens the significance of self-rule is lost," he wrote. One question drew the Dalai Lama out at greater length. The person noted that Han Chinese are victims of the same dictatorial rule that aggrieves Tibetans. "How do you view this problem? Do you have any way of maintaining good relations between Hans and Tibetans?" Problems of doubt and suspicion, the Dalai Lama wrote, are hardly limited to Hans and Tibetans. They are universal and can only be addressed through dialogue. When interaction occurs on the basis of equality, many problems can be resolved.

"When I meet people from mainland China, I always find them extremely sincere and find no barriers to communicating with them."[11]

Huge barriers exist, though, between the Dalai Lama and the overwhelming majority of Chinese, who are still subject to a synthesized view of him as an irredeemable separatist bent on returning Tibet to a theocratic tyranny. No matter which way China goes in the coming decade, as the Dalai Lama's life enters its final stretch, it seems improbable that he will gain a channel to speak directly to them. More and more Han migrants will arrive on the Tibetan Plateau, and almost inevitably Tibet will head the way of Inner Mongolia and other regions of the mainland subsumed by the vast Han majority. The race is nearly over. The "totally correct" policies of the party will carry forth, and the weather forecast will be for many more "blue sky" days. Whether the skies are truly blue is yet to be seen.

Acknowledgments

THE IDEA FOR THIS BOOK GREW FROM AN UNFORGETTABLE TRIP TO Tibet in early 2007 with two fellow foreign journalists. Since then, innumerable people have provided guidance on the issues surrounding Tibet or allowed me to pursue my research. Many of them—Chinese and Tibetan—cannot be named for their own safety. My editors at McClatchy Newspapers indulged my interest, approving several reporting trips to the Tibetan Plateau, and to Nepal to interview Tibetan refugees. They are, of course, in no way responsible for the views or errors in this book, nor are others who helped along the way.

During my time in China, I was enriched by the stimulating debate on the C-Pol mailing list managed by UCLA sinologist Richard Baum. It allowed me to read the thoughts, musings, and analysis of hundreds of the brightest minds on China. Scholars who helped me directly include Tsering Shakya at the University of British Columbia and Robert Barnett at Columbia University. I would also like to thank Nicolas Becquelin of Human Rights Watch for his feedback on China's minority policies.

The International Campaign for Tibet is lucky to have a press advocate like Kate Saunders who helped satisfy my endless requests in Dharamsala and Washington and arranged my interview with the Dalai Lama in early July 2009. Also in Dharamsala, I received much assistance from Tenzin Taklha and Chhime R. Chhoekyapa in the personal office of the Dalai Lama and from Jeremy Russell, a longtime collaborator of His Holiness.

Many contacts grew to become friends, including Dechen Pemba, who was expelled from China, and Tenzin Choephel, who guided me on lengthy hikes in the Khumbu region of Nepal and later introduced me to many young Tibetan exiles. Also in Nepal, and later in Dharamsala, Matthew Akester shared his views on Tibet. In Beijing, I met several times with Tsering Woeser, the prominent Tibetan blogger, and once with her husband, Wang Lixiong. Our journalist friends in Beijing, with whom my family and I shared many treasured moments, were of great encouragement. I'd like to thank Jasper Becker, Jonathan Watts, Richard McGregor, Barbara Demick, Peter Ford and Edith Coron, Francois Bougon, and Mick Brown in London (whom I only knew via email). Simon Elegant and Mary Kay Magistad both made helpful suggestions on key parts of the book. One of my oldest friends, John Otis, very patiently guided me in polishing my book proposal even as he was buried in writing his own book from his base in South America. I'm deeply grateful to David Weisberg, a talented writer who offered many insightful revisions and suggestions. Our friendship began in our teenage years and was rekindled in part through this project.

My agent, Robert Guinsler of Sterling Lord Literistic, helped greatly, and it was a pleasure to work with Editorial Director Carl Bromley of Nation Books. Copyeditor Beth Wright cast a fine eye over the text, and project editor Sandra Beris at Perseus Books Group ushered the text through the final stages to print.

Lastly, the work was made infinitely easier by the assistance of my wife, Tanya, who listened to me rattle on about Tibet and then patiently read each chapter, offering loads of practical advice. Our lengthy conversations over the course of a year were the catalyst for new ideas and helped clarify my own thoughts. In my very biased opinion, she rivals the Dalai Lama for compassion and good cheer. Our daughters, Michelle and Sofia, also endured my many absences on weekends. We were all deeply affected by China, just as the Middle Kingdom shaped the lives of my maternal grandparents, who steamed toward Shanghai nearly a century earlier, setting in motion a lengthy family fascination with Asia.

Notes

Introduction

1. Carsten A. Holz, "Have China scholars all been bought?" *Far Eastern Economic Review* (April 2007) 36, www.feer.com/articles1/2007/0704/free/p036.html.

Chapter One

1. Tenzin Taklha, personal email to the author, May 27, 2009.

2. Today, followers of Tibetan Buddhism dwell across the Tibetan Plateau and in many other areas of the Himalayas, including northern Nepal, Bhutan, and states of northern India such as Arunachal Pradesh and parts of Himachal Pradesh and Sikkim. Tibetan Buddhism is also practiced in Mongolia and a corner of Russia that includes Kalmykia, Buryatia, and Tuva.

3. In this section all quotations from His Holiness the Dalai Lama are from my interview with him, Dharamsala, July 1, 2009.

4. His Holiness the Dalai Lama, speech to the Foreign Correspondents Club of Japan, Tokyo, Nov. 3, 2008.

5. This was highlighted in the Dec. 23, 2009, issue of the weekly newsletter from Access Asia, a market research firm with offices in Shanghai, Kuala Lumpur, and Bristol, England.

6. Lee Davidson, "Huntsman Pleased with Obama in China," *Deseret News*, Nov. 17, 2009, www.deseretnews.com/article/705345147/Huntsman-pleased-with-Obama-in-China.html (accessed Jan. 12, 2010).

7. "The Chinese Celebrate Their Roaring Economy, as They Struggle with Its Costs," Pew Global Attitudes Project, July 22, 2008, pewglobal.org/reports/display.php?ReportID=261 (accessed Jan. 16, 2010).

8. "Coal Mine Deaths Drop 15% in 2008," Xinhua News Agency, Jan. 28, 2009.

9. The Laogi Research Foundation, a nonprofit rights group, lists 909 known reform-through-labor (RTL) camps but estimates that more than 1,000 of the camps exist. It says forty to fifty million people have passed through the camps, which were modeled on the Soviet Gulag system, since 1949. See www.laogai.org.

10. Liu later wrote of our meeting, which occurred on Jan. 28, 2007, for the Chinese dissident website *Boxun*, which is hosted outside of the mainland to avoid censorship. His posting was later translated at the *EastSouthWestNorth* blog, www.zonaeuropa.com/200701.brief.htm (accessed Jan. 13, 2010).

11. Foreign Ministry spokesman Qin Gang made the remarks at a press briefing on Nov. 12, 2009. A government transcript of the briefing is available at mw.china-embassy.org/eng/fyrth/t626745.htm (accessed Jan. 15, 2010).

12. Alan Wachman, "China's Lincolnophilia," *The China Beat* blog, Nov. 27, 2009, www.thechinabeat.org/?p=1193 (accessed Jan. 15, 2010). Wachman teaches international politics at the Fletcher School of Law and Diplomacy at Tufts University.

Chapter Two

1. Both those cases and other instances of harassment are documented on the website of the Foreign Correspondents Club of China at www.fccchina.org.

2. I had to teach Robin how to play the game, which is common on playgrounds in North America. If one of us made a shot, the other had to duplicate the same shot from the same position, and if he missed, he'd accumulate a letter from the word "horse." The first one to get the five letters loses.

3. Central Tibetan Administration, *Tibet: A Human Development and Environment Report* (Dharamsala: CTA Department of Information and International Relations, 2007), 272.

4. Warren W. Smith Jr., *China's Tibet? Autonomy or Assimilation* (Lanham, MD: Rowman & Littlefield, 2008), 34.

Chapter Three

1. Robert Lee, *Tools of Empire or Means of National Salvation? The Railway in the Imagination of Western Empire Builders and Their Enemies in Asia*, University of Western Sydney, Macarthur, Feb. 11, 2003, http://www.york.ac.uk/inst/irs/irshome/papers/robert1.htm.

2. United Nations Development Programme, "Show the World," press release on promotion of ethnic culture, Jan. 8, 2009.

3. Rebiya Kadeer, with Alexandra Cavelius, *Dragon Fighter: One Woman's Epic Struggle for Peace with China* (Carlsbad, CA: Kales, 2009), 256.

4. Author's interview with Rebiya Kadeer, Washington, DC, Dec. 16, 2008.

5. Ibid.

6. Ibid.

7. Kadeer, *Dragon Fighter*, 265.

8. Is it Uighur or Uyghur? Most U.S. news organizations prefer the former, although some Uighur organizations use the alternative latter spelling, in which case follow their preference. The quote is from the author's telephone interview with Alim Seytoff, Dec. 17, 2008.

9. Jeff Stein, "The Long Arm of China's Secret Police Reaches into the U.S.," *Congressional Quarterly*, Oct. 6, 2006.

10. "Police Destroy Terrorist Camp, Killing 18," Xinhua News Agency, Jan. 8, 2007. (The agency uses a sinicized spelling of the governor's name, calling him Nuer Baikeli.)

11. Mission of the People's Republic of China to the European Union, "Truth of the '7.5' Riot in Urumqi, Xinjiang Uyghur Autonomous Region," *Newsletter* 20, Aug. 25, 2009, www.chinamission.be/eng/sthd/t580613.htm (accessed Jan. 27, 2010).

12. Information Office of the State Council of the People's Republic of China, *History and Development of Xinjiang*, May 2003, www.china.org.cn/e-white/20030526/index.htm.

13. James A. Millward and Peter S. Perdue, "Political and Cultural History of the Xinjiang Region Through the Late Nineteenth Century," in *Xinjiang, China's Muslim Borderland*, ed. S. Frederick Starr (Armonk, NY: M. E. Sharpe, 2004), 38.

14. Author's telephone interview with Nicholas Bequelin, researcher for Human Rights Watch, Apr. 10, 2008.

15. Graham E. Fuller and S. Frederick Starr, *The Xinjiang Problem* (Baltimore: Central Asia-Caucasus Institute, School of Advanced International Studies, Johns Hopkins University, 2003), 18.

16. The Uighurs are not the largest Muslim group in China. The Hu Muslims, who are deeply Sinicized and do not have their own language, may number around nine million, although exact figures are not publicly available. Hu Muslims are concentrated in Ningxia Hu Autonomous Region, Gansu, and eastern Qinghai, but they have migrant networks all over China and have expanded them in Tibet with zeal since the 1980s. Religious restrictions on Hu Muslims are not as severe as on Uighurs.

17. "China Imposes Ramadan Security Crackdown in Muslim Northwest," Agence France-Presse, Sept. 4, 2008, afp.google.com/article/ALeqM5hdEdZru3e81VgdCojb XbfRomKfhg (accessed Jan. 25, 2010).

18. Lydia Wilson and Poppy Toland, "Xinjiang: China's 'Other Tibet,'" *AlJazeera.net*, Mar. 25, 2008, english.aljazeera.net/news/asia-pacific/2008/03/200852518481940 9441.html (accessed Jan. 26, 2010).

19. Maria Casadei, "Remembering Kashgar," *Far Eastern Economic Review*, May 2009.

20. "Uygurs Decry 'Reconstruction Project' Set to Change the Face of Old Town in Kashgar," *South China Morning Post*, Dec. 30, 2009.

21. "Ethnic Clash in Guangdong," *YouTube.com*, reposting of a video provided by Radio Free Asia, June 29, 2009, http://www.youtube.com/watch?v=6_PJTO2koPM (accessed Jan. 26, 2010).

22. Jonathan Watts, "Old Suspicions Magnified Mistrust into Ethnic Riots in Urumqi," *Guardian* (London), July 10, 2009, www.guardian.co.uk/world/2009/jul/10/china-riots-uighurs-han-urumqi (accessed Jan. 25, 2010).

23. Lucy Hornby, "Needle Attacks and Rumours Spread in China's Xinjiang," *Reuters*, Sep. 11, 2009, uk.reuters.com/article/idUKTRE58A0OG20090911?sp=true (accessed Jan. 25, 2010).

24. Uyghur Human Rights Project, "Four New Death Sentences issued in East Turkestan," press release, Jan. 27, 2010, www.uhrp.org/articles/3479/1/-Four-new-death-sentences-issued-in-East-Turkestan-cell-phone-users-punished-for-sending-harmful-texts-/index.html (accessed Jan. 26, 2010).

25. Edward Wong, "China Nearly Doubles Security Budget for Western Region," *New York Times*, Jan. 14, 2010.

26. Author's interview with Xinna, Hohhot, China, Oct. 30, 2008.

27. Ibid.

28. Telephone interview with Nabuq by a news assistant in McClatchy's Beijing Bureau, Nov. 3, 2008. The news assistant will be left unidentified to prevent possible reprisals.

29. Author's telephone interview with Enghebatu Togochog, Oct. 28, 2008.

30. "Uiles' Statement of Jan. 2nd, 2010," *Xinna on Human Rights in Southern Mongolia* blog, Jan. 5, 2010, free-hada-now.org/blog/.

31. Author's interview with Dalai Duren in Hohhot, Oct. 31, 2008.

32. Author's interview with Sengge Renqin in Beijing, Nov. 5, 2008.

33. His Holiness the Dalai Lama, speech to the Foreign Correspondents Club of Japan, Nov. 3, 2008.

34. Author's interview with Xinna.

35. "Huge Mineral Resources Found on the Tibet-Qinghai Plateau," Xinhua News Agency, Feb. 13, 2007, as carried on *China Daily* website, www.chinadaily.com.cn/bizchina/2007–02/13/content_833286.htm.

36. "China and Britain Ready to Exploit Tibet's Natural Resources," *Sunday Telegraph* (London), July 27, 2008, www.phayul.com/news/article.aspx?id=22092&t=1.

Chapter Four

1. Alexandra David-Neel, *My Journey to Lhasa: The Personal Story of the Only White Woman Who Succeeded in Entering the Forbidden City* (1927; reprint, London: Virago, 1969), 257.

2. Peter Whitfield, *Cities of the World: A History in Maps* (Berkeley: University of California Press, 2005), 97.

3. Sudip Mazumdar, "Course Correction," *Newsweek*, Jan. 27, 2010.

4. Tim Johnson, "Tibetans See 'Han Invasion' as Spurring Violence," McClatchy Newspapers, Mar. 28, 2008.

5. U.S. Department of State, *2008 Human Rights Report: China (Includes Tibet, Hong Kong, and Macau)*, Feb. 25, 2009, www.state.gov/g/drl/rls/hrrpt/2008/eap/119037.htm (accessed Nov. 20, 2009).

6. Gyalo Thondup, news conference, Dharamsala, Nov. 19, 2008.

7. Author's interview with Kelsang Gyaltsen in Dharamsala, Nov. 21, 2008.

8. "Memorandum on Genuine Autonomy for the Tibetan People," statement by Dalai Lama's envoys to negotiations with China, Nov. 16, 2008. The author was given a printed copy in Dharamsala, but a digital version is available at www.savetibet.org/policy-center/topics-fact-sheets/memorandum-genuine-autonomy-tibetan-people.

9. "Differences Remain with Dalai Lama, Official Says," *People's Daily Online*, Dec. 10, 2008, english.peopledaily.com.cn/96054/96056/6550801.html (accessed Feb. 3, 2010).

10. "Door for Talks with Dalai Lama Still Open, National Sovereignty Non-Negotiable: CPC official," Xinhua News Agency, Feb. 1, 2010, news.xinhuanet.com/english2010/china/2010–02/01/c_13159016.htm (accessed Feb. 2, 2010).

11. Tim Johnson, "Corpses Litter the 'Death Zone' Near Everest's Summit, Frozen for Eternity," McClatchy Newspapers, May 16, 2007, www.mcclatchydc.com/117/story/16188.html (accessed Nov. 25, 2009).

12. Tim Johnson, "Climbing the Often-Lethal Slopes of Mount Everest—Feat or Folly?" McClatchy Newspapers, May 16, 2007, www.mcclatchydc.com/117/story/16190.html (accessed Nov. 25, 2009).

13. Gyalo Thondup, news conference.

14. Opening statement by Jampa Phuntsok (Qiangba Puncog in Chinese transliteration), chair of the Tibet Autonomous Region, press conference at the State Coun-

cil Information Office, Beijing, Mar. 17, 2008, munich.china-consulate.org/ger/
xwdt/t416203.htm (accessed Nov. 19, 2009).

15. Ma Ting, "A Look-back on March 14," *Messenger*, a publication of China Radio International, Mar.–Apr. 2008, 14–15.

16. U.S. Department of State, *2009 Report on International Religious Freedom*, Washington, DC, Oct. 26, 2009.

17. Ye Xiaowen, "Time for Reflection as the Dust Clears," in *Materials on the March 14 Incident in Tibet* (Beijing: Foreign Languages Press, 2008), 13.

18. Author's interview with Tsering Woeser in Beijing, Dec. 15, 2009.

19. Ibid.

20. Ibid.

21. Ibid.

22. Following the release of the report, authorities shut down the Open Constitution Initiative on charges of "tax evasion." The Beijing Justice Bureau stripped the licenses of fifty-three lawyers associated with the group.

23. Li Kun, Huang Li, and Li Xiang, *An Investigative Report into the Social and Economic Causes of the 3.14 Incident in Tibetan Areas*, Open Constitution Initiative, May 2009, English translation of Chinese original at www.savetibet.org.

24. Author's interview with Tsering Woeser.

Chapter Five

1. Author's interview with Mingma Temba Sherpa, Kunde Hospital, Feb. 10, 2008.

2. Tibetan Centre for Human Rights and Democracy, *Human Rights Situation in Tibet, Annual Report 2009*, 49, www.tchrd.org/publications/annual_reports/2009/ar_2009.pdf (accessed Feb. 4, 2010).

3. Author's interview with Tenzin Tsundue, Dharamsala, Nov. 19, 2008.

4. Tenzin Tsundue, general email to author and other followers, Feb. 16, 2008.

5. Author's interview with Tenzin Tsundue.

6. Author's interview with Tenzin Tsundue.

7. Ibid.

8. Tenzin Tsundue, *Semshook: Essays on the Tibetan Freedom Struggle* (Dharamsala: TibetWrites, 2007), 83.

9. Author's interview with Tenzin Tsundue.

10. Ibid.

11. Website of the Tibetan Youth Congress, www.tibetanyouthcongress.org/aboutus.html (accessed June 17, 2009).

12. "TYC, a Terrorist Organization Much Catastrophic [*sic*] Than Bin Laden's, Say Netizens," *People's Daily Online*, Apr. 10, 2008, english.peopledaily.com.cn/90001/90780/91342/6390216.html (accessed July 9, 2010).

13. Author's telephone interview with Tsewang Rigzin, Mar. 25, 2008.

14. More than a thousand Tibetan soldiers serve in secretive units of the Indian army, often in the Special Frontier Force, widely known as the SFF, which has been guarding Indian borders for nearly five decades. Others serve in the Indo-Tibetan Border Police (ITBP). Little is known publicly about the history of the Tibetan soldiers other than anecdotal evidence that recruitment often takes place outside the gates of Tibetan schools at graduation time. Tibetan soldiers in the Indian army see their service as keeping hopes for Tibetan independence alive. A stanza from one

Hindi song sung by Tibetans in the Vikasregiment of the SFF gives some flavor of their hopes (from www.tibetwrites.org/?Not-their-own-wars):

We are the Vikasi
The Chinese snatched Tibet from us
and kicked us out from our home
Even then, India
kept us like their own
One day, surely one day
we will teach the Chinese a lesson
Whenever opportunities arise
we will play with our lives.

15. Author's interview with Tsewang Rigzin, Nov. 20, 2008.

16. Ibid.

17. Ibid.

18. "Police: Offensive Weapons Found in Tibetan Temples," Xinhua News Agency, Apr. 2, 2008, news.xinhuanet.com/english/2008–04/02/content_7900972.htm (accessed July 15, 2010).

19. "TYC Refutes Chinese Communist Party's Allegations," *Phayul*, July 16, 2008, www.phayul.com/mobile/?page=view&c=2&id=21973 (accessed July 15, 2010).

20. Author's interview with Tsewang Rigzin.

21. Heinrich Harrer, *Seven Years in Tibet*, trans. Richard Graves (1953; reprint, New York: Tarcher, 1997), 223.

22. John Kenneth Knaus, *Orphans of the Cold War: America and the Tibetan Struggle* (New York: Public Affairs, 2000), 140–148.

23. Foreign Relations of the United States (FRUS), 1964–1968, vol. 30, Item 342, "Draft Memorandum for the 303 Committee," CIA document dated Jan. 26, 1968, and posted on the U.S. State Department website: www.state.gov/www/ about_state/history/vol_xxx/337_343.html.

24. Knaus, *Orphans of the Cold War*, 217.

25. Mikel Dunham, *Buddha's Warriors: The Story of the CIA-backed Tibetan Freedom Fighters, the Chinese Invasion, and the Ultimate Fall of Tibet* (New York: Tarcher, 2004), 317–318.

26. Joe Bageant, "CIA's Secret War in Tibet," *Military History*, February 2004.

27. Knaus, *Orphans of the Cold War*, x–xi.

28. FRUS, 1964–1968, vol. 30, Item 337.

29. His Holiness the Dalai Lama, afternoon panel discussion, Meditation and Psychotherapy conference, sponsored by Harvard Medical School Department of Continuing Education, Boston Park Plaza Hotel, May 1, 2009.

Chapter Six

1. Author's interview with Parvez Nowrojee, Dharamsala, Nov. 21, 2008.

2. Ibid.

3. Author's interview with Nisha Sarin, Dharamsala, July 2, 2009.

4. Ibid.

5. "Free Tibet! Sang [*sic*] by Dorjee Tsering (Lhaksam)," *YouTube.com*, Mar. 19, 2007, www.youtube.com/watch?v=PIQAilWoy2E.

6. Author's interview with Lobsang Wangyal, Dharamsala, July 2, 2009.

7. Void told this to my colleague and traveling companion, Clifford Coonan, who published it in his article "U.S. Singer Has Key Part in Tibet Independence Movement," *Irish Times*, Nov. 21, 2008.

8. Jamyang Norbu, "Waiting for Mangtso," *Shadow Tibet* blog, Sep. 9, 2009, www.jamyangnorbu.com/blog/2009/09/09/waiting-for-mangtso/.

9. Most notable of these is an Australian-born British writer, Michael Backman, whose article "Behind Dalai Lama's Holy Cloak," published in the *Age* (Melbourne, Australia), May 23, 2007, is sometimes cited: www.theage.com.au/news/business/behind-dalai-lamas-holy-cloak/2007/05/22/1179601410290.html.

10. Hilary Lehman, "Dalai Lama Offers 100K to FIU Religion Department," Associated Press, May 26, 2009, abcnews.go.com/US/wireStory?id=7681523 (accessed Feb. 8, 2010).

11. Daniel Erikson, "The Politics of Disaster Relief: China, Taiwan and the Haitian Earthquake," *China Brief* 10, no. 3 (Feb. 4, 2010), www.jamestown.org/single/?no_cache=1&tx_ttnews%5Btt_news%5D=36009&tx_ttnews%5BbackPid%5D=7&cHash=f7656b6af1 (accessed Feb. 8, 2010).

12. Author's interview with Tsewang Yeshi, July 3, 2009.

Chapter Seven

1. Emily Wax, "A Young Lama Weighs Tibetans' Future," *Washington Post*, Mar. 17, 2009, www.washingtonpost.com/wp-dyn/content/article/2009/03/16/AR2009031602668.html (accessed Feb. 18, 2010).

2. A copy of the letter can be seen at the website of Ogyen Trinley Dorje, whom the Dalai Lama has recognized as the Seventeenth Karmapa, at www.kagyuoffice.org/karmapa.reference.recognition.predictionletter.html.

3. Michele Martin, *Music in the Sky: The Life, Art & Teachings of the Seventeenth Karmapa, Ogyen Trinley Dorje* (New Delhi: New Age Books, 2004), 23.

4. Xinhua News Agency, Jan. 7, 2000, cited in other news service reports, such as Jeremy Page, "Lama Fled China After Visa Refusal," Reuters, Jan. 8, 2000.

5. The Karmapa gave a news conference at Gyuto Tantric Monastery in Dharamsala, India, on Apr. 27, 2001. For a transcript of the questions and answers, see www.nalandabodhi.org/hhk_transcript.html.

6. Interview of His Holiness the Seventeenth Karmapa by several foreign correspondents, Gyuto Tantric Monastery, Nov. 22, 2008.

7. *Religion & Ethics Newsweekly*, PBS, July 11, 2008, www.pbs.org/wnet/religionandethics/episodes/july-11–2008/karmapa-lama/36/.

8. Interview with His Holiness the Karmapa, Nov. 22, 2008.

9. His Holiness the Dalai Lama, press conference at the Foreign Correspondents Club of Japan, Tokyo, Nov. 3, 2008.

10. Patrick Symmes, "Tibet's Rising Son," *Newsweek*, Feb. 21, 2009, www.newsweek.com/id/185796/page/1 (accessed Feb. 16, 2010).

11. Quotations in this paragraph are from the author's interviews, Dharamsala, Nov. 22, 2008.

12. His Holiness the Dalai Lama spoke to foreign reporters in Amritsar, India, on the occasion of the Elijah interfaith dialogue between prominent Jews, Hindus, Sikhs, Muslims, Christians, and Buddhists, Nov. 27, 2007, afp.google.com/article/ALeqM5i6FXsaCp58kaPjnMBrSTyWaAn8gw (accessed July 24, 2010).

13. His Holiness the Dalai Lama, news conference, Dharamsala, Nov. 23, 2008.

14. "Reincarnation of Living Buddha Needs Gov't Approval," Xinhua News Agency, Aug. 4, 2007, www.chinadaily.com.cn/china/2007–08/04/content_5448 242.htm (accessed May 16, 2010).

15. The Karmapa was speaking in Tibetan, and the translation comes from Wasfia Nazreen, "Karmapa Appeals for Wildlife Conservation," *Phayul.com*, June 30, 2009, www.phayul.com/news/article.aspx?id=25036.

16. Author's interview with His Holiness the Karmapa, Dharamsala, July 4, 2009.

17. Author's joint interview with His Holiness the Karmapa, Dharamsala, Nov. 22, 2008.

18. Author's interview with His Holiness the Karmapa, July 4, 2009.

19. Rashmee Roshan Lall, "Video War Games Satiate My Feelings of Aggression," *Times of India*, Sep. 20, 2009, timesofindia.indiatimes.com/news/sunday-toi/all-that-matters/Video-war-games-satiate-my-feelings-of-aggression/arti-cleshow/5032672.cms (accessed Feb. 18, 2010).

20. Rashmee Roshan Lall, "I'm Very Passionate About Supporting the Middle Path: Karmapa," *Times of India*, Sep. 21, 2009.

21. Anand Sankar, "The Karmapa Breaks His Silence," *Business Standard* (Mumbai), May 23, 2009.

22. Lall, "I'm Very Passionate."

23. Claude Arpi, "Trying to Guess Why the Karmapa's Tour Was Cancelled," *Claude Arpi* blog, Apr. 7, 2010, claudearpi.blogspot.com/2010/04/trying-to-guess-why-karmapas-tour-was.html (accessed May 15, 2010). Also, "India Says No to U.S. Tour of Tibetan Monk," *Times of India*, July 15, 2010, timesofindia.indiatimes.com/india/India-says-no-to-US-tour-of-Tibetan-monk-/articleshow/6171681.cms (accessed July 24, 2010).

24. "Title Claimant to Approach NEMPF for Intervention on Karmapa Issue," *Voice of Sikkim*, Feb. 11, 2010, voiceofsikkim.com/2010/02/12/title-claimant-to-approach-nempf-for-intervention-on-karmapa-issue/ (accessed Feb. 16, 2010).

25. David Van Biema, Patrick E. Cole, and Jefferson Penberthy, "Battle of the Future Buddhas," *Time*, May 2, 1994.

26. Charles Bell, *The Religion of Tibet* (1968; reprint, Delhi: Book Faith India, 1998), 131–132.

27. Alexander Norman, *Holder of the White Lotus: The Lives of the Dalai Lama* (London: Little, Brown, 2008), 319–321.

28. Ibid., 324.

Chapter Eight

1. China issued a statement to the UN Human Rights Council on July 17, 2007, in response to a query from Asma Jahangir, the special rapporteur for freedom of religion or belief. The Council report carrying the statement can be seen here: www2.ohchr.org/english/bodies/hrcouncil/docs/7session/A-HRC-7–10-Add1.doc.

2. Direct quotations from Yabshi Pan Rinzinwangmo (Renji) and details of her life story are from the author's interviews in Beijing, May 21, July 10, and July 27, 2009, as well as one follow-up meeting on Mar. 15, 2010, and numerous email exchanges with her assistant, Christopher Thomas, which often clarified and amplified her statements.

3. Jampal Gyatso, *The Panchen Lama*, unpublished English translation by Rachel W. Schlesinger of a work originally in Tibetan and Mandarin, 127.

4. Ibid.

5. Author's interview with Renji, May 21, 2009.

6. Ibid.

7. In an email to the author dated July 6, 2010, Renji's personal aide, Christopher Thomas, elaborated that political calculations may have played less of a role than human emotions:

After Madam Deng gave the example that one of Premier Zhou's nephews married a Mongolian, it was clear that Madame Deng supported these types of weddings. That said, our office feels it is more correct to view Madame Deng's statement and Princess Rinzinwangmo's great grandfather's change of heart as the realization that Princess Rinzinwangmo's mother and father's marriage was exemplary of the type of unity and coming together that the country needed. It is not correct to only analyze the marriage union as "beneficiary." That is too calculating. In addition, our office feels it is unlikely that such a simple statement made by Madame Deng would have completely swayed Princess Rinzinwangmo's great grandfather. He must have already felt certain emotions of support in his heart.

8. Penor Rinpoche, who passed away in Mar. 2009, responded to questions about Seagal in Sep. 1999 in a document, "Statement by H.H. Penor Rinpoche Regarding the Recognition of Steven Seagal as a Reincarnation of the Treasure Revealer Chungdrag Dorje of Palyul Monastery," www.facebook.com/note.php?note_id=10597 2685673&ref=mf. Penor Rinpoche adds in the statement that he received no donation from Seagal in exchange for declaring him a *tulku*.

9. Christopher Thomas, email to author, Oct. 20, 2009.

10. Author's interview with Li Guangyong, July 29, 2009.

11. "Renji, The Lama's Daughter," *Facebook.com*, zh-cn.facebook.com/notes .php?id=22946312326 (accessed July 2009).

12. The original article in *People's Daily* on Aug. 6, 2009, was in Chinese, although it was translated and commented on by Roland Soong in his *EastSouthWestNorth* blog, www.zonaeuropa.com/20090806_1.htm (accessed Feb. 22, 2010).

13. *The Cadence of Life*, 2008, DVD, produced for Princess Yabshi Pan Rinzinwangmo, ISRC CN-H09–06–321–00/V. Transcript of original Mandarin by office assistant at McClatchy Newspapers' Beijing Bureau.

14. Robert Barnett, "Historical Introduction," in *A Poisoned Arrow: The Secret Report of the Tenth Panchen Lama* (London: Tibet Information Network, 1997), xiii.

15. Nicholas D. Kristof, "The Panchen Lama is dead at 50; Key figure in China's Tibet policy," *New York Times*, Jan. 30, 1989, nytimes.com/1989/01/30/obituaries/ the-panchen-lama-is-dead-at-50-key-figure-in-china-s-tibet-policy.html (accessed July 29, 2010).

16. Gyatso, *Panchen Lama*, 142.

17. Dawa Norbu, "Preface," in *A Poisoned Arrow*, xxvi.

18. Author's interview with Renji, May 21, 2009.

Chapter Nine

1. Leo Lewis, "Tibetan Mastiff Is 'Most Expensive' Dog After £352,000 Sale in China," *Times Online*, Sep. 11, 2009. timesonline.co.uk/tol/news/world/asia/article6828862.ece (accessed July 24, 2010).

2. The lyrics come from an unpublished paper by friends who have declined to put forth their real names for fear of repercussions at a major university in Beijing where they work.

3. Ibid.

4. Daniel J. Miller, "The World of Tibetan Nomads," 2007, a chapter in an as-yet unpublished book, *Drokpa: Nomads of the Tibetan Plateau and Himalaya*, www.scribd.com/doc/16359460/The-World-of-Tibetan-Nomads (accessed Oct. 16, 2009).

5. Sudha Ramachandran, "Yarchagumba! It's Caterpillar Cocktail Time," *Asia Times Online*, July 26, 2008, www.atimes.com/atimes/South_Asia/JG26Df02.html (accessed Oct. 20, 2009).

6. Jiang Rong, *Wolf Totem* (New York: Penguin, 2008), 476.

7. "Tibetans Burn Wild Animal Skins in Tibet to Encourage Wildlife Preservation," International Campaign for Tibet, Feb. 14, 2006, www.dalailama.com/news.25.htm.

8. "Tibetan Broadcasters Ordered to Wear Fur," Radio Free Asia, Apr. 29, 2006, newsblaze.com/story/20060429212925nnnn.nb/topstory.html.

9. "Resettlement Policies Threaten the Survival of Tibetan Nomads," Free Tibet, freetibet.org/about/nomadic-lifestyle-under-threat (accessed July 24, 2010).

10. U.S. State Department, *2008 Country Report on Human Rights Practices in China, Tibet, Macau and Hong Kong*, www.state.gov/g/drl/rls/hrrpt/2008/eap/119037.htm.

11. Ibid.

12. Jonathan Fenby, *The Penguin History of Modern China: The Fall and Rise of a Great Power 1850–2009* (London: Penguin, 2008), 396.

13. "All Tibet's Farmers, Herdsmen to Move in Affordable Housing by 2010," Xinhua News Agency, Dec. 1, 2009, chinatibet.people.com.cn/6829088.html (accessed Dec. 2, 2009).

14. The news agency report on Sichuan appears to have been deleted from the internet, but there is a Reuters story about the report, "China Sets Plan to Settle 470,000 Tibetan Herders," Oct. 11, 2008, www.reuters.com/article/latestCrisis/idUSSHA149502 (accessed July 13, 2010). See also the Agence France-Presse report on a Xinhua story about nomads in Qinghai, "100,000 Tibetan Nomads Ordered to Settle in Towns," Oct. 1, 2007, afp.google.com/article/ALeqM5guapJRda-NSrCy_q7Qn3W4ONfoyg (accessed July 13, 2010).

15. "Issues Facing Chinese-Occupied Tibet," TGIE Department of Information and International Relations fact sheet, 2008.

16. Wang Wenchang, "Rural Management: The Way Out for Tibetan Rural Areas," *China Tibetology* 1, 2008.

17. Jamyang Kyi, "They," blog entry in Tibetan, translated and reposted on the *High Peaks Pure Earth* blog, Nov. 10, 2008, www.highpeakspureearth.com/2008/11/they-by-jamyang-kyi.html (accessed Nov. 13, 2009).

18. Ibid.

19. Ibid.

20. The letter by Republican Sen. Gordon Smith of Oregon and Democratic Sens. John Kerry of Massachusetts and Russell Feingold of Wisconsin was sent to Secretary of State Condoleezza Rice on May 21, 2008, coinciding with Jamyang Kyi's release by authorities. In their letter, they said the Tibetan singer in both her writing and her music had sought "to steer clear of content which could be construed as

challenging Beijing's control over Tibet." See www.tibet.net/en/flash/2008/0608/06A0608.html (accessed Oct. 20, 2009).

21. Author's interview with Jamyang Kyi, Oct. 14, 2009.

22. Ibid.

23. Ibid.

24. Ibid.

Chapter Ten

1. The Free Tibet Campaign with headquarters in London posted photos of dead Tibetans that it said showed police used lethal force to quell disturbances in Aba. Along with graphic photos, it cited witnesses saying at least thirteen Tibetans were killed. The release is at www.freetibet.org/newsmedia/pictures-dead-kirti-monastery.

2. Initial reports like this Reuters story, "Tibetan Monk Sets Himself on Fire—Activist Group" (Feb. 27, 2009, uk.reuters.com/article/idUKPEK233080 [accessed July 13, 2010]), did not report that the monk survived but subsequent reports made that clear.

3. Author's interview with Taiwanese nun, Oct. 12, 2009.

4. Liu Peng, "A Crisis of Faith," *China Security* 4, no. 4 (Autumn 2008): 26.

5. Raoul Birnbaum, "Buddhist China at the Century's Turn," in *Religion in China Today*, ed. Daniel L. Overmyer, China Quarterly Special Issues no. 3 (New York: Cambridge University Press, 2003), 142.

6. Maureen Fan, "In China, a Different Brand of Buddhism," *Washington Post*, Feb. 19, 2009, A19.

7. Author's interview with Taiwanese nun.

8. Tibetan Centre for Human Rights and Democracy (TCHRD), "Destruction of Serthar Institute: A Special Report," 2002, www.tchrd.org/publications/topical_reports/destruction_of_serthar-2002/ (accessed Nov. 12, 2009).

9. Author's interview with Dawa, Oct. 13, 2009.

10. TCHRD, "Two Monks Commit Suicide in Amdo Ngaba," *Phayul.com*, Apr. 4, 2008, www.phayul.com/news/article.aspx?id=20319 (accessed Nov. 4, 2009).

11. TCHRD, *Monk Suicides on the Rise in Buddhist Tibet*, report submitted to the U.N. Special Rapporteur on the Freedom of Religion or Belief, June 7, 2009, www.tchrd.org/press/2009/pr20090607.html (accessed Nov. 4, 2009).

12. Congressional-Executive Commission on China, *Special Topic Paper: Tibet 2008–2009*, Oct. 22, 2009, 77.

13. Estimates of the Muslim population in China routinely go higher. The Pew Forum on Religion and Public Life issued a comprehensive report on the size of the world Muslim population in 2009 that estimated 21.6 million Muslims in China. See Pew Forum on Religion and Public Life, *Mapping the Global Muslim Population: A Report on the Size and Distribution of the World's Muslim Population*, Oct. 1, 2009, pewforum.org/docs/?DocID=451 (accessed Nov. 6, 2009).

14. Daniel H. Bays, "Chinese Protestant Christianity Today," in Overmyer, ed., *Religion in China Today*, 182.

15. The Karl and Ada Scheufler Papers are archived at the Yale University Divinity School Library, 409 Prospect St., New Haven, CT 06511.

16. Yenping Conference Reports, Fukien province, Methodist Episcopal Church, Board of Missions of the Methodist Church, New York, 1922–1924.

17. Mao Zedong, Opening Address to the First Plenary Session of the Chinese People's Political Consultative Conference, Sep. 21, 1949, www.international.ucla.edu/eas/documents/mao490921.htm.

18. Author's interview with Rev. Sun, Nov. 27, 2006.

19. Ibid.

20. Author's interview with Su Baixin, Nov. 27, 2006.

21. Author's interview with Weiping Shaw, Nov. 27, 2006.

22. Author's interview with Zheng Jianping, Nov. 28, 2006.

23. Author's interview with Xu Jiashan, Nov. 28, 2006.

24. Author's interview with He Guanghu, Renmin University, Beijing, Dec. 2006.

25. Ibid.

26. "China Highlights Role of Buddhism in Promoting Social Harmony," Xinhua News Agency, May 10, 2006, au.china-embassy.org/eng/xw/t251589.htm (accessed Nov. 6, 2009).

27. Benjamin Kang Lim, "China Hopes Buddhist Forum Will Counter 'Threat' Theory," Reuters, Mar. 27, 2006, www.buddhistchannel.tv/index.php?id=46,2484,0,0,1,0 (accessed Nov. 6, 2009).

28. Author's interview with He Guanghu.

Chapter Eleven

1. "Dignitaries Met: 2005–2010," *Dalailama.com*, www.dalailama.com/biography/dignitaries-met (accessed July 14, 2010).

2. Deborah Solomon, "The Priest: Questions for Archbishop Desmond Tutu," *New York Times Sunday Magazine*, Mar. 7, 2010, www.nytimes.com/2010/03/07/magazine/07fob-q4-t.html (accessed July 14, 2010).

3. His Holiness the Dalai Lama, speech to the Foreign Correspondents Club of Japan, Tokyo, Nov. 3, 2008.

4. Joseph Kahn, "Murdoch's Dealings in China: It's Business, and It's Personal," *New York Times*, Jun. 26, 2007, www.nytimes.com/2007/06/26/world/asia/26murdoch.html?_r=1 (accessed July 14, 2010).

5. Iyer made the remark at a public town hall meeting on May 3, 2009, titled "His Holiness the Dalai Lama & Mary Robinson: Wisdom & Compassion for Challenging Times." The video of the event is at www.dalailama.com/webcasts/post/47-wisdom—compassion-for-challenging-times.

6. Matthieu Ricard, "Compassion in Practice," in *Understanding the Dalai Lama*, ed. Rajiv Mehrotra (New Delhi: Penguin Books India, 2004), 81.

7. His Holiness the Dalai Lama, "Ethics for Our Time" lecture, University of California, Santa Barbara, Apr. 24, 2009.

8. Dalai Lama, Q & A following morning lecture, "The Nature of Mind," University of California, Santa Barbara, Apr. 24, 2009.

9. Richard Blum, Remarks, Greek Theater, University of California, Berkeley, Apr. 25, 2009.

10. His Holiness the Dalai Lama, "Peace Through Compassion" lecture, Greek Theater, University of California, Berkeley, Apr. 25, 2009.

11. Nazario told this story at a San Francisco breakfast on Apr. 26, 2009, for The Forgotten International, a nonprofit that combats poverty and suffering worldwide. The Dalai Lama also spoke at the event, which brought together several hundred supporters.

12. His Holiness the Dalai Lama, speech at benefit for The Forgotten International, San Francisco, Apr. 26, 2009.

13. His Holiness the Dalai Lama, lecture, Apr. 25, 2009.

14. Author's interview with Tenzin Taklha, June 26, 2009.

15. His Holiness the Dalai Lama, "Educating the Heart" lecture, Memorial Church at Harvard University, Apr. 30, 2009.

16. His Holiness the Dalai Lama, remarks, "Meditation and Psychotherapy: Cultivating Compassion and Wisdom," Harvard Medical School conference, Boston, May 1, 2009.

17. His Holiness the Dalai Lama, "On Wisdom" conference session, May 1, 2009.

18. His Holiness the Dalai Lama, "On Compassion" conference session, May 1, 2009.

19. His Holiness the Dalai Lama, *My Land and My People* (1962; reprint, New York: Warner Books, 1997), 33.

20. Heinrich Harrer, *Seven Years in Tibet* (1953; reprint, London: HarperCollins, 2005), 252–253.

21. Daniel Goleman, "Inside the Mind of the Dalai Lama," *Bigthink.com*, bigthink.com/ideas/14680 (accessed Apr. 19, 2010).

22. William J. Cromie, "Meditation changes temperatures: Mind controls body in extreme experiments," *Harvard University Gazette*, Apr. 18, 2002, www.news.harvard.edu/gazette/2002/04.18/09-tummo.html (accessed Mar. 3, 2010).

23. "Dalai Lama Visits LA, Speaks at Universal," *KTLA.com*, Feb. 22, 2010, www.ktla.com/news/landing/ktla-dalai-lama,0,4903728.story (accessed Mar. 3, 2010).

24. His Holiness the Dalai Lama, lecture, Apr. 24, 2009.

25. Author's interview with graduate student, Waldorf Astoria Hotel, New York, May 5, 2009.

26. Evan Osnos, "Angry Youth: The New Generation's Neocon Nationalists," *New Yorker*, July 28, 2008.

27. His Holiness the Dalai Lama, speaking at a meeting with Chinese scholars, students, and dissidents at Waldorf Astoria Hotel, New York City, May 5, 2009.

28. Ibid.

29. The Dalai Lama made the remark about the Communist Party losing its communist ideology at the Forgotten International talk in San Francisco, Apr. 26, 2009; the remark about Chinese leaders referring to their approach as "scientific" came at a lecture on "Ethics and Enlightened Leadership" at the Massachusetts Institute of Technology's Center for Ethics and Transformative Values, Apr. 30, 2009; the final quote came from his meeting with overseas Chinese in New York City, May 5, 2009.

30. His Holiness the Dalai Lama, remarks, "Meditation and Psychotherapy" conference.

31. David Pilling, "Lunch with the FT: Ai Weiwei," *Financial Times*, Apr. 23, 2010, www.ft.com/cms/s/2/f04810fc-4e62–11df-b48d-00144feab49a.html (accessed July 24, 2010).

Chapter Twelve

1. See the webpage of the UCLA Buddhist Studies Center, www.international.ucla.edu/buddhist/about/.

2. Sam Blakeslee, "The Journey," *New Times* (San Luis Obispo, CA), 1998.

3. I received a copy of the letter that was originally sent by Consul General Gao to Hector de la Torre, a Democratic assembly member from the Los Angeles area.

4. A copy of the letter was provided to me by Blakeslee's office in Sacramento. Blakeslee mentioned the Clark letter in the March 2009 issue of a digital newsletter on his website, www.arc.asm.ca.gov/member/33/newsletter/09_03_22.htm (accessed July 14, 2010).

5. "London School Regrets Honoring Dalai Lama," *China Daily*, July 8, 2008, www.chinadaily.com.cn/china/2008–07/08/content_6826398.htm (accessed July 15, 2010).

6. Office of Tibet, London, "University Did Not Say Sorry to China for Degree," *Phayul.com*, July 11, 2008, www.phayul.com/news/article.aspx?id=21921 (accessed July 15, 2010).

7. "University Cancels Dalai Lama's Degree," *ABC News Online*, Aug. 11, 2009, abc.gov.au/news/stories/2009/08/11/2652886.htm?section=australia (accessed July 15, 2010).

8. "The Dalai Lama's Message to the 5th International Conference of Tibet Support Group," *Phayul.com*, May 11, 2007, phayul.com/news/article.aspx?id =16505&article=The+Dalai+Lama's+message+to+the+5th+International+Conference+of+Tibet+Support+Group (accessed July 25, 2010).

9. "Brussels Stunned as Beijing Cancels EU-China Summit," *Euroactiv.com*, Apr. 16, 2009, www.euractiv.com/en/foreign-affairs/brussels-stunned-beijing-cancels-eu-china-summit/article-177550 (accessed July 15, 2010).

10. "Golden Girl Lifts a Nation," *China Daily*, Apr. 14, 2008.

11. Ben English, "Chinese Rent-a-Crowd 'Inflamed' Olympic Torch Tensions," *Daily Telegraph* (Sydney), Apr. 25, 2008, www.dailytelegraph.com.au/news/nsw-act/rent-a-crowd-inflamed-torch/story-e6freuzi-1111116157886 (accessed July 15, 2010).

12. Australian parliamentary delegation, news conference, Dharamsala, India, July 3, 2009.

13. Isabel Hilton, "Dissolution of Paradise: The Options for Tibetan Refugees Are Narrowing as China Flexes Its Muscles in Landlocked Nepal," Comment Is Free, *Guardian* (London), Sep. 9, 2009, www.guardian.co.uk/commentisfree/2009/sep/09/tibetan-refugees-in-nepal (accessed July 15, 2010).

14. "Police Prevent Tibet Photo Exhibition," *bdnews24.com*, Nov. 1, 2009, bd-news24.com/details.php?id=146052&cid=2 (accessed July 15, 2010).

15. "Dalai Lama Ban Halts Conference," BBC News, Mar. 24, 2009, news.bbc .co.uk/2/hi/africa/7960968.stm (accessed July 15, 2010).

16. Shishir Nagaraja and Ross Anderson, *The Snooping Dragon: Social-Malware Surveillance of the Tibetan Movement*, University of Cambridge Computer Laboratory technical report, March 2009, 5, www.cl.cam.ac.uk/techreports/UCAM-CL-TR-746.pdf.

17. "Cybersecurity and GhostNet," podcast, *Connect2canada.com*, June 18, 2009, www.connect2canada.com/connect-lien/podcast-balado/?storyId=28007 (accessed July 15, 2010).

18. Nagaraja and Anderson, *The Snooping Dragon*, 7.

19. Ibid., 3.

20. Vito Pilieci, "The GhostNet Buster," *Ottawa Citizen*, Apr. 25, 2009.

21. "Cybersecurity and GhostNet."

22. Nagaraja and Anderson, *The Snooping Dragon*, 3.

23. Qin Gang, press conference, Beijing, Mar. 31, 2009.

24. Georges Dreyfus, "The Shuk-den Affair: Origins of a Controversy," *Journal of the International Association of Buddhist Studies* 21, no. 2 (1998). The article was redistributed digitally in revised form; see www.dalailama.com/messages/dolgyal-shugden/ganden-tripa/the-shugden-affair and www.dalailama.com/messages/dolgyal-shugden/ganden-tripa/the-shugden-affair-i (accessed July 15, 2010).

25. "Interpol Alert Against Killers of Dalai Lama's Aide," *Press Trust of India*, Jun. 17, 2007, www.indianexpress.com/story_print.php?storyId=33892 (accessed July 15, 2010).

26. "The Dalai Lama's Demons," video, *France 24*, Aug. 8, 2008, www.france24 .com/en/20080808-dalai-lama-demons-india-buddhism-dorje-shugden (accessed July 15, 2010).

27. His Holiness the Dalai Lama in *People & Power* video (with English translation), *Al Jazeera English*, Sep. 30, 2008.

28. "Writ Petition Under Article 226 of the Constitution of India," submitted by the Dorjee Shugden Devotees Charitable and Religious Society to the High Court of Delhi, Apr. 8, 2008.

29. "The Tibetan Situation Today: Surprising Hidden News," Western Shugden Society, 2008, media.westernshugdensociety.net/Tibetan_Situation_Today.pdf.

Chapter Thirteen

1. Adam Yauch interview, *Dreams of Tibet*, PBS *Frontline Online*, 1999, www.pbs.org/wgbh/pages/frontline/shows/tibet/interviews/.

2. Richard Gere, speech at American Himalayan Foundation fund-raising dinner, Dec. 8, 2009.

3. Tiffany Rose, "Richard Gere: Don't Call Me Babe," *Independent* (London), Feb. 18, 2005.

4. Melvin McLeod, "Richard Gere: My Journey as a Buddhist," *Shambhala Sun*, May 1999, www.shambhalasun.com/index.php?option=com_content&task =view&id=1882 (accessed Dec. 21, 2009).

5. Ibid.

6. Gere, American Himalayan Foundation dinner.

7. Ibid.

8. Mollie Rodriguez of The Gere Foundation, email to author, Oct. 3, 2009.

9. "Sharon Stone's Cold-Blooded Speech About China earthquake," YouTube video, www.youtube.com/watch?v=DYoZEn9vlzE&feature=player_embedded (accessed Dec. 22, 2009).

10. Clifford Coonan, "Dior Drops Sharon Stone After Quake Comments," *Independent*, May 30, 2008. The original Xinhua story seems to have been taken off the internet, but the characterization of Stone by Xinhua was picked up in news stories in a wide variety of outlets including the *Guardian*, *Times of London*, and *New York Times*.

11. Cathy Horyn, "Actress Stone and Dior Differ Over Apology," *New York Times*, June 1, 2008, www.nytimes.com/2008/06/01/fashion/01stone.html (accessed Dec. 22, 2009).

12. "Bjork's 'Tibet' Show to Be Probed," Xinhua News Agency, Mar. 8, 2008, www.china.org.cn/entertainment/2008—03/08/content_11961803.htm (accessed Dec. 22, 2009).

13. Dan Washburn, "Oasis: China Cancelled Gigs Due to Band's Tibet Ties," *shanghaiist* blog, Mar. 3, 2009, shanghaiist.com/2009/03/03/oasis_china_canceled _gigs_due_to_ba.php (accessed July 29, 2010).

14. "The Dalai Lama Lip Jiggle," *Memphis Flyer*, Sep. 23, 2009, www.memphis-flyer.com/TheDailyBuzz/archives/2009/09/23/the-dalai-lama-lip-jiggle (accessed Dec. 27, 2009).

15. Myron Lowery, "Commentary: Why Fist-Bumped the Dalai Lama," *CNN.com*, Sep. 24, 2009, edition.cnn.com/2009/POLITICS/09/24/lowery.fist.bump/ (accessed Dec. 27, 2009).

16. Pico Iyer, "Making Kindness Stand to Reason," 1998 essay, republished in *Understanding the Dalai Lama*, ed. Rajiv Mehrotra (New York: Viking, 2004), 62.

17. Nancy Stohs, "Dalai Lama Digs into Veal, Pheasant," *Milwaukee Journal-Sentinel*, May 15, 2007, www3.jsonline.com/story/index.aspx?id=605615 (accessed Jan. 15, 2010).

18. Norm Phelps, "An Open Letter to the Dalai Lama," June 15, 2007, www.all-creatures.org/letters/20070615-np.html (accessed Mar. 22, 2010).

19. Dennis Conkin, "Dalai Lama Urges 'Respect, Compassion and Full Human Rights for All,' Including Gays," *Bay Area Reporter*, June 19, 1997.

20. Author's interview with Lodi Gyari, Dec. 30, 2008, Washington, DC.

21. Ibid.

22. Gwen Ifill, "Lawmakers Cheer Tibetan in Capitol Rotunda," *New York Times*, Apr. 19, 1991.

23. Author's interview with Lodi Gyari.

24. "Dalai Lama and Bush Meet 'Like Old Friends,'" *CNN.com*, May 21, 2001, edition.cnn.com/2001/WORLD/asiapcf/east/05/23/dalai.bush.02/ (accessed Dec. 28, 2009).

25. Laura Bush, *Spoken from the Heart* (New York: Scribner, 2010), 359.

26. "U.S. Congressional Gold Medal Ceremony," DVD, International Campaign for Tibet and Garthwait & Griffin Films, 2008.

27. Ibid.

28. Ibid.

29. Ibid.

30. Ibid.

31. Gere, American Himalayan Foundation dinner.

32. "Mobile Phone Penetration Rate Reaches 54.3%," *People's Daily Online*, Dec. 29, 2009, english.people.com.cn/90001/90778/90860/6855171.html (accessed on Dec. 29, 2009).

33. *US-China Trade Statistics and China's World Trade Statistics*, US-China Business Council, 2008.

34. Tim Johnson, "The News Media and Tibet," *China Rises* blog, June 30, 2006, washingtonbureau.typepad.com/china/2006/06/the_news_media.html.

35. Dave Lyons, who wrote a blog titled *Mutant Palm* from a base in southern China, wrote to my blog on July 2, 2006. Lyons, a frequent critic of my blog posts, later began a project to compile a digital library of significant and endangered Chinese internet content, including content from chat rooms later censored, for future generations of researchers.

36. When monks at the Drepung Monastery near Lhasa got word that the Dalai Lama was awarded the Congressional Gold Medal in Oct. 16, 2007, some were

stirred to action. They put up prayer flags to mark the medal. Chinese security agents arrested three of them and sealed the monastery off for more than a week. See "Lhasa Monks Held, Questioned After Dalai Lama's Medal," Radio Free Asia, Oct. 29, 2007, www.rfa.org/english/news/politics/tibetan_monks-20071029.html. Grievances over those arrests were one of the sparks for the Mar. 2008 pan-Tibet uprising, which led to further arrests at Drepung, and some of those detained received jail terms of up to fifteen years.

Epilogue

1. As this book was going to press, Li Xiaobo won the Nobel Peace Prize. The Nobel committee commended him for "his long and nonviolent struggle for fundamental human rights in China" while the Chinese government noted that Liu was a convicted criminal and declared the award "blasphemy against the Peace Prize."

2. Ai Weiwei's Tweet (in Chinese), Feb. 11, 2010, twitter.com/aiww/statuses/8962515702.

3. These figures were mentioned by Yu Jianrong, chair of the Social Issues Research Center of the Rural Development Institute of the China Academy of Social Sciences, in a speech to the Beijing Lawyers Association on Dec. 26, 2009. Part of the translation of the speech was posted at chinadigitaltimes.net/2010/03/yu-jianrong-maintaining-a-baseline-of-social-stability-part-i/ (accessed on June 9, 2010).

4. Sharon LaFraniere, "China Aims to Stifle Tibet's Photocopiers," *New York Times*, May 20, 2010, www.nytimes.com/2010/05/21/world/asia/21tibet.html?src=twt&twt=nytimestech (accessed May 21, 2010).

5. "China to Achieve Fast-Paced Development, Lasting Stability in Tibet," Xinhua News Agency, Jan. 23, 2010, news.xinhuanet.com/English/2010–01/23/content_12859870.htm (accessed Jun. 8, 2010).

6. Ibid.

7. "Sichuan-Tibet Railway to Start Construction in Sept," *China Daily*, Sep. 1, 2009, www.chinadaily.com.cn/china/2009–09/01/content_8641571.htm (accessed on June 8, 2010).

8. "Downstream from China," *Travellers' Tales—The FEER Blog, Far Eastern Economic Review*, Feb. 24, 2007, feer.wsj.com/tales/?p=429 (accessed on June 8, 2010).

9. Author's interview with Richard Baum, Nov. 29, 2005.

10. The report *China 2020* can be downloaded at cgascenarios.wordpress.com/china/.

11. I used translations by Perry Link, a former Princeton professor of Chinese literature who more recently taught at the University of California, Riverside. Link, who was coauthor of the *Tiananmen Papers* about the party's response to the 1989 democracy protests, published the Twitter Q & A with the Dalai Lama in a blog on the website of the *New York Review of Books* on May 24, 2010, under the headline, "Talking About Tibet: An Open Dialogue Between Chinese Citizens and the Dalai Lama," www.nybooks.com/blogs/nyrblog/2010/may/24/talking-about-tibet/ (accessed May 26, 2010).

Index